P9-CND-781

JUN 0 6 2011

VOGUE® KNITTING

Knitopedia™

VOGUE® KNITTING

Knitopedia™

the ultimate
A to Z for knitters

sixth&spring  books

Sixth&Spring Books
161 Avenue of the Americas
New York, NY 10013

Executive Editor
CARLA SCOTT

Managing Editor
WENDY WILLIAMS

Senior Editor
MICHELLE BREDESON

Contributing Editors
ERIN SLONAKER
ELAINE SILVERSTEIN
KRISTINA SIGLER

Art Director
DIANE LAMPHRON

Book Design
CHI LING MOY

Editorial Assistant
MARINA KASTAN

Vice President, Publisher
TRISHA MALCOLM

Creative Director
JOE VIOR

Production Manager
DAVID JOINNIDES

President
ART JOINNIDES

Copyright © 2011 by Sixth&Spring Books
All rights reserved. No part of this publication may be reproduced or used in any
form or by any means—graphic, electronic, or mechanical, including photocopying,
recording, or information storage-and-retrieval systems—without written permission
of the publisher.

The written instructions, photographs, designs, projects and patterns are intended
for the personal, noncommercial use of the retail purchaser and are under federal
copyright laws; they are not to be reproduced in any form for commercial use. Permission is granted to photocopy patterns for the personal use of the retail purchaser.

Library of Congress Cataloging-in-Publication Data

Vogue knitting knitopedia.
    p. cm.
  Includes index.
  ISBN 978-1-933027-61-6
  1. Knitting--Encyclopedias. I. Vogue knitting international. II. Title: Knitopedia.
TT820.V62526 2011
746.43'203--dc22

                        2010028847

Manufactured in China

1 3 5 7 9 10 8 6 4 2

First Edition

CONTENTS

INTRODUCTION

It is with immense pleasure that we finally bring to birth this book that has been over five years in development. We brainstormed our initial topics years ago, revised the list, shelved the book, brought it back to life, edited the list again and re-edited the material again. We were overwhelmed at different points and daunted by the huge undertaking of creating as comprehensive an A to Z as possible. At other times we were just excited by the possibility of bringing such a tome to print.

I really believe that no encyclopedic work can ever be fully complete, and this book has confirmed that. The scope of possible material is endless. In choosing what to include, we approached our selection of entries from the *Vogue Knitting* point of view—otherwise we would be researching and writing for the next fifteen years. Many categories are covered, including techniques, fibers, influential people, industry organizations, types of garments, knitting traditions, fashion luminaries, yarn and needle companies and stitch patterns. We've pulled from our archives from the 1930s through the 60s, and from issues since our re-launch in 1982. The entries include topics that are near and dear to *Vogue Knitting*, now close to its thirtieth year in print in our modern phase.

Over the years we have come to know the best of the talented people in the knitting world, and we have included essays by many of them in which they offer their personal take on the topics they have devoted their lives to pursuing. We are forever grateful to them as well as being in awe of their wisdom and dedication.

To all those who have contributed to *Vogue Knitting* over the decades—staff members, designers, writers, art directors, editors, photographers, support staff, interns and upper management—we thank you. You have all had a part in creating this world we love so much, and in the words that follow on these pages.

Trisha Malcolm
Editorial Director, *Vogue Knitting*

ABBREVIATIONS

Abbreviations are shortened forms of knitting terms, stitches, techniques and actions used in printed patterns or knitting descriptions. They refer to the side of the work (right or wrong side), the type of stitch (knit, purl), actions taken on the stitch (slip, yarn over, bind off), measurements, repetition of pattern steps and so on.

Although there is a movement toward standardization, abbreviations do vary from pattern to pattern and publisher to publisher. American abbreviations can be different from those used in other countries, as well. Be sure you know what each abbreviation in a pattern means before you begin to knit. As a general rule, most knitting books and magazines will define all abbreviations in the appendix.

Common Knitting Abbreviations

alt	alternate
approx	approximately
beg	begin(s), beginning
bet	between
bl	back loop(s)
BO	bind off
CA, CB, etc.	color A, color B, etc.
CC	contrasting color
ch	chain, chain stitch
cm	centimeter(s)
cn	cable needle
CO	cast on
cont	continue(s), continuing
dec	decrease(s), decreasing
dpn	double-pointed needle(s)
fl	front loop(s)
foll	follow(s), following
g	gram
inc	increase(s), increasing
k, K	knit
k1-b, k-b	knit one stitch in row below
k1fb, k1f&b, kfb	knit into the front and back of a stitch; also called bar increase
k2tog	knit two stitches together
kwise	knitwise
LC	left cross
LH	left-hand
lp(s)	loop(s)
m	meter(s)
m1, M1	make one: increase one stitch
M1 p-st	make one purl stitch
MC	main color
mm	millimeter(s)
oz	ounce(s)
p, P	purl
p1fb, p1f&b, pfb	purl into the front and back of a stitch
p2sso	pass two slipped stitches over
p2tog	purl two stitches together
pat(s), patt(s)	pattern(s)
pm	place marker
prev	previous
psso	pass slipped stitch over
pwise	purlwise
RC	right cross
rem	remain(s), remaining
rep	repeat(s), repeating
rev	reverse
rev St st	reverse stockinette stitch
RH	right hand
rib	ribbing
rnd(s)	rounds
RS	right side
s2kp, S2KP	slip two stitches together knitwise, knit one stitch, pass the two slipped stitches over the knit stitch
sc	single crochet
sk	skip
sk2p, SK2P	slip one stitch, knit two stitches together, pass the slipped stitch over the two stitches knit together
skp, SKP	slip one stitch, knit one stitch, pass the slipped stitch over the knit stitch
sl	slip
sl 1k, sl1k	slip one stitch knitwise
sl 1p, sl1p	slip one stitch purlwise
sl st	slip stitch(es)
spp	slip one stitch, purl one stitch, pass the slipped stitch over the purled stitch
ssk	slip two stitches knitwise one after another, then knit these two stitches together
ssp	slip two stitches knitwise one after another, then purl these two stitches together through the back loop
sssk	slip three stitches knitwise one after another, then knit these three stitches together
st(s)	stitch(es)
St st	stockinette stitch
tbl	through back loop(s)
tog	together
WS	wrong side
wyb, wyib	with yarn in back
wyf, wyif	with yarn in front
yd	yard(s)
yfwd	yarn forward (same as yo)
yo, yon	yarn over
yo2, yo (2)	yarn over twice
yrn	yarn around needle (same as yo)
*	repeat the directions between the asterisks as many times as indicated
**	repeat the directions between the double asterisks as many times as indicated
[ ]	work instructions within brackets as a group as many times as indicated
( )	work instructions within parentheses in the place directed
"	inches

ACRYLIC

A synthetic fiber made from a polymer (polyacrylonitrile), acrylic has been used in the manufacturing of yarns for handknitting and crochet since the 1950s. Acrylic yarn is widely available, inexpensive, and comes in a wide range of weights. Advantages of acrylic yarn include its wool-like appearance, lightness, softness, elasticity and moth- and mildew-repellent qualities. In addition, acrylic is hypoallergenic, so it is suitable for those with sensitivities to wool. The fibers take dye well and are colorfast, and acrylic yarns are machine washable and dryable, making them ideal for children's garments, afghans and other frequently laundered items.

Disadvantages include its tendency to pill and generate static charges. Because acrylic fiber is heat sensitive, knit or crocheted items must be pressed or steamed with caution and are generally not flame retardant. In addition, acrylic does not insulate as well as natural fibers. It is often blended with natural fibers. For example, acrylic fiber can add strength to short-staple cotton or lower the cost of expensive fibers such as wool. Some cheaper acrylic yarns can be rough, but in general acrylic has great softness. *See also* FIBER CHARACTERISTICS; FIBER CONTENT

ADDI TURBO

Known for slick, immaculate nickel plating and the smooth joins of their cords, this original line of circular needles from the German manufacturer Addi is aptly surnamed "Turbo"—they're arguably the needle knitters turn to most often when there's a need for speed. Not only does yarn slip effortlessly over Turbo needles and cords, but the needles are strong and are resistant to the accidental bending, pitting and scratching that plague lesser-quality metal models (of, for example, aluminum). The company also makes a sizeable range of bamboo and laceweight needles and recently introduced a coveted "Addi Turbo Click" system of interchangeable needles. Addi is distributed in America by Skacel Knitting of Seattle.

ADORNO, JENNA

See KNITTY.COM

AFGHAN

The term *afghan* to describe a small- to medium-sized knit or crocheted blanket first appeared in the knitting lexicon in 1833. Much like patchwork quilts make good use of fabric scraps, afghans began as a thrifty use for leftover yarn. Bits and pieces were stitched into colorful squares, and when enough blocks were accumulated, the squares were sewn together to form bedspreads, shawls, lap robes and throws. The colorful patterned look of the finished pieces (so the legend goes) resembled rugs imported from Afghanistan. Today's afghans tend to be more carefully thought-out pieces that are put together with the use of written patterns and varied knitting/crochet techniques. They are often created as one piece. The term *afghan* is used interchangeably with the word *throw*. *See also* SEAMING

AFGHAN WEIGHT

In the Craft Yarn Council's Standard Yarn Weight System, afghan weight is a yarn weight equivalent to worsted weight, or one that knits up at approximately 16 to 20 stitches per 4 inches (10cm) over size 7 to 9 needles. *See also* YARN WEIGHT

ALICE SPRINGS BEANIE FESTIVAL

This annual gathering of yarncrafters is held in the historic "oasis" town of Alice Springs, located in the middle of Australia's

Swatch knit in acrylic yarn

Skein of acrylic yarn

Knitted afghan designed by Nicky Epstein (from *Cover Up With Nicky Epstein*, Sixth&Spring Books, 2007)

vast inland desert. Begun in the early 2000s to sell beanies crocheted by local aboriginal women, the festival evolved into an extended-weekend event of large scale. Prizes are awarded for best decorative beanies, or caps, but the event also involves a colorful celebration of life and craft, including market booths, workshops, children's activities, caravan camping and music. The festival is a treat for visitors because of its exotic, isolated locale and the attendance of hundreds of Australian crafters of indigenous descent.

ALLEN, PAM (1949–)
Pam Allen is a knitwear designer, author and the former editor in chief of *Interweave Knits*. Allen began her knitting career designing for several magazines, including *Woman's Day* and *Vogue Knitting*. She authored the bestselling *Knitting for Dummies* (Wiley, 2002) and in 2003 took the helm of *Interweave Knits*, where she grew both the talent pool and

Internet presence. Allen and *Interweave* editor Ann Budd collaborated on Interweave's successful series of *Style* books, including *Scarf Style* (2004), *Wrap Style* (2005), *Lace Style* (2007) and *Bag Style* (2007). Allen left *IK* in 2007 to become creative director of Classic Elite Knits. In that role, she sourced new yarns, designed color palettes and created a pattern collection that included projects she sent to subscribers in a weekly e-newsletter. Allen left Classic Elite at the end of 2009 to start her own yarn company, Quince and Company, with partners Bob Rice and Carrie Bostick Hoge.
See also BUDD, ANN; DESIGNERS; *INTERWEAVE KNITS*

ALPACA FIBER
This soft, long-staple (4–11-inch/ 10–28cm) fiber is produced by the *Vicugna pacos*, a member of the camelid family. Native to the South American highlands, alpacas have been domesticated for thousands of years and are prized for their soft, lustrous fleece. The majority

of the world's alpaca fiber originates in Peru, Bolivia and Chile; the commercial center of the alpaca industry is Arequipa, Peru.

Because alpaca fleece occurs naturally in a wide range of shades from white to creams, browns, grays and blacks, traditionally much alpaca yarn was used in its natural color. It takes dye well, however, and today is available in a variety of colorful shades. The fiber is hollow and is lighter in weight than wool, as well as warmer and silkier to the touch. Alpaca contains little to no lanolin and thus can be worn by those with wool allergies. Unlike other camelids, alpacas do not produce coarse guard hairs, so each animal yields several pounds of fiber a year, enough for several garments.

There are two main types of alpaca: Suri and Huacaya. While Suri alpaca is considered to have the softest fleece, the Huacaya is more common, and the bulk of commercially produced alpaca yarn (about 90 percent) is

Huacaya. The long fiber of Suri alpaca grows parallel to the body and hangs down the animal's sides in curly ringlets. The fiber of Huacaya alpacas grows perpendicular to the body and is shorter and more crimped than that of the Suri; it forms a lock structure that surrounds the body with fiber, giving the animal a fluffy, spongy appearance.

Knitting With Alpaca
Alpaca yarns for knitting and crochet are available in a range of weights, from laceweight to bulky. Knitting with pure alpaca yarn results in a soft fabric that drapes well. The long staple imparts an almost furry quality to the finished garment. Because of its lack of resilience, pure alpaca tends to lose its shape when stretched and is often blended with wool to gain elasticity. Another popular blend is alpaca and silk.
See also FIBER CHARACTERISTICS; FIBER CONTENT; LANOLIN; STAPLE; YARN WEIGHT

Swatch knit in alpaca yarn

Suri alpaca

Family of Huacaya alpacas

ALPINE REGION KNITTING

More commonly known as Bavarian or Tyrolean knitwear (the latter term coined by James Norbury and Margaret Agutter in in *Odhams Encyclopedia of Knitting* in 1957), the knits of the Alpine regions of Austria and Germany are richly textured, with twisted traveling stitches that have their roots in hosiery patterns from the eighteenth and nineteenth centuries. Jackets made from cut and sewn felted pieces were common in the region; knitted Alpine-style sweaters, however, probably originated in the twentieth century. The technique is similar to that of Aran patterns, giving rise to the theory that Alpine sweaters are precursors to Aran fishermen's designs. *Twisted-Stitch Knitting* by Maria Erlbacher (Schoolhouse Press, 2009) presents a wealth of stitch patterns and patterns for traditional Alpine stockings, pullovers and cardigans. *See also* ARAN KNITTING; FOLK KNITTING; KNIT/PURL PATTERNS; TRAVELING STITCHES; TWISTED-STITCH PATTERNS

ALT

Abbreviation for *alternate*.

AMERICAN/ENGLISH-STYLE KNITTING

This popular knitting method is characterized by the knitter holding the working yarn in the right hand and using the right needle to pull the strand through to create a knit stitch. This style of knitting is also described as throwing, right-hand carry or right-handed knitting.

The American/English and Continental/German knitting styles are the two main types of Western knitting. In these methods, the stitches are mounted on the needle so that the leading leg of the loop over the needle is at the front. In both methods, the knitter forms a knit stitch by inserting the needle from front to back, passing the yarn under the right needle and drawing the new loop through to make a knit stitch. To make a purl stitch, the knitter inserts the yarn into the front loop of the stitch from back to front, passes the yarn over and under the needle and pulls the loop through. *See also* CONTINENTAL/ GERMAN-STYLE KNITTING; EASTERN KNITTING; KNIT STITCH; PURL STITCH; STITCH MOUNT; WESTERN KNITTING

AMERICAN FOLK ART MUSEUM

Located in New York City, the American Folk Art Museum (folkartmuseum.org) illuminates American history and culture through folk art and crafts. The permanent collection includes many textile works, including samplers, quilts, coverlets and a knitted Shaker rug.

AMERICAN RED CROSS KNITTING CAMPAIGNS

When America entered World War I in 1917, the American Red Cross launched massive nationwide volunteer knitting campaigns with the goal of supplying soldiers on

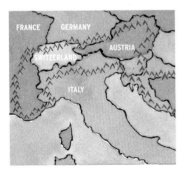
The Alpine region of Europe

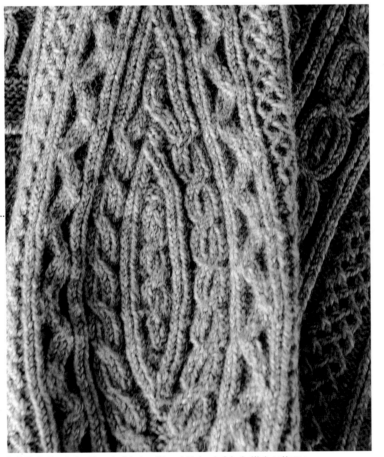
Detail photo of stockings knit in traditional Alpine twisted-stitch patterns

Poster promoting the Red Cross's "Our Boys Need Sox: Knit Your Bit" campaign

the European front with warm clothing. Thousands of American women stitched wool socks, sweaters, scarves, bandages, helmets and wristlets from instruction booklets and patterns that had been approved by the armed forces. Children learned to knit through Red Cross programs, usually starting with simple knitted washcloths. By September 1918, in an effort to ease the yarn shortage, the War Industries Board ordered American yarn retailers to turn over their entire stock of khaki, gray, heather, natural and white wool to the Red Cross.

The war's end did not halt the Red Cross knitting effort. In 1925, the organization requested 30,000 sweaters for disabled veterans. Screen star Mary Pickford began knitting sweaters between movie takes and urged "the thinking men and women of America to form a solid block behind the unselfish workers of the Red Cross."

World War II saw another surge in volunteer knitting. In January 1942, the War Production Board designated the Red Cross the clearing agency for all knitting, granting the organization priority status for receiving wool, which like meat, sugar and gasoline, was in short supply. The Red Cross supplied patterns for sweaters, socks, mufflers, fingerless mitts, toe covers for casts, residual limb covers and other garments.

Red Cross knitters continued to supply the military with wool hats as late as 1964. Soldiers stationed at remote outposts such as Greenland and Labrador claimed the wool hats, handknitted by volunteers, were warmer than the mass-produced synthetic versions supplied by the army. The Red Cross keeps an archive of free patterns from the war effort on its website, redcross.org/museum/exhibits/knits.asp.
See also CHARITY KNITTING

AMIGURUMI

These small-scale stuffed toys or dolls can be knitted but are most frequently crocheted. They originated in Japan, but their popularity quickly spread worldwide on the Internet via blogs and crafting websites. Amigurumi may take the form of animals, anthropomorphized versions of inanimate objects, or imaginary creatures. Their main aesthetic is cuteness. The dolls are usually constructed in sections by using a single crochet stitch worked in a spiral; the sections are then sewn together. Amigurumi are frequently embellished using beads, embroidery or felt appliqués to make features or extremities.
See also TOYS

ANDES REGION KNITTING

Knitting and spinning traditions developed early in the Andes region of South America. Pre-Hispanic and modern textiles from Peru and Bolivia are considered among the finest and most varied in the world. Knitting was most likely introduced to the Andes by the Spanish and Portuguese, but the indigenous peoples quickly adapted the craft to their own traditions, creating caps and leggings that replicated their woven clothing. The intricately patterned tasseled knit caps, or *chullos,* of Peru are perhaps the most recognizable of Andean designs, but knitters of the region also make beautiful sweaters and accessories. Men and women both wear the caps and knit them, looping skeins of yarn around their necks to maintain an even tension and working circularly with sets of five very thin double-pointed needles that are often handmade from baling wire. The intricate, colorful patterning is done with intarsia, and slight hooks on the ends of the needles make it easier to pull up the stitches.

Native alpaca and sheep introduced by the Spanish provided the fleece for the early designs, but by the twentieth century the men were stitching their traditional designs with factory-produced synthetics. The traditional fibers are beginning to creep back, however, as yarn

Crocheted amigurumi, designed by Ana Paula Rimoli, representing two symbols of the Chinese zodiac: the tiger (left) and the rooster (right)

The Andes region of South America

Peruvian man wearing chullo and knitting

manufacturers from around the world have begun sourcing handspun alpaca and organic, color-grown cottons from Peruvian spinners and dyers.
See also FOLK KNITTING; INTARSIA; SPANISH KNITTING

ANGORA FIBER

Angora is the name given to the downy coat of the domestic longhair Angora rabbit, of which there are three main varieties: English, French and German. The term *angora*, when used for fiber, always refers to rabbit hair, not to the fiber of the Angora goat (which produces mohair fiber). The name is derived from Ankara, the city in Turkey where both the Angora goat and the Angora rabbit are thought to have originated. Much commercial angora is now raised in Asia, although Germany and France still produce high-quality angora yarns.

Angora fibers are hollow, soft and fine, giving the finished fabric a light, floaty feel; a fluffy, furry appearance, referred to as a *halo*;

and a silky hand. The hollow fibers produce an insulating effect, and angora is said to be eight times warmer than wool. It is reputed to have therapeutic qualities useful for conditions such as joint pain and poor circulation.

The best angora fiber is plucked or combed during the rabbits' seasonal molt, about four times a year. Each animal produces around eight ounces annually, about enough to make one garment. Plucking is labor-intensive and time-consuming, and today virtually all large-scale commercial angora is shorn, resulting in shorter fibers and a finished fabric with less loft. Rabbits are clean animals with few sweat glands and no lanolin, so the fiber can be spun with virtually no cleaning. Angora fiber occurs in natural shades from pure white to chocolate brown and also takes dye well.

Knitting With Angora

Pure angora yarn lacks resilience, so it is commonly blended or plied

with other fibers, especially wool, for elasticity and durability. It is slippery on the needles, and because of its fluffiness, it gives little stitch definition. Angora is frequently used for knitting trims and collars to add details of softness and fluff to a garment. For pure angora items, it is best to knit loosely so the angora halo has room to expand or "bloom." The cool cycle of a commercial dryer can be used to fluff up angora items that have flattened during storage. Angora yarn tends to shed, especially the lesser-quality yarns.

Because of its softness, angora yarn is often used for baby items. Periodically angora sweaters have been popular in women's fashion, most notably in the 1950s, when virtually every woman had at least one fluffy angora sweater.
See also FIBER CHARACTERISTICS; FIBER CONTENT; LANOLIN

APPROX

Abbreviation for *approximately.*

ARABIC KNITTING

This general term covers the earliest known type of knitting, practiced by the nomadic peoples of North Africa. Arabic knitting was worked on oblong or circular frames, the former being used for carpets, tent flaps and clothing and the latter for sandal socks. The technique used for these patterns resembled spool knitting, as if with a knitting nancy, with nails ringing a hole in a spool or bobbin. Cord was looped around the nails, then passed over a length of wool that had been wound around the inside of each nail. Winding the cord in a counterclockwise direction produced a twisted loop. When working on a frame, the hook was used to lift the loops over one another. The knitter worked in a circular motion on the round frame or in a backward motion on the oblong frame. In Arabic knitting, every pattern stitch on every row was twisted.
See also FOLK KNITTING; KNITTING NANCY

Angora rabbit

Swatch knit in angora yarn

This crocheted angora stole appeared in the Fall/Winter 1952 issue of the *Vogue Knitting Book.*

ARAN KNITTING

In modern knitting terms, *Aran* denotes a flat-constructed garment featuring a central panel, usually worked in an intricate cable design with a textured background, flanked by symmetrical side panels. More specifically, the term refers to a style of knitting developed in the Aran Islands of Inishmore, Inishmaan and Inisheer, located off the mouth of Ireland's Galway Bay. Legend has it that the Aran knitting style and its distinctive cable patterning are rooted in Celtic symbolism, and that these patterns, which symbolize blessings and protections, were handed down through generations of seafaring families, with each family having its own patterns and stitch combinations. The women would knit these patterns into the sweaters their men wore to sea— and thus be able to identify a drowned husband, father or brother, should his body wash ashore. There's little evidence, however, that Aran fishermen

wore the style before the middle of the twentieth century. There's no written record or photograph showing the style worn by Aran fishermen prior to the 1940s, and the Aran's flat-panel construction (less sturdy than the circular construction of the traditional gansey), creamy white color and complex patternwork (too labor-intensive for a garment subject to so much wear, tear and need of replacement) would have made it impractical for months spent at sea. In addition, knitters living on the island in the 1940s state that the gansey was the style traditionally knitted on the islands.

The most plausible explanation (and the one accepted by most experts) of the origins of the Aran sweater is that it developed from the traditional Scottish gansey, with Aran women learning the skills from their Scottish counterparts, in particular the "herring lassies" who went to the isles to gut, fillet and pack for the fishing industry. These young women spent the lulls between

boats knitting and no doubt passed along their skills. Another theory, proposed by the Churchill scholar Rohana Darlington, is that the Aran style actually originated in America, by way of Austria. In this version, two young women from the Aran Islands emigrated to America in 1906, settling in Boston. There they learned intricately patterned Bavarian-style knitting from a German or Austrian immigrant. Returning to Aran some time later, they brought home these newfound stitch patterns and combined them with the traditional gansey structure used on the islands.

In the 1930s early examples of what would come to be known as the Aran sweater began appearing in Irish shops. In 1936, journalist Heinz Egar Kiewe "discovered" a cream-colored Aran sweater in the Country Shop in Dublin, a store run and supplied by Countryworkers, Ltd., a cooperative movement working to preserve Irish handicrafts. Inspired in part by the Robert Flaherty film *Man of Aran*

(1934), Kiewe devoted the next thirty years to promoting and producing Aran sweaters, all the while romanticizing the origins of a "tradition" of knitting that dated back "thousands of years." Savvy marketers began capitalizing on the legend, and the popularity of the Aran grew. By the end of the 1930s both merchants and yarn manufacturers were marketing and manufacturing Aran designs. By 1946, in search of new patterns for the sweaters, retailers began sponsoring Aran design competitions. The sweaters became popular in postwar Britain. A pattern for an Aran sweater designed by Elizabeth Zimmermann appeared in the *Vogue Pattern Book* in 1958, helping to popularize the style in the United States. The Aran endures today, as does the myth of its beginnings. Today, the term *Aran sweater* (sometimes "Irish sweater") refers to a garment worked in an intricate pattern of cables and embossed stitches, often with bobbles, and consisting of a center panel flanked by

The Aran Islands, which gave Aran knitting its name, are located in Galway Bay, off the Irish coast.

This Aran sweater designed by Elizabeth Zimmermann first appeared in the *Vogue Pattern Book* in 1958.

Ever-Changing Aran

by Alice Starmore

Of all the knitting techniques, Aran is the easiest for knitters to experiment with and use to create their own variations and designs.

The components of the style are all straightforward and well within the range of anyone who can knit and purl. The technique of crossing stitches over each other to form cables and to make shapes that travel across the fabric is simplicity itself. Knit-and-purl patterns, twisted stitches, bobbles and openwork add further texture and can be applied at will. I would like to think that I have helped to restore the exuberant creativity that is so evident in the work of the early Aran knitters of the 1930s and 40s.

As an author and teacher I have explained and published my view of the Aran pattern concept in detail. Anyone with more than a passing understanding of knitting can see that rope cables and cabled traveling zigzags represent the conceptual and technical basis for what we now call Aran patterns. They are the starting point from which most Aran patterns logically develop, and they were present on the Aran Islands in fisher ganseys from around 1900 onwards, several decades before Aran sweaters appeared.

Aran knitting was commercialized virtually at its inception, and this impeded creativity, because commercialization imposed a relatively small group of stitch patterns, which were set in a basic style suitable for mass production. It is understandable that, under these circumstances, Aran patterns and design would become simplified, but I believe that another effect was to mask the dynamic potential of the concept.

I regard Aran knitting as a concept rather than as a fixed body of set images, and as a designer, I enjoy taking the concept wherever I want to go with it. It may be geometry, nature, geography, history or indeed any theme that sparks my desire to create new patterns and designs. I am always interested in creating new forms of expression with enduring techniques such as Aran knitting, and I encourage other knitters to set aside fears of defying tradition and invite them to add their own influence to this fabled style.

Alice Starmore is a designer, author and founder of Virtual Yarns (virtualyarns.com). A recipient of a Winston Churchill Fellowship, she is an authority on the knitting traditions of Ireland, Scotland and the Norse regions.

symmetrical side panels.
See also ALPINE REGION
KNITTING; ARAN WEIGHT;
BOBBLES; CABLE PATTERNS;
CABLES; FOLK KNITTING;
GANSEY

ARAN WEIGHT

A medium-weight yarn, Aran
weight is classified with the
number 4 on the CYC Standard
Weight System. It typically knits
up at 18 stitches to 4 inches
(10cm) on size 7 to 9 needles. This
weight category also includes
worsted and afghan-weight yarn
and is considered the most popular
yarn group, particularly for new
knitters.

The term *Aran yarn* typically
refers more specifically to a natural
(undyed) wool yarn of this weight
that is used for making Aran-type
garments.
See also ARAN KNITTING; YARN
WEIGHT

ARGYLE

This classic diamond colorwork
pattern in a diagonal
checkerboard arrangement gets
its name from the Argyll region of
western Scotland, home to Clan
Campbell and the plaids from
which the argyle design
supposedly derives. The earliest
argyle stockings were made from
tartan cloth cut on the bias, but
knitters devised a method for
creating knit hose in tartan
patterns. One of the earliest
references to this patterned knit
hose comes from a Lady
Mackenzie, who, in J.H. Dixon's
Guide to Gairloch and Loch Maree
(1886), describes employing, in
1837, a "lady from Skye who was
staying at Kerrysdale to instruct
twelve young women in the
knitting of nice stockings with
dice and other fancy patterns."
Lady Mackenzie went on to
institute a formal manufacture of

such stockings, employing the
dyers, spinners and knitters of
Gairloch to do so.

Traditional Scottish argyle
stockings were worked flat and
seamed up the back using intarsia;
they do not use stranding the way
Fair Isle does. Individual colors
were worked from bobbins or
butterflies, and once a section was
completed, the bobbin or butterfly
was left behind and a new one
picked up. Many modern-day
patterns use duplicate stitch to
create the overlying pattern of
diagonal lines. If the argyle repeat
is small enough, Fair Isle argyle
can be worked in the round.
See also BOBBIN; COLORWORK;
DUPLICATE STITCH; FAIR ISLE
KNITTING; INTARSIA; SOCKS

ARMHOLE SHAPING

The increases and decreases made
to shape the armhole of a sweater
are referred to as *armhole shaping*.
Armholes can be straight, square,
angled or even shaped for a set-in
or raglan sleeve. Usually the same
armhole shaping is used for the

front and back pieces of the
sweater. Here is a guide to all the
basic shape categories.

Straight Armhole/Set-in Sleeve

This sleeve top has a straight
edge. Sewn along the straight
edge of the body pieces, it forms a
T-square look. The width of the
top of the sleeve is the total depth
of the front and back armholes.
Since the armhole isn't shaped,
the armhole depth should be
dropped a minimum of 2½–3
inches (6.5–7.5cm) from the actual
body measurement to ensure an
easy, non-clinging fit. To place the
sleeve accurately, divide the top-
of-sleeve measurement by half,
and place markers this number of
inches down from the shoulders
on front and back. Sew the
shoulders, then sew the tops of
the sleeves to the armholes
between the markers.

A straight sleeve is usually knit
from the cuff edge to the top
edge. This sleeve can also be
worked from seam to seam. The

The pattern for this men's argyle sweater appeared in the Spring/Summer 1955 issue
of the *Vogue Knitting Book*.

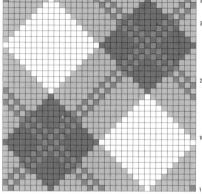

34-st rep

Swatch knit in an argyle pattern, with
accompanying color chart

advantage of this method is that the stitches run in the same direction as the body when sewn to the sweater and therefore the stitch or color pattern appears as a continuous motif.

To design a sleeve of this type, cast on about 1 inch's (2.5cm's) worth of stitches. As you work, continue to cast on stitches at the right edge (for left sleeve) and the left edge (for right sleeve) until the desired sleeve length (minus the cuff) is reached. Work until the short edge is the needed width at the wrist. Then bind off the stitches to correspond to those cast on. The long edge must measure the total armhole depth and is sewn to the armhole edges of the front and back. Pick up stitches along the short edge for the cuff ribbing and work the usual way.

Square Armhole/Straight Sleeve

This sleeve is similar in appearance to the straight style, but with less bulk at the

underarm. It is particularly well suited to the addition of shoulder pads. The average width to bind off for the armhole is 2 inches (5cm). You must work a corresponding 2 inches (5cm) straight at the sleeve top after you complete all sleeve increases. Sew the top (bound-off edge) of the sleeve to the straight edge of the armhole, and then sew the 2 inches (5cm) that was worked straight on the sleeve to the 2 inches (5cm) of the armhole bind-off.

For both this style and the straight armhole/set-in sleeve, you can pick up stitches along the straight edge of the armhole and work the sleeve down to the cuff edge.

Angled Armhole/Sleeve

Very common in classic menswear and full-fashioned sweaters, this armhole shaping is often accompanied by a straight front shoulder and a deep, sloped back shoulder. Again, it gives a broader line at the top of the

sleeve without the bulk of a straight sleeve. Since the armhole is angled, it provides more ease of movement. The average decrease for this armhole is also 2 inches (5cm) over a 2-inch (5cm) slope, with corresponding sleeve decreases. The straight portion of the sleeve top must match the straight sections of the front and back armholes.

Shaped Armhole/Set-in Sleeve

The set-in sleeve is not only the most classic form of shaping, but offers numerous style possibilities, from a very shallow but broad cap (most frequently used in men's sweaters and easy-fitting women's sweaters) to a very high but narrow cap (used for close-fitting women's sleeves). Set-in sleeves, however, are also the most difficult to plan out. They require careful calculation, graphing and sometimes even ripping out before you get a perfectly shaped sleeve to fit into the front and back of an armhole.

Here are a few tips on shaping the most basic armhole/sleeve cap:

Usually, the front and back armholes are decreased 2–3 inches (5–7.5cm) in from the edge and over a slope of 2 inches (5cm) or more. To get the curve of the armhole, you bind off approximately 1 inch's (2.5cm's) worth of stitches at once, then decrease the remaining stitches gradually. You begin the sleeve cap by making bind-offs and decreases corresponding to those used on the front and back armholes. After that, the shape of the sleeve cap varies. When you look at the sleeve cut in half lengthwise, the measurement of the depth of the sleeve cap, plus one half the top of the sleeve cap, must add up to the armhole depth of the front or back. The top of the cap can be 2–5 inches (5–12.5cm) in width and is bound off all at once. Once you determine the width at the top, divide that measurement in half and subtract it from the armhole length of the front or the back. This

Armhole Shaping

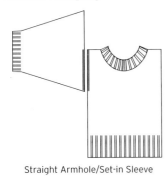

Straight Armhole/Set-in Sleeve

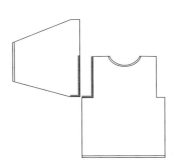

Square Armhole/Straight Sleeve

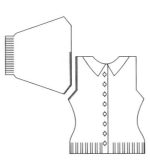

Angled Armhole/Sleeve

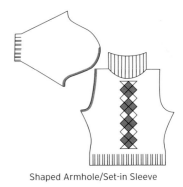

Shaped Armhole/Set-in Sleeve

measurement will be the depth of the sleeve cap.

Puffed sleeves also fall into this category. The armhole shaping is the same as described above. The sleeve cap differs only in that it is deeper and wider at the top, usually by 1–3 inches (2.5–7.5cm), depending on how puffed you want the sleeve to be. Gather the extra fabric at the top of the sleeve before setting it into the armhole.

Raglan Armhole/Sleeve

A raglan armhole is usually seen as a straight line angled from the underarm to the neck. Sometimes ½ inch (1.5cm) or so is bound off straight at the armhole before beginning the raglan shaping. The sleeve raglan must match the front and back raglan shaping (that is, it must have the same number of rows). The top of the sleeve forms part of the neck [figure A].

For an easier fit at the front neck, you can make the front neck and armhole shorter than the back neck and armhole by 1 inch (2.5cm) [figure B]. When you do this, you must work the sleeves with a slanted top so that they fit the front and back armholes. In other words, one side of the sleeve raglan is longer (to correspond to the back), and the other side is shorter (to correspond to the front). To shape the top 1–2 inches (2.5–5cm), you bind off stitches from the front (shorter) edge. The front edge of the left sleeve is at the beginning of the wrong-side rows. Conversely, the front edge of the right sleeve is at the beginning of the right-side rows.

Frequently, raglan decreases are worked 2 to 3 stitches inside each edge for a decorative finish, called full-fashioning.

Saddle Yoke Armhole/Sleeve

The same shaping principle for the set-in sleeves applies to the armhole and sleeve of the saddle shoulder style. The only difference is that the front and back armholes are shorter by 1–1½ inches (2.5–4cm) to accommodate the saddle shoulder portion of the sleeve. The top of the sleeve, which is worked straight to fit along the top of the shoulder edge, is usually 2–3 inches (5–7.5cm) wide. The top of the saddle shoulder will also form part of the neck.

Dolman Sleeve

The dolman sleeve, which was recently fashionable, has always been a classic shaping for evening sweaters and other lightweight dressy sweaters. Actually an extension of the main body pieces, the dolman is worked by increasing stitches, then casting on stitches in larger numbers to obtain the desired curve. It is important to plan the shaping carefully with a graph or paper pattern.

Sleeve Length

It's often difficult to determine sleeve lengths on any of the styles without shaped sleeve caps. The lengths will vary from style to style depending on the width of the body pieces. For the most accurate calculation, measure from your own center-back-neck to wrist (or wherever you want the sleeve to end) and subtract about 2 inches (5cm) for stretch. Divide the width of the back-neck measurement in half and add it to the shoulder measurement. Subtract this number from your center-back to wrist measure, and you'll know how long to make your sleeve.

Setting in Sleeves

A neatly set-in sleeve is one of the marks of distinction of a knitting perfectionist. In each of the examples outlined here, the setting in of sleeves requires some pre-planning and skill. The sleeve almost always has more fabric to be eased into the armholes, either because of its curves or simply because the stretching of the stitches across is greater than the elasticity of the rows lengthwise.

Sew in sleeves after the shoulder seams have been joined and before the side and sleeve

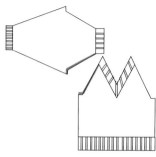

Raglan Armhole/Sleeve (figure A)

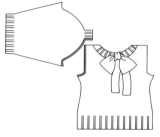

Raglan Armhole/Sleeve (figure B)

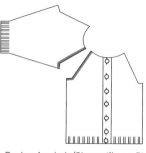

Saddle Yoke Armhole/Sleeve

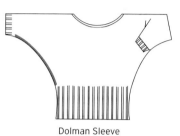

Dolman Sleeve

Nineteenth-century sampler of Azores lace doilies

seams are sewn. That way you can lay the pieces out flat and be sure that the sleeve caps are eased evenly into the armhole.

Line up the center of the sleeve cap with the shoulder seam and the two sets of armhole bind-offs (or armhole markers). Then baste with a contrasting yarn or use T-pins to pin the remainder of the sleeve cap into the armhole, easing in extra sleeve fabric.

Whether you use the invisible seam, crochet slip-stitch method or your own finishing method, be sure that the seam is worked with small, fairly close stitches for a neat and even appearance that will hold up through many years of washing and wearing.
See also SLEEVES

ARMSCYE
See SET-IN SLEEVE

ART OF KNITTING, THE
See MAGAZINES AND JOURNALS (U.K.)

ASSEMBLING
Once the knitted pieces for a project have been completed and blocked to the proper size, they must be sewn together; this is called *assembling*. The general sequence of sweater assembly follows this order: First, connect the shoulders and finish the neck edge. Next, sew in the sleeves. Finally, sew continuously from the end of the body of the sweater to the underarm and then down the sleeve to cuff edge.

See also ARMHOLE SHAPING; BACKSTITCH (SEAMING); BLOCKING; COLLARS AND NECKBANDS; SEAMING; WEAVING IN

AUERBACH, LISA ANNE
See GUERRILLA KNITTING

AUSTRIAN KNITTING
See ALPINE REGION KNITTING; FOLK KNITTING

AZORES LACE
These fine medallion lace patterns were developed in the Portuguese Azores islands. Incredibly delicate in design and detail, the lace patterns of the Azores, also known as Pita lace (for the aloe fibers from the *Agave americana*, known as *pita* in Portuguese, from which it is sometimes knitted), are created with a single thread using traditional lace knitting stitches.
See also FOLK KNITTING; LACE KNITTING

The Azores are located in the Atlantic Ocean roughly 1,000 miles from the coast of Portugal.

BACK LOOP

The part of a stitch that is at the back of the needle, or farthest from the knitter, is referred to as the *back loop*.

See also KNIT THROUGH THE BACK LOOP; STITCH MOUNT

BACKSTITCH (EMBROIDERY)

Backstitch is an embroidery stitch used for outlining and for creating straight lines.

See also EMBROIDERY

BACKSTITCH (SEAMING)

Backstitch is a seaming technique that is suitable for most garments; it is often used for sweater assembly and is worked from the wrong side of the fabric. Since a backstitch seam is not worked at the edge of the fabric as are some other seaming techniques, it is very strong. It can also be used to take in fullness. Backstitch creates a seam allowance, which should not exceed ⅜ inch (1cm).

See also ASSEMBLY; SEAMING

Backstitch (Seaming)

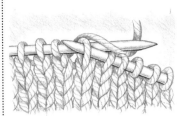

1. With the right sides of the pieces facing each other, secure the seam by taking the needle twice around the edges from back to front. Bring the needle up about ¼ inch (.5cm) from where the yarn last emerged, as shown.

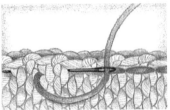

2. In one motion, insert the needle into the point where the yarn emerged from the previous stitch and back up approximately ¼ inch (.5cm) ahead of the emerging yarn. Pull the yarn through. Repeat this step, keeping the stitches straight and even.

Backwards Knitting

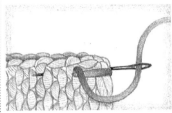

1. To practice knitting backwards on stockinette, purl to the middle of the row. Turn the work around. The yarn will be coming from the left needle as shown. To continue the row, insert the tip of the left needle into the back of the stitch on the right needle.

2. Wrap the yarn over the top of the left needle counterclockwise and draw through a loop as shown. If you wrap the yarn incorrectly, the result will be a twisted stitch.

BACKWARDS KNITTING

Backwards knitting, or knitting back backwards, is the technique of knitting from the left edge to the right edge of a piece instead of flipping the fabric over and purling. This technique can only be used with patterns such as stockinette, in which each row is composed of only one type of stitch. Backwards knitting eliminates the need to turn the work, and as such can eliminate changes in tension and save time. It is especially useful for short rows, entrelac and bobbles.

BALL

A ball is a unit of yarn measure; when wound up (not in hanks), the yarn resembles a ball. It can come in any size, from very small (less than 100 yards/90m) to oversized (1,000-plus yards). A *center-pull ball* of yarn has been wound so that the working yarn is pulled from the inside of the ball. Much commercial yarn is available in this presentation, which is easy to knit from and tends not to become

---

Backstitch (Embroidery)

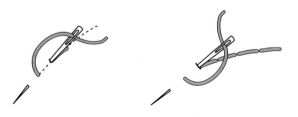

Draw the needle up. In one motion, insert the needle a little behind where the yarn emerged and draw it up the same distance in front. Continue from right to left by inserting the needle where the yarn first emerged.

Yarn wound into a ball

Winding a Center-Pull Ball

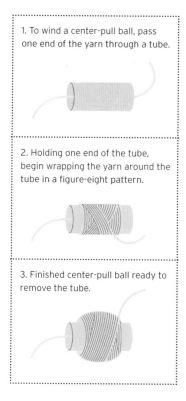

1. To wind a center-pull ball, pass one end of the yarn through a tube.

2. Holding one end of the tube, begin wrapping the yarn around the tube in a figure-eight pattern.

3. Finished center-pull ball ready to remove the tube.

tangled. Yarn that comes in hanks can be wound into a center-pull ball using a skein winder, by hand or via the combination of a swift and an electric or mechanical ball winder.

To wind a center-pull ball by hand without a swift, place the open hank of yarn around a chair back or have someone hold it loosely around his or her wrists with arms outstretched. Use a small cardboard or paper tube to begin the ball (coiling the yarn label into a tube works well). Pass the end of the yarn through the tube and begin wrapping the yarn around it in a figure eight pattern until the entire skein is wound. Slip the ball off the tube and begin knitting with the inside end of yarn.
See also BALL WINDER; HANK; PUT-UP; SKEIN; SWIFT

BALL WINDER

A small purchased machine, a ball winder is usually cranked by hand, used in conjunction with a swift to wind a hank of yarn into a ball. Made of plastic or wood, the tool is clamped to a table for stability. A ball winder replaces the more tedious method of winding a ball by hand and produces a center-pull ball, which is easy to knit from.

To use a ball winder, secure both a swift and ball winder on a sturdy table or other surface, a few feet apart. Place the hank of yarn on the swift, opening the swift up as much as possible so there is tension on the hank. Insert the outside end of yarn into the slot in the core of the winder, and slowly turn the crank to wind the ball. When the hank is completely wound, carefully remove the ball from the winder.

Ball winder

Most hand knitters and yarn shops employ hand-cranked ball winders, whereas in commercial settings an electric one is likely to be used. The resulting shape is a squat cylinder, often referred to as a "yarn cake."
See also BALL; HANK; SWIFT

BALTIC KNITTING

The Baltic nations of Latvia, Lithuania and Estonia have rich and diverse knitting traditions. Lace, cables and especially colorwork are all well represented in the region's folklore. Located on the Baltic Sea, these countries

An assortment of traditional Baltic mittens shows a rich variety of colors and patterns.

have long been a center of trade and are within reach of other important centers of stranded color knitting, such as Scandinavia and Fair Isle. According to one theory, the better-known Fair Isle colorwork patterns are based on a shawl from the Baltics. What is certain is that both Latvia and Estonia are known for socks and mittens handknit in brilliant stranded color patterns.

Estonia, the northernmost of the Baltic states, has a rich knitting heritage and is best known for its colorful geometrically designed mittens, the patterns for some of which date back to the sixteenth century. Socks are also a part of the Estonian knitting heritage. Both are ornamented with clocks and color patterns. Local traditions include more than two hundred mitten patterns.

Haapsalu, a town on the west coast of Estonia, is known for its lace shawls and scarves, which feature bobble-like "nupps" and patterns inspired by nature. In her book *Knitted Lace of Estonia*

(Interweave, 2008), Nancy Bush explores the lace-knitting traditions of this region and provides patterns for recreating authentic Estonian lace designs.

Latvia is perhaps best known for its exquisitely patterned mittens whose symbols and colors were marks of group and district affiliation. Marriageable girls were judged by both the quality and quantity of their knitting. The symbols used in Latvian mitten designs derive from ancient mythology. Interpretation of these symbols varied from district to district, as did the preferences for design combinations and colors. However, certain underlying principles are present in all Latvian designs: Several colors are employed in a single piece, both for aesthetic and practical purposes (multiple stranding made for a warmer fabric); the design elements are symmetrical; and the background is not considered part of the design.

See also COLORWORK; FOLK KNITTING; MITTENS; SOCKS

BAR INCREASE

The bar increase is performed by knitting into both the front and back of a stitch. Also abbreviated "k1fb," "k1f&b" or "kfb," it produces a distinct horizontal "bar" across the first stitch, giving rise to this name.
See also ABBREVIATIONS; INCREASE; K1FB, K1F&B, KFB

BASKETWEAVE STITCH

One of many stitch patterns, basketweave stitch is a highly textured pattern stitch composed of knit and purl stitches that forms a solid fabric with a checked design. It is one of the first knit/purl stitch patterns that a beginner might learn.

The simplest basketweave patterns have multiples of even numbers of stitches (usually 6, 8, or 10) that are divided into knit and purl blocks. More complex basketweave or checked patterns use uneven numbers of knit and purl stitches or combine garter stitch or seed stitch in the blocks instead of plain knit or purl.

Bar Increase

The bar increase is a visible increase. A horizontal bar will follow the increased stitch on the knit side of the work, whether you work the increase on the knit or the purl side.

1. To increase on the knit side, insert the right needle knitwise into the stitch to be increased. Wrap the yarn around the right needle and pull it through as if knitting, but leave the stitch on the left needle.

2. Insert the right needle into the back of the same stitch. Wrap the yarn around the needle and pull it through. Slip the stitch from the left needle. You now have 2 stitches on the right needle.

The countries of Estonia, Latvia and Lithuania comprise the Baltic region.

Basketweave swatch knit on a multiple of 8 stitches

Basketweave patterns are good for scarves, because many are reversible. They are also used to add interest to plain stockinette knitted items or as trims. Basketweave patterns can be used as borders or welts on knitted garments or blankets.

The pattern for the basketweave swatch shown on the previous page is knit on a multiple of 8 stitches and is worked as follows.

Row 1 (RS) Knit.

Rows 2–6 *K4, p4, rep from * to end.

Row 7 Knit.

Rows 8–12 *P4, k4; rep from * to end.

Rep rows 1–12.

See also BORDERS; GARTER STITCH; KNIT/PURL PATTERNS; KNIT STITCH; PURL STITCH; SCARF; SEED STITCH; STOCKINETTE STITCH; WELT

BATHING SUITS, KNITTED

Patterns for handknitted bathing suits began popping up in publications such *Weldon's Practical Knitter* as early as 1897 and continued to appear until about 1951. The heyday for handknitted swimsuits came in the late 1930s. Although designers carefully chose stitches to combat the heaviness of handknitted fabric and its tendency to sag when wet, ultimately the suits proved both impractical and unsatisfactory. Early commercial swimwear was machine-knitted with wool and synthetic elastic

fibers. The introduction of Lycra in 1960 all but put an end to handknitted bathing suits, though crocheted bikinis (for sunning, not swimming) were popular in the 1970s. New yarns with better elasticity have revived interest in swimsuit patterns, and many can be found in both knitting magazines and on the Internet. *See also* WELDON'S PRACTICAL NEEDLEWORK

BAVARIAN KNITTING

See ALPINE REGION KNITTING; FOLK KNITTING

BEADED KNITTING

Not the same as the similarly named bead knitting, beaded knitting is a technique in which beads are spaced at planned or random intervals and fall over stitches rather than between them. Beads are added by threading them onto the working yarn and can be worked with

This knitted bathing suit was featured in *Vogue's Knitting Book* in 1947.

Beaded Knitting (from wrong side)

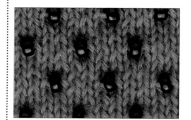

You can add beads in stockinette stitch on wrong-side rows by making a knit stitch (a purl on the right side of the work) on either side of the bead to help anchor it.

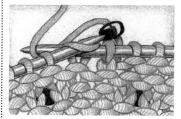

From the wrong side: On a purl (wrong-side) row, work to one stitch before the point you wish to place a bead. Knit this stitch. With yarn still at back of the work, slip the bead up to the work and knit the next stitch.

Beaded Knitting (from right side)

On right-side rows, beads are placed without the purl stitches on either side. The bead will lie directly in front of the stitch. Work the stitch firmly so that the bead won't fall to the back of the work.

From the right side: Work to the stitch to be beaded, then slip the bead up in back of the work. Insert needle as if to knit; wrap yarn around it. Push bead to front through the stitch on the left needle; complete the stitch.

stockinette, garter or slip stitches. Work stitches firmly on either side of the beads to keep them in place. There is an alternative technique in which the beads are not strung on the yarn prior to beginning the knitting: The loop of a stitch is drawn through the bead and doubled, and the loop is then placed on the right-hand needle without being worked.

See also BEAD KNITTING; BEADS; EMBELLISHMENTS

BEAD KNITTING

Not to be confused with beaded knitting, bead knitting is a technique in which beads are placed between every stitch so that the beads completely cover the knitted stitches. Also known as *purse knitting,* this technique developed in the eighteenth and nineteenth centuries, when it was used (as it is today) for purses and other elaborately decorated items. Intricate patterns can be worked by threading beads in reverse of the

design, then working them into the knitting.

See also BEADED KNITTING; BEADS; EMBELLISHMENTS

BEADS

Beads are small objects made of glass, wood, plastic, clay, gems or crystal that have a hole in them. Beads can be worked into your knitted pieces with beaded or bead-knitting techniques or sewn onto a completed project. There are many creative ways to add beads to your knitted pieces. Use them to enhance a neckline or hem, create an allover pattern, or form pattern indentations, such

as at the center and sides of cables or in the openings created by eyelet stitches. Match the beads to the yarn, keeping in mind that the yarn must be able to pass through the hole and the end effect is that they will add weight to the knitted piece and may cause stitches to stretch.

See also BEAD KNITTING; BEADED KNITTING

BEG

Abbreviation for *begin(s)* or *beginning.*

BELL SLEEVE

See SLEEVES

BERET

See HATS

BERGEN MUSEUM

Founded in 1825 and now part of the University of Bergen, the Bergen Museum houses one of the largest collections of natural and cultural history in Norway. Norwegian folk costumes, including cardigans, mittens, hats and stockings knit in traditional patterns, are part of the collection.

See also SCANDINAVIAN PATTERNS

BERGERE DE FRANCE

Bergère de France is a French

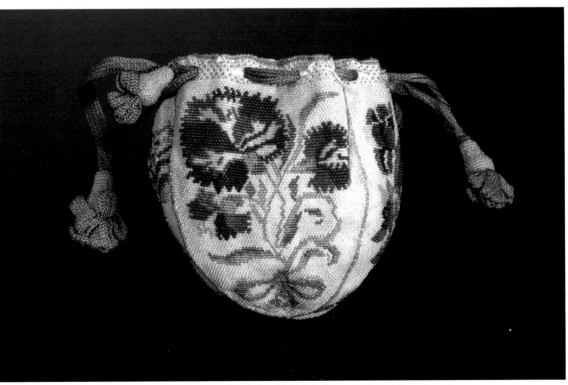

An excellent example of bead knitting, this silk bag was knit in Great Britain in the early nineteenth century.

manufacturer that has been producing luxury hand-knitting yarns since 1946. The company emphasizes close interaction with its retailers to ensure that the proper image and ambiance surround its products. The company gives its retailers different ways to sell its lines: via promotion of pattern magazines (Bergère's design department turns out about 250 patterns per year), promotion of themed pattern booklets, single yarn collections or complete display packages. The company's new collection of natural yarns, Origins, is a natural extension of the ecologically friendly philosophy of manager Vincent Glorion. Bergère also emphasizes its special wrapper packaging, which is translucent to keep displays looking tidy and to prevent the fibers from being handled directly by customers. Bergère's yarns include merino, bamboo, silk and blends featuring cashmere, merino/alpaca, cotton/soy and mohair, each in a wide variety of colorways. Bergère's manufacturing facility in France is respectful to the environment, having been designed to lower the consumption of electricity and make the dyeing as clean as possible. Even the heat generated by the high temperatures of liquids used in its machines is used to heat the plant.

BERNAT

Bernat is a brand of the manufacturer Spinrite Yarns in Stratford, Ontario. Bernat's yarns are widely available to North American knitters via crafts chain stores and needlework mail-order catalogs. The yarns are perceived as economical for family knitting, and the many patterns available for the yarns reflect those aesthetics—afghan knitters, for example, find many resources on Bernat's website. Bernat's fibers include blends of alpaca, bamboo, corn, cotton, mohair, nylon, acrylic, silk, soy and wool. Because so many knitters had contacted Bernat about how and where they could donate knitted goods for charitable causes, Bernat recently introduced a secondary website, BernatCares.com, which features an extensive resource of charities in need of knitted products for many different causes. Sara Arblaster of Bernat put it this way: "We wanted to link these passionate, avid knitters and crocheters with charities in their neighborhoods." The company is also actively involved in the yarn industry, taking part in organizations such as the Craft Yarn Council (CYC) to influence the direction of crafts in our culture.

BET

Abbreviation for *between*.

BIND-OFF

On the last row of knitting, the bind-off secures the stitches together and keeps the work from unraveling; it is also called the cast-off, especially in Britain.

A bound-off edge can be attached to other pieces of knitting, or it can stand on its own. The bound-off edge should be elastic but firm. To avoid a too-tight bound-off edge, bind off with a needle one or two sizes larger than the size used used for the previous rows. Unless the pattern instructions state otherwise, bind off in the stitch pattern used for the piece.

In addition to finishing knit pieces, binding off is used to shape armholes, necks and shoulders. It can be used to create the first row of a buttonhole or three-dimensional stitch patterns.

Some bind-offs are multipurpose, such as the basic knit bind-off or the basic purl bind-off. Others serve special functions, such as the three-needle bind-off, which brings two edges together to make a neat, flexible join and is most commonly used to attach equal numbers of live stitches at the shoulder of a sweater.
See also CAST-ON; FINISHING TECHNIQUES; SHAPING; THREE-NEEDLE BIND-OFF

An assortment of beads suitable for knitting, including (left to right) E-beads, seed beads, faceted beads and pony beads

Basic Knit Bind-off

This is the most common bind-off method and the easiest to learn. It creates a firm, neat edge.

1. Knit two stitches. *Insert the left needle into the first stitch on the right needle.

2. Pull this stitch over the second stitch and off the right needle.

3. One stitch remains on the right needle as shown. Knit the next stitch. Repeat from * until you have bound off the required number of stitches.

Basic Purl Bind-off

The purl bind-off creates a firm edge and is used on purl stitches.

1. Purl two stitches. *Insert the left needle from behind the right needle into the back loop of the first stitch on the right needle as shown.

2. Pull this stitch over the second stitch and off the right needle.

3. One stitch remains on the right needle as shown. Purl the next stitch . Repeat from * until you have bound off the required number of stitches.

BISON FIBER

See BUFFALO FIBER

BL

Abbreviation for *back loop(s)*. *See also* BACK LOOP

BLACK SHEEP GATHERING

See SHEEP AND WOOL FESTIVALS

BLISS, DEBBIE (1952-)

This London-based knitwear designer has twenty-plus books and her own line of yarn to her name. Although she designs many garments for adults, Bliss is best known for her knits for babies and children.

Bliss discovered knitting while studying fashion and textiles. She experimented with soft-sculpture pieces and was hired as contributing editor on a book called *Wild Knitting* (Mitchell Beazley/A&W Publishers, 1979), after which she began accepting handknitting commissions from magazines and book publishers. It was the birth of her son, Will, in 1985—daughter Eleanor came along in 1990—that got her thinking about and knitting baby clothes. *Baby Knits* (Ebury Press/St. Martin's Press) hit shelves in 1988 to great acclaim. Bliss followed it with nearly two dozen more books, including *How to Knit* (1999), *Debblie Bliss Home* (2005), *Baby Knits for Beginners* (2003) and *Essential Baby* (2007), all published by Trafalgar Square

Books, and *Design It, Knit It* (2009) and *Design It, Knit It Babies* (2010), both published by Sixth&Spring Books.

In the midst of this prolific publishing career, Bliss designed baby clothes for Marks & Spencer and newborn ready-to-wear for Baby Gap. She now has a line of yarn that bears her name and an eponymous magazine, and she continues to travel widely, giving talks at yarn shops in the U.K., the United States and elsewhere, while developing pattern booklets to support her yarn and add to her ever-growing bibliography. *See also* DESIGNERS; MAGAZINES AND JOURNALS

BLOCKING

Blocking is the process of wetting, pressing or steaming finished knit pieces to give them their permanent size and shape and set the stitches.

Most knitted pieces should be blocked before seaming to flatten and smooth the edges as well as even out the stitches. In addition, you can lightly steam seams from the wrong side to flatten them once they are sewn. You can also block a finished garment, such as a sweater or shawl, after you have worn it. Each time a garment is washed it will likely need to be re-blocked in order to maintain the proper size.

Before blocking, read the instructions on the yarn label about fabric care. Some synthetic yarns shouldn't be steamed, and some novelty yarns and highly textured yarns should not be blocked at all. Long-hair fibers such as mohair and angora become matted if you press them. If you are uncertain about how a yarn will react when blocked, experiment with a swatch before blocking your knitted pieces.

Materials for Blocking

Gather the following supplies to successfully block:

• A flat surface or blocking board large enough to hold one full piece of knitting; an ironing board works for small pieces

• A padded covering that will hold pins

• Rustproof pins, such as T-pins or glass- or plastic-headed pins that will not leave marks on knitting, or blocking wires

The Blocking Process

If you are wet blocking, soak the pieces first per the following instructions. If you are steam blocking, proceed with the dry pieces. Block pieces right-side up so you can see the results as you work. Begin pinning the pieces to the blocking surface at key areas such as shoulders, the bust/chest just below the armholes and at lower-edge points. When blocking a shawl or scarf, pin down the corners first.

Keep all pieces straight and even as you pin them, smoothing them from the center out. You may want to mark the center of each piece at its widest point. Then you can measure from this point to place your first crucial pins. Make sure the width and length measurements are accurate before you place pins at closer intervals. Place the pins so they are close enough to avoid marks or create scalloped edges when the pieces dry. Do not pin ribbed areas that are intended to pull in.

If you have two matching pieces, such as cardigan fronts, block them side by side to ensure that the measurements of both pieces are accurate.

Wet Blocking

Wet blocking is done without steaming or pressing. Wet the pieces either by submerging them in cool water before laying them on your blocking surface, or by spraying them with tepid or cold water after pinning (the latter technique is often referred to as *cold blocking*). If you submerge your pieces in water, let them soak for at least 30 minutes so that the fibers are fully saturated. Drain the water and squeeze—do not wring—to get most of the water out. Gently roll the piece in a towel to remove excess water. The pieces should be damp but not dripping before pinning. Pin them out while wet. Always allow your pieces to dry completely before unpinning and seaming them.

Steam Blocking

You can block with an iron or hand-held steamer rather than completely saturating the work with water. Note that it is the heat and moisture that smooth and even out the pieces, *not* the pressure of the iron. Never place the iron directly on your finished piece; instead, hold it above the piece and slowly work over the entire area. Let the steam dampen each piece completely. Curled work will unfurl before your eyes as the steam penetrates the fiber.

To protect the knitted piece from intense heat, place a pressing cloth between the iron and the knitted piece. You can steam block by using either a dry pressing cloth with a steam iron or by using a wet pressing cloth with a dry iron.

Set the temperature of your iron carefully to match the type of fiber in the yarn—check the care label. Cottons can withstand warmer temperatures than wool. Synthetics need very cool iron settings.

See also ASSEMBLING; BLOCKING WIRES; CARE; FIBER CONTENT; PINS; YARN LABELS

BLOCKING WIRES

A set of flexible wires can be used for blocking a completed section of knitting to fit the desired dimensions. The flexible wires, usually made of stainless steel to prevent rusting, make it easy to

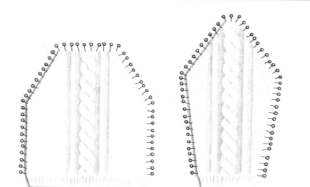

Knitted pieces pinned for blocking. When blocking pieces that will be joined, such as sweater fronts and sleeves, make sure the measurements match the schematic.

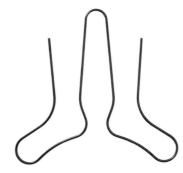

Sock blockers are helpful for shaping socks after knitting. Place damp socks on blockers, shape to fit and let dry.

block a long straight edge, such as the side of a lace shawl. The wire is inserted into the outer edge of the completed item by carefully weaving it in and out of the fabric. Even scallops can be effectively blocked with blocking wires by catching the points of the scallops with the wire. This will hold them equidistant from the edge. The wire itself is pinned to the blocking board or other flat surface, not the work, to fit the dimensions called for in the pattern. The work is then steamed. Blocking wires can be purchased at yarn shops or through catalogs and websites specializing in knitting accessories.
See also BLOCKING

BLOGS
See INTERNET

BLUE SKY ALPACAS
Blue Sky Alpacas got its start when Linda Niemeyer entered the world of yarns and knitting by purchasing a pregnant alpaca and breeding a small herd on her Minnesota farm. Since those days, her alpacas have become pets, but they still represent the down-to-earth lifestyle that Niemeyer espouses. Blue Sky has leapt and bounded ahead, now importing its fibers from Peru and Bolivia. The company sources from sustainable resources and pays a fair wage to its suppliers, bringing a sense of social responsibility to all of its ventures: Niemeyer says her basic philosophy is that "having a great product isn't enough, you need to have integrity behind it." That ethos marries with products of impeccable quality and on-target fashion sensibilities. Knitters love Blue Sky for its soft pastels, latte shades and creamy, super-bulky organic cottons and wools that beg to be touched. The collection now includes over thirty colors as well as blends of silk, wool, bamboo and merino. Blue Sky has also delved into knit-related accessories. All of these products are artfully presented: Even the company's swatch cards are constructed as clever idea kits. Blue Sky Alpacas is maintaining a unique presence in the luxury yarn sector.

BO
Abbreviation for *bind off*.
See also BIND-OFF

BOBBIN (COLORWORK)
This term is born out of sewing, where the bobbin is a small plastic piece that holds the secondary source of thread. In knitting and crocheting, a bobbin is a larger plastic piece used to hold a short length of yarn. The term can also be used to describe a smaller ball of yarn used in addition to the main yarn, especially in colorwork. Bobbins are most typically used when knitting multicolored patterns such as argyles or intarsia.
See also ARGYLE; COLORWORK; INTARSIA

BOBBIN (SPINNING)
The bobbin is the spool onto which yarn is spun by a spinning wheel or machine. Often the bobbin has flanges on the ends to keep the yarn from slipping off. The type of mechanism used to spin determines the manner in which yarn is guided onto the bobbin(s), as well as the tension with which it is wound. Yarn is then unwound from the bobbin, either as a ply that is joined with other plies, or directly into balls, skeins or hanks.
See also SPINNING

BOBBLE
A three-dimensional stitch, the bobble (sometimes called a *popcorn*) is made by working multiple increases in one stitch, sometimes working a few rows over these increased stitches, and then decreasing back to one stitch. The increased stitches will puff out from the body of the work, as they are all inhabiting one stitch space, and the result is a three-dimensional bobble.

Bobbles can be knit in stockinette or reverse stockinette stitch, and their size depends on the number of stitches made out

Bobbins for colorwork come in different shapes and styles.

Make Bobble

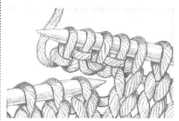

Five-stitch bobbles

1. To knit a 5-stitch bobble, make 5 stitches in one stitch as follows: [Knit the stitch in the front loop and then knit in the back loop without slipping it from the left needle] twice, knit in the front loop once more. Slip the stitch from the left needle.

2. [Turn the work and purl these 5 stitches as shown, turn the work and knit 5] twice.

3. With the left needle, pull the second, third, fourth and fifth stitches one at a time over the first stitch and off the needle. One bobble has been made.

of the first stitch and the number of rows worked on the increased stitches. Bobbles can be combined with cables, as in Aran knitting; they can be used individually or in groups; or they can be arranged to form rows of vertical and horizontal lines. They can also be knitted separately and sewn onto a garment.
See also ARAN KNITTING; CABLES; REVERSE STOCKINETTE STITCH; STOCKINETTE STITCH

BODY FIT

When describing how a knitted garment fits in relation to the body, the term "body fit" is often used. Knitted garments are usually categorized as very close-fitting (body-hugging), close-fitting (body-contoured), standard-fitting (body-skimming), loose-fitting (straight-hanging) or oversized (full, roomy).
See also EASE

BOHUS KNITTING

The knitting cooperative established in Sweden in 1939 called itself Bohus Knitting. Founded by Emma Jacobsson, the wife of the governor of the Swedish province of Bohuslan, the Bohus Stickning ("Knitting") provided work for the wives of unemployed stonecutters and farmers. By 1947, the cooperative employed some 870 knitters, who produced fine-gauge handknits inspired by, but not limited to, traditional Swedish patterns. Production began with

plain socks and gloves in strong wools but soon moved on to sweaters in fine wool and angora blends. Knit back and forth in stranded colorwork patterns that employ a minimum of three to four colors in a single row (some designs contain as many as seven colors), the sweaters are prized examples of Swedish handicraft. Bohus designs were presented to visiting dignitaries and exported on a large scale.

Emma Jacobsson, who had a fine-arts background, designed many of the original Bohus patterns, eventually bringing in a

gifted team of designers to work with her. Along with their famed colorwork, Bohus designs often used purl stitches to add texture, further complicating their construction. The increasing skill needed to create the patterns and the delicacy of the wool employed to make them, combined with a postwar economic boom, resulted in a gradual decline in the numbers of Bohus knitters. When Jacobsson retired in 1956, no replacement could be found for her; Bohus Stickning closed in 1969. The Bohus knitting tradition continues, however, in workshops

Classic Bohus sweaters

and classes taught around the world. Patterns for authentic Bohus sweater designs can be obtained from Sweden's Bohuslan Museum.
See also FOLK KNITTING; SWEDISH PATTERNS

BOHUSLAN MUSEUM
See BOHUS KNITTING

BOHUS STICKNING
See BOHUS KNITTING

BORDERS

The stitch pattern placed at or near an edge of a knitted piece to give it stability or design interest is called a border. Unlike edgings, which are worked in a strip and attached to the finished item, borders are knitted in and worked with the item.

Most knit-in borders are constructed from simple stitches such as ribbing, seed stitch or garter stitch. The best stitches to use for borders are those that lie flat, such as ribbing or seed stitch. You can also construct knitted-in borders from lace or eyelet patterns, slip-stitch patterns, cables or other knit/purl combinations. Most borders are placed at horizontal or vertical edges, but they also can be inserted within garments or knitted items, as in the case of ribbing that falls at the waist of a fitted sweater.
See also COLLARS AND NECKBANDS; EDGINGS; EMBELLISHMENTS; EYELET

Borders

Ribbing on a curve: To shape an armhole and make the band at the same time, rib 2 stitches, then decrease one stitch. On right-side rows, keep increasing one stitch at the edge (in rib) and decreasing inside the ribbing edge until the armhole is shaped and the desired stitches are in the rib pattern.

Seed stitch: This is a good choice for a border on a stockinette stitch body, since it has the same row gauge as stockinette stitch. Also, a seed stitch pattern makes a nice flat edge.

Bias: Leave this stockinette stitch band flat or fold it in half to the inside and sew it in place. On right-side rows, slip the first stitch knitwise, work a make one increase, work to the last 2 stitches of the band, knit 2 together. On wrong-side rows, purl all border stitches.

PATTERNS; GARTER STITCH; KNIT/PURL PATTERNS; LACE KNITTING; RIBBING; SEED STITCH; SLIP-STITCH PATTERNS

BOUCLÉ

Bouclé is a looped yarn deriving its name from the French word meaning "curled." Considered a novelty yarn, a strand of bouclé looks like a length of loops of similar size, which can range from tiny circlets to large curls. The looped effect is created during the manufacturing process by plying together two strands, one spun much looser than the other. In a simple bouclé, the looser strand forms the loops and the tighter strand acts as the anchor. Another method employs a binder and two looped plies. Traditionally, bouclé yarns were made primarily of mohair or wool, although other blends have become popular, including cotton, silk and linen.

While the fabric created by knitting with bouclé yarn has an interesting texture, the downside is that needles are easily caught in the loops, and the loops allow for little stitch definition. Bouclé yarns are therefore best suited for simple stitches like stockinette and garter.
See also NOVELTY YARN; PLY

BOYE NEEDLES

The Boye company developed very early in the twentieth century as part of a Minnesota cabinetmaker's effort to create the best cases possible for traveling sewing-needle salesmen. After a number of years, James Boye's inventiveness led him to develop his own large line of needles, thimbles, hooks and more. Thus Boye Needle Company became one of America's biggest needle and hook makers, enjoying preeminence alongside the Bates line throughout the twentieth century. Eventually the company was acquired by Wrights Products and is still one of the largest sellers of steel and aluminum stitching and knitting tools, as well as offering the unique Balene knitting needles that mimic the texture of whale ivory. Boye's

Swatch knit in a bouclé yarn

interchangeable NeedleMaster System harks back to James Boye's original efforts to provide all-in-one solutions for the domestic knitter.

DE LA BRANCHARDIERE, RIEGO

See BRITISH KNITTING

BRIOCHE

A general term that refers to stitch patterns that form a plush, textured fabric with a cellular structure, brioche stitch patterns can be knit in one of two ways. In the first method, you knit into a knit stitch one or more rows below the stitch on the left-hand needle. In the second method, a yarn over is combined with a slip stitch and a decrease (k2tog). Both methods start with a preparation row done in needles larger than those used for the rest of the pattern.

Brioche patterns are loose and stretchy, and many are the same on both sides. When knit on large needles, this stitch produces a lacy pattern that is particularly good for shawls, scarves and baby blankets. When knit on smaller needles, it makes a warm fabric suitable for garments such as hats, scarves and legwarmers.

In some knitting books and references, brioche patterns are also called Shaker knitting patterns. Brioche stitch is also sometimes known as fisherman's rib. *Knitting Brioche* (North Light Books, 2009) by Nancy Marchant explores this technique in detail.

The swatch shown below is knit with the "knit one below method" over an odd number of stitches.
Row 1 (WS) Knit.
Row 2 *K1, k1-b; rep from *, end k1 (mark this row as RS).
Row 3 K2, *k1-b, k1; rep from *, end k1.
Rep rows 2 and 3.
See also KNIT/PURL PATTERNS

BRITISH KNITTING

Knitting probably took hold in Britain in the fifteenth century, but the knitting styles most associated with the region— Shetland lace, Fair Isle, Aran and the ever-practical gansey—didn't emerge until the 1800s. An act of parliament passed in 1488 set the price of both felted and woolen caps, evidence that these knitted items must have been produced for some time previously. During the Elizabethan era, knitted stockings were a source of industry, exported to Holland, Spain and Germany. The queen herself had a notorious taste for elegant silk knitted stockings, but the pieces that adorned her royal legs were imported from Spain, and Mrs. Montague's Pattern, the famous lace stitch said to have been invented by Elizabeth's "silk woman," is based more in folklore than fact. During Elizabeth's time,

Swatch knit in brioche stitch

The British Isles

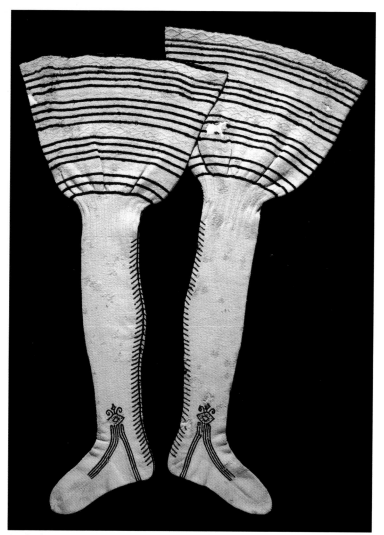

A pair of seventeenth-century Englishman's stockings

William Lee invented the first knitting machine, reportedly after watching his wife toil over knitted stockings, but the queen allegedly refused to grant him a patent for fear of putting the country's handknitters out of work. This story may or may not be true, but it's fairly certain that Lee's invention would have found little favor in an era when so many depended on knitting for their livelihood. The knitting frame, a first step toward machine knitting, was not introduced for another hundred years.

On the farms and crofts and in the fishing villages of the British countryside, knitting was a cruder, more practical pursuit. The few idle moments these people had were put to good use knitting plain, unpatterned stockings and other articles that were used to clothe the family or sold or traded in exchange for food and goods. Everyone in the family—male and female, young and old—was expected to turn out at least one pair of stockings each week. As the empire grew through colonization, it brought knitting to other reaches of the globe, including the Americas, India, China and Japan.

Victorian ladies, like their poorer counterparts, also knitted, but they made fine garments, typically of lace. Many of these garments were highlighted during the Great Exhibition of 1851, a huge event that celebrated British industry. During the Victorian era the first commercial knitting patterns appeared on a large scale. Pioneers in the writing and publishing of patterns were Jane Gaugain, Frances Lambert, Miss Watts, Cornelia Mee and Mlle. Riego de la Branchardière, all of whom began to publish around 1840. *Weldon's Practical Needlework* began publication in 1888 and continued through the 1920s.

Britain suffered severely, both on the battlefield and at the home front, during the two World Wars of the twentieth century, and many commodities—including wool— were in extremely short supply. It is a little-known fact that Britain cornered the worldwide market in wool early in World War I; as a result, British soldiers were better clad than their German counterparts and better able to survive winter conditions. Knitting for the troops was a veritable mania during this period.

During the war years, "make do and mend" was the rallying cry as everyone was encouraged to knit both for conservation and for the aid of the army and navy. In the 1940s and 1950s, new innovations in yarn color and styles fed a war-weary market hungry for fashionable designs and brighter colors. Knitting was taught in schools as a useful skill, not a hobby, and patterns for clothing and blankets, toys and household goods were provided with the idea that these items could be sold for profit. In the 1970s Britain led a kind of handknitting revolution with Patricia Roberts, Kaffe Fassett and others blazing new trails for knitters. Debbie Bliss is a modern British knitwear designer who has attained much acclaim.
See also ARAN KNITTING; ARGYLE; CHANNEL ISLANDS PATTERNS; DALES KNITTING; FAIR ISLE; FASSETT, KAFFE; GANSEY; MACHINE KNITTING; SHETLAND LACE; VICTORIAN KNITTING; *WELDON'S PRACTICAL NEEDLEWORK*

Classic Fair Isle V-neck pullover

BROWN SHEEP

One of the largest fiber mills in America, Brown Sheep spins wool, cotton and other fibers sourced solely from the United States. The company was launched in 1980 when Harlon Brown and his wife first purchased spinning equipment in Mitchell, Nebraska. Their first yarn line, "Top of the Lamb," was a major success and is extremely popular to this day. Their son Robert Brown began to experiment with dyes and other natural fibers like mohair, and from this the top-selling "Lamb's Pride" line was created, growing to include over seventy solid and shaded colors. The company continues to add new fibers to its collection, and today carries over fourteen different yarn lines in various weights and fibers, including Waverly Wool, a plied yarn developed just for needlepointers. Believing that jobs and manufacturing need to stay in the United States, Brown Sheep's current owner Peggy Wells upgraded the mill in 2003 with modern equipment and technology. Since all production and fibers used are domestic, the Brown Sheep brand is often the yarn of choice for those who prefer to purchase all-American products. Brown Sheep has also ventured into the realm of pattern leaflets.

BUDD, ANN (1956-)

Knitwear designer and author Ann Budd has been affiliated with Interweave Press since 1989. Among her books (all published by Interweave) are the best-selling *The Knitter's Handy Book of Patterns: Basic Designs in Multiple Sizes & Gauges* (2002)— a collection of sweater templates that can be mixed and matched to create a customized garment— and its sequel *The Knitter's Handy Book of Sweater Patterns* (2004). *Getting Started Knitting Socks* (2007) applies the same build-on-the-basics approach to footwear. She is considered a go-to reference source for budding designers. Budd is well known for her sock designs, and with fellow Interweave editor Anne Merrow she compiled *Favorite Socks* (2007). She lives in Boulder, Colorado, and has been designated a master knitter by the Knitting Guild Association. *See also* ALLEN, PAM; DESIGNERS; MAGAZINES AND JOURNALS; *INTERWEAVE KNITS*

BUFFALO FIBER

The coarse guard hairs and downy undercoat of the American bison, also known as American buffalo, a member of the bovid (Bovidae) family and the genus *Bison,* are spun into a knittable fiber. The thick outer guard hair provides insulation to the large animal during the winter and molts away in the spring.

Ancestors of the American bison originated in Eurasia and migrated over the Bering Strait to North America approximately 25,000 years ago. As recently as three hundred years ago, up to 50 million head of buffalo roamed the American West. They thrived especially in the Great Plains, where they provided food, shelter, clothing and spiritual importance to the Plains Indians and other Native American tribes. In the late 1800s the animals were over-hunted to meet the demand for buffalo skins. Large-scale slaughter of once-thriving herds reduced their numbers to just a few hundred and placed the buffalo on the brink of extinction.

Thanks to the efforts of a few enterprising ranchers, the numbers of American bison began to increase at the end of the nineteenth century, and today approximately 250,000 bison live on ranches, where they are raised mainly for meat and hides, while 100,000 remain in the wild in national parks and other protected areas.

Native Americans used the coarser guard hair fiber for rope and the finer downy undercoat as stuffing for insulation and in yarn for weaving. The guard hairs of a buffalo fleece are hollow, while the softer, shorter hairs are solid and covered in scales. The hair

Buffalo

Skeins of buffalo-fiber blended with cashmere, silk and Tencel

contains no lanolin and is therefore both hypoallergenic and mothproof. Buffalo down is a very warm, insulating fiber with a short staple length of about one inch and with more bounce than other luxury fibers. The yarn is produced as a byproduct of the buffalo-meat industry.
See also FIBER CHARACTERISTICS; LANOLIN; STAPLE

BULKY

The second-highest category in the CYC's Standard Weight System, bulky yarn scores a 5 on the scale. This category includes yarns labeled craft, chunky and rug yarn. It typically knits up at 12–15 stitches to 4 inches (10cm) on size 9–11 needles. Bulky yarns work up quickly and are suitable for beginners and for quick projects such as hats, scarves, blankets and chunky sweaters. Once largely available in acrylic, wool and cotton, today's bulky yarns are also produced in a range of luxury fibers and blends.
See also YARN WEIGHT

BULLION STITCH

Bullion stitch is an embroidery stitch in which the yarn or thread is coiled around the needle to give the effect of tiny cords or worms on the surface of the fabric.
See also EMBROIDERY; FINISHING TECHNIQUES

BUSH, NANCY (1951-)

A knitting designer who imbues her work with an art historian's sense of reverence, reference and scope, Nancy Bush is best known for her sock and Estonian patterns. She has a degree in art history, and it was her interest in textiles that led her to study weaving in Sweden, where she picked up knitting from other students.

Bush is one of the country's premier sock designers— though she admittedly hardly ever wears or makes handknit socks for herself—having written three books on the subject, incorporating into both text and patterns meticulous research on sock-knitting traditions and construction. *Folk Socks* (Interweave, 1994) focused on the European folk culture of footwear; *Knitting on the Road: Sock Patterns for the Traveling Knitter* (Interweave, 2001) includes patterns inspired by her travels in the United States and abroad; and *Knitting Vintage Socks* (Interweave, 2005) translates for the modern knitter nineteenth-century socks originally published in the *Weldon's Practical Needlework* monthly newsletters from the late 1800s. Bush has also delved deeply into Estonian techniques. In 2008 her book *Knitted Lace of Estonia* was published (Interweave, 2008).
See also DESIGNERS; SOCKS; *WELDON'S PRACTICAL NEEDLEWORK*

BUTTON BAND

The strip of fabric or area on a sweater, cardigan or jacket front on which buttons are sewn is commonly called the button band. Button bands may be worked horizontally or vertically. Generally, on women's garments, the button band is on the right side of the garment; on men's garments it is on the left side. Button bands can be reinforced with grosgrain ribbon for stability after the knitting is complete.
See also BORDER; BUTTONHOLE BAND; BUTTONHOLES; BUTTONS; EDGINGS; FINISHING TECHNIQUES

BUTTONHOLE BAND

The separate strip of fabric or area on a sweater, cardigan or jacket front on which buttonholes are placed is called the buttonhole band. The band may be worked vertically or horizontally or folded over. Generally, on women's garments the buttonhole band is on the left side; on men's garments it is on the right. Buttonhole bands can be reinforced with grosgrain ribbon for stability after the knitting is complete.
See also BORDERS; BUTTON BAND; BUTTONHOLE; BUTTONS; EDGING; FINISHING TECHNIQUES

Bullion Stitch

Bring the needle up through the fabric. Reinsert it as shown and wrap the yarn around it four to six times. Holding the yarn taut, pull the needle through. Reinsert the needle a short distance from where it emerged and pull through again.

BUTTONHOLES

Buttonholes come in many styles, including horizontal, vertical and eyelet button loops. They can also be created by slipping a button through a yarn over in lace stitch patterns or through very loosely knit stitches. The buttonhole should be just large enough to slip the button through. Knitted fabric stretches, so a buttonhole that is too large will eventually allow the button to slip loose. When making buttonholes, remember that bound-off stitches must be offset by casting on in either the same row or the next row. Yarn overs must be offset by decreases. The first row of a buttonhole is worked on the right side of the piece unless stated otherwise in the pattern. There are several methods for working buttonholes; instructions for a few of the most popular are given here.

When working the button band before the buttonhole band, mark button placements on the button band with contrasting yarn or safety pins and use that to determine buttonhole placement.

Two-Row Horizontal Buttonhole

The two-row buttonhole is made by binding off a number of stitches on one row and casting them on again on the next. The last stitch bound off is part of the left side of the buttonhole. The single cast-on makes the neatest edge for the upper part of the buttonhole. Some versions have techniques to strengthen the corners. All the horizontal buttonholes shown here are worked over four stitches.

One-Row Horizontal Buttonhole

The horizontal one-row buttonhole is the neatest buttonhole and requires no further reinforcing. It is shown here worked from the right side (lower buttonhole) and from the wrong side (upper buttonhole).

Eyelet Buttonhole

Eyelet buttonholes are small and are ideal for small buttons and children's garments.

Vertical Buttonhole

Vertical buttonhole slits are made by working two sections with separate balls of yarn at the same time or individually. If the latter, work the first side to desired depth (end at buttonhole edge). Work second side with one row fewer, ending on wrong side. Turn work, cut second ball of yarn. Then, with yarn from first side, rejoin by working across all stitches. Finish and strengthen by making a horizontal stitch at upper and lower joining points (use yarn from joining).
See also BUTTON BAND; BUTTONHOLE BAND; BUTTONS; EYELET; FINISHING TECHNIQUES; YARN OVER

Two-Row Horizontal Buttonhole

This buttonhole is frequently called for in knitting instructions.

1. On the first row, work to the placement of the buttonhole. Knit 2, with the left needle, pull one stitch over the other stitch, *knit one, pull the second stitch over the knit one; repeat from the * twice more. Four stitches have been bound off.

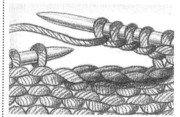

2. On the next row, work to the bound-off stitches and cast on four stitches using the single cast-on method. On the next row, work these stitches through the back loops to tighten them.

One-Row Horizontal Buttonhole

Top: worked from wrong side
Bottom: worked from right side

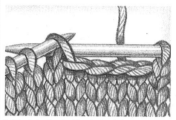

1. Work to the buttonhole, bring yarn to front and slip a stitch purlwise. Place yarn at back and leave it there. *Slip next stitch from left needle. Pass first slipped stitch over it; repeat from the * three times more. Slip the last bound-off stitch to left needle and turn work.

2. Using the cable cast-on with yarn at the back, cast on 5 stitches as follows: *Insert right needle between first and second stitches on left needle, draw up a loop, place the loop on left needle; repeat from * four times more, turn.

3. Slip the first stitch with the yarn in back from the left needle and pass the extra cast-on stitch over it to close the buttonhole. Work to the end of the row.

Eyelet Buttonholes

One-stitch eyelet:
Row 1 Work to the buttonhole, knit 2 together, yarn over.
Row 2 Work the yarn over as a stitch on next row.

Two-stitch eyelet:
Row 1 Work to the buttonhole, knit 2 together, yarn over twice, slip, slip, knit (ssk).
Row 2 Work the yarn overs as follows: Purl into the first yarn over and then purl into the back of the second yarn over.

Vertical Buttonholes

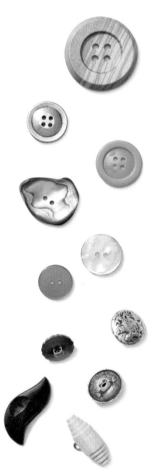

Seed stitch: Vertical buttonholes can be worked on narrow bands. This type of buttonhole is not suited for large buttons or stress and is best used for decorative purposes, such as on pocket flaps. Seed stitch is ideal for vertical buttonholes since it lies flat.

Double buttonholes: Since stockinette stitch rolls inward, vertical buttonholes should only be used on stockinette stitch for double bands as shown here. To make a neater edge, add a selvage stitch on either side of the slit.

Closed double buttonholes: When the band is complete, fold it, match the buttonholes and reinforce them by embroidering with the buttonhole stitch. Note that the band is worked with a slip stitch at the center to make a neater folding edge.

BUTTONS

These everyday fasteners are used frequently on knitted garments. The choice of buttons should complement a garment, not detract from it. Although buttons are applied after garment is completed, whenever possible choose them during the planning stage. Size, color and material are all important factors to be considered. Some patterns call for buttons to be crocheted or knit from the same or complementary yarn as the garment.

See also BUTTON BAND; BUTTONHOLE BAND; BUTTONHOLES

Buttons come in two-hole, four-hole, shank and toggle styles and in a variety of materials including wood, plastic, metal and shell.

C

CABLE CAST-ON

The cable cast-on forms a sturdy yet elastic edge. It is perfect for ribbed edges. This cast-on is worked with two needles.

See also CAST-ON; KNITTING ON

Cable cast-on edge

Cast on 2 stitches using the knitting-on cast-on. *Insert the right needle between the 2 stitches on the left needle.

Wrap the yarn around the right needle as if to knit and pull the yarn through to make a new stitch.

Place the new stitch on the left needle as shown. Repeat from the *, always inserting the right needle in between the last 2 stitches on the left needle.

CABLE NEEDLE

Not the same as a knitting needle, a cable needle is a short (about 3–4 inches/7.5–10cm) long, slightly curved or straight needle made of plastic, metal or wood that is pointed at both ends. A cable needle is used to hold stitches temporarily when working a cable. It can be shaped with a bend in the middle or look like the letter *U,* with one end of the U longer than the other to keep stitches from sliding off.

Cable needles come in a range of sizes that coordinate with differnt yarn weights, and it's best to use a cable needle with a smaller diameter than that of the working needles. In knitting instructions, *cable needle* is often abbreviated as "cn."

See also CABLE PATTERNS; CABLES

CABLE PATTERNS

When cables are combined to form patterns of ropes, braids or waves, they are referred to as cable patterns. In some cable patterns, the cables are arranged in vertical columns; in others they form an allover design.

Most often, cable patterns are worked on backgrounds of reverse stockinette stitch, but vertical, rope-like, or braided cables can also be separated by seed or moss stitch, garter stitch, ribbing, checked patterns or other textured stitches. Small cables alternated with columns of purl stitches can also be used as ribbing. Stockinette cables worked on a stockinette ground don't have as much contrast and can be an interesting and appealing design as well.

Cable patterns enhance any type of knitted garment. Cable patterns can be positioned vertically or horizontally, or they can be inserted as panels. Cables also are often incorporated into knitted afghans and pillows. Aran sweaters combine cables in various sizes, often with bobbles, seed or moss stitch and other textured stitches.

See also AFGHAN; ARAN

KNITTING; BOBBLE; CABLES; MOSS STITCH; RIBBING; SEED STITCH; STOCKINETTE STITCH; TRAVELING STITCHES; TWISTED-STITCH PATTERNS

CABLES

The term *cable* is used for a type of textured, traveling stitch pattern formed by crossing stitches from one position to another and knitting the stitches out of order. Cables are usually knit on a background with a contrasting stitch pattern (such as a stockinette-stitch cable on a reverse stockinette background).

Typically, equal numbers of stitches are crossed in cables. However, cables can also be formed by crossing uneven numbers of stitches. The smallest cables, also called twisted stitches, are constructed by crossing only 2 stitches, although most cables are formed by crosses over 4, 6, 8 or 10 stitches.

A cable (also called a *cross*) is usually formed by using an extra needle, called a cable needle, to

Three types of cable needles

This classic cable is simply constructed by placing a left-twisting cable and a right-twisting cable side by side.

Another classic pattern, the moss-stitch diamond, is formed by moving the sides of the cable close together, then apart.

hold the stitches to be crossed to either the front or back of the work. Then the next group of stitches is knit, and finally the stitches from the cable needle are knit. Stitches placed to the front of the work will form a left-slanting cable pattern; stitches placed in back of the work will form a right-slanting cable. This technique is illustrated at right for a cable crossed over 6 stockinette stitches.

Many knitters choose to create cables without a cable needle, employing various techniques that involve slipping the stitches that would be held, working the cable stitches, then transferring the slipped stitches back to the left needle, usually in a careful motion that leaves the stitches off either needle for a moment. Those who become adept at it find it to be much faster than using a cable needle.

See also ARAN KNITTING; CABLE NEEDLE; CABLE PATTERNS; REVERSE STOCKINETTE STITCH; STOCKINETTE STITCH; TRAVELING STITCHES

Front (or Left) Cable

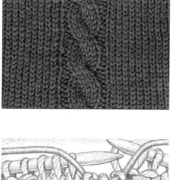

1. Slip the first 3 stitches of the cable purlwise to a cable needle and hold them to the front of the work. Be careful not to twist the stitches.

2. Leave the stitches suspended in front of the work, keeping them in the center of the cable needle where they won't slip off. Pull the yarn firmly and knit the next 3 stitches.

3. Knit the 3 stitches from the cable needle. If this seems too awkward, return the stitches to the left needle and then knit them.

Back (or Right) Cable

1. Slip the first 3 stitches of the cable purlwise to a cable needle and hold them to the back of the work. Be careful not to twist the stitches.

2. Leave the stitches suspended in back of the work, keeping them in the center of the cable needle where they won't slip off. Pull the yarn firmly and knit the next 3 stitches.

3. Knit the 3 stitches from the cable needle. If this seems too awkward, return the stitches to the left needle and then knit them.

CAMELHAIR

The fiber from the Bactrian, or two-humped, camels raised in the desert steppes of central Asia, including China, Mongolia and Russia, is used in yarn. Like most of the fiber-producing camelids (a group of animals that includes llamas and alpacas as well as camels), camels produce a two-layer coat. The long (up to 15-inch/40cm), coarse guard hairs are scratchy and used primarily for rugs and kilims. The shorter (about 5-inch/13cm) soft down undercoat and the fiber of the baby camel are the sources of the desirable fiber that is used in the manufacture of camelhair coats and handknitting yarns. The fiber is collected when the animals molt or shed their hair in the late spring. Each animal can produce up to 5 pounds of fiber a year. Camelhair is virtually impossible to bleach and difficult to dye, so it is most often used in its natural shade, the caramel-like brown color we know as "camel."

See also FIBER CHARACTERISTICS; FIBER CONTENT

Swatch knit with camelhair yarn

CAMPS AND RETREATS

Immersive knitting experiences away from everyday commitments and stresses are popular with knitters of all ages. Led by experts and typically held in a hotel or campground, these programs run from a weekend to a week and vary widely in price, depending on accommodations, offerings and the star wattage of the presenters.

The preeminent and longest-running program is Knitting Camp (schoolhousepress.com/camp.htm), which is held in Wisconsin and was started by Elizabeth Zimmermann in 1974. Knitting Camp is now run by the late designer's daughter, Meg Swansen.

Two designers who regularly host their own knitting retreats include Tara Jon Manning (tarahandknitting.com), who headlines Mindful Knitting, long weekends combining knitting, yoga and meditation in Vermont; and Canadian designer Lucy Neatby (tradewindknits.com), who themes her weeklong summer sessions around a particular garment like socks. Many local yarn shops also hold summer-camp programs, and groups online form them from time to time.
See also INTERNET; SWANSEN, MEG; TRAVELING WITH KNITTING; ZIMMERMANN, ELIZABETH

CAP

See HATS

CAPE

Any sleeveless outerwear garment that extends from the shoulders to the high hip or below is a called a cape. Capes are usually fastened at the neck with a clasp, button or tie. Knitted or crocheted capes can be worked in any number of yarns and stitch patterns.
See also CAPELET; PONCHO; SERAPE

CAPELET

As the name suggests, a capelet is a short cape, falling from the shoulder to about mid-arm or elbow. Simple shaping and abbreviated length make this type of garment a favorite of both beginners and more experienced knitters looking for quick-finishing projects. Styles range from simple rectangles sewn up with two side seams and an opening for the head, to designs featuring more complex colorwork, lace and cabled patterns.
See also CAPE; PONCHO

CAP SLEEVE

See SLEEVES

CARDIGAN

A cardigan is a sweater that is open in the front, usually closing with buttons. A fashion classic (Coco Chanel and Elsa Schiaparelli helped bring them into style), cardigans can be knit in any number of silhouettes, from close and clingy to comfortably loose, single-breasted or double-breasted, with or without closures, and with various necklines, including crewneck and V-neck.
See also SWEATER

Cardigans

Crewneck cardigan

V-neck cardigan

Cape

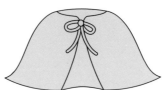

Capelet

CARDING

The combing process that prepares fibers for spinning is known as carding. Carding is the final step in the preparation of fibers after washing and picking out any foreign materials. Carding can be done by hand using a pair of hand carders, or by machine using a drum carder, a hand-cranked mechanical device. Each tool has rows of metal teeth that align the fibers. Commercial carding employs the same principle mechanized on a large scale.

Carded fiber is formed into a tube (also called a roving), or a matt (also called a batt). There are two methods of carding or lining up the fibers, woolen and worsted, which determine how the yarn is spun. In the woolen method, wool fibers of varying lengths are loosely combed and removed from the carders in a batt and rolled into a fluffy "rolag" for spinning. In the worsted method, the fibers are further combed and are of a more uniform length. The resulting yarn is smoother and stronger than woolen-spun yarn.

Hand spinners, dyers and felters view carding as both a necessary step and a creative process. Fiber is usually carded before it is dyed, but carding can also be used to mix dyed fibers before spinning. Similarly, fibers can be carded together to create fiber blends, such as wool and mohair or wool and silk.
See also DYEING; FELTING; FIBER CHARACTERISTICS; FIBER CONTENT; SPINNING

CARE

Instructions for caring for your yarn, including the preferred cleaning method, will be recommended by the manufacturer on the ball band label. To maximize the life of your garment, always follow these recommendations. Ideally, knit a gauge swatch before beginning your project and wash or clean it by the recommended method. In the case of wool, for example, not all wool is machine washable, and if washed improperly, unwanted felting can occur. In general it is best to wash and rinse with water of the same temperature to prevent shock or accidental felting. To care for your finished handknits, follow the advice for the yarn. Each time a piece is

International Care Symbols Used on Yarn Labels

	Hand wash, normal		Do *not* bleach
	Hand wash in cool water		You may iron on low heat
	Machine wash in warm water		Do *not* use an iron to press or steam
	Tumble dry, normal		Dry clean with any commercially available solvent
	Dry flat		Do *not* dry clean
	You may use chlorine bleach		Dry clean only with the following solvents: perchloroethylene mono-fluorinerichloromethane or hydrocarbon-based solvents

Hand Carding

1. First, distribute the fibers evenly over one carder and hold it in your left hand as shown.

2. Next, take the second carder in your right hand and brush it gently across the left-hand carder several times.

3. Most of the fibers are now on the right-hand carder. Push the botton edge of the right-hand carder against the left-hand carder as shown to transfer the fibers to the left-hand carder.

4. Repeat step 2. To remove the fibers trapped in the teeth of the left-hand carder, push the bottom edge of the left-hand carder against the right-hand carder to transer the fibers. If necessary, transfer the right-hand carder to your left hand and repeat the process until the fibers lie straight up and down. Remove the fibers and roll them into a rolag. It is now ready for spinning.

washed it might need to be re-blocked.

See also BLOCKING; FIBER CHARACTERISTICS; FIBER CONTENT; SUPERWASH WOOL; YARN LABEL

CARON

Caron International is one of the world's largest providers of hand-knitting yarns, latchhook kits and knitting machines. The company's yarn lines are bywords for crafts retailers: Simply Soft, One Pound and NaturallyCaron are huge sellers nationwide, offering maximum yardage for the price. In 2002, the company was reinvigorated by Cari Clement, who was brought in as director of fashion and design when she sold her company, Bond America, to Caron. Clement's career in knitwear was extensive: She had owned retail yarn stores, had designed and published hundreds of knitting patterns in top magazines and was an expert in the knitting machine. After joining Caron, Clement quickly took Caron in socially conscious directions: She secured grant money from USAID for a program called Rwanda Knits, which assists Rwandan women to form self-sustaining knitting cooperatives and earn a living wage. Caron then brought in television-celebrity-knitter Vickie Howell as a company spokesperson and designer, gaining a more hip and personable image. The company launched an e-commerce site, Caron.com. Caron is also branching out into more upscale territory with NaturallyCaron.com, yarns that blend bamboo and merino with acrylic and are supported by patterns from some of the knitwear industry's trendsetting designers.

CARRILERO, PIERRE
See PIERROT

CASCADE YARNS
Wool lovers know: No matter what you're knitting, you can always turn to Cascade for a reliable, sturdy, hardy, non-itchy worsted-weight wool that handles beautifully on the needles, felts up like a dream and can always be found in "that perfect color."

A family-owned business located in Tukwila, Washington, Cascade was founded in the late 1980s by Bob and Jean Dunbabin. At the time, most handknitters were using acrylic yarns, as expensive imported merino or coarse wool were the commonly available choices for those who wanted to use wool. The Dunbabin's search for a soft yet affordable wool took them to Peru, where they found the perfect wool from which they produce their Cascade 220 yarns.

While Cascade 220 is their best-known line, that is only part of the story. The company also sells Lana d'Oro, Eco Wool, Eco Alpaca and a variety of wool, alpaca, cottons and other high-quality fibers and blends under its own label. It also imports Di.Ve', a colorful Italian fashion yarn line, Bollicine, King Cole and Madil. There is almost no type of fiber that Cascade does not carry: bamboo, angora, cashmere, alpaca, silk, Tencel, microfiber and superwash finishes are among its many offerings. A substantial number of patterns for Cascade yarns can be found on the company's website, as can designer Nicky Epstein's distinctive range of nickel and brass buttons.

CASHMERE
Cashmere is the fiber from the undercoat of the Kashmir goat, and it is widely considered the ultimate luxury fiber. Today most cashmere comes from rugged mountainous regions of Tibet, Mongolia, Afghanistan, Iran and China and is still produced as it has been for centuries by nomadic herders. Like many other fiber-producing animals,

Swatch knit with cashmere yarn

Herd of Kashmir goats

cashmere goats have a dual coat. The long, coarse guard hairs are generally unsuitable for handknitting yarn. It is the soft undercoat, with its shorter length, that provides the fibers used for luxury cashmere yarns. The animals are combed or shorn in the spring. Each animal produces only about 100 grams (4 ounces) of usable fiber per year. This fiber is lighter in weight than wool but possesses greater insulating ability. In recent years cashmere yarn has become increasingly popular among handknitters, both in pure form and in blends. It is pleasant to knit with, and the finished product improves with age and washing, so knitters can rationalize the expense by considering it an investment.

Knitting With Cashmere

Cashmere has less elasticity than wool and therefore drapes rather than bounces back. It is soft against the skin and is suitable for a wide range of garments. It doesn't irritate sensitive skin and

is often used for baby items.
See also FIBER CHARACTERISTICS; FIBER CONTENT

CAST-OFF
See BIND-OFF

CAST-ON

Before knitting can commence, the stitches must be placed on the needles. The process of placing the loops or stitches on the needle to form the foundation row for knitting is called casting on. There are many ways to cast on, some worked with one needle and some worked with two.

The cast-on row can greatly affect the overall work, and the various cast-on methods have different qualities that can complement the stitch pattern of the knitted item. Some common cast-on methods are the single cast-on, long-tail cast-on, knitting-on cast-on and cable cast-on. Versions that allow for easy removal of the cast-on (for adding features later, for example)

are called provisional cast-ons. There are dozens of methods of casting on, the product of various ethnic traditions and of knitters' ingenuity.
See also CABLE CAST-ON; LONG-TAIL CAST-ON; SINGLE CAST-ON; KNITTING ON.

CAST ON (MAGAZINE)

Cast On is the quarterly magazine published by The Knitting Guild Association (TKGA) and available to individual or corporate members. The magazine emphasizes knitting education, offering many lessons and tutorials in addition to guild news, information about the TKGA Master Knitting Program, garment and home décor designs to knit and feature articles. The magazine was first published in 1984; editors have included Susan Hamilton, Mindi Efurd, Barbara Scott, Michelle Antle, Jennie Merritt, Pauline Schultz, Charlotte Morris, Dee Neer and Jane Miller.
See also KNITTING GUILD

ASSOCIATION, THE; MAGAZINES AND JOURNALS; MASTER KNITTING PROGRAM

CAST-ON PODCAST
See PODCASTS

CC
Abbreviation for *contrasting color*.
See also COLORWORK

CENTER-PULL BALL
See BALL

CH
Abbreviation for *chain* or *chain stitch*.
See also CHAIN; CHAIN STITCH

CHAIN

In crochet, the foundation row, called a chain, is formed by making a series of loops that are linked together. In knitting, crocheted chains are most commonly used as provisional cast-ons.
See also CHAIN STITCH; CROCHET, PROVISIONAL CAST-ON

Chain

1. Make a slipknot and place it on the hook. Draw the yarn through the loop on the hook by catching it with the hook and pulling it toward you.

2. One chain stitch is complete. Lightly tug on the yarn to tighten the loop if it is very loose, or wiggle the hook to loosen the loop if it is tight. Repeat from step 1 to make as many chains as required for your pattern.

3. To count the number of chain stitches made, hold the chain so that the Vs are all lined up. Do not count the loop on the hook or the slipknot you made when beginning the chain. Each V counts as one chain made.

CHAIN STITCH

Chain stitch is a type of embroidery stitch that forms a chain of links for outlining or filling. *See also* EMBROIDERY; LAZY DAISY STITCH

CHANGING COLORS

Color designs ranging from simple stripes to intarsia to Fair Isle knitting require color changes at the selvages or within the knitted piece. It is necessary to find smooth and consistent methods to attach yarn of a color different from the working yarn while knitting. The following step-by-step illustrations show how to change colors at the selvage, mid-row and how to carry colors along the side. *See also* FAIR ISLE KNITTING; INTARSIA; JOINING YARNS; WEAVING IN

Chain Stitch

Draw the needle up and *insert it back where it just came out, taking a short stitch. With the needle above the yarn, hold the yarn with your thumb and draw it through. Repeat from *.

Changing Colors at the Selvage

1. Wrap first the old and then the new yarn knitwise and work the first stitch with both yarns.

2. Drop the old yarn. Work the next 2 stitches with both ends of the new yarn.

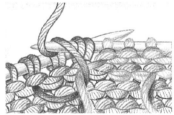

3. Drop the short end of the new color and continue working with the single strand. On the following rows, work the 3 double stitches as single stitches.

Changing Colors Mid-Row

1. Work to 3 stitches before where you want to join the new yarn. Work these stitches with the yarn folded double, making sure you have just enough to work 3 stitches.

2. Loop the new yarn into the loop of the old yarn, leaving the new yarn doubled for about 8 inches (20cm). Knit the next 3 stitches with the doubled yarn. Let the short end of the new yarn hang and continue knitting with one strand.

3. On the next row, carry the first yarn across the back of the work from where it was dropped on the previous row and twist it together with the second yarn. Work the doubled stitches as single stitches.

Carrying Colors Along the Side

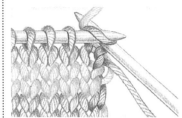

1. When changing colors with narrow, even-numbered stripes, drop the old color. Bring the new color under the old color, being sure not to pull the yarn too tightly, and knit the next stripe.

2. When working thicker stripes (generally more than 4 rows), carry the old yarn up the side until it is needed again by twisting the working yarn around the old yarn every couple of rows, as shown.

CHANNEL ISLANDS PATTERNS

Certain gansey designs originated in the Channel Islands of Guernsey and Jersey. The trading of knitted goods from the Channel Islands dates back to the reign of Elizabeth I. Mary, Queen of Scots, is rumored to have worn a pair of white gansey-knit stockings to her execution. Channel Island knitters were esteemed for their skill with yarn and needles and the fine workmanship and finishing of their garments. During the seventeenth and eighteenth centuries, knitted goods were shipped from the islands to England, France and beyond. Trade declined in the nineteenth century, but the islanders continued to create knitted goods for themselves.

Though there is some debate on the subject, the Channel Islands are generally recognized as the birthplace of the gansey (sometimes called *guernsey*), the thick, boxy sweater worn by fishermen throughout Britain.

Channel Island styles have a decorative edge created with a knotted cast-on. The shaping begins with a short welt, slit at the sides to provide freedom of movement. Once the welt was worked, the fronts and backs were joined and the body was knit in the round to the underarm, with underarm gussets for ease. The work was divided again for the armholes, and in some instances a shoulder strap was added at each side. Other sweater designs incorporate a small half-gusset at the neck edge. The body is usually done in stockinette with simple knit and purl combinations sometimes appearing on the chest. In later years, more complex cables were added, often extending to the upper arm. The sweaters became a fashion item in 1880s and a fashionable version was even worn by women.
See also BRITISH KNITTING; CABLES; FOLK KNITTING; GANSEY; KNIT/PURL PATTERNS; STOCKINETTE STITCH; WELT

CHARITY KNITTING

Stitching for a cause is a popular pursuit amongst knitters. Knitters are a particularly philanthropic lot, donating impressive amounts of time, money and knitted or crocheted goods to worthy organizations. Hundreds of charities exist solely to collect knitted items for people and animals who are ill or in need, either close to home or halfway around the world. Knitting guilds and groups, local yarn shops and bloggers often sponsor charity drives; yarn manufacturers and retailers sometimes donate a portion of the proceeds of the sale of a certain product to charities of choice. Knitters respond to tragedies by picking up needles to restock victims' wardrobes or send loving feelings to victims and their families. Hospitals, shelters and places of worship frequently need handknit garments and blankets and rely on local knitters—both individuals and those participating in community-service projects—to provide them.

Lists of knitting charities can be found at WoolWorks (woolworks.org/charity.html), the Daily Knitter (dailyknitter.com/charity.php), Lion Brand Yarn's Charity Connector (lionbrand.com/charityconnection.html) and Knitting for Charity (knittingforcharity.org). Warm Up America! recruits volunteers to knit or crochet small rectangles, which are joined to create afghans. The afghans and other knitted items are distributed in the volunteers' communities. Always check with a charity before sending knitted items; they often have specific guidelines.
See also AMERICAN RED CROSS KNITTING CAMPAIGNS; INTERNET; WARM UP AMERICA!

CHARTS

Traditional patterns are written out longhand, but patterns can also be represented visually by means of a chart. Charts give a visual guide to how a finished motif will look and are often easier to follow than written

The Channel Islands are located in the English Channel between England and France.

Lace chart and swatch knit from chart

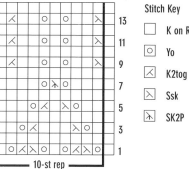

instructions, so they are commonly used for lace, colorwork and cable patterns. Charts are presented as grids, with each square representing one stitch and each row of squares representing one row. Every stitch is given a visual representation with a different symbol; the symbols vary from publisher to publisher but there are similarities and some standards.

Right-side rows are read from right to left, and wrong-side rows are read from left to right. When working circularly, all rows are read from right to left. Charts are almost always read from bottom to top, unless otherwise indicated in the pattern. Different colors used in the pattern are indicated by colors or symbols. A key will indicate which color or stitch each pattern symbol represents. Most charts feature repeat lines to indicate stitch repeats of the motif or pattern. These are the equivalent of the "repeat from *," or "[ ]" used in written instructions.

See also CABLE PATTERNS; COLORWORK; GRAPH PAPER, KNITTER'S; GRAPHING; LACE KNITTING; SYMBOLS

CHENILLE

Chenille yarn produces a fabric similar to corduroy or velvet. Chenille yarn is made of short lengths of spun fiber held together by two tightly plied threads. The short lengths are called the pile, and the plied threads are the core. The production of chenille requires two steps: the twisting of the two core threads around the pile, and the cutting of the pile to produce an even, smooth yarn. The resulting yarn is soft and fuzzy.

Chenille yarn is often used in woven upholstery fabrics, throws and decorative items, and to a lesser extent in commercially produced knitwear. Cotton and rayon are the most commonly used fibers for chenille yarns employed by handknitters; both silk and wool chenille are also available but are more costly. Because of its softness, cotton chenille is popular for baby items, especially blankets and stuffed animals. Chenille yarn lacks resilience and so is unsuitable for garments and other items requiring elasticity.

Because the manufacturing process for chenille yarn requires a lot of twist to bind the pile into the core, the resulting excess twist isn't always released at the spinning mill. This can cause the yarn to twist when it is knit. In addition, small loops can appear in the fabric after the knitting is completed. These loops are called "worming." Inexpensive chenille yarns tend to shed as well as to worm.
See also FIBER CHARACTERISTICS; FIBER CONTENT

CHEVRON STITCH

Chevron stitch is an embroidery stitch that creates a zigzag line.
See also EMBROIDERY

CHIA, WENLAN
See TWINKLE

CHIN, LILY M. (1961-)

Lily Chin is prolific designer and author equally adept at crochet and knitting; she is one of the fiber world's most recognizable ambassadors. Among her high-profile appearances in the general media are a 2003 guest spot on the *Late Show with David Letterman,* during which she crocheted a sweater in 40 minutes (midi-length on the 6-foot-2 Letterman), and a 2005 appearance on the fabled "poncho" episode of *The Martha Stewart Show,* in which Chin crocheted, on live TV, a dog's version of the poncho Stewart wore on her release from prison.

Chin is deeply steeped in the fashion industry, growing up in the "schmatta [rag] business," she told *Vogue Knitting* in 1991. When she was eight she learned the basics of her craft from her mother, a Chinese immigrant who had a Seventh Avenue sample-making company. She became a full-time designer in 1988, creating runway pieces for Ralph Lauren, Isaac Mizrahi, Diane von

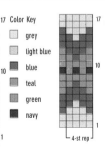

Color Key
- ☐ grey
- ☐ light blue
- ■ blue
- ☐ teal
- ■ green
- ■ navy

14-st rep

4-st rep

2-st rep

2
1

Fair Isle color charts and knitted swatch

Swatch knit from chenille yarn

Chevron Stitch

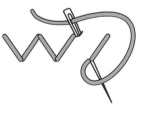

Make a line of diagonal stitches from right to left; then, pulling the needle through the same holes, make a line of diagonal stitches from left to right.

Furstenberg and Vera Wang as well as commercial designs for The Gap and Victoria's Secret.

Chin is also the national spokesperson for the Orphan Foundation of America's Red Scarf Project and a *Vogue Knitting* Master Knitter who received the TNNA Jubilee Award in 2005 for contributions to the knitting industry. That year she launched her own yarn line, the Lily Chin Signature Collection, with skeins named for neighborhoods in her beloved hometown of New York, where she lives with her husband, an architecture critic.

See also DESIGNERS; MAGAZINES AND JOURNALS; NATIONAL NEEDLEARTS ASSOCIATION, THE

CHOOSING YARN

Most patterns specify a yarn, but you can make substitutions provided you select a suitable one. To do this, you'll need some familiarity with the different types of yarns and the fiber they are made from and an understanding of gauge and yarn substitution. For example, suppose the yarn specified in a pattern for a cabled sweater is 100-percent wool with a tight twist. If you substitute an unplied or woolen-spun yarn, you will not achieve the same effect. You might be better off with a blend that contains some wool or with a mercerized cotton of the same weight as the original yarn. Learning more about different fiber characteristics will also help you select yarns for your own designs.

See also FIBER CHARACTERISTICS;

FIBER CONTENT; GAUGE; GAUGE SWATCH; YARN LABELS; YARN SUBSTITUTION; YARN WEIGHT

CHULLO

See HAT; ANDES REGION KNITTING

CHURCH OF CRAFT

See GUERRILLA KNITTING

CIRCULAR KNITTING

Knitting need not only be worked back and forth in flat pieces; it can also be worked in rounds or spirals, usually on sets of three, four or five double-pointed needles or on circular needles. Circular knitting produces a tube that is open at the top and bottom. It is used to construct traditional seamless sweaters, such as Fair Isle sweaters, ganseys or Scandinavian sweaters, as well as other tubular garments, such as hats, socks, gloves and mittens.

Many knitters like to work in the round because the right side of the work is always facing and because seamless garments require less finishing than garments constructed out of flat pieces. Sweaters knit in the round are more difficult to block than flat-knitted pieces and are often more difficult to shape or adjust.

Circular knitting can be done with a circular needle or double-pointed needles (dpns).

See also CAST-ON; CIRCULAR NEEDLES; COLORWORK; DOUBLE-POINTED NEEDLES; FLAT KNITTING; FAIR ISLE KNITTING; HATS; SOCKS; STEEKS

Knitting With Circular Needles

Cast on as you would for straight knitting. Distribute the stitches evenly around the needle, being sure not to twist them. The last cast-on stitch is the last stitch of the round. Place a marker here to indicate the end of the round.

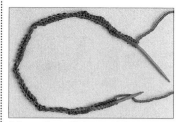

If the cast-on stitches are twisted, as shown, you will find that after you knit a few inches the fabric will be twisted.

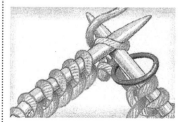

1. Hold the needle tip with the last cast-on stitch in your right hand and the tip with the first cast-on stitch in your left hand. Knit the first cast-on stitch, pulling the yarn tight to avoid a gap.

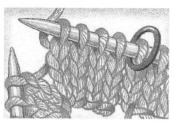

2. Work until you reach the marker. This completes the first round. Slip the marker to the right needle and work the next round.

Knitting With DPNs

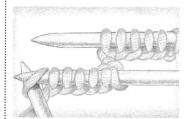

Cast-on with three needles

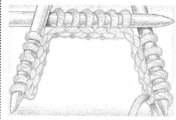

1. Cast the required number of stitches onto the first needle, plus one extra. Slip this extra stitch to the next needle as shown. Continue in this way, casting the required number of stitches onto the last needle.

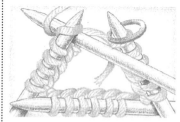

2. Arrange the needles as shown, with the cast-on edge facing the center of the triangle (or square).

3. Place a stitch marker after the last cast-on stitch. With the free needle, knit the first cast-on stitch, pulling the yarn tightly. Continue knitting in rounds, slipping the marker before beginning each round.

CIRCULAR NEEDLES

Circular needles are used for knitting in the round (circular knitting) and for large flat pieces. One circular needle consists of a flexible plastic wire joined seamlessly at each end to a needle tip made of plastic, metal, bamboo or wood. Circular needles, commonly called "circs," are available in various lengths (16–36 inches/40–90cm) and in virtually all needle sizes.

Circular needles have several advantages over straight needles. First, they better balance the weight of the knitting, allowing it to rest in the knitter's lap. Their flexibility makes it easier to knit in constricted spaces where long straight needles would be awkward. Another advantage is that they allow a garment to be knit in one piece, eliminating the need for seaming.
See also CIRCULAR KNITTING; DOUBLE-POINTED NEEDLES; FLAT KNITTING; INTERCHANGEABLE NEEDLES; NEEDLE TYPES

CLASP

A clasp is a device with interlocking parts, such as a hook and eye, used to hold two parts of a garment together, usually the fronts of a sweater. Clasps are sewn onto a garment after it is completed and can be hidden or decorative.
See also CLOSURES

CLASSIC ELITE

Truly one of America's most classic yarn companies, Classic Elite is a distributor of hand-knitting specialty yarns. The best known of its yarns is its brushed "La Gran" mohair. The company took root in the 1940s when Ernest Chew became a partner at Warley Worsted Mills, in the mill town of Lowell, Massachusetts. Warley was already manufacturing fine mohair at the time. In 1980, Chew founded Classic Elite as the marketing arm of the mill and expanded its handknitting yarns to include cottons, silks, alpacas, wools and natural fiber blends. In

1985, Ernest's daughter-in-law Pat Chew took over the business and continued to grow its mainstay, La Gran, into a range with over 70 colors. Pat emphasized patterns to support the yarn lines, publishing about 150 designs yearly, and founded its Luxury Fibers Division. The company eventually stopped milling its own yarn, though it is still headquartered in its historic mill. In 2008, Betsy Perry, sales and marketing director for the company since 2003, purchased Classic Elite Yarns. Perry has brought new knitters to the brand by partnering with young, fresh designers like Twinkle and Jil Eaton to develop yarn lines and Jared Flood to develop pattern books.
See also ALLEN, PAM; NICHOLAS, KRISTIN

CLEANING

See CARE

CLOCHE

See HATS

CLOSURES

Objects used to fasten a knitted garment, such as buttons, zippers, clasps, or hooks and eyes, are collectively known as closures. Closures, especially decorative ones, are often the finishing touch to a handknit garment.
See also BUTTONS; CLASP; FINISHING TECHNIQUES; ZIPPER

CLOVER NEEDLES

Clover USA is a forward-thinking company that sells crafts supplies for the needlearts with a colorful spirit of fun. Its knitting sector includes a vast selection of bamboo needles and ingenious notions, including tools for embellishments such as pompoms and flowers—indeed, Clover is an excellent source for cross-crafters interested in quilting and sewing. The firm's website is extensive, offering online shopping with Shopatron fulfillment. Clover also provides craft projects and inspiration with patterns and newsletters. The company operates a division in Japan, and

Circular needles come in a wide variety of materials, sizes and lengths.

thus distributes the Japanese line of Takumi bamboo knitting needles, as well as tools to make flower knots, button knots and other traditional Asian accents.

CM

Abbreviation for *centimeter(s)*.

CN

Abbreviation for *cable needle*.
See also CABLE NEEDLE

CO

Abbreviation for *cast on*.
See also CAST-ON

COATS & CLARK

In 1952, two venerably old Scottish companies, J. & P. Coats and the Clark Thread Co., merged to form Coats and Clark. Both of these industrial companies already had manufacturing facilities in America dating to the mid-nineteenth century. Today Coats & Clark is one of the world's largest textile and thread manufacturers, with products sold in over 150 countries, and it continues to innovate through ongoing research and product development, exploring new fibers and fabrics as well as their applications for consumer and industrial use. One of the most popular lines that Coats & Clark carried included Moda Dea, a fashionable novelty yarn with unique textures and vivid colors, which, although successful, has been retired. Red Heart Yarn, a subsidiary of Coats, has been a very successful bargain-priced yarn for over 65 years, and the Coats & Clark website has a listing of many free Red Heart yarn patterns. In 1998 TLC Essentials, also introduced by Coats, set a new standard in worsted-weight acrylics. Unlike "soft" yarns, the TLC Essentials resist splitting. Brooklyn designer Debbie Stoller recently joined forces with Coats, where her new line of 100-percent natural and affordable yarns have elicited a lot of excitement among knitters.

COLE, DAVE

See GUERRILLA KNITTING

COLLARS AND NECKBANDS

The section around the neck of a garment is called a collar or neckband. In knitting, a distinction is sometimes made: A neckband is knit by picking up stitches, whereas a collar is knit separately and sewn on.

Collars are often worked in ribbing on needles one or two sizes smaller than those used for the body of the garment. They can be worked back and forth in rows on straight needles by sewing one shoulder seam, picking up and knitting stitches along the neck edge, and then sewing one side of the neckband along with the remaining shoulder seam. Alternatively, a collar can be picked up and worked on circular or double-pointed needles after both shoulder seams have been sewn. A third option is to work the collar separately and sew it to the garment.

When picking up stitches around a neckband, it is important to work evenly so that the band will not pucker or stretch. Place pins, markers or yarn every 2 inches (5cm) around the neckline and pick up the same number of stitches between each pair of markers. If your pattern specifies the number of stitches to be picked up, divide this number by the number of sections to determine how many to pick up in each section.

Collars can be shaped with short rows, increases or decreases, or by casting on or binding off stitches. Noncurling stitches such as garter stitch and seed stitch will keep a collar's edges from rolling. If you wish to work a collar in stockinette stitch, you will need to add an edging or border to make it lie flat or knit it as a turned collar, with the result being double thick.

There are many collar and neckband styles to choose from

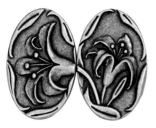

Two clasps designed by Nicky Epstein

when designing a sweater; the most popular are illustrated on the next page. Your choice of neckline should be in keeping with the style of your sweater, taking yarn and stitch pattern into consideration. Neckline depth and shape may be limited by stitch or color pattern (and vice versa); for instance you may not want to interrupt some motifs at the beginning of the neck shaping.

Cowl Neck

A cowl neck is wider and longer than a turtleneck and may be worked in a stitch other than ribbing. To widen the collar, work increases, change to a larger needle or do both.

Crewneck (Single)

This type of neckband is worked to the desired depth and bound off loosely in pattern.

Crewneck (Double)

Work as for single crewneck to double the desired depth. Bind off in pattern and sew the bound-off edge to the inside of the neck.

Henley

Work the placket, then join the shoulders and pick up stitches all around the neckline. Work back and forth to desired depth.

Polo (Basic)

Polo collars are often joined to plackets. Work placket first, then join shoulders. Begin picking up stitches in center of one side of placket and end in center of the other side. Work back and forth, making the collar deep enough to lie flat when folded over.

Polo (Front-Split)

Pick up stitches, beginning at the center front neck. Join and work as for a crewneck for ½ to 1 inch (1.5–2.5cm), ending at the center. Work back and forth to the desired length, adding one or two stitches to balance both sides of the collar.

Side-Split Collar

Similar to a cowl, but worked back and forth instead of in the round, a side-split collar may be worked in ribbing or plain stockinette. To create an overlap, either cast on a few stitches or pick up a few stitches at each side of the join.

Square Neck

Join shoulders and pick up stitches all around. Mark corner stitches. Work every round as follows: Work to one st before marked st, * sl the next st and the marked st tog knitwise, k1, pass 2 sl sts over knit stitch; work to one st before next marked st; repeat from *, then work to end of round.

Square-Neck Shawl Collar

This collar is knit separately and sewn on. It may be knitted either vertically or horizontally and is usually worked in ribbing or garter stitch.

Turtleneck

A turtleneck is an extension of a crewneck. Turtlenecks are usually ribbed. Change to larger needle sizes as you progress to make the collar lie smoothly.

V-Neck

A V-neck may be worked with an odd or even number of stitches. In either case, first join the shoulders and pick up stitches all around the neck. For an even number of stitches, place a marker at the center of the V. Work every round as follows: Work to 2 sts before marker, ssk, slip marker, k2tog, work to end of round. For an odd number of stitches, place a marker before and after the center stitch. Work every round as follows: Work to 2 sts before first marker, ssk, slip marker, work center stitch, slip marker, k2tog, work to end of round.

V-Neck (Crossover)

Pick up an odd number of stitches around the neck, beginning and ending at center front. Work back and forth without joining. When neckband is desired length, bind off. Sew front of band in place, with the left side overlapping the right.

Wrapped Collar

The wrapped, or overlapped, collar is a modified shawl collar that is knit separately and sewn in place. Begin by casting on a number of stitches equal to the entire neck measurement plus the desired amount of overlap. Work short-row shaping on both ends of the collar to create the shape. Sew the cast-on edge to the neckline.

See also BORDERS; COWL; EDGINGS; NECK EDGING; PICKING UP STITCHES; PLACKET, RIBBING; V-NECK SHAPING

Collars and Neckbands

Cowl Neck

Crewneck

Henley

Polo (Basic)

Polo (Front-Split)

Side-Split Collar

Square Neck

Square-Neck Shawl Collar

Turtleneck

V-Neck

V-Neck (Crossover)

Wrapped Collar

Knitting Color

by Brandon Mably

What is it about color that is so fascinating?

Recently I had a reminder of the power of color. In a New York City department store, I saw a towering display of mirrors, furniture, ornaments, statues in marble, wood and textiles in a hundred different shades of white. The whole display resembled an ice palace. Then I turned to face an entire wall, 20 feet high, studded with saffron, orange and marigold flowers interlaced with bright pink rose petals. That towering wall, every inch covered with three-dimensional flowers in shades of toasty orange broken up by vivid pinks, was a vivid contrast to the white space I had experienced just before. Visions like this stop me in my tracks and come back to me again and again to feed my imagination and remind me of the power of color.

It's fun to experiment with color in your knitting. Here's one way: Pick a postcard of a painting that really moves you. Examine the color combination used: Is there a balance of several colors or does one color predominate? Turn the card upside down so that your eye will focus on the colors rather than the design of the card.

Next, choose a variety of yarn in colors from the card. Cast on approximately 30 stitches and begin to knit a color swatch that gives you the feeling of the original color image.

For example, look at the painting of vibrant sunflowers to the right. The thing that struck me when I first saw it is how the yellow blossoms pop out against the rich dark browns and touches of burgundy. Next I noticed how the royal magenta tones of the vase glow against the wall of pea green and how the cool greens are woven throughout. After examining the painting in this way, I knitted a swatch based on the colors in it. I used a tumbling blocks pattern, which allowed me to separate out the dark, light and medium tones and combine them in different ways. Note that this is my personal interpretation: If you knitted a swatch based on this image, it might be quite different from mine. Working in this instinctive way can be very rewarding, so please have a go at it yourself. You just might find yourself empowered to combine colors in unique and surprising ways.

Brandon Mably (brandonmably.com) is a member of the Kaffe Fassett Studio. His designs have been featured in all major knitting publications, and he is the author of *Knitting Color* (Sixth&Spring Books, 2006).

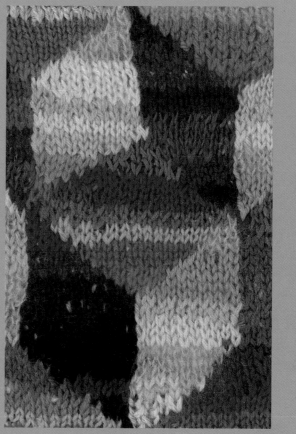

This still life of sunflowers by Kaffe Fassett (left) inspired the colors in the knit swatch (above).

COLOR BLOCK

See INTARSIA

COLOR THEORY

This body of practical guidance to color mixing and the impact of specific color combinations, as first outlined by Leon Battista Alberti (c. 1435) and Leonardo da Vinci (c. 1490) and later by Isaac Newton (1704), can be indispensable to designers. Knitwear designers are artists and, consciously or unconsciously, they use the same principles that painters and colorists use when mixing colors to create a pleasing palette.

Before Newton's discovery of the light spectrum, color theory was formulated in terms of primary colors—red, yellow, blue—which were found to be the foundation for mixing all other colors, and were used for centuries by dyers, printers and painters when mixing pigments. Newton refined the system, mapping a color wheel of twelve colors: the primaries (red, yellow and blue), the secondaries, which result from mixing two primaries (red + blue = violet; red + yellow = orange; blue + yellow = green), and the tertiaries, which result from mixing a primary and a secondary color (yellow-orange, red-orange, red-violet, blue-violet, blue-green and yellow-green). "Complementary" colors lie opposite each other on the color wheel.

Color Wheel

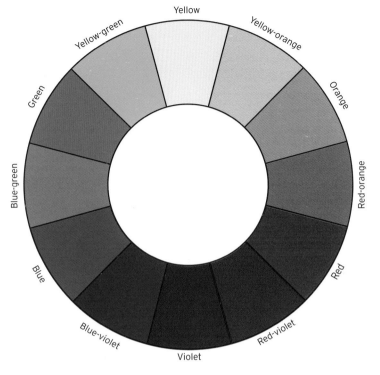

All colors are combinations of these basic hues. Black and white are not part of the spectrum, but pigments do occur in nature that approximate the values of black and white and can be mixed with hues to darken or lighten them.

Color Qualities

Every color has three qualities: hue, saturation and value. *Hue* is the name of the color; *saturation* is the intensity; *value* is the range from light to dark. In addition, colors are also described in terms of temperature: Warm colors include the reds, oranges and yellows. Cool colors include violets, blues and greens.
See also COLORWORK

COLORWAY

A colorway is the specific color pattern of a variegated, or multicolored, yarn: It is the color name describing a yarn that incorporates more than one shade. For example, a hand-painted yarn with four hues and an overall red look may have the word "red" in its colorway name, or it may have a more expressive colorway name such as Cherry Vision. Tweeds can also be colorways.

COLOR WHEEL

See COLOR THEORY

COLORWORK

See ARGYLE; BOBBIN (COLOR-WORK); FAIR ISLE KNITTING; INTARSIA; MOSAIC PATTERNS; SLIP-STITCH PATTERNS

COMBINED KNITTING

This style of knitting uses elements of both Eastern and Western knitting. Combined knitting is mostly used by Russian and Eastern European knitters and their descendants in North America.

The stitch mount is the same as in Eastern knitting, in that the leading leg of the loop over the needle is at the back, and the trailing leg is at the front.

For the knit stitch, the right needle is inserted into the back loop, as in Eastern knitting. The yarn is wrapped under and then over the right needle, and the stitch is pulled off the left needle.

For the purl stitch, however, the right needle is inserted into the front loop from back to front, as in Western knitting. The yarn is then wrapped under and over the needle, and the stitch is pulled off the left needle. This technique necessitates working into the back loop on the return row.
See also AMERICAN/ENGLISH-STYLE KNITTING; CONTINENTAL/GERMAN-STYLE KNITTING; EASTERN KNITTING; KNIT

STITCH; PURL STITCH; STITCH
MOUNT; WESTERN KNITTING

CONT

Abbreviation for *continue(s)* or
continuing.

CONTINENTAL/GERMAN-STYLE KNITTING

The Continental style is a popular
knitting method in which the
knitter holds the working yarn
in the left hand. The left hand
controls the yarn tension and
wraps the yarn around the needle.
This style of knitting is also
described as picking, left-hand
carry or left-handed knitting.

Like American/English-style
knitting, Continental/German-style knitting is a type of Western
knitting, in that the stitch mount
is the same.
See also AMERICAN/ENGLISH-STYLE KNITTING; KNIT STITCH;
PURL STITCH; STITCH MOUNT;
WESTERN KNITTING

CONVERSION TABLE

See NEEDLE SIZE

COOKIE A

See KNITTY.COM

COPYRIGHT

In American law, a copyright is
the legal right that automatically
belongs to the creator of an
original creative or intellectual
work, which allows him or her
the exclusive right to display,
reproduce and distribute that
work. However, the law does
allow the use of copyrighted
material by others for "fair use,"
such as criticism or scholarship.
For works created after 1977, a
copyright is automatically in place
from the moment of creation until
seventy years after the author's
death, at which point the work
enters the public domain and can
be used and copied freely.

In knitting, copyrights are most
frequently encountered on printed
patterns. A copyrighted pattern
cannot be reproduced (as by
photocopying) or displayed (as on
a blog or other website). However,
a copyright of a pattern applies
only to the pattern itself, and not

to garments or other items
created using the pattern, *unless
otherwise specified*. Garments
created using copyrighted
patterns, then, can be freely
displayed and sold or otherwise
distributed.

CORDS

Drawstring, ties or lacings are all
often added as embellishments to
knitted pieces. Ribbons, leather
strips and knitted cord can be
woven or laced into eyelets, lace
stitches, frog closures or dropped-stitch spaces. Two types of cords
made from yarn are twisted cord
and I-cord.

Twisted Cord

To created a twisted cord, cut
two long strands of yarn at least
three times the desired length of
the cord. Attach the strands to
something stationary, such as
a doorknob, and twist the free
ends many times until the yarn
begins to kink up on itself. Fold
the pieces in half and knot the
ends together.

I-cord

I-cord is knit with double-pointed
needles. Knit as shown below.
See also KNITTING NANCY

To make I-cord, cast on anywhere from
3 to 5 stitches, *knit, do not turn. Slip
the stitches back to the beginning of
the row. Pull the yarn tightly from the
end of the row. Repeat from * until the
I-cord is as long as desired. Bind off.

Combined Knitting

The stitch mount for combined knitting

Knit stitch in combined knitting

Purl stitch in combined knitting

CORRECTING COMMON MISTAKES

Errors such as dropped stitches, accidentally twisted stitches, mistakenly knit or purled stitches, split stitches and running stitches can be corrected without unraveling completely. If you have knitted only a few rows past the error, you can work back to it stitch by stitch ("tinking"). If you don't discover the error until you have worked many rows, it is often possible to drop individual stitches above the error and unravel or "ladder" them back to the mistake. The instructions shown here demonstrate how to make these kinds of corrections.

See also FROGGING; TINK; UNRAVELING

Twisted Stitches

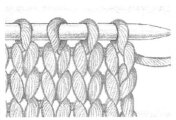

A twisted or backward stitch is created either by wrapping the yarn incorrectly on the previous row or by dropping a stitch and returning it to the needle backward.

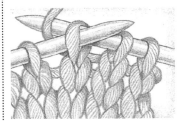

To correct the backward knit stitch, knit it through the back loop.

A backward purl stitch looks different from a regular purl stitch in that the back loop is nearer the tip of the needle than the front loop.

To correct the backward purl stitch, purl it through the back loop.

Picking Up a Dropped Stitch

1. This method is used when a knit stitch has dropped only one row. Work to where the stitch was dropped. Be sure that the loose strand is behind the dropped stitch.

2. Insert the right needle from front to back into the dropped stitch and under the loose horizontal strand behind.

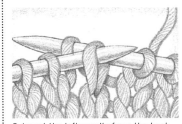

3. Insert the left needle from the back into the dropped stitch on the right needle, and pull this stitch over the loose strand.

4. Transfer this newly made stitch back to the left needle by inserting the left needle from front to back into the stitch and slipping it off the right needle.

Picking Up a Running Stitch

A running stitch is one that has dropped more than one row. It is easiest to pick it up with a crochet hook. For a knit stitch, be sure the loose horizontal strands are in back of the dropped stitch.

Insert the hook into the stitch from front to back. Catch the first horizontal strand and pull it through. Continue up until you have worked all the strands. Place the newest stitch on the left needle, making sure it is not backwards.

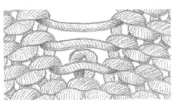

Before picking up a dropped purl stitch, be sure the loose horizontal strands are in front of the stitch.

Insert hook into the stitch from back to front. Pull the loose strand through the stitch. Continue up until you have worked all the strands. Place the newest stitch on the left needle, making sure it is not backwards.

CORTRIGHT, LINDA

See MAGAZINES AND JOURNALS

COSH, SYLVIA

See FREEFORM
KNITTING/CROCHET

COTTON

The most widely used plant (or cellulose) fiber, cotton is one of the oldest known textile fibers, and evidence of cotton cloth dating back to ancient times has been found in Mexico, Egypt and India. Up to four thousand fine, fluffy cotton fibers grow around each seedpod, or boll, of the cotton plant (genus *Gossypium*). The biggest commercial producers of cotton include China, the United States, India, Turkey and Brazil. Quality varies and is graded by length of fiber, or staple (from ⅜"–2¼" [9.5–57mm]). Egyptian, Sea Island (Georgia) and Pima are considered the finest varieties.

Conventional cotton farming and processing employs extensive use of chemicals, including pesticides, insecticides, herbicides, fertilizers, bleaches, sizing and dyes. There is a growing trend toward organic cotton production, especially among small-scale growers.

After harvesting, cotton bolls are fed through a gin, which removes the seeds and short waste fibers (linters). The remaining fibers are blended, cleaned, carded, combed and spun. Much commercially produced cotton yarn is mercerized, a process named for its inventor, John Mercer. The spun yarn is treated with caustic soda (sodium hydroxide) and stretched, making it smoother, stronger, more lustrous and less prone to shrinkage than untreated yarn. And because it absorbs and holds dye better, richer color saturation is achievable in mercerized cottons. Mercerized cotton plies beautifully and has good stitch definition when knit. Unmercerized cotton is softer and less dense and does not wear as well. The yarns are often single-ply and have a more string-like quality. Novelty cotton yarns include cotton chenille and slubby spins. One major benefit of cotton yarn is its wicking quality. Unlike wool, which holds body heat, cotton draws heat and moisture away from the body, making it well suited for clothing worn in hot climates and seasons. Additional benefits of cotton include its hypoallergenic properties, lack of itchiness, strength, resistance to moth damage and ease of care. Potential disadvantages include the weight of cotton and its lack of resilience, which can make for a droopy garment. Because cottons yarns tend to be less resilient than wool, blends are an option: Wool adds softness and warmth; synthetic fibers can decrease weight and add elasticity, while linen can add texture. Knitting a strand of fine elastic thread along with the yarn can help alleviate looseness, especially in ribbing.

Most cotton yarns are machine washable. If a garment has lost its original shape, machine drying can help restore it. Cotton garments can be wet blocked or steam blocked.
See also FIBER CHARACTERISTICS OF; FIBER CONTENT

COUNTERPANE

The term *counterpane* is used to refer to a particular style of fancy knitting in white cotton thread popular during the nineteenth century in Europe and the United States; it was used on coverlets for beds. Most knitted counterpanes are constructed out of shapes that are knitted separately and sewn or crocheted together. Common pattern stitches are of knit and purl, ribbing, lace, yarn overs and deeply embossed leaves, shells and flowers. Knitted or crocheted edgings are then sewn or knitted on to the assembled piece.

COVIELLO, JAMES (1966-)

An acclaimed ready-to-wear designer who makes a point of incorporating handknits into his Seventh Avenue collections,

Swatch knit with cotton yarn

Cotton boll

Cotton field

James Coviello travels to Peru four times a year to convene with the knitters who realize his intricate, feminine designs.

A native of Fairfield, Connecticut, Coviello studied at New York's Parsons The New School for Design and learned to knit shortly after leaving school, when he wanted to add knit hats to his burgeoning hat collection. These were sold at Neiman Marcus and Barneys and were a staple of the runway shows of Calvin Klein, Oscar de la Renta and Todd Oldham. Coviello's knitwear career further took wing in 1991 when Anna Sui hired him to design hats and knits for her first runway show. Coviello's first solo show took place in 2000; his ready-to-wear collections ever since have relied heavily on knitwear and woven garments. His frequent contributions to *Vogue Knitting* are indicative of his design ethos: gently rugged femininity with lots of texture—cables, bobbles, ribbons, ruffles—in fashion-forward fibers and color palettes.

"Given all of the yarns and stitches that exist," he said, "the ideas are limitless if you're a good knitter." *See also* DESIGNERS; MAGAZINES AND JOURNALS

COWICHAN KNITTING

Warm, waterproof multicolored sweaters made by women of the Coast Salish tribe of southern Vancouver Island, Canada, and prized for their skillful construction and longevity are known simply as Cowichans. European settlers introduced sheep to Vancouver Island sometime in the mid-1850s; the Cowichan native community began shearing sheep and preparing the raw wool to knit clothes and blankets not long after. The women of the Cowichan Valley were soon embellishing sweaters with stranded colorwork patterns made in the naturally occurring creamy whites, browns and black of the local sheep. The harsh climate requires clothing that will stand up to outdoor living and protect the wearer from the elements. For that reason, the fleeces are carefully carded and spun by hand to preserve the wool's natural oils and water-resistant qualities. The sweaters are knit in the round with seams only at the shoulders. Because there are few seams to split, with proper care a true Cowichan can hold up for a lifetime of wear.

Over time, the Cowichan style was modified to incorporate a shawl collar and stylized motifs of eagles, deer, birds, fish, whales and the thunderbird, all taken from Native American, Scottish and Icelandic sources. Zippers can be found on some authentic Cowichan designs, but they are always sewn in by hand with the sweater fronts worked separately. (Cheaper imitation sweaters simply cut open the front of the sweater and sew in a zipper.)

At one time, Cowichan sweaters were sold and traded and had great economic importance for the Coast Salish. Women knit to keep food on the table, and the sweaters soon became a highly prized form of art, often presented by the Canadian government as gifts to heads of state. The reputation of the sweaters (and their hefty price tag) has inspired manufacturers to copy them and attempt to pass off the fakes as authentic. In reality

The Cowichan Valley is located on Vancouver Island, British Columbia, Canada.

Cowichan sweaters at a Junior Chamber of Commerce hobby show in the Cowichan Valley, 1950

only about 800 true Cowichan sweaters are created per month, each one handcrafted by a native knitter from Vancouver Island or the lower mainland. An authentic Cowichan will be hand-numbered and will bear a label that provides a registration number and authenticates the garment as a genuine "Cowichan Indian Knit."

The Cowichan sweater is the inspiration for the official Olympic sweater of 2010, worn at the games in Vancouver, Canada.
See also FOLK KNITTING; GANSEY

COWL

Though primarily defined as a type of collar or neckline, cowls can also be worked as separate accessories. By knitting only a short tube—often featuring a texture pattern or colorwork—a cowl can replace a scarf. They can be made large for wrapping around the head and neck or snug to cover only the exposed neck.
See also COLLARS AND NECKBANDS; SCARF

CRAB STITCH

The crab stitch is a single crochet stitch worked in reverse, from left to right. It can be used as an edging for knitted fabric to prevent curling and to provide a decorative border.
See also SINGLE CROCHET

CRAFTIVISM

See GUERRILLA KNITTING

Crab Stitch

Work a backward single crochet edge the same as a single crochet, but from left to right rather than right to left.

This variation is worked by making a backward single crochet in one stitch, making a chain one, and skipping a stitch.

1. Pull through a loop on the left edge. Chain one. *Go into the next stitch to the right. Catch the yarn as shown and pull it through the fabric, then underneath (not through) the loop on the hook.

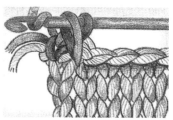

2. Bring the yarn over the top of the crochet hook and around as shown, then draw the yarn through both loops. Repeat from *.

CRAFT YARN COUNCIL (CYC)

CYC is the trade association of the craft-yarn industry, founded in 1981 to "raise awareness of yarns" and known until 2010 as CYCA (Craft Yarn Council of America). The CYC's membership—composed of yarn manufacturers and distributors, knitwear and crochet designers and publishers of craft books and magazines—provides 85 percent of the yarn and knitting-related merchandise and publications sold annually in the United States.

CYC has an active educational component for both career and recreational knitters. Its Certified Instructors Program (CIP) is a three-level program that trains professional knitting/crochet instructors. The curriculum incorporates seventeen hours of classwork that cover techniques, design guidelines, principles of teaching and lesson planning. At least fifteen hours of volunteer student teaching is expected; thousands of CIP volunteers have taught 1 million people to knit or crochet. Hobby knitters can take advantage of CYC's educational arm by visiting one of the council's targeted websites: learntoknit.com and learntocrochet.com focus on the basics for beginners, while knit911.com and crochet911.com highlight FAQs for newbies. The council's charitable efforts are equally robust. In 1995 CYC assumed sponsorship of Warm Up America!, which distributes to people in need afghans assembled from donated 7-by-9-inch knit and crocheted squares.

CYC is the only organization to conduct biannual surveys about knitting and crocheting habits and trends. Stats are also at the heart of its Standards and Guidelines for Crochet and Knitting, compiled by CYC members in April 2003 and updated as necessary. These guidelines, adopted by fiber manufacturers, publishers and designers, assure a uniformity of yarn, needle, hook and pattern labeling no matter the source of a project. For more about CYC and its many programs, visit craftyarncouncil.com.
See also CHARITY KNITTING; EASE; WARM UP AMERICA!; YARN SUBSTITUTION; YARN WEIGHT

CRANE, JOSIAS
See FLORENTINE JACKET

CREATIVE KNITTING
See MAGAZINES AND JOURNALS

CREEL, BROOKE CHENOWETH
See KNITTY.COM

CREWNECK
See COLLARS AND NECKBANDS

CROCHET GUILD OF AMERICA
See KNITTING GUILD ASSOCIATION, THE

CROCHET HOOKS

The tool used for the craft of crochet, a crochet hook is a short needle with a hook on one end, traditionally made of steel, ivory or bone, now usually made of plastic, aluminum, wood or bamboo. Crochet hooks are available in a wide range of sizes from very small for lacework to very large for use with big yarns or to create very open fabric. Like knitting needles, crochet hooks are sized in American (U.S.) sizes and metric sizes.

Crochet hooks have a variety of applications for handknitting, including picking up dropped stitches, seaming and adding edgings.
See also CROCHETING; NEEDLE TYPES

CROCHETING

The craft of creating fabric by looping thread or yarn with a hooked tool, crochet is similar to knitting in that the stitches are formed by pulling one loop of yarn through another, and it usually

Crochet Hook Size Chart

U.S.	METRIC
B/1	2.25mm
C/2	2.75mm
D/3	3.25mm
E/4	3.5mm
F/5	3.75mm
G/6	4mm
7	4.5mm
H/8	5mm
I/9	5.5mm
J/10	6mm
K/10½	6.5mm
L/11	8mm
M/13	9mm
N/15	10mm

involves a single thread or yarn running in horizontal courses. In crochet, only one loop is active at a time, whereas in knitting a series of loops is active. The base row for crochet is a free-floating series of loops, or chains, whereas the base row for knitting is a series of loops cast on to the knitting needle.

According to Richard Rutt, the history of crochet has been studied less than that of knitting. Crochet appears to spring from a technique called "shepherd's crook knitting" in eighteenth-century Britain. Beginning in the 1800s, crocheted lace became a substitute for more costly bobbin and tatted laces in Europe and America. With the advent of inexpensive manufactured threads, crochet became a popular domestic pastime, especially during the Victorian era, and patterns for crocheted doilies, purses and potholders were published in women's magazines.

Crochet for Knitting

In knitting projects, crochet is most often used as a finishing or edging technique. Crocheted edges add stability to knitted fabric and can help prevent curling. Popular stitches for edgings include single crochet, crabstitch and picot. Crocheted buttons are frequently called for in knitting patterns. Seams on knitted garments may also be crocheted together in a method similar to three-needle bind-off.
See also CROCHET HOOK; CRABSTITCH; SEAMING; SINGLE CROCHET

CROSS

See CABLES

CROSS-OVER COLLAR

See COLLARS AND NECKBANDS

CROSS STITCH

Cross stitch is a basic embroidery stitch that forms a series of Xs on the surface of the fabric. Cross stitch may be used to create an allover pattern lines or geometric designs.
See also DOUBLE CROSS STITCH; EMBROIDERY

CYC

See CRAFT YARN COUNCIL

CYCA

See CRAFT YARN COUNCIL

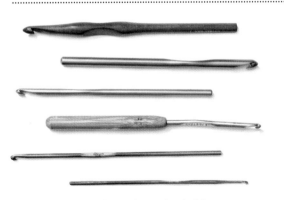

Crochets hooks in different sizes and materials

Cross Stitch

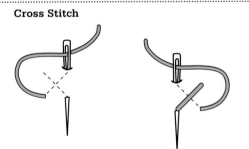

Pull the thread through and make a diagonal stitch. Bring the needle up and make a diagonal stitch in the opposite direction. You can also make a parallel row of half cross stitches, then work back across this set in the opposite direction.

D

DALES KNITTING

The rural handknitting industry that flourished in the Yorkshire Dales region of northern England gave rise to what is known as Dales knitting. Now, gloves knitted in the Dales style are iconic. By the end of the eighteenth century, the advent of the knitting machine and the rise of factories had all but eliminated England's rural knitting industry. In the Yorkshire Dales, however, handknitting remained a means of livelihood through the beginning of the twentieth century. In fact, with a span of more than three hundred years, the domestic knitting industry in the Dales was the longest-lived in England.

Both men and women in the Dales knit as they went about their daily business, wearing a belt into which they tucked a knitting sheath or stick. A hole in the center of the stick held the right needle rigid. Most of the work was done by the left needle, which allowed the knitter to work faster and produce a tighter, more even tension. Carriers, who operated from towns in southern England, would travel to the Dales, collecting knitted stockings and delivering a new lot (or "bumps") of wool for the next assignment.

Stitching was a communal affair, and neighbors would gather in the evenings for parties.

The signature Fair Isle–style gloves created by the Dales knitters are made with two different colors of yarn, black and red being the most common combination. The fingers tend to be decorated with a midge-and-fly pattern and the palms in a pattern that is known as shepherd's plaid. In addition, the knitter's name and date of completion are usually knitted into the cuff.
See also BRITISH KNITTING; FAIR ISLE KNITTING; KNITTING SHEATH

DARNING

A method for invisibly mending worn areas or holes in fabric, darning is most associated with fixing holes in socks, but it is applicable to any hole.

The specific technique you choose for darning will depend on the type of repair. If the fabric is worn out, it can be reinforced with duplicate stitch and a thinner yarn. If there is a hole, you must fill it in with new stitches. To do this, attach vertical or horizontal threads, then re-form the knit stitches using a tapestry needle,
See also DUPLICATE STITCH

Darning Worn Stitches

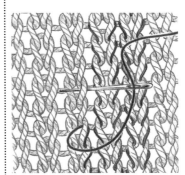

Vertical Reinforcement

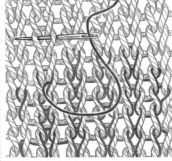

Horizontal Reinforcement
Use a tapestry needle threaded with a thinner yarn than that used to knit the item, or divide the plies of the original yarn. Use duplicate stitch to cover the worn-out stitches.

Darning Holes

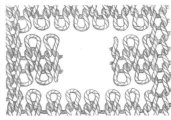

If the stitches are broken, you must re-form them using horizontal or vertical threads. First, pull out worn or broken threads to make a square hole. Increase the size of the hole by 2 or 3 stitches and fold these inside to make a neat edge. Sew down the narrow hems.

Repairing Vertical Damage

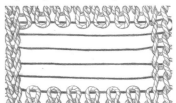

1. Attach horizontal threads, working from the sides of the square hole that you have hemmed in. These threads, which should be loose enough not to pull the hole, will form the base for the new darned stitches. You need one thread for each knitted row you will be replacing.

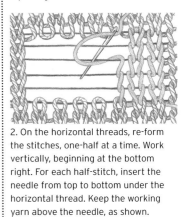

2. On the horizontal threads, re-form the stitches, one-half at a time. Work vertically, beginning at the bottom right. For each half-stitch, insert the needle from top to bottom under the horizontal thread. Keep the working yarn above the needle, as shown.

To prevent the top and bottom stitches of the hole from dropping, insert the needle under the yarn and into the stitch that corresponds with the one you are re-forming. Turn your work upside down to construct the other half-stitch in the same way.

Repairing Horizontal Damage

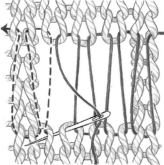

1. Attach vertical threads, working from the top and bottom of the square hole that you have hemmed in. Follow the direction of the arrows to position the vertical threads so that they make a V between the stitches at the top and bottom of the hole. You need two vertical strands for each row of darned stitches.

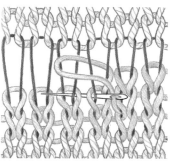

2. On the vertical threads, work horizontally to re-form the stitches. Begin at the bottom right edge of the hole. Use the row of stitches at the bottom edge of the hole to anchor your first darned row. Note that you also need to catch the rightmost and leftmost stitches on the vertical sides of the hole to anchor the sides of the darned patch. For each new darned stitch, bring the needle to the right side between the two threads. Then insert the needle under the left-hand thread of that stitch and the right-hand thread of the next stitch. Continue in this manner, working from right to left.

On the next row, turn the work upside down. Re-form the stitches on this row by bringing the needle through to the right side between the two vertical threads that come out of a newly made stitch in the row below. Insert the needle from right to left under these two threads. Then insert the needle between the threads and under the left-hand thread of the stitch below and the right-hand thread of the next stitch, as shown. Repeat these two rows to fill in the hole.

DAYNE, BRENDA

See PODCASTS

DEC

Abbreviation for *decrease(s)* or *decreasing*.
See also DECREASES

DECREASES

There are several methods used to decrease the number of stitches, usually one or two at a time, to narrow a piece of knitting. Decreasing is used in lace knitting to compensate for the yarn overs that form the holes, to shape sleeve caps and shoulders, to create necklines and to shape the body of a sweater, among other uses.

There are many different ways to decrease a stitch, and patterns typically specify the one you should use. When no specific instruction is given, or when you are designing your own garment, your choice in any given situation depends on the purpose the decrease will serve. For example, decreases can slant to the left, slant to the right, or be vertical. When shaping an armhole, you might want to work a left-slanting single decrease on the right-hand side of the garment and a right-slanting single decrease on the left-hand side of the garment, to emphasize the slope of the shaping. If you place the decreases one or two stitches in from the edge, the decreases become a decorative detail. This type of visible decreasing is called "fully fashioned" decreasing. Placing decreases away from the edge also makes it easier to seam the pieces together.

Decreases do not have to be visible. A simple decrease, such as knitting two stitches together, can be placed at the edge of the knitting so that it will be invisible once the pieces are sewn together. Most decreases are worked on the right side of the knitting, but sometimes it is necessary to place them on the wrong side, such as when the decreases are worked on every row.

Paired Decreases

When placing decreases on opposite sides of a garment or on the opposite side of a group of stitches, it's customary to pair them so that they slope in opposite directions. For example, it is common to pair the left-slanted ssk decrease with the right-slanted k2tog decrease.
See also INCREASES; KNIT STITCH; LACE KNITTING; PURL STITCH; SLEEVES; SWEATER

Basic Single Left-Slanting Decrease (k2tog tbl/p2tog tbl)

Knitting (or purling) 2 stitches together through the back loops is a decrease that slants the stitches to the left on the knit side of the work. It is abbreviated as k2tog tbl (or p2tog tbl).

With the right needle behind the left needle, insert the right needle through the back loops of the next 2 stitches on the left needle. Knit these 2 stitches together.

With the right needle behind the left needle, insert the right needle into the back loop of the second stitch, and then into the back loop of the first stitch on the left needle, which twists the 2 stitches. Purl these 2 stitches together.

Basic Single Right-Slanting Decrease (k2tog/p2tog)

Knitting (or purling) 2 stitches together is the easiest decrease and one that every beginner must learn. This basic decrease slants to the right on the knit side of the work. It is abbreviated as k2tog (or p2tog).

Insert the right needle from front to back (knitwise) into the next 2 stitches on the left needle. Wrap the yarn around the right needle (as when knitting) and pull it through. You have decreased one stitch.

Insert the right needle into the front loops (purlwise) of the next 2 stitches on the left needle. Wrap the yarn around the right needle (as when purling) and pull it through. You have decreased one stitch.

Single Left-Slanting Decrease (skp)

This decrease slants the stitches to the left on the knit side of the work. It is abbreviated as SKP or sl 1, k1, psso (slip one stitch, knit one stitch, pass slip stitch over knit stitch).

1. Slip one stitch knitwise, then knit the next stitch. Insert the left needle into the slipped stitch as shown.

2. Pass the slipped stitch over the knit stitch and off the right needle.

Single Left-Slanting Decrease (ssk)

This decrease slants the stitches to the left on the knit side of the work. It is abbreviated as ssk (slip one, slip one, knit two together).

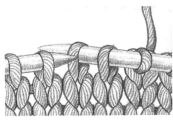

1. Slip 2 stitches knitwise, one at a time, from the left needle to the right needle.

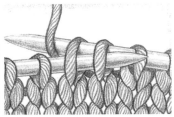

2. Insert the left needle into the fronts of these 2 slipped stitches as shown and knit them together.

DESIGN

To take a design for a sweater from concept to execution, you'll need to consider several elements: silhouette (the outside line and general shape of your garment), fit (how closely or loosely the garment lies to the body and the approximate finished measurements), type of garment (will it be casual or elegant, for everyday wear or special occasions?), stitch pattern, yarn and color. Design is evolutionary in nature, so there's no real rule of order for any of these elements: You might start with an idea for a particular shape or style of sweater before you choose a yarn, or you might find the yarn first and then start thinking about how to best use it.

Sketching out a silhouette of your design will help you get a clearer picture of the finished piece and how to go about creating it. A simple line drawing that portrays the proportions you want for your finished sweater and any pattern details will do. If you are using an established pattern, you can trace its outline from the photograph or illustration, then make alterations to the outline. Once you've got your idea of the general silhouette, you can begin to think about fit and the approximate finished measurements for your design. Begin with a simple style, getting ideas for size, shape and silhouette from an existing sweater. Lay the sweater out flat and measure it, making notes of the measurements and any changes you'd like to make.

A successful knit design requires that the fiber's weight and hand be suited to the silhouette and the type of the garment. Thinner yarns drape well and are better suited to showing off intricate stitch and color patterns. Thicker yarns create extra weight and a firmer fabric; a fuzzy mohair may hide the details of fancy stitchwork. Your choice of stitch pattern will affect both the way the yarn behaves in the garment and the final outcome of your design. For example, seed stitch or another allover stitch pattern will have a heavier, bulkier look than stockinette; ribs will give a garment a closer fit. Color is also a consideration. Dark shades may make it hard to see some stitch patterns, while lighter colors may make a garment look larger.

A swatch is the place to try out all of these variations; make sure yours is large enough to see the actual results of your efforts. The standard 4-by-4-inch swatch may be too small to show you the final look of highly textured stitch patterns or large-scale colorwork. A swatch will give you a feel for how the yarn you've chosen will behave within the stitch pattern you plan to use. You may find, for example, that the details of the cables you've planned are lost in the fuzzy yarn you've selected or that the fabric is working up stiffer or softer than you'd like. Sleeves, armholes, necklines and collars must be considered in relation to the other elements of your design. For example, a tailored, fitted look should employ a set-in sleeve, while a thick yarn may require a square or angled armhole to reduce bulk. At the neck, lacy patterns often look best with a narrow edging or picot; turtlenecks and half-zips are nice options for rugged outdoor sweaters. A drapey yarn may call out for a relaxed cowl, while a more structured fabric may look best with a tailored collar.

Once you have planned the conceptual details of your design, you can move on to the more technical details of yarn amounts, gauge, shaping and assembly. Use a worksheet to organize your thoughts and then create a step-by-step plan for what will eventually become your pattern. *See also* ARMHOLE SHAPING; BODY FIT; BORDERS; COLLARS AND NECKBANDS; CHOOSING YARN; EASE; EDGINGS; GAUGE; GAUGE SWATCH; MEASURE-MENTS; SHAPING; SLEEVES; YARN REQUIREMENTS; YARN WEIGHT

DESIGNERS

Designers create patterns for knitted garments that will be published by yarn manufacturers, books and magazines and via the Internet. Many have formal fashion-design training, while others are knitting enthusiasts who turned their hobby into a business. Traditionally, designers have contracted with publishers and yarn companies to distribute their work; today, many independent designers continue in that vein yet also sell their patterns directly to knitters online. It's not unusual for even well-known knitting designers to have day jobs, as making a living wage by designing depends on a large-scale output. Organizations such as the Association of Knitwear Designers (knitwear-designers.org) and the Canadian Knitwear Designers & Artisans (canknit.com) address the professional needs of handknitting designers. *See also* ALLEN, PAM; BLISS, DEBBIE; BUDD, ANN; BUSH, NANCY; CHIN, LILY M.; COOKIE A; COVIELLO, JAMES; ELLIS, PERRY; EPSTEIN, NICKY; FALKENBERG, HANNE; FASSETT, KAFFE; FOALE, MARION; GAUGHAN, NORAH; HARDING, LOUISA; HOWELL, VICKIE; INTERNET; KAGAN, SASHA; LOWE, CATHERINE; MABLY, BRANDON; MAGAZINES AND JOURNALS; MASON-DIXON KNITTING; NEWTON, DEBORAH; NICHOLAS, KRISTIN; OKEY, SHANNON; PARKES, CLARA; PATTERNS; PATRICK, MARI LYNN; PEARL-MCPHEE, STEPHANIE; PIERROT; SCHULZ, HORST; SHARP, JO; SINGER, AMY R.; SLICER-SMITH, JANE; STARMORE, ALICE; STOREY, MARTIN; STOVE, MARGARET; SWANSEN, MEG; TERIOKHIN, VLADIMIR; TWINKLE; WALKER, BARBARA; ZIMMERMANN, ELIZABETH

On Design

By Mari Lynn Patrick

To create a design, by definition, is to make tangible a deep personal truth.

The heart and soul of the designer as artist is nourished by the process of designing, and it is a force that cannot be stopped. Design will out.

I know this to be true for me. My chosen career has been in handknitting design. And the process of handknitting has become the passion that drives my life.

There are no aspects of the process that I like more or less than others. Each step both builds on my past designs and leads to future ones. My personal process can be summed up as follows:

Saturate Yourself in Your Interests

For me, those interests are fashion, world events, music, foreign languages, film, food and more. Rich conversation and keeping an open mind also make up a great part of who I am. As I'm excited and stimulated by my many interests, I gain the energy I need to accomplish my work. My love of fashion particularly informs my designs, in silhouette, fabric and colorwork. That being said, timeliness is crucial to the fashion mix and of more interest to me than trend. Time and work spent on knitting must translate to years of loving wear.

Make the Knitting Techniques the Focus of the Design

Each piece I design tends to emphasize knitting technique—ribbing, shaping, pleats, stitch or color pattern—and I want to make that technique shine. In a sense, the technique becomes the major design element. Written instructions will definitely guide the knitter along in the knitting process, but the garment has to tell the whole story of both technique and body fit.

Never Do the Same Thing Twice

This is my own personal motto. Because I try to live up to it, I never get bored and I can keep moving forward, always perfecting my work and my vision of what knitting can be.

Immerse Yourself in the Repeat

This is where your heart and soul come into play and where your own experience as a knitter determines the complexity or the simplicity that you strive to achieve. Knit and knit again, and don't put your work down until you have knit for long stretches and can see the piece unfold. Lay it flat on the floor as you work and measure to be sure you are keeping to gauge. Adjust the gauge if you can or tear it out if you must and start again. But don't stop knitting.

As you immerse yourself in pattern repeats, particularly new ones that you add to your skill repertoire, you will gain confidence to continue to expand your knitting vocabulary. And as you learn, your skills will grow and expand, and knitting will become a true love.

Plan It Out Schematically

Before starting to knit, use graph paper to make a pattern template or schematic drawing. Take into consideration the drape and bulk of the knitted fabric as well as the properties of your chosen yarn. These will all dictate the shape of the pattern pieces that add up to create the body fit. Sculpting the final shapes is where experience comes into play—how heavy will the knitted fabric be? How will it drape? How much will the ribbing pull in? How will the yarn affect the stitch pattern? I never look at my past schematics or anyone else's at this stage. Instead, I look

inside my own experience and "get in the zone," where there is always an answer to be found.

Write It Out

Write out the pattern instructions from beginning to end before you begin to knit. Use your stitch gauge and the schematic pattern pieces to plot each segment, inch by inch. Keep in mind the overall design, even while you concentrate on the particulars. By learning to invest yourself in the technical aspects before you begin knitting, your knitting vocabulary will expand.

There are not many things in life that are as personal as knitting, as basic and complex at the same time. There are few things that continue to live on for as long after we have finished with them. Remember that by knitting you are marking time with a gift—long hours spent knitting become the fruit of hard work, and the finished object tells the story of time well spent.

Learning to design your own knits will increase your enjoyment of knitting exponentially. There are few things in life more satisfying and rewarding than creating something by hand, except perhaps the knowledge that what you have created is your own unique vision.

Mari Lynn Patrick is a prolific designer whose original works are in high demand by all the major knitting publications. One of her designs appeared in the premiere issue of *Vogue Knitting* in 1982.

DK (OR DOUBLE KNITTING) WEIGHT

Light worsted-weight yarn, called DK (or double knitting) weight yarn, is classified as "Light" and takes a category 3 rating on CYC's the Standard Yarn Weight System. DK-weight yarn knits up at 22 to 24 stitches to 4 inches (10cm) over stockinette stitch on U.S. size 5 to 7 (3.75 to 4.5mm) needles. This weight was formerly known as Germantown, after the Germantown Yarn Mill outside of Philadelphia, Pennsylvania.
See also YARN WEIGHT

DOUBLE-BREASTED

When a garment has two rows of fasteners (usually buttons) down the front, it is called double-breasted. Usually only one row of buttons is functional and the other row is merely decorative. This style is common in men's suit jackets, but can be employed in knitwear designs as well, such as cardigans and coats.
See also CARDIGAN

DOUBLE CROSS STITCH

This embroidery stitch consists of one cross stitch superimposed over another.
See also CROSS STITCH; EMBROIDERY; FINISHING TECHNIQUES

DOUBLE KNITTING

Double knitting is a method that creates double-sided fabric. Double-knit fabric may be created in either of two ways: by working a slip-stitch pattern that is identical on both sides (shown below) or by knitting two fabrics at the same time with two yarns on one set of needles. The latter method uses twice as much yarn as single-face knitting. Double knitting creates a thick fabric suitable for blankets and outerwear. Though it shows as stockinette on both sides, the double thickness prevents the natural curling that would otherwise occur with stockinette stitch, creating nice flat hems and edgings on garments. Double knitting can be accomplished using straight, circular or double-pointed needles.

The pattern given here should be worked for at least 1 inch (2.5cm) for the double knitting to become apparent; for bulky yarns, work at least 2 inches (5cm).

Double Stockinette Stitch

(Worked over an odd number of sts)
Row 1 (RS) K1, * wyib sl 1, k1; rep from * to end.
Row 2 *K1, * p1, k1; rep from * to end.
Repeat rows 1 and 2.
See also KNITTED FABRIC

DOUBLE-POINTED NEEDLES

Short needles with points on both ends are called double-pointed needles (abbreviated as *dpns*). They are sold in sets of four or five and are used for circular knitting, especially for small circumferences. Made of wood, plastic, metal or bamboo, double-pointed needles are available in different lengths, from about 4 to 15 inches (10–40cm), and in a range of needle sizes.

Just as many straight lines can approximate a circle, so do double-pointed needles work to create the tube of circular knitting. The stitches are divided equally among three (or four) needles, and instead of working back and forth, each needle is worked in succession in a clockwise direction, with the fourth (or fifth) needle acting as the right-hand needle for each segment. Tension is crucial when working with double-pointed needles; too loose and a gap can appear at the junction between needles, creating a visible "ladder" along the work. To prevent this, pull tightly at the junctions and keep tension as even as possible.

Double-pointed needles are believed to be the oldest type of knitting needles and can be seen in several fourteenth-century paintings that show the Madonna working on a piece of knitting. Long dpns are still used in Shetland for traditional knitting.

Double Cross Stitch

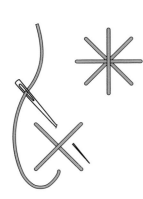

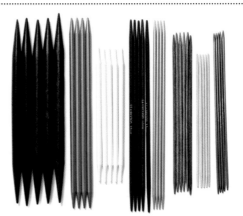

Double stockinette stitch swatch

Double-pointed needles in sets of four and five, made from a variety of materials

With the advent of circular needles, dpns fell out of favor for much knitting in the round but remain the needles of choice for small items such as hats, socks and gloves.

See also CIRCULAR KNITTING; FAIR ISLE KNITTING; HATS; LADDER; MITTENS; NEEDLE SIZE; NEEDLE TYPES; SOCKS

DOWDE, JENNY

See FREEFORM KNITTING/CROCHET

DPN

Abbreviation for *double-pointed needle(s).*
See also DOUBLE-POINTED NEEDLES

DRESS

A basic of any woman's wardrobe, a dress is a woman's garment consisting of a bodice, waist and skirt in one piece. Knitted dresses can be loose and flowing or short and closely fitted to the body, and every style in between. Care must be taken when planning a knit dress to find a yarn that will not be too heavy and will drape appropriately.

DROP SHOULDERS

See SHOULDER SHAPING

DROP SPINDLE

In spinning, a drop spindle is the small tool, usually made of wood, that is used for twisting or spinning fibers, especially wool, into yarn by hand. Drop spindles get their name from the action the spinner performs when using them. Spindles are the most primitive spinning tools and can be traced back at least five thousand years, to ancient Egypt and the Middle East.

A drop spindle is made up of two parts: the shaft and the whorl, with a hook or notch at one end. It functions not unlike a spinning top: The weight of the whorl sets it spinning. A guide or starter yarn, or *lead,* is tied to the shaft and wrapped around the top or hooked around the hook. The carded wool is twisted around the lead to begin and the spindle drops and spins, twisting the fibers into yarn. After a length is completed and the spindle reaches the floor, the yarn is wrapped around the shaft and the process is repeated.
See also SPINNING

DROP-STITCH PATTERNS

Occasionally, stitches will be deliberately dropped down to create decorative ladders in a finished piece of knitting; these are called drop-stitch patterns. The swatch shown below is knit over a multiple of 10 stitches plus 6.

Rows 1 and 2 Knit.
Row 3 (RS) K6, *yo, k1, [yo] twice, k1, [yo] 3 times, k1, [yo] twice, k1, yo, k6, rep from * to end.
Row 4 Knit, dropping all yo's off needle.
Rows 5 and 6 Knit.
Row 7 K1; *yo, k1, [yo] twice, k1, [yo] 3 times, k1, [yo] twice, k1, yo, k6; rep from * end k1.
Row 8 Rep row 4.
Rep rows 1–8.
See also LADDER

DRYING

Hand-knitted garments require careful attention when drying. Dry them flat on a towel or rack and away from heat or sun. If blocking, use original dimensions of garment to shape. If there are wrinkles in a dried garment, use a damp pressing cloth and a cool iron on the wrong side of the knit and lightly press or steam, never touching the iron to the yarn. Never iron acrylic yarn.
See also BLOCKING; CARE; FIBER CHARACTERISTICS; FIBER CONTENT

DUPLICATE STITCH

This embroidery technique is specific to knitting, where the V stitches are sewn over with another color to mimic colorwork or to fix an error. Duplicate stitch can be used alone to place small areas of color on a knitted piece in place of intarsia or to place motifs in a precise location after the fact, when placement can be better determined. Duplicate stitch can be combined with other color

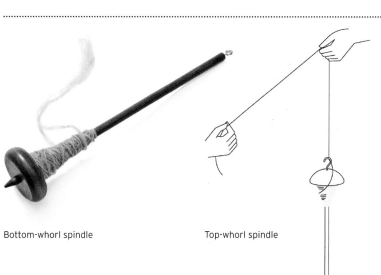

Bottom-whorl spindle

Top-whorl spindle

Swatch knit in drop-stitch pattern

knitting methods, such as Fair Isle or intarsia. Minor mistakes in Fair Isle can be corrected using duplicate stitch—an errant stitch or two, but not whole stretches of knitted fabric.
See also COLORWORK; EMBELLISHMENTS; EMBROIDERY; FAIR ISLE KNITTING; INTARSIA

DUTCH HEEL

See HEELS

DUTCH KNITTING

It's not clear when knitting first arrived in Holland, but in the seventeenth and eighteenth centuries the Dutch were creating embossed patterns in twisted stockinette on a reverse stockinette ground. It's likely that the embossed, patterned quilting for which the Dutch were famous influenced the development of their knitting patterns, because most of the traditional knit stitches mimic those found in Dutch quilts. The most famed of these pieces is shown above—an impressive

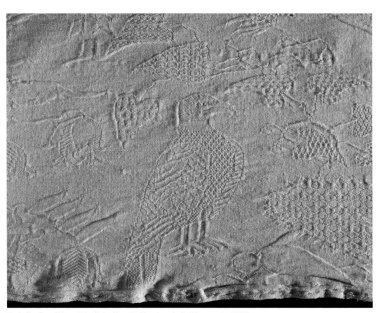
Detail of petticoat knit in the Netherlands in the early 1700s

knitted cotton petticoat covered in embossed birds, animals, flowers and trees. Now in the collection of the Victoria & Albert Museum in London, it is easily mistaken for an elaborate work of embroidery.
See also FOLK KNITTING; VICTORIA & ALBERT MUSEUM

DYEING

Dyeing is the process in which yarns or fibers are colored. Both

vegetable and chemical dyes are used to give yarns color, from something as simple as black tea, Kool-Aid or food coloring to as complex as a manufactured pigment. Yarn is usually dyed in batches (called lots) and can be colored by hand or through mass production. A solution of dye is mixed and yarn is dip dyed, submerged completely or the solution is "painted" on using

brushes or squeeze bottles. Space dyeing is a technique for dyeing yarn in sections of different colors. The dyes must be fixed with a mordant; because each color requires a different mordant, they don't bleed into each other.
See also CARDING; DYE LOT; HAND-PAINTED YARN

DYE LOT

When yarn is dyed, each particular batch of yarn that has been dyed at the same time is given a number or letter—its specific dye lot. Dye lots are indicated on the ball band of commercial yarns and on the labels of hand-dyed yarns (where applicable). When purchasing yarn for any knitting project, make sure to always buy enough yarn of the same dye lot in order to complete the entire project. Even though a given color uses the same dye formula, lots can vary visibly, and the difference may be so slight that it is only evident after the project has been completed.
See also DYEING; YARN LABELS

Duplicate Stitch

To cover a knit stitch in duplicate stitch, bring the needle up below the stitch to be worked.

Insert the needle under both loops one row above, and pull it through.

Insert it back into the stitch below and through the center of the next stitch in one motion.

The Netherlands (commonly known as Holland) is on the North Sea between Germany and Belgium.

EASE

The difference between a garments's bust/chest measurement and the actual measurement of the wearer is known as ease. Ease may be positive (the garment's dimensions are larger than the wearer's) or negative (the garment's measurements are smaller than the wearer's). Ease allows for freedom of movement and helps to create a particular silhouette. Ease is determined by subtracting your actual body measurement from the garment's finished measurements. For example, if you are making a sweater sized for a 40-inch (101cm) bust and the finished garment measures 45 inches (114cm), the sweater will have an oversized fit. Negative ease does not necessarily indicate that the work will be constricting, however; the stretch of the finished garment should be taken into consideration to determine if it is desirable to have it stretch or not.

The chart shown above, from the Craft Yarn Council, gives the recommended amount of ease for various fits of garments.

Fit and Ease Chart

FIT	AMOUNT OF EASE
Very close-fitting	Actual chest/bust measurement or less
Close-fitting	1-2"/2.5-5cm
Standard-fitting	2-4"/5-10cm
Loose-fitting	4-6"/10-15cm
Oversized	6"/15cm or more

See also BODY FIT

EASTERN KNITTING

A style of knitting common in Eastern Europe, the Islamic world and South America, Eastern knitting is characterized by the orientation of the stitch mounts: The leading leg of the stitch is at the back of the needle and the trailing leg is in front. The yarn may be held in either hand.

To make a *crossed* knit stitch, the Eastern knitter holds the yarn to the back, inserts the right needle into the front of the stitch, wraps the yarn over and then under the needle and pulls the yarn through. To make a purl stitch, the knitter inserts the needle into the front loop from back to front, wraps the yarn under and then over the needle and pulls the yarn through. This also produces a crossed stitch.

It is also possible to knit *uncrossed* stitches in Eastern knitting. Using the procedure described for a crossed knit stitch when knitting in the round produces identical results to Western knitting. In flat knitting, uncrossed knit stitches can be made by inserting the right needle into the back of the loop, wrapping the yarn over, then under the needle and pulling it through.

Many Eastern knitters control the yarn tension by wrapping the working yarn around their neck and manipulating it with their thumb. Knitting historian Richard Rutt lists three characteristics that distinguish Eastern knitting from Western: the stitch mount, as described above; the use of colorwork patterns that include curlicues and twists, as opposed to the more geometric Western designs; and knitting socks from the toe up rather than from the top down. In the general category of Eastern knitting he includes the ethnic traditions of the Balkans, Albania, Greece and Turkey as well as lands farther east, such as the Caucasus, India and Afghanistan.

See also AMERICAN/ENGLISH-STYLE KNITTING; CIRCULAR KNITTING; CONTINENTAL/GERMAN-STYLE KNITTING; KNIT STITCH; PURL STITCH; SOCKS; WESTERN KNITTING

ECHELMAN, JANET

See GUERRILLA KNITTING

EDGE STITCH

See SELVAGE

Eastern Knitting

Stitch mount in Eastern knitting

Position of the yarn and needles for the uncrossed Eastern knit stitch

Position of the yarn and needles for the uncrossed Eastern purl stitch

EDGINGS

As its name implies, an edging is a decorative strip for the edge of a knitted item. Generally edgings are worked separately and then attached. An edging may be attached in several different ways: It may be knit entirely separately and sewn or crocheted on; stitches along one side of the edging may be picked up and used to begin the body of the garment; or stitches along the side of the garment may be left live and the edging stitches knit together with those live stitches. An edging typically has one straight edge, which is used to attach it to the knitted piece. The other edge can be straight, indented, wavy, pointed or looped. Rather than using the term "edging," some knitting books and references distinguish between borders knit onto a piece of knitting and borders that are knit separately and sewn on.

In vintage knitting, edgings were used to embellish tablecloths, bed linens, baby clothes and doilies. Many vintage and modern patterns use edgings that contrast with and enhance the lace patterns used for the main area of the garment.

See also BORDERS; EMBELLISHMENTS; LACE STITCHES; SHAWL; SHETLAND KNITTING

ELIZABETH'S PERCENTAGE SYSTEM
See EPS

ELLIS, PERRY (1940-1986)

Perry Ellis was a designer who led the knitwear resurgence in the late 1970s and early 1980s. By infusing his fashion collection with cables, colorwork, playful polka dots, "exploded" patterning, tweedy wool yarns and slouchy shapes, he transformed the handknit sweater into an integral element of modern sportswear. One of the A-list fashion designers to contribute handknitting designs to *Vogue Knitting* when that publication relaunched in 1982, he also knitted his designs so knitters could stitch their own Perry Ellis garments. Since his death in 1986, the company he founded has transformed to a textile liscensing and marketing firm in Miami, Florida, with holdings of many important brands of casual clothing and knitwear.
See also DESIGNERS

EMBELLISHMENTS

Decorative details added to a knitted piece fall under the catchall term *embellishments*. Knitting can be enhanced with appliqué or embroidery, beads or sequins, cords or fringe, pompons or tassels, borders or edgings. Embellishments allow you to add a personal touch to your knitting.
See also BEADED KNITTING; BEAD KNITTING; BORDERS; CORDS; DUPLICATE STITCH; EDGINGS; EMBROIDERY; FRINGE; POMPOM

EMBROIDERY

Embroidery adds an interesting dimension to finished knit pieces and is most effective on simple stitch patterns such as stockinette. It can be done with yarn, embroidery thread or needlepoint thread. Choose a yarn or thread that is smooth enough to go through the knitted fabric and appropriate for the knitted piece—a too-thick yarn will stretch out your stitches, and a too-thin one will disappear into the fabric. Work evenly and not too tightly, using a blunt needle with an eye large enough to accommodate the yarn. Do not make a knot to secure the yarn; instead weave the end into

Garter stitch band: Work this band by picking up 2 stitches for every 3 rows along a straight edge. Knit every row to desired length. Bind off.

Pick up and knit border: This border makes a good, firm, narrow edge and is sometimes called "mock crochet." Pick up the stitches and then bind them off on the next row. Or knit one row and then bind off.

These gloves designed by Kristin Nicholas (from *Color by Kristin*, Sixth&Spring Books, 2009) are embellished with several embroidery stitches: French knots, spiderweb stitch, lazy daisy stitch and fern stitch.

Enrich Your Knitting

by Nicky Epstein

As a knitwear designer for over twenty years, I've used just about every knitting technique and worked in every genre to create hundreds of knitting fashions for magazines, yarn companies, my students and, of course, for my books.

One of my favorite genres is embellishment. Embroidery, ruffles, edgings, appliqué, cords, frogs, closures—I love them all. They're all wonderful design tools, and I have always been fascinated by the way an embellishment can enhance a knitted piece. I discovered them early in my career and enjoy exploring innovative ways to use them; I incorporate them in many of my pieces to add richness, dimension and individuality.

When I design a garment, of course I first think about its function, the basic shape, the yarn and the stitch pattern that will best serve my vision. Once that is set, the fun begins. I let my imagination roam free and I consider how to take the piece from ordinary to something special.

What better way to make a piece truly your own than to make use of some of those little extras? While you don't want embellishments to take over the design, the judicious use of embellishments is a great way to express your creativity and kick your work up a notch. For me, as a designer, it's a wonderful way to distinguish my work. Many embellishment techniques look difficult (like some in my books) but are actually surprisingly easy to do. *Webster's* defines "embellish" as "adorn, decorate, enrich," and I agree. Embellishment enriches our work. It's creatively rewarding, therapeutic and great fun!

To me, a knitted piece without embellishment is like a day without chocolate.

Nicky Epstein (nickyepstein.com) is a designer, teacher and author of more than a dozen best-selling books on knitting and crochet, including *Knitting on the Edge, Knitting on Top of the World* and *Knitting a Kiss in Every Stitch* (all from Sixth&Spring Books) and *Knitting Block by Block* (Potter Craft, 2010).

the place you begin and end your embroidery.

See also BACKSTITCH (EMBROIDERY); BULLION STITCH; CHAIN STITCH; CROSS STITCH; DOUBLE CROSS STITCH; DUPLICATE STITCH; EMBELLISHMENTS; FRENCH KNOT; LAZY DAISY STITCH; SPIDERWEB STITCH; STOCKINETTE STITCH

ENGLISH KNITTING

See AMERICAN/ENGLISH-STYLE KNITTING; BRITISH KNITTING

ENTRELAC

A knitting technique that creates a fabric with a trellis or woven look, *entrelac* comes from the French word *entrelacer*, which means to interlace or intertwine. To work an entrelac pattern, you knit each rectangular area on its own rather than work across an entire row. Starting from a row of base triangles, you pick up stitches from one of the triangle's sides to form the first row of rectangles; you then form subsequent rectangles, one at a time, by picking up stitches from the rectangle below them. Rows of right-sloping rectangles alternate with rows of left-sloping rectangles, giving the knitting its woven appearance.

Entrelac can be knit using one or more colors. The rectangles can be constructed using stockinette stitch or any other stitch pattern, such as garter stitch, seed stitch, lace stitches or ribbing.

See also COLORWORK; PICKING UP STITCHES

Base Triangle Row

1. Cast on desired sts (in this example a multiple of 10 sts) and work each triangle as foll: *K2, turn, p2, turn. K3, turn, p3, turn. K4, turn, p4, turn. Cont in this way until you have worked k9, turn, p9, turn. k10. Do *not* turn.

2. Leaving the first triangle on the right-hand needle, work the second triangle over the next 10 sts as in the previous step; that is, repeat from *.

3. Rep from * across row until all sts have been worked from the left-hand needle. Note how the triangles made after the first one curl up. Turn.

First Row—First Corner Triangle

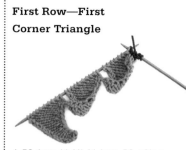

4. P2, turn, k1, M1, k1, turn. P2, p2tog, turn, k2, M1, k1, turn. P3, p2tog, turn, k3, M1, k1, turn. P4, p2tog, turn, k4, M1, k1, turn. Cont in this way until you have worked p8, p2tog, turn, k8, M1, k1, turn. P9, p2tog. Do *not* turn.

Right-Side Rectangles

5. *Pick up and p 10 sts along side of triangle. Beg with a RS row [k10, turn, p9, p2tog, turn] 9 times. k10, turn, p9, p2tog. Do *not* turn. Rep from * to last triangle.

Second Corner Triangle

6. Pick up and p 10 sts along side of last triangle. Turn. K1, k2tog, k7, turn, p9, turn. K1, k2tog, k6, turn, p8, turn. K1, k2tog, k5, turn, p7, turn. Cont in this way until you have worked k1, k2tog, turn, p2, turn. K2tog. Do *not* turn.

Second Row—First Wrong-Side Rectangle

7. *Pick up and k 9 sts along side of triangle. Beg with a WS row [p10, turn, k9, ssk (shown here), turn] 9 times. P10, turn, k9, ssk. Do *not* turn.

Subsequent Wrong-Side Rectangles

8. *Pick up and k 10 sts along side of rectangle. [P10, turn, k9, ssk, turn] 9 times. p10, turn, k9, ssk. Do *not* turn.

9. Rep from * across the row. Cont to rep the first and second rows to desired length, end with a second corner triangle completed—one st remains on the right-hand needle. Do *not* turn.

10. Pick up and k 9 sts along side of triangle. Beg with a WS row, *p10, turn, k7, k2tog, turn, p9, turn, k2tog, k6, k2tog, turn, p8, turn, k2tog, k5, k2tog, turn, p7, turn, k2tog, k4, k2tog, turn, p6, turn, k2tog, k3, k2tog, turn, p5, turn, k2tog, k2, k2tog, turn, p4, turn, k2tog, k1, k2tog, turn, p3, turn, [k2tog] twice, turn, p2, turn. [K2tog] twice, pass first st over second st—1 st remains on the right-hand needle.

Rep from * across row, picking up sts along edge of rectangle instead of triangle.

Fasten off rem st.

EPS

These initials are the abbreviation for Elizabeth's Percentage System, a method for calculating the number of stitches in each part (body, border, yoke, neck, cuffs, sleeve tops) of a sweater that is knit in the round. Elizabeth is Elizabeth Zimmermann, who first revealed the system in her book *Knitting Without Tears* (Scribner, 1971). It was later refined by her daughter, Meg Swansen, in an article in *Vogue Knitting*'s Winter 2001/02 issue. EPS relates the parts of a sweater to one another and allows knitters to design custom garments using simple calculations.

The first step in using EPS is to determine the desired chest circumference of the finished sweater and the stitch gauge. The total number of stitches needed for the chest circumference is the basic number you use to determine the number of stitches in all other parts of the sweater. To knit the sweater body, cast on 90 percent of the basic number of stitches for a ribbed bottom border or 95 percent for a hemmed border. Once you have completed the border, increase gradually to the full stitch count and knit even to the underarms. Put the body aside to knit the sleeves.

For each sleeve, cast on 20 percent of the basic number of stitches. After completing the ribbing, increase gradually over the first third of the sleeve until you have approximately 33 percent of the basic number. Knit to the desired length to the underarm.

Before joining the body and sleeves, set aside 8 percent of the body stitches at each side of the body and on each sleeve to be joined for the underarm and hold these stitches on lengths of waste yarn. The beginning of the yoke will have approximately 150 percent of the basic number of stitches. You may work a pair of short rows at the bottom of the back yoke, or you may work even until the yoke is half the desired depth.
See also CIRCULAR KNITTING; DESIGN; GAUGE; GRAFTING; SWANSEN, MEG; ZIMMERMANN, ELIZABETH

EPSTEIN, NICKY (1952–)

Nicky Epstein is a prolific designer and author who has stitched on, over and beyond the edge of knitting. Epstein, author of the best-selling *Knitting on the Edge* series (Sixth&Spring Books), is well regarded for her tapestry-like and three-dimensional designs. Intarsia pictorials and sculptural embellishments in the form of embroidery, appliqués, twisted I-cords and felted flowers are just a few of her signature touches.

Family members taught Epstein the basics of knitting as a young child, but when she was fourteen a Spanish woman who moved to the neighborhood became her advanced-level tutor. She and Epstein swapped lessons, with the latter teaching English in return for courses in colorwork and motif knitting. After studying retail advertising and fine art at the Columbus College of Art and Design, Epstein worked as an art director and stylist.

Since 1981, she has published upward of fifty designs per year in all the major knitting magazines and numerous book compilations, and that doesn't count her many books. She also writes a regular column for *Vogue Knitting*.
See also DESIGNERS; EMBELLISHMENTS; *VOGUE KNITTING*

ERRORS
See CORRECTING COMMON MISTAKES

ESCH FRAGMENTS

The oldest datable pieces of knitted fabric on record are known as the Esch Fragments. Discovered by L.J.A.M. Van der Hurk in a late-second-century grave at Esch in southern Holland, the two fragments measure about ¾ inch square and are made of woolen yarn. The gauge of both pieces is about 20 stitches to the inch (8 stitches to the centimeter). Both fragments were backed with another sturdier material—perhaps leather—suggesting that they were ornamental. Two bronze rods were found in a box near the fragments. In 1966, textile technologist J. E. Leene determined that the structure of the fragments resembled stockinette, but in the course of his examinations, one fragment was nearly destroyed, and the other began crumbling in 1973. The rods found with the piece may have been knitting needles or pieces of jewelry—Van der Hurk was unable to determine whether they were the right size to produce such a fine stitch.
See also HISTORY OF KNITTING

ESTONIAN KNITTING
See BALTIC KNITTING

EYELASH YARN

Eyelash yarn describes a type of yarn, known as a novelty yarn for its fun and less practical qualities, that has a furry appearance. Eyelash is constructed of varying lengths of spun or metallic fiber or ribbon held together by two or more tightly plied threads; it is often made out of synthetic materials. The fibers can be up to several inches long, and when knit up the fabric takes on a furlike or feathery appearance. It is not recommended for detailed work or for fine garments, as the yarn is too busy to show detail.
See also NOVELTY YARN; YARN TYPES

EYELET

In knitting, an eyelet is a hole formed by a yarn over, usually paired with a decrease to maintain the stitch count.

See also DECREASES; EYELET PATTERNS; INCREASES; LACE PATTERNS; YARN OVER

EYELET PATTERNS

Certain openwork patterns constructed by pairing yarn overs with decreases to create small holes or groups of holes are called eyelet patterns. These patterns are similar to lace patterns but in general have a less open look.

Most eyelet patterns are constructed by using yarn overs on a stockinette background. The yarn typically is wrapped once over the needle, although multiple yarn overs can be used to make larger holes. The yarn over is paired with a decrease to restore the original stitch count.

Eyelets can be arranged horizontally, vertically or diagonally and grouped in geometric shapes, such as diamonds or triangles. When a series of eyelets is placed horizontally or vertically, it can accommodate ribbons or cords.

Eyelets also can be used as small buttonholes.

Eyelet patterns work well for baby garments and blankets. They also give garments a lacy look, and they can be combined with more open lace patterns. Here are three examples of eyelet patterns.

Pattern A

(multiple of 8 stitches plus 1)
Row 1 (RS) *P1, k3; rep from *, end p1.
Rows 2, 4 and 6 K1, *p3, k1; rep from * to end.
Row 3 *P1, k2tog, yo, k1, p1, k3; rep from *, end p1.
Row 5 Rep row 1.
Row 7 *P1, k3, p1, k2tog, yo, k1; rep from *, end p1.
Row 8 Rep row 2.
Rep rows 1–8.

Pattern B

(multiple of 3 sts plus 2)
Row 1 (RS) K3, *yo, k2tog, k1; rep from *, end k2.
Rows 2 and 4 K1, p to last st, k1.
Row 3 *K1, yo, k2tog; rep from *, end k2.

Row 5 K2, *yo, k2tog, k1; rep from * to end.
Row 6 Rep row 2.
Rep rows 1–6.

Pattern C

(multiple of 6 sts plus 2)
Note On rows 4 and 8, work double yos of preceding row as 2 separate sts.
Row 1 (RS) P1, *p1, yo, ssk, k2tog, yo, p1; rep from *, end p1.
Row 2 K1, *k1, p4, k1; rep from *, end k1.
Row 3 P1, *p1, k2tog, yo twice, ssk, p1; rep from *, end p1.
Row 4 K1, *k1, p2, k1, p1, k1; rep from *, end k1.
Row 5 P1, *k2tog, yo, p2, yo, ssk; rep from *, end p1.
Row 6 K1, *p2, k2, p2; rep from *, end k1.
Row 7 P1, *yo, ssk, p2, k2tog, yo; rep from *, end p1.
Row 8 K1, *k1, p1, k2, p2; rep from *, end k1. Rep rows 1–8.
See also DECREASES; EYELET; FAGGOTING; LACE KNITTING; LACE PATTERNS; YARN OVER

Pattern A

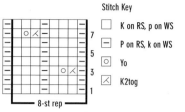

Stitch Key
☐ K on RS, p on WS
— P on RS, k on WS
○ Yo
╱ K2tog

Pattern B

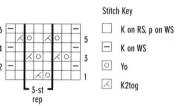

Stitch Key
☐ K on RS, p on WS
— K on WS
○ Yo
╱ K2tog

Pattern C

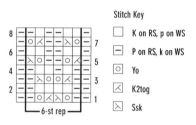

Stitch Key
☐ K on RS, p on WS
— P on RS, k on WS
○ Yo
╱ K2tog
╲ Ssk

Swatch knit in eyelash yarn

  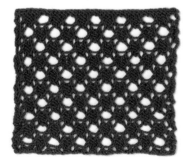

Three examples of eyelet patterns (from left to right): pattern A, pattern B, pattern C

FABRIC

See KNITTED FABRIC

FAGGOTING

Considered a type of lace, faggoting describes a basic lace-knitting stitch pattern that consists only of yarn overs paired with decreases. Faggoting produces a fabric that looks like netting. A distinction is sometimes made between faggots and eyelets: In faggoting the holes are vertically or horizontally adjacent; eyelet patterns produce holes that are next to one another.

Some faggoting patterns are worked on the right side only, with a purl row on the wrong side. Other faggoting patterns are worked in every row. In the stitch pattern shown below, the yarn overs and decreases are in every row. Different decreases produce fabrics with unique appearances.

Faggoting is used in shawl knitting, often to separate the main body of the shawl from the edging. It may also be used in any type of lace garment or knitted item.

The swatch below is knit over an odd number of stitches.

Row 1 (RS) *K2tog, yo; rep from *, end k1.
Row 2 *P2tog, yo; rep from *, end p1.
Rep rows 1 and 2 for basic faggoting.
See also DECREASES; EYELET PATTERNS; EYELET; LACE KNITTING; LACE STITCHES; SHAWL; SHETLAND KNITTING

FAIR ISLE KNITTING

Although the name for this style of patterned colorwork comes from its origins on Fair Isle, a tiny island halfway between Orkney and Shetland, the term is now used generally for any colorwork pattern that contains no more than two colors in any one row.

Although Fair Isle designs are complicated in appearance, the execution of Fair Isle technique is fairly simple. No more than two colors are worked in a single row, and the nonworking color is stranded along the back of the work. Traditional pieces are knit

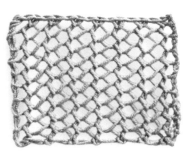

Swatch knit in basic faggoting pattern

Fair Isle is a tiny island between the Orkney and Shetland Islands of Scotland.

Fair Isle Stranding: One-Handed

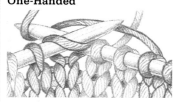

1. Drop the working yarn. Bring the new color (now the working yarn) over the top of the dropped yarn and work to the next color change.

2. Drop the working yarn. Bring the new color under the dropped yarn and work to the next color change. Repeat steps 1 and 2.

Fair Isle Stranding: Two-Handed

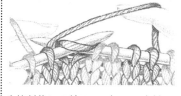

1. Hold the working yarn in your right hand and the nonworking yarn in your left hand. Bring the working yarn over the top of the yarn in your left hand and knit with the right hand to the next color change.

2. The yarn in your right hand is now the nonworking yarn; the yarn in your left is the working yarn. Bring the working yarn under the nonworking yarn and knit with the left hand and to the next color change. Repeat steps 1 and 2.

Weaving Long "Floats"

1. Hold working yarn in right hand and yarn to be woven in your left. To weave yarn above a knit stitch, bring it over right needle. Knit stitch with working yarn, bringing it under woven yarn.

2. The woven yarn will go under the next knit stitch. With the working yarn, knit the stitch, bringing the yarn over the woven yarn. Repeat steps 1 and 2 to the next color change.

Twisting Long "Floats"

Twist the working yarn and the carried yarn around each other once. Then continue knitting with the same color as before.

The Prince of Wales (shown in this portrait from 1926) helped popularize the Fair Isle sweater.

in the round, so the pattern is always visible to the knitter and work progresses quickly.

The most pervasive legend surrounding Fair Isle's origins claims that in 1588, shipwrecked sailors of the Spanish Armada brought the colorful geometric patterning to the islands, but little hard evidence supports the story. More likely, the geometric patterns associated with the technique made their way from nearby Norway, where a similar colorwork style was popular. Some on the island credit a patterned shawl brought back from the Baltics for the distinctive Fair Isle patterning. The original Fair Isle patterns took their color from the naturally occurring browns and creams of the island's sheep, brightened with dyes made from madder, indigo and lichen. Colors made from commercial dyes worked their way into the patterns beginning in the 1850s.

While the stranded gansey-style sweater is what comes to mind when most of us think of Fair Isle knitting, hats, stockings and scarves were what knitters originally turned out. Fair Isle sweaters as we know them didn't appear until around 1914. In 1922, a widely circulated photograph of the Prince of Wales wearing a V-neck Fair Isle sweater on the green at St. Andrews put the patterns in fashion. Since then, the style has never really gone out of fashion, and today's designers enjoy playing with new colors, patterns and interpretations of classic Fair Isle design.
See also ARAN KNITTING; COLORWORK; FOLK KNITTING; GANSEY

FALICK, MELANIE (1963-)

Melanie Falick is an editor and writer who has profoundly influenced the way knitting books are published in the United States. Her book *Knitting in America* (Artisan, 1996), in which she visited with thirty-eight of the country's most creative fiber artists, was the first knitting title to merit full coffee-table-book treatment. It featured exquisite photography and production values, and Falick was sent on an unprecedented seventeen-city tour to promote the book.

Falick learned to knit as a child but picked it up seriously when she was 25. After studying French and linguistics in college, she took a job at *Chocolatier* magazine that led her to editing cookbooks and writing for lifestyle magazines, which led in turn to a trip to Russia to do an article on Orenburg lace. On her frequent trips she'd seek out yarn shops and bookstores, and she realized that there were no beautiful knitting books being published in America.

In 1999 Falick became editor in chief of *Interweave Knits*, which she left in 2003 to move to publisher Stewart, Tabori & Chang, where she is currently the editorial director of her own imprint, STC Craft/Melanie Falick Books, which has a strong catalog of beautiful knitting and craft books.
See also DESIGNERS; *INTERWEAVE KNITS*

FALKENBERG, HANNE (1943-)

The garments of this popular Danish knitwear designer bear the sensibility of a clever geometric Nordic modernism, yet reference other cultures and cross generational boundaries. Offering playful colors, avante-garde shapes and often accessible, simple patterning, Falkenberg's fashion has remained youthful and on-trend through the decades. Having authored over 800 patterns, Falkenberg in 1994 broke away from reliance on the yarn, fashion and knitting-magazine industries in a

self-proclaimed "emancipation" by launching her "My Own Collection" of knitwear kits in her own line of tastefully colored Shetland wool. The kits soon became renowned for their striking color combinations, their easy knittability, and their exclusivity, thus justifying Falkenberg's instincts in declaring her independence.
See also DESIGNERS

FAMILY CIRCLE EASY KNITTING

See MAGAZINES AND JOURNALS

FAROE KNITTING

The Faroe Islands are a group of islands that belongs to Denmark and is roughly equidistant from Iceland, Scotland and Norway. The islands gave rise to their own knitting style. The word *faroe* means "sheep," and these woolly creatures have a long connection to life on the islands. An old saying goes, "Wool is Faroe's gold," and for hundreds of years, wool was as important an export

for the Faroe Islands as fish is today. Men generally spun the wool, but the production of clothing was left to the women. The earliest Faroe knits were felted, most likely to bolster the wind and water resistance of the lanolin, which was deliberately left in the spun wool. The sweater style that we recognize as Faroese

today was probably developed sometime in the mid-eighteenth century. The construction resembles that of Icelandic and Scandinavian designs, but the style is distinctly that of the islands. Faroe sweaters are patterned with small geometric shapes that are usually worked in narrow bands of alternating colors

on an off-white ground. In later years, the knitters began incorporating wider bands into the work. Examples of the different pattern bands were labeled with their traditional names and shown in a national exhibition in Copenhagen in the 1920s. Queen Alexandra saw them on display and was so taken with their beauty that she requested they be compiled into a book. This was done in 1932, and the knitters of the islands still draw upon the designs today.
See also COLORWORK; FOLK KNITTING

FASSETT, KAFFE (1937-)

Why use one color when two, nine, seventeen or twenty-six will do the trick? Such seems to be the question Kaffe Fassett asks himself before beginning every project. A master of colorwork in every artistic endeavor with which he is involved—knitting, painting, needlepoint, quilting, mosaics and costume and set design—Fassett has said that he thinks of himself

The Faroe Islands are located in the North Atlantic between Iceland, Scotland and Norway.

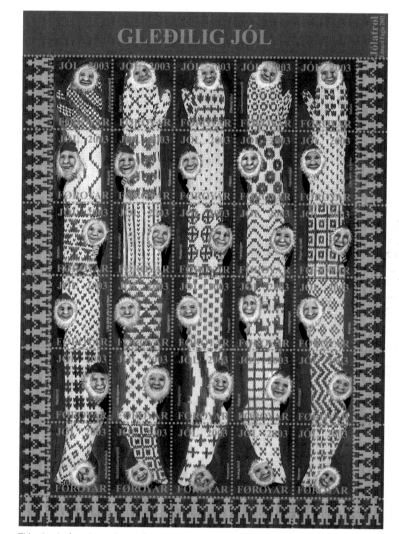

GLEÐILIG JÓL

This sheet of postage stamps from the Faroe Islands depicts "Christmas trolls"–knitted items that aren't ready for Christmas–painted by artist Edward Fuglø.

as "an artist who is interested in pattern and color, in whatever form it comes in."

Fassett was born in San Francisco and grew up in an artistic home near Big Sur, California. At nineteen he received a scholarship to study painting at the School of the Museum of Fine Arts in Boston, where he attended class for three months before England beckoned and, eventually, convinced him to stay; he settled in London in 1964. During a 1968 trip to a Scottish woolen mill with fashion designer Bill Gibb, Fassett became fascinated with the interplay among the shades of yarn he saw. He purchased twenty different-colored skeins and a set of needles and learned to knit on the train ride back to London. The next year his first design, a waistcoat, was featured in *Vogue Knitting*. He did some commercial-knitwear designing for Gibb and Missoni but soon found that handknitting was more suited to his vision and palette. Not surprisingly, given the number of

colors he employs in any one project, he knits his yarn ends in as he goes, greatly accelerating what would otherwise be an interminable finishing process.

Since 1981 he has collaborated closely with Rowan Yarns, and in 2007 he launched his own line of yarns, hand-picking the colors. Fassett was the first fiber artist to merit a solo show at London's venerable Victoria & Albert Museum, and his work has been exhibited at museums throughout Europe, Asia and North America. Other notable achievements include designing theatrical sets and costumes for the Royal Shakespeare Company, giving marketing and design advice to Oxfam for weaving villages in India and Guatemala, appearing in the 2007 documentary *Real Men Knit* and mentoring knitwear designer Brandon Mably.

Fassett's knitwear designs have been collected by Barbra Streisand, Lauren Bacall, Shirley MaClaine and other notables, and he has designed sweaters for

Peruvian Connection, the online and catalog retailer.

A prolific artist with many interests, Fassett is equally known for his work in quilting. His books include *Glorious Knits* (Three Rivers Press, 1992), *Kaffe Fassett's Pattern Library* (Ebury/Taunton, 2003), *Kaffe Knits Again* (Potter Craft, 2007) and many more titles on patchwork and quilting.

Today, Fassett and Mably travel the globe teaching workshops in which they demonstrate and share their mastery and love of color. *See also* COLOR THEORY; DESIGNERS; MABLY, BRANDON; *VOGUE KNITTING*

FEATHER STITCH

Feather stitch is an embroidery stitch used for outlining. When creating this stitch, it is helpful to hold the yarn or thread down with the left thumb to keep it a bit slack. This gives it an undulating look. *See also* EMBROIDERY

FELTED YARN

Wool yarn can be felted after

spinning and then heat-dried. The felted yarn is then balled. The process thickens the fiber and stabilizes it for uniformity of dye uptake. Felted yarn is traditionally used for loop-pile and cut-pile carpets because it yields a thick surface, but it is also sometimes used for handknitting. *See also* FELTING; FIBER CHARACTERSTICS

FELTING

The process of using water and agitation to mat together protein fibers, especially wool, to produce a fabric, is called felting. Technically, *felting* applies to raw fiber, while *fulling* is the felting of knitted fabric. However, *felting* is now the common term for both methods.

The basic process for felting knitted pieces involves washing them in a washing machine, preferably a top-loader, using a small amount of detergent and very hot water. Some knitters toss in a pair of jeans or a clean sneaker to increase the agitation

Kaffe Fassett on the cover of a special men's issue of *Vogue Knitting* in 2002.

Feather Stitch

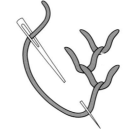

Bring the needle up. Insert the needle to the right on the same level and take a small stitch to the center. Insert the needle to the left on the same level and take a stitch to the center.

of the machine. Another common practice is to place the pieces to be felted in a pillowcase or mesh laundry bag to reduce the amount of lint in the washing machine. The scaly structure of the protein fiber causes the fibers to swell up, curl around and adhere to each other, forming a matlike fabric. All protein fibers—alpaca, angora, cashmere, mohair, silk, wool—will felt if given this treatment. Felted knit fabric is strong, durable, very dense and very warm, and it is well suited to making bags, hats, slippers, toys, household decorations and many other knitted objects.

Nearly all people who have done laundry have had the unfortunate experience of felting something by accident because they washed a wool sweater. Not merely shrunk, a felted sweater is now composed of a new material, and fiber that is felted can never be unfelted.

See also CARE; FIBER CHARACTERISTICS; FULLING; FULLING FACTOR; WOOL

FERN STITCH

Fern stitch is an embroidery stitch that consists of three straight stitches of equal length radiating from the same central point. The stitch is repeated to create a straight or curved line.

See also EMBROIDERY; STRAIGHT STITCH

FIBER CHARACTERISTICS

The qualities a particular fiber possesses greatly influence the qualities of yarn spun from that fiber. Fibers are either filaments (continuous strands) or staples (short strands).

The three main classifications for fiber are protein (animal fibers), vegetable (plant fibers) and synthetic. Animal and plant fibers begin as staples, whereas synthetic fibers are created first as filaments and then cut into staples, which are then spun to create yarn.

Animal fibers include wool, mohair, alpaca, cashmere, angora and silk. Plant fibers include cotton, linen and hemp. Synthetics include nylon, acrylic and polyester. Animal fibers tend to be warm, breathable, elastic, durable and receptive to dye. Because of their protein content, all are also susceptible to moth damage. Plant fibers are composed of cellulose and, compared with animal fibers, are cooler to wear but less elastic and resilient. The fibers of bamboo and corn are now used in the development of yarn. Some new fibers, such as those from soy and milk, contain protein but are similar to plant fibers. Synthetic fibers are artificially produced from various coal and petroleum products; most were developed in the World War II era because of shortages of natural raw materials. They tend to be easy to care for and inexpensive, but they also lack elasticity and breathability.

Different fibers have their own unique characteristics, including softness, drape, elasticity and overall feel. Animal fibers can be felted, for instance, whereas the smooth structure of plant fibers and synthetics makes fulling or felting impossible.

See also ACRYLIC; ALPACA FIBER; ANGORA FIBER; BUFFALO FIBER; CAMELHAIR; CARDING; CASHMERE; COTTON; DYEING; FELTING; FIBER CONTENT; FLAX; FULLING; HEMP; JUTE; LINEN; MERINO FIBER; MOHAIR FIBER; NONTRADITIONAL YARNS; ORGANIC KNITTING; POLYESTER; QIVIUT; SILK; SPINNING; STAPLE YARNS; WOOL; YAK FIBER; YARN SUBSTITUTION

FIBER CONTENT

The percentage breakdown of fibers within a yarn, such as "100% wool" or "75% merino, 20% silk, 5% nylon," describes its fiber content. The fiber content of yarns is indicated on the label or ball band. Yarn manufacturers are responsible for accurate reporting of fiber content under the Wool Labeling Act, and yarns can be tested to analyze their makeup.

See also FIBER CHARACTERISTICS; YARN LABELS; YARN SUBSTITUTION; YARN WEIGHT

Two identical swatches knit out of a woolen-spun pure wool yarn, before (left) and after (right) felting. Note the difference in size as well as the loss of stitch definition in the felted swatch.

Fern Stitch

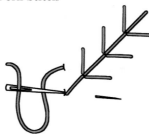

Bring the thread up and make a straight stitch. Bring thread up to the left of the starting point and into the center. In the same motion, make a stitch to the right.

FICTION, KNITTING IN

Over the centuries, knitting has wound its way into everything from poetry to pulp fiction. The poems of George Gascoigne ("The Steel Glass," 1575) and the stories of Edmund Howes (dating from 1615) mention the craft, but the grand dame of fictional knitters is without question Madame Defarge of Charles Dickens's *A Tale of Two Cities* (1859), whose needles click away the count of heads dropping from the guillotine. Defarge is never seen without her knitting, and Dickens's chapter titles—"Knitting," "Still Knitting," "The Knitting Done"—attest to the symbolic significance of her busy fingers. Pressed to reveal what she is knitting, she replies, "Many things…. For instance, shrouds." Like the mythical Fates, whose spinning determines the span of a person's life, Madame Defarge's knitting carries a death sentence—and the record of evil deeds—for the heartless aristocrats she despises. As her husband says, "It would be easier for the weakest poltroon that lives, to erase himself from existence, than to erase one letter of his name or crimes from the knitted register of Madame Defarge."

Knitting forms a subtle but continuous thread in the nineteenth-century Victorian novel. It's mentioned only once in Jane Austen's Regency comedies of manners, when the genteel but impoverished Mrs. Smith learns to knit from a lower-class acquaintance (*Persuasion*, 1817). Mrs. Smith's goal is to make pretty little nothings to sell to the frivolous rich; she uses the money to aid very poor families in her neighborhood. In George Eliot's novels, knitting is the sign of an earnest, industrious, down-to-earth woman. Mrs. Poyser, the hardworking farmer's wife in *Adam Bede* (1859) prefers knitting to all other work because it's a task she can accomplish as she patrols her busy farmhouse dairy and kitchen, keeping an eye on her servants and children. In *Middlemarch* (1872), all the worthy women knit: Mrs. Farebrother, the vicar's mother, and the estimable Mrs. Garth are just two examples.

As tireless in her pursuit for justice as yarn and needles is Miss Jane Marple, Agatha Christie's formidable sleuth and the central character in *A Pocket Full of Rye* (1953), *A Murder Is Announced* (1950) and several other mystery novels. (Christie also used the motif of a knitting secret in her tale of Middle East derring-do, *They Came to Baghdad*, 1951). Time after time, the grandmotherly Miss Marple draws out information by placidly sitting and knitting (selfless soul that she is, she never knits anything for herself, instead turning out endless items for babies). She's not the only knitting detective. Miss Maud Silver, the creation of Patricia Wentworth and another boon to Scotland Yard, begins each of her tales (*Miss Silver Intervenes*, 1943; *Through the Wall*, 1950; and *The Silent Pool*, 1954; to name a few) with gently clicking needles. Knitting so fast that socks seem to revolve as she works them, Miss Silver always gets her man.

Other fictional knitters, while equally dedicated to their needles, are not always on the right side of justice. In Ruth Rendell's short story "A Needle for the Devil" (1996), Alice Gibson discovers knitting as a way to control her violent temper, only to marry a man who can't bear to watch her knit. Deprived of her therapy, Alice lies awake at night dreaming of projects she can't start and growing increasingly unsettled, until at last she finds a new use for her knitting needle—with consequences fatal to her husband. In *Tuesday the Rabbi Saw Red* (2003), Harry Kemelman supplies readers with an industrious knitter, only in this case the murder is not the result of knitting deprivation, but an essential part of the modus operandi.

Other knit-themed fiction focuses on the craft's healing nature. Tita, the main character in Laura Esquivel's 1989 novel *Like Water for Chocolate*, knits a seemingly endless afghan to thwart both sadness and sexual frustration, while in *The Knitting Circle* (2007), author Anne Hood (who turned to knitting when her own young daughter died from a rare form of strep) introduces Mary Baxter, who, still reeling from the death of her five-year-old daughter, finds solace in the click of needles and the company of a knitting club. The fictional yarn shop Walker & Daughter is the setting for Kate Jacobs's *The Friday Night Knitting Club* (2007), in which single mom Georgia has her hands full with both her yarn shop and her teenage daughter. Georgia's regular customers gather once a week to work on their latest projects and share experiences in love and life. On Seattle's fictional Blossom Street, the customers and proprietor of A Good Yarn, the touchstone for Debbie Macomber's popular series (*The Shop on Blossom Street*, 2004, and others), find happiness, friendship and fulfillment amid skeins and stitches. In *Knitting Under the Influence* (2006), Claire LaZebnik blends needles with chick lit by chronicling the tangled lives of Los Angeles women who reexamine their sense of self as knitted sweaters, baby blankets and bikinis take shape.
See also FILM, KNITTING IN

FILM, KNITTING IN

Characters can be seen knitting in films of all genres, be it action, comedy, drama or suspense. In many cases knitting is used to define a character, such as the loving grandma in *Willy Wonka and the Chocolate Factory* (1971) or the flighty Holly Golightly in *Breakfast at Tiffany's* (1961), who knits an enormous red scarf as she listens to foreign language tapes. In other instances, knitting highlights a character's mood, such as the anxious handwork of the women in *Gone With the Wind* (1936) or the endless afghan that trails the main character, Tita, in *Like Water for Chocolate* (1992). Whatever it is intended to show, the clicking of needles has had more than its share of screen time. In *Holiday* (1938), Katharine Hepburn portrays a quiet older sister who uses her knitting as a means to eavesdrop on conversations. The Claymation dog Grommit, despite his lack of thumbs, shows great knitting proficiency stitching a scarf while waiting for Wallace's return in *Wallace and Grommit: The Curse of the Were-Rabbit* (2005). Blanche, the trapped sister in *What Ever Happened to Baby Jane?* (1962), knits while plotting her escape. In fact, when Joan Crawford was asked about the differences between herself and Bette Davis, she stated, "Bette likes to rant and rave. I just sit and knit. She yelled, and I knitted a scarf from Hollywood to Malibu." Bette Davis herself knits away during an illicit affair in *Now,*

Voyager (1942). In *Brokeback Mountain* (2005), Ennis's wife, played by Michelle Williams, knits as she stews over her husband's "camping trips" with another man. In *Lady and the Tramp* (1955), precious pup Lady runs off with a baby bootie that her owner is knitting as a way of expressing her worry that she'll soon be replaced in her masters' affections.

The choice of project and knitting method among big-screen knitters is as varied as the films in which they appear. Grandma Georgina knits Charlie a scarf in 1971's *Willy Wonka and the Chocolate Factory*; in the 2005 Tim Burton remake *Charlie and the Chocolate Factory*, she opts for a crocheted version. Scarlett Johansson's character tries on her scarf in progress at the beginning of *Lost in Translation* (2003). Morticia knits a three-legged bodysuit in *The Addams Family* (1991) movie, and Suzanne Pleshette creates a dog sweater for the title character in *The Ugly Dachshund* (1966). Kate Hudson clicks away on circulars in *Alex & Emma* (2003), while in *Harry Potter and the Chamber of Secrets* (2002), Harry and the Weasleys stumble across needles that knit by themselves. In *Spider-Man 3* (2007), Peter's aunt employs an uncomfortable but elegant style of knitting (taking a break from the crochet she displayed in the

previous *Spider-Man* flicks). In *Phone Call from a Stranger* (1952), Bette Davis busily turns out socks on dpns.
See also FICTION, KNITTING IN

FINGERING WEIGHT
A super-fine-weight yarn, fingering weight takes number 1 on the CYC Standard Yarn Weight System chart. Fingering includes sock, baby and lace yarns. In Great Britain, this weight is commonly referred to as two- or three-ply yarn. It typically knits up at 27–32 stitches to 4 inches (10cm) in stockinette stitch on U.S. size 1–3 needles. Some fingering-weight yarns are categorized as 0 (33 to 40 stitches to 4 inches/10cm on U.S. size 000 to 1 needles).

Traditionally, fingering weight was used for fine ladies' garments, such as dresses and skirts and baby garments, but today it is most popular for lace and socks.
See also YARN SUBSTITUTION; YARN WEIGHT

FINGERLESS GLOVES
See GLOVES

FINGERLESS MITTENS
See MITTENS

FINISHING TECHNIQUES
The skills needed to finish a garment or other item after all pieces are knit, finishing techniques include binding off,

grafting (Kitchener stitch), blocking, seaming and weaving in ends.
See also ASSEMBLING; BIND-OFF; BLOCKING; BUTTON BAND; BUTTONHOLE BAND; BUTTONS; CLOSURES; EMBROIDERY; GRAFTING; SEAMING; WEAVING IN ENDS

FISHERMAN PATTERNS
See ARAN KNITTING; FOLK KNITTING; GANSEY

FISHERMAN'S RIB
See BRIOCHE

FL
Abbreviation for *front loop(s)*.

FLAT KNITTING
Knitting worked in rows instead of rounds, knit on pairs of straight needles or by working back and forth on one circular needle is called flat knitting. A flat-knitted piece has four edges: the cast-on and bound-off edges and the two sides. Flat pieces must be seamed to form the garment.

Some knitters prefer flat knitting, and some prefer working in the round. Colorwork is more difficult to do working flat because working with two colors while purling is not as practiced and thus not as easy, plus there are more ends to weave in. However, it is generally easier to shape sweaters that are knitted flat rather than in the round and to manage

complex patterns or design elements. And knitting the front and back of a sweater separately allows you to make size adjustments if necessary. For example, if the back seems a bit too small, you can adjust the width of the front to compensate.
See also CIRCULAR KNITTING; NEEDLE TYPES; SELVAGE

FLAX

The plant that produces linen fiber is called flax *(Linun ustatissimum)*. Flax is also the source of linseed or flaxseed oil. The long fibers in the stem of the flax plant have been used to make cloth at least as far back as ancient Egypt.

Flax fiber is extracted from the skin of the stem of the plant in a lengthy process that involves threshing the plant to remove the seeds, soaking (called "rotting" or "retting") the stalks to loosen them from the core, beating *(scotching)* them to further break down and separate the fibers and combing them through a bed of nails, or hackles. This process separates the fibers into two types: *line,* the long fibers used for spinning linen, and *tow,* the short, tangled fibers used for towrope.
See also FIBER CHARACTERISTICS; LINEN

FLORENTINE JACKET

Knitted, patterned silk jackets dating from the seventeenth century are referred to as Florentine jackets. Knit with two colors, often with purl stitches enhancing the brocade effect, the jackets were sewn from squares of knitted fabric. Though they are often referred to as Italian, their actual origin is in dispute. The square pieces from which they were constructed and the long floats on the reverse side suggest that the jackets are products of machine knitting rather than handknitting. The waistcoats were likely made by framework knitters who were imitating woven brocades. Some believe that the technique was developed in Spain and replicated in England. Two Englishmen, Josias Crane and J.P.

This exquisite silk jacket was knit in Italy, or possibly England, in the early 1600s.

Porter, patented the technique in 1768, introducing a machine that created brocade patterns such as those used in the jackets.

Though the origins of the Florentine jackets may be in dispute, there's no argument that they were worn well into the eighteenth century. A London paper dating from 1712 reports the theft of such a waistcoat, and Colonial American newspapers from the mid-eighteenth century also make mention of them.
See also ITALIAN KNITTING

FO

Shorthand for "finished object," FO is the term often used by knitting bloggers to describe completed projects.
See also INTERNET

FOALE, MARION (1939-)

Foale is a fashion designer, author and knitwear designer with a major influence in both the fashion and knitting worlds, who earned acclaim for her work early in her life: In 1960, while Foale attended the Royal College of Art on a fellowship, one of her designs was selected as Queen Elizabeth II's mantle for an Order of the British Empire ceremony (the queen still wears the piece). In 1961, Foale joined with fellow student Sally Tuffin to create the fashion design firm Foale and Tuffin, which became a major player—with the collaboration of Mary Quant and Betsey

Johnson—in London's emergent pop or mod fashion movement. These designers brought a youthful energy and spirit of fun into knitwear that the industry had never seen before. In the 1980s, Foale transitioned to an independent career as a knitwear designer, opening a shop in Marylebone High Street to sell her creations (in finished form) and authoring *Marion Foale's Classic Knitwear: A Beautiful Collection of 30 Original Patterns* (Rodale Press, 1985), a collection of simple shapes that helped stoke the 1980s mini-boom in home hand knitting. Foale's hand-knitted sweaters are still sold at exclusive boutiques worldwide. In the mid-'00s Foale and her daughter sold yarns and patterns online under the Foale name.

FOLK KNITTING

As with other "folk" pursuits, folk knitting is used to describe the knitting of a particular region or people, usually in a distinct style that uses indigenous materials. Most folk knitting evolved in tandem with the region's tools and materials. Folk garments are usually ornamented with motifs drawn from local culture and often worn during holidays or as part of a traditional costume. Folk knitting resists generalizations because it varies so greatly.
See also ALPINE REGION KNITTING; AMERICAN FOLK ART MUSEUM; ANDES REGION

KNITTING; ARABIC KNITTING; ARAN KNITTING; ARGYLE; AZORES LACE; BALTIC KNITTING; BAVARIAN KNITTING; BOHUS KNITTING; BRITISH KNITTING; CHANNEL ISLANDS PATTERNS; COWICHAN KNITTING; DALES KNITTING; DUTCH KNITTING; FAIR ISLE KNITTING; FAROE KNITTING; GANSEY; GERMAN KNITTING; HISTORY OF KNITTING; ICE-LANDIC KNITTING; NORWEGIAN KNITTING; ORENBURG LACE; SETESDAL SOCKS; SHETLAND LACE; SPANISH KNITTING: SWEDISH KNITTING; TARTAN KNITTING; TURKISH PATTERNS; WELSH KNITTING

FOLL

Abbreviation for *follow(s)* or *following.*

FOOD FIBERS

See NONTRADITIONAL YARNS

FOUNDATION ROW

Depending on the pattern, the foundation row can be defined in two ways: 1) the cast-on row; 2) the first row of a multi-row stitch pattern, especially when the first row sets up the remaining pattern repeat rows but is not itself repeated. An example would be a row of knit and purl stitches that sets up the pattern for a cable. In some patterns, the foundation row is referred to as the preparation row.
See also CAST-ON

FREEFORM KNITTING/CROCHET

To work "freeform" is to employ an improvised fiber art that depends

Freeform knitted and crocheted design by Prudence Mapstone

Elsa Schiaparelli's famed *trompe l'oeil* Bow-Knot sweater

not on a pattern but on a stitcher's individual creativity and facility with needles, hook or both. The yarny equivalent of jazz, freeform uses as its building block the "scrumble," typically a small knitted or crocheted swatch of any shape and color scheme, often embellished with separately stitched motifs, beads, wire, feathers, novelty yarn and the like. Crocheted items can be added to a knitted scrumble base and vice versa. Scrumbles can be flat or three-dimensional, abstract or representational and can stand alone as a piece of art or jewelry or be sewn together to form a larger garment, handbag or accessory. Because freeform does not specify yardage quantities and utilizes a variety of yarns, it is often touted as an imaginative and efficient way to use up stash yarn.

The term *scrumble* was coined by the late Sylvia Cosh and James Walters, the British crochet team who collaborated from 1977 through Cosh's death in 2000 and coauthored *The Crochet Workbook* (St. Martin's Press, 1989). The best-known freeformers of the 2000s, Australians Prudence Mapstone and Jenny Dowde, have both published acclaimed books on the technique, including Mapstone's self-published *Freeform: Serendipitous Design Techniques for Knitting and Crochet* (2002) and Dowde's *Freeform Knitting and Crochet* (Sally Milner Publishing, 2004).

Groups such as the International Freeform Crochet Guild (freeformcrochet.com) and the International Freeform Fiberarts Guild (intff.org) promote the medium, the latter mounting online themed exhibits to which industry designers and hobbyists contribute: "Earth, Wind, Air, and Fire," "Tree of Life/Tree of Peace," and "60 Odd/A Fiber Odyssey" incorporated scrumbles that both depicted still lifes and people and amorphously evoked thematic concepts.
See also INTERNET; SCRUMBLE

FRENCH HEEL

See HEELS

FRENCH KNITTING

As with other regional knitting techniques, French knitting refers to the knitting styles and traditions established in France. But it has an alternative definition, quite unrelated, as that of knitting done on a knitting nancy.

The French were the first to integrate knits into couture, building on the popularity of sweaters, which had been steadily increasing since World War I. Elsa Schiaparelli, an Italian-born designer who came to prominence in Paris and was considered the founder of graphic knitwear, took this trend and created a fashion sensation when she introduced the Bow-Knot sweater in 1927. In her design, a white yarn was used to "weave" a collar, floppy bow and cuffs into a black sweater. She was preceded by Coco Chanel, who created the costumes for the Diaghilev ballet *Le Train Bleu* in 1924. Most of the dancers, depicting flappers and their boyfriends, wore handknitted bathing suits in a unisex design. Chanel changed the colors of the suits from typical beige or black to dazzling colors like royal blue.

In addition to its couture knits, France has a long tradition of lace knitting; many popular lace patterns in use today still have French names.
See also BATHING SUIT, HAND-KNITTED; KNITTING NANCY; RYKIEL, SONIA; SCHIAPARELLI, ELSA

FRENCH KNOT

A small embroidered knot often used to add depth and dimension to knitted pieces.
See also EMBROIDERY

French Knot

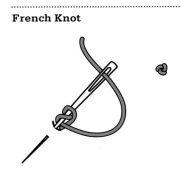

Bring the needle up and wrap the thread around it once or twice, holding the thread taut. Reinsert the needle close to where the thread emerged.

FRINGE

Fringe are the lengths of loose or knotted yarns applied to the edges of finished garments. Fringe can be created in a number of ways; the easiest method is to cut the yarn twice the desired length of the fringe, adding extra length for knotting. Insert a crochet hook through the wrong side of the edge of the finished piece and over the folded yarn. Pull the yarn through the fabric, draw the ends through and tighten.

See also EMBELLISHMENTS; FINISHING TECHNIQUES

Simple Fringe

Cut yarn twice the desired length plus extra for knotting. On the wrong side, insert the hook from front to back through the piece and over the folded yarn. Pull the yarn through. Draw the ends through and tighten. Trim the yarn.

Knotted Fringe

After working a simple fringe (it should be longer to account for extra knotting), take half of the strands from each fringe and knot them with half the strands from the neighboring fringe.

FROG CLOSURE

A decorative fastener inspired by the knotwork fasteners on traditional Chinese garments, frogs can be purchased or made by looping cording or a fabric or knit tube (I-cord) into the desired shapes. One side of the frog is formed into a loop and the other is formed into a button that fits into the loop.

See also CLOSURES; CORDS

FROGGING

A slang term for unraveling, or ripping out, your knitting, *frogging* is derived from "ribbit, ribbit," the sound a frog makes, which "rip it, rip it" sounds like.

See also CORRECTING COMMON MISTAKES; INTERNET; UNRAVELING

FULLING

Technically, the term *fulling* refers to only the felting of a knitted fabric, though it is often used interchangeably with *felting*, and in fact the term *felting* is more commonly used for both processes. Some protein fibers, especially wool, have a scaly structure and are crimped. The scales, or fibrils, trap warm air (which is why wool is so warm), and this crimp gives the wool its resilience. Additionally, these two qualities allow the fibers to adhere during the spinning process and, with the application of heat and moisture, to full or felt. Both fulling and felting are essentially the rearrangement and shrinking of the fiber molecules. Many people discover fulling by accident when they wash a wool garment and it shrinks beyond recognition.

See also FELTING; FULLING FACTOR

FULLING FACTOR

The degree to which some protein fibers, such as wool, will felt or full is referred to as the fulling factor. The fulling factor of wool is largely dependent on the breed of sheep. The way the yarn is carded and spun also contributes to this quality: Woolen-spun yarn is more suited to fulling than worsted-spun yarn, and loosely spun yarns such as Icelandic wools have a high fulling factor.

When planning a fulled or felted project it is essential to make a swatch and put it through the fulling process before beginning to knit to calculate how much it will shrink.

See also FELTING; FULLING

FUN FUR YARN

Fun fur is a type of novelty yarn that is not real fur, but rather an eyelash fiber with a filamented nap reminiscent of fur. Fun fur yarn is usually made of artificial fibers of polyester, nylon, rayon, microfiber or polyamide, but can also comprise natural elements such as cotton, wool and linen. This type of yarn shows up frequently as trim on garments. Fun fur yarn can also be used to knit entire objects, such as hats, furry pillows or vests. Fun fur yarn is often seen as kitschy, but this is a matter of personal taste.

See also EYELASH YARN; NOVELTY YARN

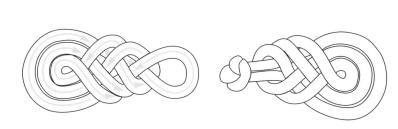

A frog closure can be made from I-cord or other cord.

Finished frog closure

G

Written in lowercase, g is the abbreviation for *gram*, a metric unit of measurement equal to approximately one-twentieth of an ounce. Many yarns are sold in 25g, 50g or 100g skeins.
See also ABBREVIATIONS; YARN WEIGHT

GANSEY

Fishermen's ganseys (also known as guernseys or jerseys) were produced throughout the ports of the Northern Atlantic, North Sea and English Channel. Traditional ganseys were knit in the round out of a smooth, combed-wool yarn, had a tight tension (approximately 30 stitches to 4 inches/10cm), and were elaborately patterned; those from Scottish fishing ports and from Holland were particularly elaborate. The origin of the fisherman's gansey is unknown. It may have been a precursor to the Aran sweater.
See also ARAN KNITTING; BRITISH KNITTING; FOLK KNITTING

GARDINER, KAY

See MASON-DIXON KNITTING

GARTER STITCH

A stitch pattern formed by knitting (or purling) every row when knitting flat, or by alternating rows of knit and purl when working circular rounds, garter stitch has bumpy horizontal ridges and forms a dense fabric that stretches more lengthwise than crosswise. It is usually the first stitch pattern knitters learn.

Garter stitch combines well with other stitches and patterns, such as cables, lace and knit-purl stitches (textured patterns). It also lies flat, so it is particularly suited for edges and borders, and as welts. It looks the same on the front and back, making it good for reversible garments such as scarves. However, it is not as tall as plain stockinette, and will distort the fabric if used in combination with stockinette-based fabrics, unless allowances are made. To knit the swatch shown below, cast on any number of stitches and knit every row or purl every row.
See also BORDERS; CABLES; EDGINGS; KNIT/PURL PATTERNS; KNIT STITCH; TEXTURED KNITTING; WELT

GAUGAIN, JANE

See BRITISH KNITTING

GAUGE

Perhaps the most crucial piece of information about a piece of knitting, gauge is the number of stitches and rows per inch, based on the size of a knitted stitch. The way you control your yarn, the size of your needles and the yarn you choose influence the size of your stitch and therefore the gauge you obtain. It can be measured simply with a ruler or tape measure, or a tool known as a stitch gauge can also be used.

Controlling the yarn as it feeds through your fingers is similar to setting the tension dial on a sewing or knitting machine to determine how tightly the thread feeds through the needle. A tight tension produces a smaller stitch than a loose tension.

Needle size and type can produce stitches of different sizes. As you increase your needle size, the size of your stitch will increase. The type of needle you use also affects your gauge. You may find that metal needles give you a different gauge than wooden or plastic needles.

Row gauge can be as important as stitch gauge, particularly in shaping pieces, such as sleeves. If you do not have the correct row gauge, you may not get the correct length after working the specified number of increases or decreases. If you are using a full body chart for a sweater, you must work the exact number of rows on the chart. Your piece will be too long or too short if your row gauge differs from the recommended gauge. In addition, some sweaters are worked from side to side, and the row gauge will determine the width. Both row and stitch gauge are essential for proper fit.

Garter-stitch swatch

Each swatch shown here was made in stockinette stitch with the same number of stitches and rows, but using three different needle sizes, from (left to right) smaller to larger. The smaller the needle, the smaller the swatch, and the larger the needle, the larger the swatch.

A True Classic

by Debbie Bliss

I have a love affair with the gansey.

The classic shape and stitch patterning of the gansey has formed the basis of many of my designs, and I am fascinated by its history. By using this classic style in my work I feel part of a history that has been passed down through generations.

"Gansey" is the name given to a hard-wearing, practical garment that was knit in most every fishing community in northern Europe, especially throughout Britain and the Channel Islands. Many of the stitch patterns were regional, as in the Polperro from Cornwall in southwestern England or the Whitby from Yorkshire in the north. All ganseys were traditionally knit in the round with sleeves knitted down from the shoulder, meaning you could easily reknit a sleeve when the cuffs got worn or sea damaged. (This is something I like to do with children's sweaters to get more wear out of them as little arms grow.) Ganseys weren't just practical garments, however; there would be a Sunday best

gansey, sometimes worked in cream rather than the usual dark blue, and a bride-to-be would knit a special shirt for the groom to wear on their wedding day. The patterning on the "working" ganseys was usually kept simple, while the special occasion ones sometimes featured more elaborate stitch patterns.

On traditional ganseys, the stitch patterning is usually confined to the yoke, and this makes it a great style to use in baby or children's designs. Often when changing from the stockinette stitch bottom portion to the patterned yoke I increase the number of stitches to compensate for the fact that the textured fabric pulls in. But if, instead, you maintain the same stitch count, you produce a sweet A-line shape that is lovely for a little girl. For boys and men the classic shape is pretty much perfect. I sometimes also knit family initials into the gansey as one more link to this long and wonderful knitting tradition.

Debbie Bliss (debbieblissonline.com) is a noted designer whose work appears regularly in major knitting publications. She is also the author of over thirty books. She also has her own magazine and her own line of yarns.

Different yarns can alter gauge as well as produce different textures. Even different colors of the same yarn may result in stitches of different sizes. The stitch pattern you use may affect your gauge. Loose stitches such as lace will give a larger gauge (fewer stitches per inch) than stockinette; cables will give a smaller gauge (more stitches per inch). Your knitting style (English, Continental, Eastern, combined) may also affect your gauge.

All projects benefit from the working up of a gauge swatch to determine gauge and help to plan the project accurately.
See also GAUGE SWATCH; YARN SUBSTITUTION; YARN WEIGHT

GAUGE SWATCH

The small piece of knitting made before beginning a garment or other knitted item and used to measure your gauge is called the gauge swatch. Knowing your gauge as it compares with that of the pattern's specifications allows you to better produce well-fitting

garments. If the gauge matches that stated in the pattern, you can proceed with confidence. If it is off, changing needles or yarn may produce a gauge that is a better match. Knowing your gauge can also help you customize a pattern, even if you do not match the stated gauge. Gauge swatches are also useful for determining how a yarn blocks and whether it is colorfast.

The instructions for most garments specify a gauge swatch that is 4 inches (10cm) square. Some instructions indicate the number of stitches and rows per inch (centimeter), and you will have to calculate how many stitches you need to cast on to make the square. Generally, instructions specify what pattern stitch to use for your gauge swatch; if this is not specified, knit it in stockinette stitch.

To knit a gauge swatch, start with the needles and yarn suggested. To make it easier to measure your gauge swatch, add 2 garter stitch stitches at each edge

of your gauge swatch so it will lie flat, or knit a swatch that is larger than 4 inches (10cm).

After completing your gauge swatch and removing it from your needles, measure the number of stitches and rows to the inch. Then steam block or wet block it. When the swatch is completely dry, measure it with a tape measure or stitch gauge. Count the stitches carefully, because even small variations can make a significant difference in your finished piece. Match the blocked gauge swatch's numbers to those given in the pattern. If your gauge is smaller than the recommended gauge, use larger needles; if your gauge is larger than the recommended gauge, use smaller needles. If the gauge changes significantly from the unblocked to blocked swatches, note how much of a change it took, so that when working to specific distances ("12 inches from cast-on edge") you can work appropriately for the finished piece to come out correctly.

Swatch Knitting Tips

To determine your gauge, measure either the center 4 inches (10cm) of your swatch or measure the entire swatch and divide that measurement by the number of stitches to get the number of stitches per inch.

If you are knitting several different stitch patterns in one garment, such as an Aran or guernsey sweater, and the instructions give one gauge for all the patterns, make one large swatch incorporating all the patterns.

If you are working with a lacy pattern or with yarns that stretch, such as cotton or silk, make your gauge swatch at least 6–8 inches (15–20cm) square to account for both horizontal and vertical stretch.

Instead of binding off the last row of your swatch, place it on a stitch holder or cut the yarn and thread it through the live stitches before you remove them from the needle. Binding off may pull in the stitches at the top of the swatch

Measuring the stitch gauge of a swatch with a tape measure

Measuring row gauge of a swatch with a tape measure

Using a stitch gauge

and make it more difficult to measure gauge. If it is a lacy pattern, however, or one that tends to spread, you should bind off the last row.

Make notes about the gauge swatch in the gauge itself: Take the number of the needle size used, and work that many purls against the stockinette ground, or work (yo, k2tog) that number of times. You'll be able to determine what size needle was used for the swatch even if your notes get misplaced.

With yarns such as mohair or bouclé, it is difficult to measure individual stitches. In this case, cast on the exact number of stitches given in the gauge, work the specified number of rows, and measure the entire swatch. Or place stitch markers on either side of the stitches needed for the gauge and measure between the markers.

Gauge Swatches for Knitting in the Round

When you work stockinette stitch in the round, you knit every row and never purl. Because the size of a knit stitch differs slightly from the size of a purl stitch, the gauge for straight knitting will differ from the gauge for circular knitting. You can make a swatch without working in the round by knitting every row on a circular needle or two double-pointed needles as follows: After the first row, cut the yarn. Slide the stitches to the other end of the needle to begin a new row, without turning your work. Repeat at the end of each row. An

alternative method is to knit a narrow tube in the round as your gauge swatch.

Uses for Gauge Swatches

In addition to contributing to the success of your projects, gauge swatches have other useful purposes:
• Use them to practice borders, buttonholes, embroidery and finishes.
• Sew squares together to make afghans.
• Put swatches in a notebook to keep for future reference.
• Use them for patches or pockets.
• Test the yarn's washability or colorfastness.
• Use them to match notions such as buttons, or when shopping for clothes or fabric that will complement your knitted garment.
See also BLOCKING; GAUGE; YARN SUBSTITUTION; YARN WEIGHT

GAUGHAN, NORAH (1961–)

Armed with an undergraduate degree in biology with a concentration in studio art from Brown University, Norah Gaughan has long since stopped choosing between her right and left brain. "I think scientists can relate to art and artists to science, although it takes the right kind of personality to look across fields," she said of her bestselling book *Knitting Nature* (STC Craft, 2006). The book's nearly forty textured, cabled and asymmetrical garments are constructed from repetitive patterns and phenomena found in nature—spirals, hexagons,

pentagons, fractals, waves and phyllotaxies.

The daughter of two commercial illustrators, Gaughan grew up in a creative household, learning to crochet from her mother and grandmother at a tender age. Her mother, Phoebe Gaughan, does technical knitting illustrations (including for this book). When she was fourteen, Gaughan spent the summer with a friend in Princeton, New Jersey, who taught her to knit. Gaughan sold her first pattern at the age of seventeen, and she continued to submit designs throughout her college career. After earning her dual degree, she stayed in Providence, Rhode Island, and knit samples for

renowned local knitters Margery Winter and Deborah Newton, who were to become her mentors.

Today Gaughan is the design director for Berroco Yarns, collaborating on yarn lines, color palettes and designs for both pattern books and the company's weekly e-newsletter, "Knit Bits."

Gaughan's books include *Knitting Nature* (STC Craft, 2006) and *Comfort Knitting and Crochet: Afghans* with Margery Winter (STC Craft, 2010).
See also DESIGNERS; *VOGUE KNITTING*

GERMAN KNITTING

Needles and yarn were so much a part of early German culture that

The Visit of the Angels, Master Bertram (c. 1390)

The Visit of the Angels, painted around the year 1390 by Master Bertram of Munich, portrays the Madonna knitting on double-pointed needles. In style and materials German knitting is almost identical to what is known as Alpine region knitting. Much German knitting is worked on four or five needles in the round, and decorative, or fancy, stockings are quite popular.

The Continental method of knitting is sometimes called the German method, and, because it was associated with Germany, it went out of favor in English-speaking countries during World War II. Its reintroduction in the United States is often credited to Elizabeth Zimmermann.
See also ALPINE REGION KNITTING; CONTINENTAL/ GERMAN-STYLE KNITTING; FOLK KNITTING; ZIMMERMANN, ELIZABETH

GILBERT, KATE
See KNITTY.COM

GLOVES
Coverings for the hands enclosing each of the five fingers separately, as opposed to one space for the thumb and another for the rest of the fingers (called mittens) are known as gloves. Their prime purpose is to keep hands warm in cold weather, but gloves also serve as evening accessories, especially when stitched in pretty lace patterns. Most sources date the origin of knitted gloves to the early Middle Ages, and it is possible that some bishops were using

these items as early as the seventh century. The Cluny Museum in Paris houses one silk liturgical glove believed to be that of Pierre de Courpalay, the abbot of Saint-Germain-des-Prés, who died in 1334. At the Basilica of St. Sernin in Toulouse is a pair from the thirteenth century, knit in white stockinette and embellished with embroidered medallions.

Gloves are most often knitted in the round starting at the wrist. A gusset is created for the thumb, and stitches are placed on a holder to be picked up later. When the wrist and hand reach the desired length, stitches are placed on holders for each finger. Fingers and thumb are then knitted individually in the round.

Glove length is measured in "buttons." One button is equal to one French inch (approximately ½ inch longer than an American inch). Gloves are measured starting at the base of the thumb.

There are several typical styles and lengths of gloves:

Shorty
A shorty glove extends no longer than the wrist.

Gauntlet
Historically a gauntlet was a flared protective glove worn with medieval armor. Currently, in knitting, a gauntlet denotes a glove that extends well past the wrist but below the elbow. The cuff or shaft portion may flare, but the term gauntlet has become more generalized to include close-fitting, ribbed models.

Gloves

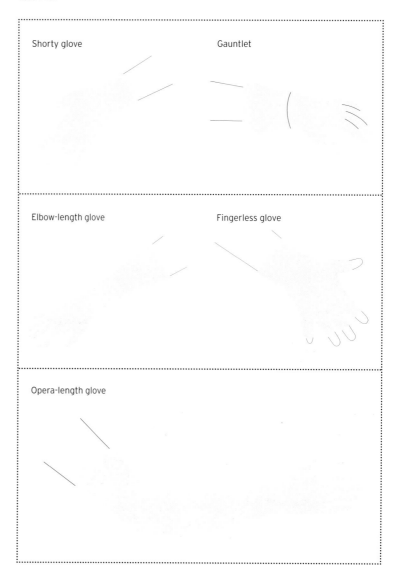

Shorty glove   Gauntlet

Elbow-length glove   Fingerless glove

Opera-length glove

Elbow-Length

The fabric of elbow-length gloves extends to the elbow; they may be part of a formal look, or can be fun and colorful, like arm warmers.

Opera-Length

The opera, or evening-length, glove extends past the elbow to cover some portion of the upper arm, or all of it. Opera gloves are usually considered formal wear.

Fingerless

The fingerless glove, favored for situations requiring dexterity, can either cover the base of each finger with a small sheath (giving a hole for each finger and thumb) or can have one general opening for the fingers, without sheaths. Fingerless gloves are usually informal dress.
See also CIRCULAR KNITTING; HISTORY OF KNITTING; MITTENS

GOAT, KASHMIR
See CASHMERE

GRAFTING

Also called Kitchener stitch, grafting joins two open edges stitch by stitch, using a yarn needle and the yarn from the work. The graft resembles a row of stitches and leaves no visible seam. It's perfect for the tips of mittens and the toes of socks, as well as any other joining that

Grafting

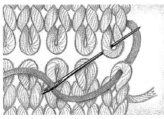

1. Insert needle purlwise into the first stitch on the front piece, then knitwise into the first stitch on the back piece. Draw the yarn through.

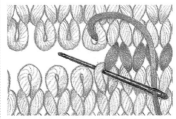

2. Insert the yarn needle knitwise into the first stitch on the front piece again. Draw the yarn through.

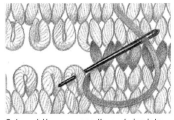

3. Insert the yarn needle purlwise into the next stitch on the front piece. Draw the yarn through.

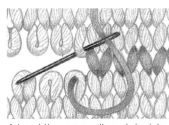

4. Insert the yarn needle purlwise into the first stitch on the back piece again. Draw the yarn through.

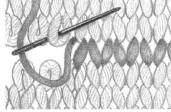

5. Insert the yarn needle knitwise into the next stitch on the back piece. Draw the yarn through. Repeat steps 2 through 5.

needs to look seamless. Because you must follow the path of the stitches with the yarn needle, grafting is best used on simple stitches such as stockinette, reverse stockinette or garter stitch that have been worked in flat, smooth yarns, making the stitches clearly visible.

Graft stitches when they are still on the knitting needle, slipping them off as you are done with them. Be sure that the needles are pointing in the same direction when the wrong sides of your work are placed together. In order to do this, you may need to work one fewer row on one needle or reverse one of the needles, depending on the pieces you are working.

When grafting garter stitch, it is important that the purl stitches of the front piece face the knit stitches of the back piece.
See also FINISHING TECHNIQUES; SEAMING

GRAPHING

The creation of charts for knitting, graphing is used for colorwork, stitchwork—such as lace and cable patterns—and beading. Charts are a visual way to represent a pattern and can be easier to read than written instructions. Each square in a chart represents one stitch. In color charts, each color is represented by the colors

themselves, or by symbols for each color and a corresponding key. Likewise, stitchwork charts use symbols for the stitches (knit and purl) indicated on the graph paper.
See also CHARTS; GRAPH PAPER, KNITTER'S

GRAPH PAPER, KNITTER'S

Unlike standard graph paper, knitter's graph paper is specifically designed for charting knitting patterns. Whereas standard graph paper has a square grid, knitter's graph paper has different grids depending on the proportion of knit stitches (for example, 5 stitches and 7 rows to the inch, or 6 stitches and 8 rows to the inch) so that the charted pattern accurately reflects how the knitted item will look. It allows the knitter to design patterns to a specific gauge.
See also CHARTS; GRAPHING

GUERNSEY
See GANSEY

GUERRILLA KNITTING

An early twenty-first century movement (sometimes called "craftivism"), guerrilla knitting combines political activism, performance art and public crafting to effect social change. Guerrilla knitting can take the form

of an organized event, such as a sit-in/knit-in to protest a particular action; a piece of art that conveys the creator's principles; or a group that assembles to promote knitting itself. It is often used to rebel against consumerism, mass production, globalism and conformity. The biannual journal *KnitKnit* follows this movement closely, featuring artists who use knitting to make political and artistic statements.

The Revolutionary Knitting Circle was founded in Calgary, Alberta, Canada, in 2000 to bring about "constructive revolution," arming its members, according to its manifesto, with "tools to liberate local communities from the shackles of global

corporatism." Several offshoot groups formed throughout North America and Europe. The Revolutionary Knitting Circle was the force behind a number of Global Knit-In protest rallies in various cities during the 2002 G8 Summit held in Genoa, Italy. Members have marched against the wars in Iraq and Afghanistan wearing armbands with peace symbols knit into them and holding stitched banners reading "Peace Knits."

The Iraq War was responsible for other notable examples of guerrilla knitting: Artist Lisa Anne Auerbach has repeatedly knit her stance on the war into her artwork, including her "Quagmire" blanket and body-count mittens, the latter

Knitter's graph paper divided into 5 stitches and 7 rows to the inch.

a stranded pattern incorporating the number of American soldiers killed in Iraq on a given date. For her art installation titled "The Red Sweater Project," Nina Rosenberg suspended fifteen-hundred-plus miniature red sweaters, knit by volunteers across the country, in a tree outside her San Francisco home, each signifying an American casualty. Danish artist Marianne Jorgensen sewed pink squares knit by a thousand volunteers into a patchwork cozy for a WWII combat tank. Dave Cole has knit teddy bears out of Kevlar and, to mark the anniversary of 9/11, he knit a giant American flag using utility poles manipulated by excavators as needles. Cole was one of twenty-seven artists represented in the 2007 exhibit "Radical Lace and Subversive Design" at New York City's Museum of Art and Design, which also included Janet Echelman's hand-knotted net rendering of a mushroom cloud suspended from the ceiling and Freddie Robins's full-body gray jumpsuit pierced with knitting needles and bearing the words "Craft Kills."

The Church of Craft, a nondenominational, secular gathering started in 2000 in San Francisco, urges its members to embrace a lifestyle in which "any and all acts of making have value to our humanness." Knitta is a collection of Houston knitters who, under rap-star-style aliases like P-Knitty, the Notorious N.I.T. and Purl Nekklas, tag utility poles, signage and public memorials with colorful knit swatches, graffiti-style. *Anticraft,* an online magazine, specializes in subversive patterns like a knitted voodoo doll.

A more pointed petition came from MicroRevolt's Cat Mazza, who spearheaded an international initiative to knit squares that were assembled into a blanket bearing the Nike swoosh and present it to Nike's CEO to petition for fair labor practices. Guerrilla knitters have banded together locally to draw attention to animal-rights causes, knitting symbolic "wetsuits" for bottlenose dolphins after the U.S. Navy proposed using the aquatic mammals to patrol a Pacific Northwest submarine base, and tiny sweaters for penguins affected by an oil spill in Phillip Island near Melbourne, Australia.

GUILDS

Groups of knitters who meet to knit for charitable and personal purposes in a social, sometimes educational, setting are often called *guilds.* Knitting guilds date to the thirteenth century; more recently, as knitting became women's work, women have gathered to knit, most prominently during critical times when knitting could provide

comfort on a national level—the Civil War, the Great Depression, World War II. So while it is not a new concept, simultaneous stitching and socializing has become increasingly popular in recent years.

The Knitting Guild Association (TKGA), the national organization dedicated to promoting knitting in the United States, sponsors local and regional chapters around the country. Particularly active local knitting guilds include Chicago's Windy City Knitting Guild, the Greater Boston Knitting Guild, the Atlanta Knitting Guild, the Greater St. Louis Knitters' Guild and New York's Big Apple Knitters Guild. These regional and local groups organize social meetings, charitable knitting drives, lectures by guest instructors and fashion shows; they also teach others to knit. Comprehensive lists of local knitting guilds by state can be found on the TKGA website (tkga.com). The Crochet Guild of America (CGOA) publishes a monthly print newsletter and offers e-news, educational resources, a message board and a list of local chapters on its website (crochet.org).

Many yarn shops sponsor weekly or monthly knitting clubs. Hundreds of informal knitting clubs and "Stitch 'n Bitch" groups gather nationwide. Membership in informal knitting

groups can range from the single digits up through triple digits. Meetup.com, the Knitty Coffeeshop (knittyboard.com), *Knitter's Review* (knitters review.com) and Ravelry (ravelry.com) all have forum features through which cyberknitters can locate nearby stitchers and arrange to meet in person. Knitters often blog about their group activities, which many see as a great resource for learning new techniques and finding out about patterns and designers they may not have heard of otherwise.

See also CHARITY KNITTING; INTERNET; *KNITTER'S REVIEW;* KNITTING GUILD ASSOCIATION, THE; *KNITTY.COM;* RAVELRY; STITCH 'N BITCH

GUSSET

Small, shaped areas set into a garment to provide additional ease, gussets are sometimes placed at the underarm areas of sweaters to improve fit. In top-down handknitted socks, the gusset is the area where the number of stitches is gradually reduced to the original stitch count after the heel is shaped. It is also the area on mittens or gloves where space is provided for the thumb.

See also GLOVES; MITTENS; SOCKS

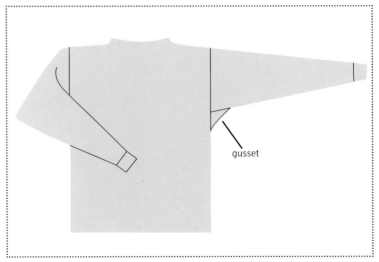

Sweater with sleeve gusset

HALTER

A sleeveless garment that is held up by a strap around the neck, leaving the back and shoulders bare, a halter may be a stand-alone garment or describe the top of a dress. Handknitted halters are usually intended as lightweight summer garments or as evening wear. A halter top may be knit in the round or constructed out of a flat piece that joins at the back.

HANDARBEIT & HOBBY

An important international trade expo held yearly in Cologne, Germany, Handarbeit presents to wholesale and retail buyers a wide range of handicrafts. Knitting, embroidery, yarn and notions, tapestry, home textiles

The pattern for this halter-style wool bathing suit appeared in the Fall/Winter 1951 issue of the *Vogue Knitting Book*.

and sewing machines are among the products exhibited. Fashion shows, social events and workshops make Handarbeit a rewarding destination for professionals in all walks of the knitting-design industry.

HAND-PAINTED YARN

When yarn has been dyed by applying the pigment with a brush or squeeze bottle in a painterly fashion, rather than by being submerged in a dye bath, it is advertised as having been hand-painted. This technique allows a dyer to individualize a skein of yarn so that it becomes a one-of-a-kind creation. Numerous colors appear in each skein, and the transitions between colors are subtle and random, unlike those of space-dyed yarn, which repeat in a regular pattern.

The pre-dampened yarn is placed on a flat surface and the dyer applies the colors by squeezing or painting the mixed pigments in a random fashion. The dyed yarn is steamed to fix

the color. When knit, hand-painted yarn takes on an unplanned, impressionistic appearance that unfolds as it is knit.
See also DYEING; FIBER CHARACTERISTICS

HAND-SPINNING
See SPINNING

HANK

A put-up in which the yarn is wound into a coil or circle is called a hank. String is tied around it in several places to keep it from tangling, and it is loosely twisted so it winds around itself into a compact bundle. When open, the hank presentation is ideal for dyeing, as the maximum surface is exposed but the hank won't unravel in the dye bath.

Yarn that comes in hanks must be wound into balls before knitting, either by hand or using a ball winder and swift. Most yarn stores will wind purchased yarn for you for free, but swifts and ball winders are easily purchased for home use as well. A hank will

have a label with the same information that is on a ball band, although hanks from hand spinners or small-production hand dyers often don't have as much information as commercially produced yarn does.
See also BALL; BALL WINDER; PUT-UP; SKEIN; SWIFT

HARDING, LOUISA (1967-)

Louisa Harding is an English knitwear designer and author of the distinctively photographed *Miss Bea* series (Holmfirth/C&T Publishing) of children's storybooks incorporating patterns for garments worn by the characters. Harding became established as a designer at Rowan Yarns in the 1990s, then went on to produce the *Miss Bea* books, using her own family members as models, as well as authoring other highly praised books of refreshing, romantic designs. She has achieved great popularity for knitwear that conveys her quintessentially delicate, floral, and sometimes

Hand-painted yarns

Hank of yarn

Nature's Inspiration

by Elaine Eskesen

Daily walks in Maine give me a chance to see color at its best.

I might jump into a pile of leaves in the autumn and feel the sense of color that surrounds me in my natural world. My life becomes saturated with color as I recognize the beauty that inspires me. I notice the incredible color combinations in an individual flower or a field of wildflowers. I notice different moods that colors create when they're combined: the subdued rusts, golds and moss greens of a tidal pool or the vivacious purples, mauves and pinks in a lupine field.

Back in my dye studio, I remember the colors I noticed on my walk and bring them to life in another form. I hand-paint them on white wool. I mix the dyes and put each color in a dye bottle. The white yarn is a blank canvas, and each hand-painted skein is a watercolor painting. The summer wildflowers become splashes of orange, hot pink, lemon yellow and zesty green. Each skein becomes a unique creation as I put the dye on the yarn and it finds a place in relation to the other colors. It is a magical time in the studio and a place to enjoy a new adventure. The many years I have spent in my dye studio have shown me that happy mistakes often happen and that trying different color combinations each day is the best way to foster the creative process of hand-painting.

Elaine Eskesen hand-painting yarns in her studio

Elaine Eskesen is the owner of Pine Tree Yarns in Damariscotta, Maine, where she has her dye studio and a courtyard full of flowers. She is the author of *Dyeing to Knit* (Downeast Books, 2005) and *Silk Knits* (Martingale, 2007) She has written for *Interweave Knits*, *Family Circle Easy Knitting* and *Knitter's* magazines.

eccentric British vision, and for the way her books incorporate this vision in photo tableaux that portray entire "stories." Working with Knitting Fever International, she has her own Louisa Harding yarn line, and she also markets kits under her name.

HATS

A hat is a shaped covering for the head. Knit hats come in endless shapes, styles and sizes and are incredibly popular projects for knitters, especially beginners. They can be knit in the round or back and forth on straight needles and seamed at the back or sides. Hats are quick to knit, and yarn choices are as varied as the styles and shapes used to knit them, although yarn that is sportweight or heavier is most typically used.

Beanie

A beanie is a snug, often brimless, knit or crocheted cap. It is usually stitched in the round from the bottom up, and is often striped or colorfully patterned. Beanies are generally items for casual wear, and are favored headwear among snowboarders and skiers, who often crochet or knit their own.

Beret

To knit a beret, work a snug-fitting hatband, increase to create fullness above the band, and then decrease gradually at the top.

Cloche

There are several ways to shape a knit cloche; the simplest begins at the brim and is worked in the round with a series of decreases.

Watch Cap

Similar to beanies, these classic knit hats are also usually worked in the round from the bottom up with decreases at the crown. A watch cap is usually longer than a beanie and has a turned-up brim.

Chullo

This classic Peruvian cap, usually worked in stranded colorwork, is similar to a beanie with earflaps.

Helmet

Work back and forth to knit the bottom flap, then cast on additional stitches and join to work in the round to form the crown.

Stocking Cap

A beanie elongated through the use of very gradual decreases.

Ski Cap

A ski cap is a close-fitting, slightly elongated hat that tapers to a blunt point. It often has tassels attached to the crown.

Hat Styles

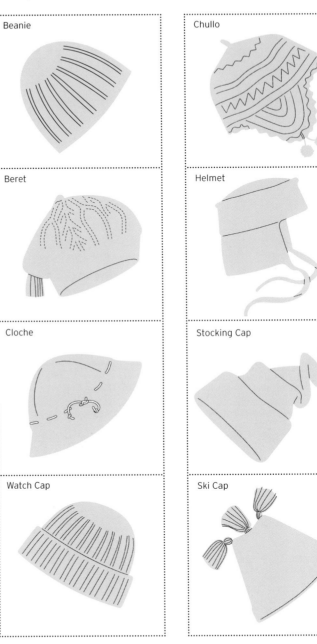

Beanie

Chullo

Beret

Helmet

Cloche

Stocking Cap

Watch Cap

Ski Cap

Mindful Knitting

by Tara Jon Manning

Mindfulness is a quality that can enrich our daily lives. But what exactly is mindfulness?

In the dictionary sense, being mindful means being aware or careful. However, being mindful, in the sense of "contemplative," has a more holistic meaning. Mindfulness becomes the experience of engaging in what is happening from moment to moment, and thereby participating fully in what is going on right here, right now.

Knowing that the quality of being present can ground and nourish us, lots of us enjoy participating in contemplative or mindful activities such as yoga, jogging, gardening or meditation. A commonality between most of these mindful activities is that they all possess an object of focus. For yogis and yoginis, it is the posture, or "asana." For runners it is the footfall, for gardeners is it the sensation of working and touching the earth, for meditators, it is the ever-constant flow of breath. For knitters it is the repeated formation of stitch after stitch as they create fabric.

Using knitting as a mindful activity allows you to focus your attention on the soothing natural rhythm that is the cornerstone of our craft—insert needle, wrap yarn, pull through a new stitch, repeat. By focusing on the continuous repetitive action, you stay in the current moment. This is Mindful Knitting. Over a period of time—say 20 minutes or so—of really watching what you are doing with your hands and how the fiber feels as it slips through your fingers, you begin to relax, to quiet your mind and to open to what is available here and now. You become conscious of a feeling of contentment as you start to get out of your own head and into your experience in the moment.

Mindful Knitting can help reveal the natural, innate calm that is within you. You leave behind your many thoughts and emotions and begin to just be. As you continue with your knitting as practice, your field of vision will begin to relax and expand, and you will see that your everyday concerns may not be as important as you think they are. You will see that there are things outside yourself that you may have been missing out on. This experience may be as simple or as profound as really seeing that the sky is a beautiful shade of blue, or that someone else needs you to direct a bit of compassion their way. Your knitting offers us a very lovely gift—the ability to cultivate your connection to the world and to others.

Designer Tara Jon Manning (tarahandknitting.com) pioneered the Mindful Knitting movement and teaches the technique at workshops and retreats. She is the author of *Compassionate Knitting: Finding Basic Goodness in the Work of Our Hands* (Tuttle, 2006), as well as several other books.

HEALTH BENEFITS OF KNITTING

There is a great deal of anecdotal evidence that knitting is good for you, and clinical studies bear this out. Researchers at the Harvard Medical School Mind/Body Institute monitored individuals who were knitting and recorded drops in heart rate of up to eleven beats per minute; this slowing, in turn, can lead to reduced blood pressure. Herbert Benson, M.D., author of *The Relaxation Response* (HarperTorch, 1976), points to the calming effect of knitting's repetitive motion, which decreases metabolism, heart rate, blood pressure and breathing rate. Health and wellness consultant Gary Scholar has incorporated knitting classes into programs for employees at the American Hospital Association and uses the craft to reduce stress in people dealing with issues ranging from chronic illness to overscheduled lifestyles.

While no clinical evidence yet exists to support the theory, plenty of knitters say their stitching habit has helped keep their hands busy during and after successful attempts to quit smoking. Cancer-support organization Gilda's Club sponsors knitting programs to help family members cope with the emotional aspects of cancer treatment, and the Duke Diet and Fitness Center recommends knitting to its weight-loss clients as a way to lower stress.

Stitchlinks is a British social network dedicated to researching and promoting the emotional and therapeutic advantages of knitting to combat depression, raise self-esteem or distract attention from chronic pain. In her book *Never Too Old to Knit* (Sixth&Spring Books, 2006), Karin Strom cites knitting's ability to lubricate stiff joints and thus bring relief to arthritis sufferers. (Support gloves and hand exercises can further aid knitters with arthritis or carpal tunnel syndrome.)

For children and teenagers with attention deficit disorder, knitting is used as a focusing tool and a way to sharpen mathematical skills, creativity and eye/hand coordination. Juvenile-detention centers teach residents to knit and crochet, then donate their output to local charities, a tack taken at many adult prisons and women's shelters throughout the United States.

Then there are knitting's meditative and contemplative aspects. It's become cliché to say "knitting is the new yoga," but many practitioners of both swear by their similar abilities to center mind and body. According to designer Tara Jon Manning, who wrote *Mindful Knitting* (Tuttle, 2004) and conducts frequent weekend retreats that combine knitting with yoga and meditation, most knitters perform mindful knitting, whether or not they're aware of it. Bernadette Murphy explored "the metaphysical and esoteric elements of this craft" in *Zen and the Art of Knitting* (Adams Media, 2002). Others tap into the spiritual centering of knitting; the Shawl Ministry advocates "knitting prayers" into shawls for friends and loved ones in need of special blessings. *See also* CAMPS AND RETREATS; CHARITY KNITTING

HEELS

The heel is not just a part of your foot, it's the part of a sock that covers the back of the foot. A heel creates the 90-degree angle that makes a sock's shape match the natural angle of the foot and ankle.

There are two basic ways to accomplish this small sculptural miracle. A square heel flap, worked back and forth across half the total number of stitches, can cover the distance from the heel to approximately the ankle bone. Then the heel is turned by working a series of short rows to form a little pouch, and, finally, stitches along the sides of the heel flap to rejoin the rounds of the sock. Heel flaps can be worked both from the top down and from the toe up. There are many different variations on this type of turned heel: the handkerchief heel, German strap heel, French heel and Dutch heel are just a few. The second basic method of forming a heel is called a short-row heel; you work a series of short rows, decreasing and then increasing numbers of stitches, starting and ending with half the total number of stitches. The resulting shape is a small pocket.

Other more specific heel shapes are detailed below.

Heels

Round heel, side view

Round heel, bottom

Round or French Heel

Work the leg to the desired length, then set aside half the total number of stitches. The heel should be worked on an even number of stitches. The heel flap may be worked in stockinette stitch or in a slip-stitch pattern.

Slip-stitch pattern

Row 2 Sl 1, purl across, turn.

Row 3 *Sl 1, k1; repeat from * to end, turn.

Repeat rows 2 and 3 until desired length.

Heel flap

Row 1 (RS) Place all the heel stitches on one needle and knit across.

Row 2 through end of heel

Work either in stockinette st (knit all RS rows and purl all WS rows), slipping the first st of every row, or in slip-stitch pattern.

Turn heel

Row 1 (RS) Sl 1, k to center, k1, ssk, k1, turn.

Row 2 (WS) Sl 1, p5, p2tog, p1, turn.

Row 3 Sl 1, k6, ssk, turn.

Row 4 Sl 1, p7, p2tog, p1, turn.

Continue in this manner, working 1 more st before the decrease in each row until all stitches have been worked, and ending with a WS row.

Square or Dutch Heel

Heel flap

Row 1 (RS) Place all the heel sts on one needle and knit across.

Rows 2 through end of heel

Either work in stockinette st (knit all RS rows and purl all WS rows), slipping the first st of every row, or work in slip-stitch pattern.

Turn heel

Row 1 (RS) Sl 1, k to center, k4, ssk, turn.

Row 2 (WS) Sl 1, p10, p2tog, turn.

Row 3 Sl 1, k10, ssk, turn.

Row 4 Sl 1, p10, p2tog, turn.

Rep rows 3 and 4 until all sts have been worked, and ending with a WS row.

Short-Row Heel

Place all heel sts on one needle and knit across.

Row 1 (WS) Purl to end.

Row 2 (RS) K to last 2 sts, wrap and turn.

Row 3 P to last 2 sts, wrap and turn.

Row 4 K to 1 st before last wrapped st, wrap and turn.

Row 5 P to 1 st before last wrapped st, wrap and turn.

Repeat rows 4 and 5 until the number of unwrapped sts equals the original number of sts multiplied by 0.4 and rounded to the nearest even number. (For example, if you began working the heel over 30 sts, repeat until 12 unwrapped sts remain.)

Next row K to next wrapped st, pick up wrap, wrap and turn. Note that this and all following wrap and turns will create double wraps.

Next row P to next wrapped st, pick up wraps, wrap and turn. Repeat these two rows until original st count is restored.

See also PICKING UP STITCHES, SHORT ROWS; SOCKS; TOE; WRAP AND TURN

HELMET

See HATS

HELPING HANDS FOUNDATION

See NEEDLE ARTS MENTORING PROGRAM; KNITTING GUILD ASSOCIATION, THE

HEMP

A bast, or skin, fiber similar to flax and jute, hemp is derived from the *Cannabis sativa* plant and traditionally used to make rope, sails and carpet backing. The fibers are prepared in a similar way to flax, but the end product is much coarser. The fibers are long—up to 18 inches. With the recent rise in interest in natural and organic fibers, hemp has become a popular fiber for clothing and for knitting.

See also FIBER CHARACTERISTICS; FLAX; JUTE

HEMS

The lower edge of an article of clothing is its hem. Knitted hems fold under to keep the knitted fabric from curling or stretching. Although most knitted garments have ribbed bottom edges rather

Square heel, side view

Square heel, bottom

Short-row heel, side view

than hems, hems add a nice drape and are thus good choices for lower edges that do not hug the body. A hem can also be used to form a casing for elastic, such as at the waistband of a skirt. It can be worked at the same time as the piece or picked up after it is complete.

The edge of the hem can be distinct (with a turning ridge) or rounded (without a turning ridge). The folded part of the hem should be worked in a smooth stitch such as stockinette regardless of the stitch pattern used for the piece, and on smaller needles. Avoid using hems on garments with openwork patterns, because the turned edge will show.

Sew the folded edge to the garment as invisibly as possible using a whipstitch, or attach it stitch by stitch from the knitting needle without binding off.

Turning Ridges

A turning ridge creates a neat edge when the hem is folded over and sewn in place. Make the ridge after the hem is the desired depth, regardless of whether it is at the top or bottom edge. Three commonly used turning ridges are the purl stitch, the picot and the slip stitch.

Purl

To work a purl stitch turning ridge, knit one row of stitches through the back loops on the wrong side. This works with any number of stitches and forms a purl ridge on the right side.

Picot

To work a picot turning ridge, work on the right side as follows: k1, *k2tog, yo; repeat from *, end k1. A picot turning ridge is worked on an even number of stitches.

Slip Stitch

To work a slip-stitch turning ridge, work on the right side as follows: k1, *sl 1 with the yarn in front, k1; repeat from * to end of row. A slip-stitch turning ridge is worked on an odd number of stitches.

Knit-in Hem

A knit-in hem reduces bulk by working the cast-on edge together with the stitches on the needle.
See also BIND-OFF; SEAMING; SWEATER

Turning Ridges

Purl turning ridge

Picot turning ridge

Slip-stitch turning ridge

Knit-in Hem

Knit-in hem

Cast on in the regular way and then work to a depth equal to the desired depth of the hem. Work a turning ridge. Work until the main piece is the same depth as the hem, ending with a wrong-side row. Then, using a spare needle and a separate ball of yarn, pick up one loop from each cast-on stitch.

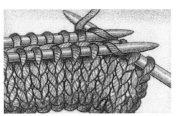

Cut the extra yarn. Fold up the hem along the turning ridge and knit the picked-up stitches together with the stitches from the main piece.

HENLEY

See COLLARS AND NECKBANDS

HISTORY OF KNITTING

Knitting probably originated on the Arabian Peninsula some three thousand years ago. Women of the nomadic tribes of the region spun yarn from sheep and goats, but the men did the actual knitting as they tended to their flocks. Among the earliest surviving knitted objects from this region is a sock with a separate toe, knit much as mittens are today. While this is accepted as a knitted piece, many other fabrics, including ancient Peruvian tapestries and metal wire decorations, resemble knitting but were actually created by various netting techniques using a kind of sewing needle. A few native peoples of the Americas developed their own knitting traditions, but the Mediterranean region seems to have been the cradle of knitting,

and we can thank traders and sailors for spreading the craft throughout the rest of the world.

Until the establishment of the Renaissance trade guilds, there is no recorded history of knitting, so our only links to the knitted past are fragments of textiles found in tombs or church treasuries. These are often too fragile to examine closely, so we can only speculate as to whether the craft was widespread or confined to a few highly skilled workers. Several altar pieces from the fourteenth century portray the Madonna knitting, but they demonstrate only that knitting was known to the painters, not whether it was the pursuit of fine ladies or an ordinary craft. The earliest recognizable garments that survive are felted caps, stockings and sleeve pieces that date from around the thirteenth century. The earliest cap knitters were professional

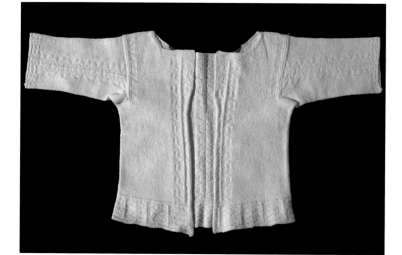

Handknitted cotton child's jacket from seventeenth-century England

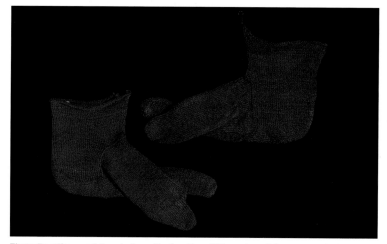

These Egyptian sandal socks from the fourth or fifth century A.D. were created with the nålebinding technique.

tradesmen licensed by the government, and their prices were strictly controlled to prevent profiteering.

At the beginning of the seventeenth century, better metalworking techniques allowed for the production of uniform knitting needles. This led to the development of knitting guilds, some of which survived well into the eighteenth century. Exclusively male and intensely competitive, the guilds (the earliest of which were for cap knitters) required a long and elaborate apprenticeship. It took six years to become a master knitter, three as an apprentice and three as a journeyman. After this, the aspiring master knitter had to produce a felted cap, a pair of stockings or gloves complete with embroidered decoration, a shirt or waistcoat and an elaborately knitted carpet—all within the

space of thirteen weeks. The Tudor and Elizabethan periods marked the golden age of handknitting—and interestingly enough, the invention of the first knitting machine.

As demand for knitted products grew, so did the spread of the craft. Skilled tradesmen were still producing fine stockings, jackets and petticoats, but in the countryside a cruder form of the craft was taking shape. Knitting was easy to learn, transport and pick up or put down at any given moment, and so farmers, fishmongers and shepherds began producing socks, stockings and caps, both to clothe their families and to sell at market. In Colonial America, knitting was also a practical pursuit, done for the most part by women and children.

The rise of the Industrial Age and improved knitting machines brought an end to the handknitting industry, though it still held on as a supplemental means of income in some rural areas. Knitting by hand, which before had been viewed as a trade practiced by the lower classes (ladies of position embroidered or did other fine needlework), became a leisure pursuit of the middle class. Improvements were made in mass-produced yarns and the availability of pattern books and magazines spread. The nineteenth century also saw the rise of many folk knitting traditions, including Aran knitting, Shetland lace and many Scandinavian designs. Knitting also became a means of improving both prospects and

morals for the poor. English reformers repeatedly suggested that street urchins be taught to knit socks as a means of avoiding the workhouse. Knitting cooperatives were established to preserve native handcraft and provide a means of self-sustenance in the British Isles, Sweden, Alaska, Canada and South America.

Popular interest in knitting had dwindled by the twentieth century, but World War II sparked a new surge in the craft as women on both sides of the Atlantic "knit their bit" for the troops, following a wartime knitting tradition that dates back to the American Civil War. Needles were certainly still

clicking throughout the 1950s and '60s, but it wasn't until the late '70s and early '80s that popular interest in the craft again emerged, fueled in part by the amazing works of knitted color and pattern that began to appear in England. Knitting came on bigger than ever in the early 2000s, thanks to the handknits that were paraded down the fashion runways and the A-list celebrities who confessed to knitting between takes on the set as well as the boom of online knitting blogs. The online community has effected a shift in the course of knitting history, with collaboration among people from different countries and the increased ability to connect with one another to share techniques, patterns and even yarn. New books, yarns, patterns and designers continue to feed our need to knit, and a long-established tradition shows no signs of fading away.

See also ALPINE REGION KNITTING; AMERICAN RED CROSS KNITTING CAMPAIGNS; ANDES REGION KNITTING; ARABIC KNITTING; ARAN KNITTING; ARGYLE; AZORES LACE; BALTIC KNITTING; BOHUS KNITTING; BRITISH KNITTING; CHANNEL ISLAND PATTERNS; COWICHAN KNITTING; DALES KNITTING; DUTCH KNITTING; ESCH FRAGMENTS; FAIR ISLE KNITTING; FAROE KNITTING; FLORENTINE JACKET; GANSEY; GERMAN KNITTING; ICELANDIC

KNITTING; ITALIAN KNITTING, JACQUARD; MUSEUMS; NÅLEBINDING; NORWEGIAN KNITTING; ORENBURG LACE; PENCE JUG; SHETLAND LACE; SPANISH KNITTING; SWEDISH KNITTING; TARTAN KNITTING; TURKISH PATTERNS; WELSH KNITTING

HOLDING THE YARN

The knitting method (American/English, Continental/German, Eastern or combined) and the knitter's preferences determine how a knitter holds the yarn and needles. The method chosen should provide good control over the yarn, an even flow of working yarn and a consistent gauge.

Two traditional methods of holding the yarn are for American/English-style knitting, in which the working yarn is held in the right hand, and for Continental/German-style knitting, in which the yarn is threaded around the left hand.

See also AMERICAN/ENGLISH-STYLE KNITTING; COMBINED KNITTING; CONTINENTAL/GERMAN-STYLE KNITTING; EASTERN KNITTING; WESTERN KNITTING

HONEYCOMB STITCH

A type of cable pattern, common in Aran knitting, in which the cables form an allover hexagonal design, is called honeycomb stitch due to its resemblance to honeycombs. The swatch shown

Knitted silk bag from Great Britain, nineteenth century

Holding Yarn: English-Style

1. Hold the needle with the stitches in your left hand as shown. Wrap the yarn around your little finger and then around the index finger on your right hand.

2. Hold the working needle with your right hand as shown, controlling the tension with your right index finger.

Holding Yarn: Continental-Style

1. Hold the needle with the stitches in your right hand. Wrap the yarn around your little finger and then around the index finger of your left hand. Transfer the needle back to your left hand.

2. Hold the working needle with your right hand as shown, controlling the tension with your left index finger.

below is knit over a multiple of 8 stitches plus 4.

4-st RC Sl 2 sts to cn and hold to back, k2, k2 from cn.

4-st LC Sl 2 sts to cn and hold to front, k2, k2 from cn.

Row 1 (RS) P2, *4-st RC, 4-st LC; rep from * to last 2 sts, p2.

Row 2 and all WS rows K2, p to last 2 sts, k2.

Rows 3 and 7 P2, k to last 2 sts, p2.

Row 5 P2, *4-st LC, 4-st RC; rep from * to last 2 sts, p2.

Row 8 Rep row 2.

Rep rows 1–8.

See also ARAN KNITTING; CABLE PATTERNS; CABLES

HOOD

A head covering attached to a jacket, coat or sweater, often optional, is known as a hood. A hood may be knit as a separate piece or pieces and sewn to a finished garment, or it may be knit from stitches picked up around the neckline.
See also HOODIE; SWEATER

HOODIE

Garments with attached hoods are sometimes referred to as hoodies in modern slang.
See also HOOD; SWEATER

HOOK, CROCHET

See CROCHET HOOK

HOWELL, VICKIE (1974–)

The host of the DIY Network television show *Knitty Gritty*

expanded knitting's demographic horizons. Debuting in 2004, the program featured Howell demonstrating cool projects (knitted boots and corsets) and techniques (Möbius, modular, Fibonacci) alongside some of the biggest names in the business, celebrity knitters and an on-set audience of stitching "knitsters." Howell's stated goal is to eliminate fusty images of knitting. She had learned to knit when she was eight, but it wasn't until she experienced the LYS phenomenon that the craft stuck. She founded the L.A. Stitch 'N Bitch chapter, an act she duplicated a couple of years later when she moved to Austin, Texas. There, in 2001, she opened several crafts-based e-businesses, including VickieHowell.com, where she blogs and pursues other business outlets. She also cofounded the Austin Craft Mafia, a consortium of women's crafts businesses that support and promote each other and each other's endeavors.

Once *Knitty Gritty* came calling and she became such a visible face of knitting, Howell quickly produced three imaginative books as well as designing for magazines, penning a celebrity-knits column in *knit.1* magazine and an eco-craft column in the healthy-parenting title *KIWI*. She at one time had an eco-friendly line of yarn, the Vickie Howell Collection from South West Trading Company, named for her favorite rockers, crafters and movie couples. Howell then moved on to become the celebrity spokesperson for NaturallyCaron.com, a line of ecological yarns with an integrated website. She is the author of a variety of books, including *Craft Corps* (Lark, 2010), *AwareKnits* (Lark, 2009), *Pop Goes Crochet!* (Lark, 2009), *Knit Aid* (Sterling, 2007), *Not Another Teen Knitting Book* (Sterling, 2006) and *New Knits on the Block* (Sterling, 2005).
See also CARON; DESIGNERS; STITCH 'N BITCH

Swatch knit in honeycomb stitch

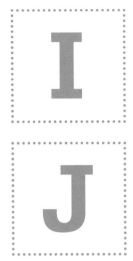

I

J

ICELANDIC KNITTING

Knitting first appeared in Iceland in the 1500s, most likely arriving from northern Europe. The craft quickly became the island's principal export and a source of income for many people. Knitting is still an important element in Icelandic culture. Children learn the basics in school, and many people spend evenings and spare time knitting the famous yoke sweater, the *lopapeysa*, for the tourist trade. Throughout rural Iceland, almost every snack stand and gas station sells handknit sweaters, mittens and hats made by the local people.

Ever since the Vikings settled the island more than a thousand years ago, Iceland and wool have been closely connected. Farmers as well as warriors, Iceland's first settlers brought their sheep with them to their new homes. Today's Icelandic sheep are direct descendants of these Viking flocks. The Icelandic sheep's fleece is made up of *tog,* a long outer hair and *pel,* a short, fine underhair. The two kinds of wool were used for very different products. Tog, which can be up to 14 inches long, was combed, drawn and spun into strong cord for sewing and weaving and was occasionally plied for rope and twine. The finest tog, similar to mohair in texture and luster, was used for knitting lacy shawls and for embroidery. Pel was used for garments. Brown and gray sheep produce the softest pel, which was preferred for underwear. (Handknit woolen underwear was common in Iceland until after World War II.) For warmth and durability, socks and mittens were sometimes knitted to three times their intended size and then felted.

Knitting with roving, or *lopi,* is relatively new. Lopi was used experimentally in machine knitting by a home knitter in 1920 and became popular for handknitting during the 1930s. Dyed lopi appeared in the 1980s. Icelanders knit with the soft unspun lopi using the Continental technique.

Much Icelandic yarn sold in America is plied and slightly twisted to accommodate the American knitter. However, twist is not necessary to keep an Icelandic sweater together, as the wool's extremely long fibers are longer than a stitch.

Icelandic lace knitting, which resembles that of Europe and America, dates from the middle of the nineteenth century. Two kinds of shawls were common, the *langsjal,* a long rectangle worked in one or several colors, and the triangular *prihyrna.* Probably the most iconic Icelandic lace knitting is the *klukka,* an elegant dress derived from women's knitted woolen underwear. The klukka (which means "clock") is composed of twelve long, narrow gores joined with a lace stitch. Today klukkur are knitted with sleeves, in all lengths from T-shirts to long evening dresses. The work is usually done on size 2 or 3 needles, using a fine single-ply woolen yarn called *eingirni.* It is common to use graded tones of a natural color—either black to gray or brown to tan—in bands at the hem, neck and sleeves, with a light-colored body.
See also FOLK KNITTING; LOPI; STAPLE

I-CORD
See CORDS

INC
Abbreviation for *increase(s)* or *increasing.*
See also INCREASES

INCREASES
Any of a variety of methods used to shape a knitted piece by adding stitches to make it larger is called an increase. Some increases are inconspicuous and do not interrupt the pattern, especially if they are formed in the edge stitch. Increases placed 2 or 3 stitches in from the edge of a piece, however, are visible and add a decorative touch.

Most increases are worked on the right side of the work, for two

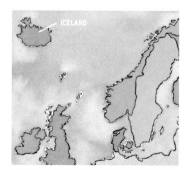

Iceland is located in the North Atlantic just south of the Arctic Circle.

Icelandic sheep

reasons. First, working on the right side allows you to see the finished look and placement of the increases. Second, it is easier to keep track of increase rows when you work them at regular intervals, such as on every right-side row.

Knitting instructions often do not specify the type of increase to use. Increases differ greatly in appearance—some have a right or left slant, some are quite visible, while others are inconspicuous— and you can choose one that gives you the effect you desire.

If you want to add one or two stitches, use increases, but if you need to add several stitches at one time at the side edge, it is better to cast on the additional stitches.

The most common types of increases are the bar increase, the lifted increase and the make one. *See also* BAR INCREASE; KNIT IN THE ROW BELOW; LIFTED INCREASE; MAKE ONE; SHAPING

INTARSIA

When colorwork is formed with blocks of color and separate balls of yarn or bobbins, not stranding, it is called intarsia. The yarns are not carried across the back of the work as in Fair Isle or jacquard colorwork, so they must be twisted around each other at each color change to avoid holes in the work.

When changing colors in a vertical line, twist the yarns on every row. When changing colors on a diagonal line, twist on every other row. If the diagonal slants up toward the right, twist the colors on the knit rows; if toward the left, on the purl rows.

Intarsia patterns must be worked flat so that each color is in the correct position on each succeeding row
See also ARGYLE; FAIR ISLE KNITTING; BOBBIN; COLORWORK

Intarsia: Changing Colors in a Vertical Line

1. On the knit side, drop the old color. Pick up the new color from under the old color and knit to the next color change.

2. On the purl side, drop the old color. Pick up the new color from under the old color and purl to the next color change. Repeat steps 1 and 2.

Intarsia: Changing Colors in a Diagonal Line

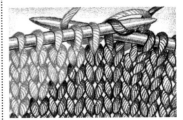

1. When working a right diagonal on the knit side, bring the new color over the top of the old color and knit to the next color change.

2. On the purl side, pick up the new color from under the old color and purl to the next color change.

1. When working a left diagonal on the purl side, bring the new color over the top of the old color and purl to the next color change.

2. On the knit side. pick up the new color from under the old color and knit to the next color change.

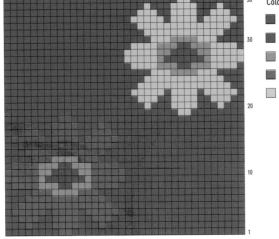

Color Key

- blue
- purple
- pink
- red
- green

Intarsia swatch with flower motif and accompanying chart

INTERCHANGEABLE NEEDLES

Interchangeable circular needles come in sets that include needle tips in a range of sizes and cords of varying lengths. The first set of interchangeable needles was the Boye Needlemaster. A number of companies currently produce sets with needle tips made of wood, bamboo, plastic, aluminum and other materials.

See also CIRCULAR NEEDLES

INTERNATIONAL FREEFORM CROCHET GUILD

See FREEFORM KNITTING/CROCHET

INTERNATIONAL FREEFORM FIBERARTS GUILD

See FREEFORM KNITTING/CROCHET

INTERNET

The flourishing online knitting community has much to do with the craft's twenty-first-century resurgence. Knitting-related sites range from knit blog/podcast and instructional how-to sites to community forums and industry outlets for selling and creating a buzz about yarn, such as e-tail yarn shops and LYS blogs. There are knitting groups for newbies, cable knitters, lace knitters, sock knitters, charity knitters, scarf knitters, sexy knitters, Elizabeth Zimmermann knitters and so on.

One of the earliest Internet-age knitting communities was The KnitList, which was founded in 1994 by Jill McAllister at the University of Minnesota. Ravelry, launched in 2007, took the knitting forum to new heights, incorporating not just a bulletin-board area where knitters could converse with each other but also a cross-referencing platform in which subscribers could post information about their personal stash and projects and search to see who was knitting the same patterns. It transformed the online knitting community, expanding on electronic networking venues that had already been formed.

Forums and Knit-alongs

Forums are important aspects of the sites of the two premier knitting e-magazines, *Knitter's Review* and *Knitty.com*, both free and available only online. *Knitter's Review* was started by Clara Parkes in 2000 as an outlet to talk about yarn. Every week she regales her 35,000 subscribers with in-depth yarn, tool and book reviews; she also hosts an annual *Knitter's Review* retreat, runs an online boutique and monitors the comprehensive forum boards. *Knitty.com*, launched in 2002 by Amy R. Singer, is a quarterly pattern-and-articles magazine that has published some of the most popular projects of the early twenty-first century.

Patterns with mass appeal often become subjects of a knit-along (KAL), an organized group effort to knit a certain project. Participants who live anywhere in the world can post comments and pictures on the knit-along blog or forum, so others working the same pattern can compare yarn choices, provide help and encouragement and share progress.

Blogs

The most vital segment of the cyber-knitting community is found in personal knit blogs, online journals in which bloggers document their knitting in words and pictures. The most prominent knit blogger is unquestionably Stephanie Pearl-McPhee, the Yarn Harlot, whose humorous musings about yarn have earned her a large cadre of devoted followers and have led to several books.

Online Commerce

Designers, yarn shops and yarn companies often have blogs on their websites, bringing a human touch to a commercial endeavor. Many brick-and-mortar shops also sell merchandise online, while a large number of online-only e-tail yarn stores have popped up to serve the needs of Internet shoppers. Etsy.com is a communal selling site where independent crafters can hawk their wares without dealing with the hassles of maintaining an individual e-storefront. Yarn companies utilize the Internet by sending out e-newsletters full of patterns and info on the latest yarns—Berroco's *Knit Bits* has a subscription base of 70,000; magazine publishers do the same thing, with *Interweave Knits' Knitting Daily* newsletter

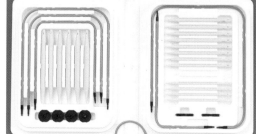

Two sets of interchangeable needles

Thoughts on the Internet

by Clara Parkes

We knitters like to take matters into our own hands, and we always have.

We prefer our own handmade socks and sweaters and hats to store-bought ones, and when we can't find a pattern we like, we improvise. This same spirit of independence is what inspired Elizabeth Zimmermann to found Schoolhouse Press all those years ago.

So it should come as no surprise that a technology facilitating even greater independence and unfettered access to a global microphone would take off like wildfire within the knitting community. Which is exactly what the Internet has done.

Knitting is primarily a solitary activity, but we're also social creatures. Give us a space and occasion, and we'll flock. We may enjoy quietly knitting at home, but we're also pleased at the prospect of getting to create with other people.

The Internet has given us the best of all worlds. We can sit in our comfy chairs with our cup of tea and snoozing cat by our side as we simultaneously tap into a massive global knitting community in which anything and everything goes. We can shop for yarn twenty-four hours a day. We can debate the merits of applied I-cord with strangers until the wee hours of the morning. The Web has forged connections that continually feed our passion for knitting.

Through this unhindered exchange of ideas, the Web has also allowed a stronger critical voice to arise. With no more than the click of the mouse, we can say whatever we want, and sell whatever we want, to the very same audience that the establishment has spent decades, and millions of dollars, trying to cultivate.

The Web short-circuited the whole established process of getting published, making and selling products, and connecting with your audience or market. In effect, it put the car keys directly in the hands of the kids. Our challenge now is to make sure we drive responsibly.

Clara Parkes is the editor and publisher of *Knitter's Review,* (knittersreview.com), the weekly online fiber magazine, and the moderator of the *Knitter's Review* forums. She is the author of *The Knitter's Book of Yarn* (Potter Craft, 2007) and a columnist for *Interweave Knits* magazine.

going out every weekday. The instructional tone taken by many industry blasts can also be found on prominent how-to sites like Knittinghelp.com, which has a substantial catalog of video tutorials, and About.com: Knitting. Knitting wikis—user-penned sites that lean toward the instructional —are also gaining in popularity.
See also CAMPS AND RETREATS; CHARITY KNITTING; *KNITTER'S REVIEW; KNITTY.COM*; PARKES, CLARA; PEARL-MCPHEE, STEPHANIE; PODCAST; RAVELRY; SINGER, AMY R.

INTERWEAVE KNITS

Launched in 1997 as a one-time special issue from the Loveland, Colorado–based Interweave Press, *Interweave Knits* is now a popular quarterly known for wearable, casual designs. It was founded by Linda Ligon; the original editors were Marilyn Murphy, later president of Interweave Press, and Judith Durant, also an Interweave book editor who shepherded the successful *One-Skein Wonders* books. The two subsequent editors continue to work at the heights of the knitting industry: Melanie Falick, with her own book imprint, STC Craft/Melanie Falick Books, and Pam Allen, later design director at Classic Elite Yarns, then principle at Quince and Company Yarns. Allen's shoes were filled in 2007 by current editor in chief Eunny Jang, a designer and knit blogger in step with the synergistic approach Interweave took in other media, such as the

Knitting Daily website and e-newsletters, the burgeoning online pattern store and the PBS television show *Knitting Daily TV,* hosted by Jang. *Interweave Knits* offers twenty to thirty projects per issue, without difficulty ratings, as well as a variety of feature articles.
See ALLEN, PAM; FALICK, MELANIE; LIGON, LINDA

INTERWEAVE PRESS
See INTERWEAVE KNITS; MAGAZINES AND JOURNALS

IRISH GALWAY BAY PATTERNS
See ARAN KNITTING; FOLK KNITTING

IRSHAD, MARIE
See PODCAST

ITALIAN KNITTING
Spanish nobles introduced knitting to Italy during the Renaissance, and once there the craft became more sophisticated. Designs became more elaborate, with floral patterning that resembled elaborate brocades. There is some debate as to whether the famed Florentine jackets (some of which can be found at the Victoria & Albert Museum) are actually Italian in origin, but there is no doubt that complex designs like these were being created in Italy in the sixteenth and seventeenth centuries.

Today Italy is an important center for yarn production. Designers, fashion editors and

yarn industry insiders flock to the trendsetting knitwear trade show Pitti Filati each year to see the latest innovations in yarn and style, and Milan is considered one of the fashion knitting capitals of the world.
See also FLORENTINE JACKET; PITTI FILATI; SPANISH KNITTING; VICTORIA & ALBERT MUSEUM

JACOBSSON, EMMA
See BOHUS KNITTING

JACQUARD
In weaving, a jacquard pattern is a complex textured fabric that often includes figural designs. The term is also used to refer to seventeenth-century knitted pieces that were knitted of two colors of silk, often employing purl stitches to enhance the textured effect. In knitting today, jacquard refers to a stranded colorwork pattern that may include any number of colors in a single row of knitting (in contrast to Fair Isle patterns, which use only two colors in any single row).
See also COLORWORK; FAIR ISLE KNITTING

JANG, EUNNY
See I*INTERWEAVE KNITS*

JERSEY
Sometimes spelled jarsey, iarnsey, iarzie or jerdsie, *jersey* used to describe a worsted (i.e., combed) wool or silk yarn. This term originated in the sixteenth century or earlier. Jersey yarn was used to make stockings, breeches and other items. Today, the term more often refers either to a knitted pullover or to a smooth knitted fabric of any sort.

It is likely that the five-ply worsted wool yarn used extensively throughout Britain and Holland to make fishermen's ganseys originally came from Jersey, which is one of the Channel Islands. In later centuries worsted yarn was made in other parts of England, and as late as 1882 *jarsey* was still the local name used for worsted yarn manufactured in Lancashire.
See also GANSEY; WORSTED WEIGHT; YARN WEIGHT

JOINING YARN
To attach a new ball of yarn to a piece of knitting is to join it. When possible, join new balls or skeins of yarn at the beginning or end of a row in flat knitting to make it easier to weave the strands into the seams during finishing. There are many ways to join new yarn; the most simple is to drop the old strand and begin using the new. Any gap or hole will be tightened up when the work is complete and ends are woven in. Some knitters tie the new yarn on with a knot, but this can come through the work and be difficult to hide

Joining at the Side Edge

To join a new yarn at the side edge, tie it loosely around the old yarn, leaving at least a 6-inch (15cm) tail. Untie the knot later and weave the ends into the seam.

Joining in the Middle of a Row

1. To join a yarn in the middle of the row, insert the right needle into the next stitch to be worked, wrap the new yarn around the right needle and start knitting with the new yarn.

2. Work to the end of the row. Tie the old and new strands together loosely before continuing so they will not unravel.

Splicing Yarn

1. To join the same color in the middle of a row, splice the two ends together by untwisting the ends of both the old and the new yarn. Cut away approximately 4 inches (10cm) from half of each set of strands as shown.

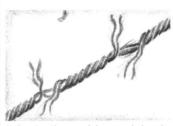

2. Overlap the remaining uncut strands and twist them together in the same direction as the yarn. Continue working with the twisted yarn, weaving in the loose ends later.

later. Other techniques for smoothly joining yarn include working 2 to 4 stitches with both yarns held together; the double thickness is hardly noticeable in the finished work if the yarn isn't too textured or thick. You can also join the same color in the middle of the row by splicing it.

If the fiber is feltable—made of 100 percent wool—the two ends can be felted together in what is called a felted join. To minimize the size of the resulting strand of yarn at the join, cut away a few of the plies and felt just the smaller ends together. Wet the ends with water (or spit) and rub vigorously between your hands until the ends have fused together into one strand. Those who use their own spit are said to be "spit-felting."

A specialized technique for creating a single strand of yarn is the Russian Join. In this technique the new strand is folded around the original strand, threaded onto a needle, and the end drawn into the shaft of the strand. The threading is repeated with the original strand, and though the result can be a bit thicker than one strand, it creates a nearly invisible join.

When attaching yarn of a different color, any of these techniques can be used, but care must be taken to match the ends exactly so that the colors are not out of place.

Sometimes joining the yarn in the middle of a row is unavoidable, as on garments knit in the round or with some colorwork patterns. Join the yarn in mid-row in an inconspicuous place, such as at the edge of a cable or in a textured stitch area. Weave in the ends neatly during finishing. Always weave the strands into the wrong side of the fabric by working them in opposite directions. If you are using a thick yarn, untwist the strands and weave them in separately.

See also CHANGING COLORS; FELTING; FIBER CHARACTERISTICS; WEAVING IN

JORGENSEN, MARIANNE

See GUERRILLA KNITTING

JUTE

Like some other plant fibers, jute is a bast, or skin, fiber. It comes from the stem of the *Cochorus* plant native to India, traditionally used for making rope and burlap. The fibers are removed from the stem of the plant in a series of steps that include retting (soaking in water to soften the plant material and separate the fibers). Like hemp, jute is strong and coarse and lacks the softness and sheen of flax.

In the craft world, jute has traditionally been used more for macramé work than for knitting.

See also FIBER CHARACTERISTICS; FLAX; HEMP

K

Abbreviation for *knit*.
See also KNIT STITCH

K1-B, K-B

Abbreviations for "knit in the stitch below." Infrequently used for "knit through back loop."
See also BRIOCHE; KNIT IN THE STITCH BELOW

K1FB, K1F&B, KFB

Abbreviations for "knit into the front and back of a stitch"; also called a bar increase.
See also BAR INCREASE; INCREASES

K2TOG

Abbreviation for "knit two stitches together."
See also DECREASES

KAGAN, SASHA (1945-)

Knit and crochet designer Sasha Kagan brings the pastoral view of the Welsh countryside to her work. Kagan grew up in the East English county of Cambridgeshire and now lives in rural Wales. She trained in painting as an undergraduate at Exeter College of Art, then went on to study printmaking at London's Royal College of Art, learning the repetitive, layered techniques she'd later apply to her knitting. She found success as a theatrical designer before relocating with her family to the country. It was then that she earned acclaim as a designer. Her modern versions of '40s-era Fair Isle knits were picked up by Browns, an influential London boutique, and orders piled in. Sasha Kagan produced knitwear garments for runways and commercial shops in both the U.K. and the United States, and Kagan's work was the focus of a one-woman show at the Victoria & Albert Museum.

Kagan contributes to all the major knitting publications and has written several books: *Knitwear* (Guild of Master Craftsman, 2008), *Crochet Inspiration* (Sixth&Spring, 2007), *Knitting for Beginners* (Carroll & Brown, 2004), *Country Inspiration* (Taunton, 2000), *The Sasha Kagan Sweater Book* (Dorling Kindersley/Ballantine Books, 1984) and *Sasha Kagan's Big and Little Sweaters* (Westminster Trading, 1987). She has also produced kits of several of her popular designs, allowing handknitters to dig into her signature twisted ribs and leafy intarsia.

Today, Kagan is giving back to the surroundings that have so inspired her work over the years, becoming active in a Welsh initiative designed to help farmers improve sheep breeding and with a burgeoning local sheep-and-wool festival, Wonderwool Wales. "For me," Kagan said to *Yarn Market News* in 2007, "the lifestyle came first; the knitting came second to support it. I think that's what makes me unique as a designer. Most important to me is to support the creative spirit."

In 2010, Kagan was the recipient of a European "Chance to Create Grant," which she used to put together a touring exhibition of textile designs from the 1960s to the present.
See also DESIGNERS; FAIR ISLE KNITTING; VICTORIA & ALBERT MUSEUM

KAL

Abbreviation for *knit-along*.
See also INTERNET

KITCHENER STITCH

See GRAFTING

KLEIN, ADINA

See VOGUE KNITTING

KNIT.1

See MAGAZINES AND JOURNALS

KNIT-ALONG

See INTERNET

KNITCAST

See PODCASTS

KNIT IN THE BACK LOOP

See KNIT THROUGH THE BACK LOOP

KNIT IN THE ROW BELOW

Abbreviated k1-b or k-b, knitting a stitch in the row below increases the stitch count by one. It is

Knit in the Row Below

With the yarn at the back, insert the right needle from front to back into the center of the stitch one row below the next stitch on the left needle. Knit this stitch. Slip the top stitch off the left needle without working it.

commonly used in brioche knitting.
See also BRIOCHE; INCREASES

KNIT 'N STYLE

See MAGAZINES AND JOURNALS

KNIT ONE, CROCHET TOO

Less formally known as K1C2, this fine-yarn wholesaler and online retailer was originally established in California in 1996. In 2003 it was sold to Hélène Rush, who relocated it to Windham, Maine. Rush had been a hand-knitting industry insider for over twenty-five years, having authored five knitting books and designed patterns for many major knitting magazines. She also served as the editor of *McCall's Needlework and Crafts* and *Cast On* magazines. K1C2 makes about thirty yarns, including "Cotonade" and the "Ty-Dy Soxx" range, and provides ecological alternative yarns of bamboo and soy. All yarns and colorways are designed by Rush in a personal, hands-on process as she evaluates the fiber and envisions patterns that will best showcase its properties. Her business philosophy is to always create yarns she would like to use herself. Following this formula, K1C2 has developed an eclectic lineup of original patterns for women, children and men, as well as carrying kits and a variety of buttons and accessories. The company also carries the Culinary Colors Collection, a ten-bottle kit that allows knitters to create their own yarn colors from nontoxic dyes.

KNIT-OUTS

Knit-Outs are yarn-arts conventions with an emphasis on public outreach, run by the Craft Yarn Council (CYC) since 1998. Staffed by volunteers and free to attend, Knit-Out & Crochet events have been held nationwide, usually in city locations guaranteed to attract a lot of foot traffic, such as New York's Union Square, the Mall in Washington, D.C. and the Twin

Cities' Mall of America. While dedicated crafters, CYC members and stitching guilds are typical attendees, the public nature of Knit-Outs assures that many passersby will stop in, learn about knitting and crochet and become future crafters. Exhibit booths are maintained by many yarn companies and knitting-pattern publishers; tutorial Learn-to-Knit/Crochet booths attract long lines; and knitwear fashion shows are a great draw. Celebrity knitting designers and media personalities often attend. No retailing is permitted, as the purpose of the Knit-Outs is simply awareness and fun.
See also CRAFT YARN COUNCIL

KNIT/PURL PATTERNS

Knit and purl stitches can be combined in almost endless combinations to create simple but beautiful patterns. The simplest knit/purl combination patterns are garter stitch and stockinette stitch. Garter stitch consists only of knit stitches (or only of purl stitches) in every row. Stockinette

stitch consists of alternating rows of knit and purl stitches.

Many well-known stitch patterns, such as ribbing, basket-weave patterns, moss and seed stitch and chevrons, are knit/purl patterns. Some knit/purl patterns are reversible, making them useful for garments such as scarves in which both sides of the fabric are visible.
See also ALPINE REGION PATTERNS; BASKETWEAVE STITCH; BRIOCHE; GARTER STITCH; KNIT STITCH; MOSS STITCH; PURL STITCH; REVERSE STOCKINETTE STITCH; RIBBING; SEED STITCH; STOCKINETTE STITCH; WELT PATTERNS

KNITSCENE
See MAGAZINES AND JOURNALS

KNIT SIMPLE
See MAGAZINES AND JOURNALS

KNIT STITCH

One of two basic stitches used to form a fabric made of interlocking loops from a continuous strand of

yarn using two or more needles, the knit stitch is the basic building block of all knitted work. The other basic stitch is the purl stitch. Each loop is called a stitch.

A horizontal series of loops in a knit fabric forms a row. Each row links together with the rows above and below, and each stitch is attached to its neighbor.

There are two basic ways to form a knit stitch: the American/English method and the Continental method. In American/English knitting, you hold the yarn in your right hand; in the Continental method, you hold it in your left.

In a normal knit stitch, you knit into the front loop of the stitch on the left-hand needle. Sometimes directions tell you to work through the back loop (tbl) instead. Most stitches are simply variations on this basic stitch.
See also AMERICAN/ENGLISH-STYLE KNITTING; CONTINENTAL/GERMAN-STYLE KNITTING; GARTER STITCH; KNIT/PURL PATTERNS; KNITTED FABRIC;

Three swatches showing different knit/purl patterns

English-Style Knit Stitch

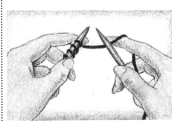

1. Hold the needle with the cast-on stitches in your left hand. The first stitch on the left needle should be approximately 1 inch (2.5cm) from the tip of the needle. Hold the working needle in your right hand, wrapping the yarn around your fingers.

2. Insert the right needle from front to back into the first cast-on stitch on the left needle. Keep the right needle under the left needle and the yarn at the back.

3. Wrap the yarn under and over the right needle in a clockwise motion.

4. With the right needle, catch the yarn and pull it through the cast-on stitch.

5. Slip the cast-on stitch off the left needle, leaving the newly formed stitch on the right needle. Repeat these steps in each subsequent stitch until all stitches have been worked from the left needle. One knit row has been completed.

Continental-Style Knit Stitch

1. Hold the needles in the same way as the English method, but wrap the yarn around your left hand rather than your right.

2. Insert the right needle from front to back into the first cast-on stitch on the left needle. Keep the right needle under the left needle, with the yarn in back of both needles.

3. Lay the yarn over the right needle as shown.

4. With the tip of the right needle, pull the strand through the cast-on stitch, holding the strand with the right index finger if necessary.

5. Slip the cast-on stitch off the left needle, leaving the newly formed stitch on the right needle. Continue to repeat these steps until you have worked all of the stitches from the left needle to the right needle. You have made one row of knit stitches.

KNITTING VS. WEAVING; PURL STITCH; STITCH MOUNT; STOCKINETTE STITCH

KNITTA

See GUERRILLA KNITTING

KNITTED FABRIC

The textile produced by continuous interlocking of one or more yarns, using two needles at a time, worked one stitch at a time, by hand or on a knitting machine, is referred to as knitted fabric. All fabrics, or textiles, are constructed of intermeshed yarns, fibers or filaments. The three broad categories of fabrics are:

Nonwoven: Fibers or filaments are bonded together by needle-punching, bonding, heat-setting or fiber felting

Woven: Yarns that intermesh in two or more directions, as in loom weaving and certain types of basketry and lace-making

Knitted: A single strand of yarn forms series of interlocking loops

Handknitted fabric can be formed using a pair of straight needles and working back and forth, row by row, to create a flat piece such as a scarf, blanket or the front or back of a garment. It can also be formed using a single circular needle or a set of double-pointed needles and working in the round to form a tube such as a hat, sock, sleeve or sweater body.

Two stitches, knit and purl, form the basis for all knitted fabric. Row after row of knit stitch makes a garter stitch fabric; a row of knit followed by a row of purl makes stockinette, the most frequently used knitted fabric. Stitches combined in a variety of ways form stitch patterns such as ribs, lace stitches, cables and textures. Knitted garment pieces are shaped as they are being made by increasing (adding) or decreasing (taking away) stitches.

Because of its loop construction, knitted fabric is stretchy and produces a flexible material, and thus garments made of it are generally comfortable to wear. In addition to sweaters, scarves, hats, socks and gloves, knitting is well suited to baby clothing. Double knitting produces a heavier, more stable fabric. In general, woven fabric is more stable and structured, making it suitable for tailored clothing such as suits, trousers and coats.

See also DOUBLE KNITTING; KNIT STITCH; KNITTING VS. WEAVING; PURL STITCH

KNITTED LACE

Knitting in which yarn overs and decreases are used to create patterns of decorative holes is called lace. Some knitters distinguish between the terms lace knitting and knitted lace. Lace knitting refers to lace patterns in which yarn overs and decreases are worked only in every other row (the right side), alternating with rows of knits or purls (on the wrong side).

In knitted lace, however, the yarn overs and decreases are worked in every row. The resulting pattern is sometimes reversible.

Knitted lace can be as simple as a basic faggoting stitch or as complex as the design shown below. Knitted lace is not necessarily more difficult than lace knitting, and many knitters downplay the distinction.

See also FAGGOTING; LACE KNITTING

KNITTER'S (MAGAZINE)

Knitter's premiered in 1984, and from the beginning this quarterly offered stylish, inclusive knitwear designs. Excellent diagrams, clear instructions and its School for Knitters section make it a very accessible read. As much of a player as *Knitter's* is on the newsstand, it tends to make even more impact when it takes its show on the road. Publisher XRX, in Sioux Falls, South Dakota, is the force behind the well-loved and well-attended Stitches events—markets, camps and classes chock-full of yarn vendors, fashion shows, stitching events and celebrity knitters.

Knitter's publisher is Alexis Y. Xenakis, who has always taken an active interest in and been an

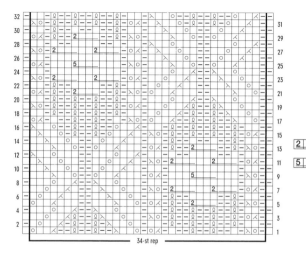

Stitch Key

□	K on RS, p on WS
−	P on RS, k on WS
○	Yo
⟋	K2tog on RS, p2tog on WS
⟍	Ssk on RS, ssp on WS
Ω	K1 tbl on RS, p1 tbl on WS
2 ⊥⊥⊥	Wrap 4 sts twice
5 ⊥⊥⊥	Wrap 4 sts 5 times

34-st rep

Knitted lace swatch

Designing Knitted Lace

by Margaret Stove

I am fascinated by our lace heritage.

How did lace patterns evolve? Perhaps the lace knitters of earlier times were inspired by nature just as I am; perhaps they followed the process I use in designing new lace stitches. At any rate, perhaps this description of that process will inspire you to experiment and come up with your own designs.

I know from my own experience that designing and knitting lace can be unpredictable. Understanding the placement and manipulation of stitches gives some control; however, as little as a change in yarn or needle size may produce surprises. There is always a "what if" factor in lace knitting, and this fascinates me.

Before I could read words my grandmother taught me to understand knitting patterns. This led to my passion for translating my own drawings of New Zealand flora into knitted lace. For example, the rata blossom is a brilliant scarlet native flower composed of a cluster of stamens and small, slightly curved leaves that has always intrigured me. I designed a lace pattern to represent this flower based on

two traditional and very familiar English laces: rose leaf and cockleshell. The design process began with an accurate drawing of the flower, which I then redrew to emphasize and simplify its shapes. I tried various configurations, turning the design to make it follow the direction of knitted fabric. Then I knit.

Typically my design process involves trying out solutions on knitted samples and fine-tuning them until I am happy with the result. The illustrations included here show the sequence from initial sketch to simplified version, turning the flower in the direction of knitting, and, finally, the fully realized lace pattern incorporated into a christening gown. I have taken the basic rata lace design and worked it into other knitted items including a shawl.

I learned a great deal from this process, and since the time I designed the rata lace, I have translated many other native New Zealand flowers into lace. With its endless variation and unpredictable results, knitted lace continues to blow my mind.

Margaret Stove (artisanlace.co.nz) is a teacher and designer whose patterns have appeared in *Vogue Knitting* and other North American, British and Australian spinning and knitting publications. She is the author of three books, including *Wrapped in Knitted Lace* (Interweave Press, 2010).

The rata flower of New Zealand was my inspiration for the rata lace pattern.

Detailed drawing of rata flower

Simplified version of drawing

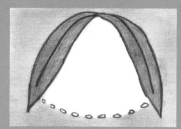

Drawing turned in the direction of knitting

This christening gown I designed incorporates the rata lace pattern. You can see the flower motif running in three vertical lines down the front of the dress.

editorial presence at the magazine. The first editor, Elaine Rowley, had a long tenure, until 1995. She was succeeded by former *Vogue Knitting* editor Nancy J. Thomas. Thomas was succeeded in 2001 by Rick Mondragon, making *Knitter's* the only major knitting magazine in America helmed by a man. Mondragon has continued as editor to this day.

See also STITCHES; THOMAS, NANCY J.

KNITTER'S REVIEW

Published by Clara Parkes, *Knitter's Review* is a weekly online magazine focused on yarn and fiber. In addition to the magazine, KnittersReview.com includes forums in which members discuss yarn, fiber and knitting-related topics and a boutique that sells knitting-related items. There is also an annual Knitter's Review Retreat, held usually in New England in November, that attracts star teachers and as many stitching enthusiasts as the site will allow.

Established in 2000, *Knitter's Review* is free to subscribers and forum members and is supported by advertising. Each Thursday morning, subscribers receive a new issue of the magazine, which may feature an in-depth yarn review, a survey of the yarn stores in San Francisco or the Hudson

Valley, a detailed description of a trade show such as TNNA, or a roundup of recent knitting- and fiber-related books. Whatever the topic, readers are sure of a lively, well-written, in-depth discussion. *See also* INTERNET; PARKES, CLARA

KNIT THROUGH THE BACK LOOP

Knitting into the back loop of the stitch on the left needle, rather than the front loop, which is the standard method, results in a twisted stitch. It is abbreviated as "tbl."

See also KNIT STITCH

KNITTING (MAGAZINE)

See MAGAZINES AND JOURNALS (U.K.)

KNITTING AIDS

Items that ease the process of knitting, such as fingerless gloves for arthritis, magnifying glasses for eyestrain and specially designed lamps for task lighting, all constitute knitting aids. Aids are especially helpful to those who have knit for many years and are suffering the effects of repetitive

movement or carpal tunnel syndrome, arthritis or failing eyesight. However, certain aids, such as proper lighting, are essential to knitters of any age or experience level.

Fingerless gloves made of elastic fabric fit snugly to support and massage the muscles and ligaments of the hand and wrist, minimizing stress, cramping and fatigue. They are non-restrictive and stimulate circulation.

Magnifying glasses for knitters are available in a variety of strengths and frame styles and are designed to ease the eyestrain that occurs while working on projects for extended periods, especially fine-gauge knitting. They are often set on stands, sometimes combined with a light.

Natural daylight is the healthiest and most comfortable type of light for the eyes, and there are lamps designed for knitters and other crafters that mimic natural daylight to reduce the eyestrain that can occur with close work. Lamps with a built-in magnifying glass are another option for knitters with failing eyesight.

KNITTING BACK BACKWARDS (KBB)

See BACKWARDS KNITTING

KNITTING CAMPS

See CAMPS AND RETREATS

KNITTING CHARTS

See CHARTS

KNITTING COMPETITIONS

From traditional county-fair/4-H best-knitted-garment-in-a-given-age-group contests to sheep-to-shawl meets at fiber festivals, to blog giveaways to serious speed-knitting tournaments held worldwide and authenticated by the *Guinness Book of World Records,* there is a knitting competition for every knitter. Some competitions specify original designs, others, an impeccably produced garment. Sheep-to-shawl contests are full-day affairs, with contestants creating wearable pieces with yarn they shear, spin and knit in a matter of hours. The Craft Yarn Council routinely holds time trials for the world's fastest knitter and crocheter; comparable guilds in the U.K., Europe, Australia and New Zealand partner with CYC at fiber-arts shows such as Germany's Handarbeit & Hobby and London's Knitting and Stitching Show to make this an international effort. The world-record holders as of 2007, recognized by the Guinness Book, are knitter Mirian Tegels of the Netherlands, who knit 118 stitches per minute, and crocheter Lisa Gentry of Chatham, Louisiana, who looped 170 stitches per minute. Held annually in London, England, and Dublin, Ireland, the Knitting and Stitching Show also features themed contests hosted by individual exhibitors; in 2010 these included "Best Little Black Dress" and a "Sew, Salvage, and Save" bag competition. Less cutthroat are contests and drawings spearheaded by yarn shops, blogs and podcasts that offer fiber goodies to shoppers, readers and listeners who enter, answer questions or donate money and/or knitted goods to a given cause.

Janet Johnson Stephens, who authored TKGA's correspondence course on knitting-judge certification and cowrote *The Blue Ribbon Manual of Competitive Needlearts Events* (Susan Yarns, 1998) with Donalene S. Poduska,

A magnifying-glass stand can be a useful knitting aid.

has suggested in an online thread that knitting competition contestants research the event before entering and thoroughly read and follow the rules. Finishing, blocking and presentation count, so concentrate on all aspects of workmanship, not just the stitches. Visit the websites of local fairs, festivals and guild shows to see entry guidelines.
See also CRAFT YARN COUNCIL; INTERNET; KNITTING GUILD ASSOCIATION, THE; KNITTING JUDGES; MAGAZINES AND JOURNALS; SHEEP AND WOOL FESTIVALS

KNITTING FICTION
See FICTION, KNITTING IN; FILM, KNITTING IN

KNITTING FRAME
Also known as peg-frame loom, a knitting frame is a group of pegs on a fixed base, usually wood, arranged in a row or a ring. Stitches are formed by treating each peg as the needle for one wale of the knitted fabric. The loops are formed by winding the yarn around a peg twice and lifting the first course of yarn over the peg and second course of yarn with a hook, needle or pointed stick. The knitting frame is a primitive precursor to the knitting machine.
See also KNITTED FABRIC; KNITTING LOOM; KNITTING NANCY

KNITTING GUILD ASSOCIATION, THE (TKGA)
TKGA is a national nonprofit organization dedicated to educating and fostering communication among knitters. Founded in 1984 in Knoxville, Tennessee, by knitter Carol Wigginton, TKGA was acquired in 2001 by the Offinger Management Company, which now administers its many activities for the 12,000-plus members from its base in Zanesville, Ohio, where Offinger also runs operations for the National NeedleArts Association (TNNA). TKGA is overseen by an advisory board of yarn manufacturers, designers and retailers. It acts as the umbrella organization for smaller, local knitting guilds across the United States; publishes the quarterly magazine *Cast On,* sent to its members and sold at member yarn shops; sponsors the Master Knitting Program and other educational correspondence courses; and, most visibly, mounts with the Crochet Guild of America a number of knit and crochet shows and conferences throughout the year. With its nonprofit wing the Helping Hands Foundation, TKGA sponsors the Needle Arts Mentoring Program, which links generations by providing young people with knitting tutors; Precious Pals, a program that provides police, fire and rescue departments with stuffed animals dressed in knitted sweaters to be handed out to comfort children in crisis situations; and the Memorial Fund for Knitters, which allows

Knitting frame

friends and families to commemorate the memories of knitters and crocheters who've died by making contributions that support TKGA educational grants and programs. Presidents of local guilds receive the quarterly TKGA e-newsletter, *Swatches,* and members have access to password-protected message boards, patterns and other information on the association's website.

See also INTERNET; MAGAZINES AND JOURNALS; MASTER KNITTING PROGRAM; NATIONAL NEEDLE ARTS ASSOCIATION, THE; NEEDLE ARTS MENTORING PROGRAM

KNITTING IN THE ROUND

See CIRCULAR KNITTING

KNITTING JOURNAL

Knitters often like to track their knitting projects in books or notebooks; their knitting journal can also be used as a place to inventory yarns and supplies or file photos and ideas for future projects. While any kind of notebook or sketchbook could be used for this purpose, several journals have been published specifically for knitting and contain pages preprinted for specific uses such recording needle inventory or favorite yarn shops. These knitting-specific journals usually include graph paper, knitting abbreviations and

other basic information. Some have pockets in which to store patterns, pages for photos of completed projects and places to attach swatches. With the advent of interactive online communities such as Ravelry, knitters now have the option of sharing their works in progress and finished

objects with the wider community. The online knitting journal means the information can be accessed anywhere, as well. *See also* INTERNET; RAVELRY

KNITTING JUDGES

Individual judges are charged with selecting the winners of

knitting competitions held at local fairs, 4-H events, or knitting-guild shows. The Knitting Guild Association (TKGA) offers a correspondence course called Certification for Knitting Judges authored by Janet Johnson Stephens, who started entering knitting competitions in the 1960s

Knitting journal from the mid-1800s showing knitted samples and handwritten notes

Knitting loom

and judging them in the '70s; she also cowrote with Donalene S. Poduska *The Blue Ribbon Manual of Competitive Needlearts Events* (Susan Yarns, 1998). The TKGA course, which must be completed within two years, delves into the criteria for judging knitted items—what to look for in technique, finishing and presentation—and highlights the various types of competitions and judging methods.
See also INTERNET; KNITTING COMPETITIONS; KNITTING GUILD ASSOCIATION, THE; SHEEP AND WOOL FESTIVALS

KNITTING LOOM

Also known as an Amish loom or knitting board, the knitting loom is a descendant of the peg-frame loom with grooved pegs spaced along a central frame. These pegs are wrapped with yarn in various ways, then the knitter uses an angled hook to pull the wrapped yarn over the top of the peg, resulting in a fabric with stitches similar to a needle-knitted item.

See also KNITTED FABRIC; KNITTING FRAME; KNITTING NANCY

KNITTING NANCY

Also know as a knitting lizzy, knitting mushroom, knitting spool, corker or peg knitter, the knitting nancy is a tool for peg knitting in the round. It produces a tubular cord (known as an I-cord, or idiot cord) and, as with a knitting frame and knitting loom, stitches are created by winding the yarn around a peg. These devices all evolved from the medieval lucet, a two-pronged wooden fork with a hole in the handle that produced a knitted cord historically used for piping on dresses.

The simplest knitting nancy is a wooden or plastic spool with four nails fastened into one end. Knitting nancies are often whimsically shaped and brightly painted to resemble a mushroom or doll and are used to teach children the concept of knitting. The cords or braids formed can be used for decorative trim, purse handles, or to make hats, bags or mats.

Variations on the theme include knitting spools with up to forty-one pegs that can be used to make hats and even socks, hand-cranked versions, available in craft stores, that produce braid rapidly, and hand-cranked versions designed to accommodate wire for jewelry making.
See also CORDS; KNITTING FRAME; KNITTING LOOM

KNITTING ON

Method of casting on stitches that uses two needles and a single length of yarn.
See also CAST-ON

Knitting-on cast-on

Knitting On

1. Make a slipknot on the left needle. *Insert the right needle knitwise into the stitch on the left needle. Wrap the yarn around the right needle as if to knit.

2. Draw the yarn through the first stitch to make a new stitch, but do not drop the stitch from the left needle.

3. Slip the new stitch to the left needle as shown. Repeat from the * until the required number of stitches is cast on.

Three styles of knitting nancies

KNITTING RETREATS

See CAMPS AND RETREATS

KNITTING SCHOOLS

Formal schools have been established to teach knitting. The first knitting schools were established in both urban and rural communities in England during the second half of the reign of Elizabeth I. Knitting was seen as both a way to keep idle hands busy and out of trouble and to give the poor a means of earning an income. In the nineteenth century English reformers urged that knitting be taught to the poor as an alternative to the workhouse. Scholars and those with an interest in preserving local handicraft traditions also established schools and cooperatives to carry on these traditions, including knitting.

In some places that have a strong knitting heritage, such as in the Shetland Islands of Scotland, knitting is still taught in the schools, but like many other arts programs, knitting classes are often in jeopardy from budget cuts. *See also* HISTORY OF KNITTING; MASTER KNITTING PROGRAM

KNITTING SHEATH

The knitting sheath is a tool used by the knitters of the Shetland Islands. One end of its carved stick was tucked into the knitter's apron or skirt, while the other end was attached to the bottom of a knitting needle. This freed up one hand, enabling the knitter to work faster. Knitting sheaths hand-carved of ivory, bone and exotic woods became collectibles during the Victorian era, when they served more of a decorative purpose than a utilitarian one. *See also* DALES KNITTING

KNITTING VS. WEAVING

Knitting is the looping of one strand of yarn to form a fabric, either by hand or machine, and weaving is the interlacement of two strands of yarn to form fabric on a loom. In general, weaving forms a more stable, less stretchy fabric than knitting. Because knitted fabric is so stretchy, it has the advantage of clinging to the body.
See also KNITTED FABRIC

KNIT TODAY

See MAGAZINES AND JOURNALS (U.K.)

KNITTY.COM

The preeminent Internet-only knitting magazine, *Knitty.com* was launched in June 2002 by Toronto-based editor/publisher Amy R. Singer. As of 2007, more than 32 million individual users had visited the site, which averages 20,000 hits a day. Advertiser-supported, *Knitty.com* is free for personal individual use and is published quarterly. Each issue contains technical articles, columns, trend features, product and book reviews, and fifteen to twenty patterns, often by up-and-coming independent web-savvy designers.

That was the case for Kate Gilbert, who designed Clapotis, the bias-knit, drop-stitch scarf that became *Knitty*'s signature pattern after it was published in fall 2004 and took the knit blogosphere by storm. Other popular patterns have included Cheryl Niamath's Fetching fingerless gloves; Jenna Adorno's beribboned, off-the-shoulder Tempting; Brooke Chenoweth Creel's toe-down Widdershins socks; and Cookie A's lacy Pomatomus socks.

Included in each issue of *Knitty* is *KnittySpin,* a zine-within-a-zine edited by designer Jillian Moreno and catering to the growing number of *Knitty* readers interested in spinning.

The broad *Knitty* readership actively posts on *Knitty*'s extensive Coffeeshop forum. *Knitty* merchandise is available through a Café Press shop linked to the site. Each page is embellished with a picture of a pink aluminum needle that belonged to Singer's grandmother Lillian, who taught her to knit at age six.
See also INTERNET; SINGER, AMY R.

Knitting sheath

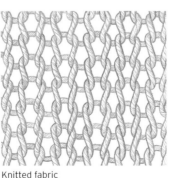

Knitted fabric

Woven fabric

KNITTYSPIN

See KNITTY.COM

KNITWISE

If an instruction calls for the needle to be inserted in the stitch—for slipping or working—as if it were to be knit, the instructions will specify "knitwise." This technique is sometimes used when decreasing or when working with color or slip-stitch patterns. Knitwise is ometimes abbreviated "kwise." Some knitting instructions will state, "slip as if to knit." Note that stitches slipped knitwise become twisted, whereas stitches slipped purlwise remain untwisted. If the pattern instruction doesn't state which way to slip a stitch, slip it purlwise, except when decreasing. When decreasing, slip knit stitches knitwise and purl stitches purlwise.

See also DECREASES; PURLWISE; SLIP-STITCH PATTERNS

To slip one stitch knitwise, insert the right needle through the stitch from front to back, as if you were knitting it. Transfer the stitch to the right needle without working it.

KOIGU WOOL DESIGNS

Koigu Wool Designs has achieved cult status for its hand-painted yarns and pattern support that shows off the spiraling rainbow hues to maximal effect. The brainchild of Estonian-born Maie Landra and her daughter and partner Taiu, Koigu is situated on the family's residential farm in Ontario. The Landras were among the first artisanal spinners in the knitting world and are still considered among the very best. At first, they used wool from their own sheep. In the mid-1990s, they began to use lighter-weight milled wool known as "Koigu Premium Merino" ("KPM") and "Koigu Painter's Palette Premium Merino" ("KPPPM"), with an ever-shifting palette of over 300 colorways. Shortly after, Linda Skolnik picked up the lines in her Patternworks catalog, and Koigu fever took off, to the degree that when yarns such as "KPPPM" arrived at stores, they often sold out before price tags could be put on. In addition to yarn, the Landras market Maie's original designs—and she has made her niche in modular garments, achieving huge success with the Charlotte's Web Scarf pattern. Knitters are also familiar with the family's third generation, Kersti, having seen her grow up along with the success of the company in Koigu's print ads.

KORS, MICHAEL (1959-)

Renowned American fashion designer Michael Kors is famous for his chic and unfussy luxury sportswear. After entering the fashion business at the age of nineteen, designing and merchandising for the upscale New York City boutique Lothar's, he struck out on his own and founded his eponymous label in 1981. Since then, Kors has expanded his brand to encompass not only women's ready-to-wear—often integrating knitwear—but also accessories, a men's collection and fragrances. In 1999 Kors received the fashion industry's most prestigious honor, the CFDA Award for Womenswear Designer of the Year, a feat he mirrored in 2003, when he won the CFDA Menswear Award.

Kors has contributed designs to *Vogue Knitting*, translating his clean, wearable knitwear into handknitting patterns. He's also one of the most recognizable faces of Seventh Avenue, thanks to his role as a judge on the popular TV reality show *Project Runway*.

See also DESIGNERS

KWISE

Abbreviation for *knitwise*.

See also KNITWISE

LACE KNITTING

The knitting technique in which yarn overs and decreases are used to create patterns of stable, decorative holes in the knitted fabric is called lace knitting. Lace knitting most likely originated in Spain, and as the technique spread throughout Europe and beyond, regional styles and techniques developed. Shetland and Orenburg, Russia, are among the regions most famed for their lace designs, but equally beautiful patterns were developed in Estonia and Iceland. All borrow motifs and techniques from each other. Until the Victorian era, lace knitting was a rural enterprise practiced by the wives of farmers and fishermen in rural and poor areas. Then in the second half of the nineteenth century came the great flowering of lace knitting, as middle-class Victorian women took up the craft and produced elaborate garments and objects for their homes.

There are several types of lace, each defined by the ground on which the lace pattern is worked (garter stitch or stockinette) and the frequency of the patterned rows containing yarn overs and decreases. Garter stitch lace is virtually identical on both sides; stockinette lace has definite right and wrong sides (the knit row being the former and the purl row the latter). Lace that is patterned on every row has a much more open and airy appearance than lace patterned every other row.

Some distinguish between true knitted lace and lace knitting. True knitted lace has yarn overs and decreases on both right-side and wrong-side rows. In lace knitting, the lace design is worked only on right-side rows. The wrong side is worked plain.

See also AZORES LACE; EYELET; EYELET PATTERNS; FAGGOTING; KNITTED LACE; LACE STITCHES; ORENBURG LACE; SHETLAND LACE; YARN OVER

LACE STITCHES

Stitch patterns used to form openwork fabric are called lace stitches. Like eyelet patterns and faggoting, lace is knit by combining yarn overs with decreases, but lace patterns are more diverse and inventive than eyelet patterns or faggoting. In eyelet patterns and faggoting, the yarn overs and decreases are adjacent. In lace stitch patterns, the yarn overs and decreases may be far apart. In addition, pairs of decreases may be arranged to point toward each other or away from each other to shape the openwork design.

Lace patterns can be used for almost any knitted item: sweaters, socks, baby clothes, shawls, hats. Lace is used in many traditional knitted garments, such as Shetland or Orenburg shawls.

See also DECREASING; EYELET; EYELET PATTERNS; FAGGOTING; LACE KNITTING; ORENBURG LACE; SHETLAND LACE; YARN OVER

This exquisite lace baby gown was knit in cotton thread in Great Britain in 1851 when it won third prize in the handknitting competition of the Great Exhibition.

LACEWEIGHT

Specifically designed for lace knitting, laceweight yarn generally has a gauge of 8 or more stitches per inch and rates a category 0 on CYC's Standard Yarn Weight System.

While other weights and qualities of yarn can be used for lace knitting, a strand of ultra-fine laceweight yarn knits up into extremely delicate, spiderweb-like fabric. Fine luxury fibers such as merino wool, cashmere and silk are popular for lace yarns.
See also YARN WEIGHT

LADDER

When horizontal strands of yarn are visible in the finished work, that vertical element is called a ladder. Ladders can be intentional or not; decorative ones are made by intentionally dropping a stitch and unraveling it several rows down. An unintentional ladder forms if you accidentally drop a stitch or if tension is not even when working in the round.
See also CORRECTING COMMON MISTAKES; DROP-STITCH PATTERNS; MAKE ONE

Ladders

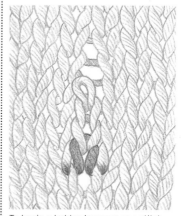

To begin a ladder, increase one stitch using a make-one increase. This forms the bottom of the ladder. Knit the number of rows required for the ladder, then drop the stitch directly above the make-one increase.

The finished ladder. The make-one stitch (shown in dark blue in both illustrations) prevents the finished ladder from unraveling any farther.

Three lace patterns (left to right): a flame-stitch pattern, a starfish motif and a feather-and-fan pattern

LADIES' HOME JOURNAL

See MAGAZINES AND JOURNALS

LAMBERT, FRANCES

See BRITISH KNITTING

LANOLIN

The greasy substance secreted from a sheep's sebaceous glands, lanolin is also known as wool fat, wool wax and *adeps lanae*. Certain breeds produce more lanolin than others. Lanolin softens wool fibers and is waterproof, so it repels water from the sheep in wet weather. Most lanolin is removed from the fleece during the cleaning process, but certain yarns intentionally retain some lanolin. For example, in Aran-type yarns, such as those used for Irish fishermen's sweaters, the water repellent properties serve a functional purpose. Lanolin is used commercially in cosmetics and in pharmaceuticals for its skin softening and healing properties. *See also* ARAN KNITTING; FIBER CHARACTERISTICS; SHEEP; WOOL

LATVIAN KNITTING

See BALTIC KNITTING

LAVENDER

Buds from this aromatic flowering plant native to the Mediterranean region can be used to repel moths from wool. When dried and sealed in pouches, lavender sachets can be placed among stored items of woolen clothing to give a fresh fragrance and deter moths. It will not kill moth larvae, so if moths are already present, thorough cleaning of the items is required. *See* FIBER CHARACTERISTICS

LAZY DAISY STITCH

This flowery embroidery stitch is used to create floral designs, such as a circle of "petals" surrounding a French knot or knots. *See also* CHAIN STITCH; EMBROIDERY; FINISHING TECHNIQUES

LC

Abbreviation for *left cross*. *See also* CABLES

LEAF STITCH

This embroidery stitch consists of two diagonal stitches radiating from a central stitch. It is sometimes combined with lazy daisy stitch to create a flower motif. *See also* EMBROIDERY; LAZY DAISY STITCH

LEE, WILLIAM (ca. 1563-1614)

Inventor of the first knitting machine. *See also* BRITISH KNITTING; MACHINE KNITTING

LEENE, J. E.

See ESCH FRAGMENTS

LEFT-HAND CARRY

See CONTINENTAL/GERMAN-STYLE KNITTING

LEFT-HANDED KNITTING

Directions for learning to knit usually assume that the learner is right-handed, and many people who are left-handed learn to knit using typical right-handed methods. Left-handed knitters who find those styles awkward can try the procedure shown below. Note that if you use the left-handed method, you will need to reverse the instructions, as almost all knitting patterns are written for the right-handed method. *See also* AMERICAN/ENGLISH-STYLE KNITTING; CAST-ON; CONTINENTAL/GERMAN-STYLE KNITTING; COMBINED KNITTING; EASTERN KNITTING; KNIT STITCH; PURL STITCH; WESTERN KNITTING

Lazy Daisy Stitch

Work in same way as chain stitch, but fasten each loop at the center with a small stitch.

Leaf Stitch

Bring up needle. With thread running under needle, insert needle to right at same level then into center in one motion.

Left-Handed Long-Tail Cast-On

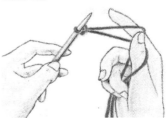

1. Make a slipknot on the left needle, leaving a long tail. Wind the tail end around your right thumb from front to back. Wrap the yarn from the ball over your index finger and secure both ends between your palm and fingers.

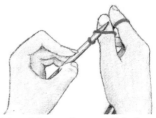

2. Insert the needle upward into the loop on your thumb.

3. Insert the needle downward into the loop on your index finger and draw it through the loop on your thumb. Repeat steps 1-3 until all stitches are cast on.

Left-Handed Knit Stitch

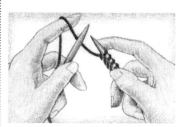

1. Hold the needle with the stitches in your right hand and the working needle and yarn in your left.

4. With the left needle, catch the yarn and pull it through the stitch on the right needle.

2. Insert the left needle from front to back into the first cast-on stitch on the right needle. Keep the left needle under the right needle and the yarn at the back.

5. Slip the stitch from the right needle to the left needle. This completes one stitch. Repeat these steps until you have worked all the stitches on the right needle.

3. Wrap the yarn counterclockwise under and over the left needle.

Left-Handed Purl Stitch

1. Hold the needle with the stitches on it in your right hand and the working needle and yarn in your left hand.

4. Draw the left needle through the stitch, bringing the yarn with it, making a new stitch on the left needle.

2. Insert the left needle from back to front into the back loop of the first stitch on the right needle.

5. Slip the stitch off the right needle. This completes one stitch. Repeat these steps until you have worked all the stitches on the right needle.

3. Wrap the yarn clockwise over and under the left needle, holding the yarn taut with your left index finger.

LEFT-SLANTING DECREASE

See DECREASES

LEGWARMERS

Tubular knit pieces, legwarmers are open on both ends and usually ribbed at the top and bottom, and are worn over the leg. Legwarmers originated in the ballet studio, where dancers slipped them over their legs as they warmed up their muscles for class or performance. The movie *Flashdance* brought them into mainstream wear in the 1980s, often in wild color combinations and even wilder textures. After a long hiatus and in a sleeker interpretation, they reemerged as a fashion accessory for the early twenty-first century. Their simple construction and minimal shaping makes them a popular project for beginning knitters, and many patterns are available in knitting books, magazines and online outlets. They can even be worn under pants for an extra layer of warmth with no one the wiser.

LENGTH, ADJUSTING

You can shorten or lengthen the body or sleeves of a garment either before or after knitting. Both techniques are explained below.

Adjusting Length Before Knitting

If you want to knit a particular pattern but decide to adjust the length in some way, make the adjustment in an area that requires no shaping. For example, to make sleeves longer, add the required number of rows after all the increasing is completed (for sleeves knit bottom-up) or before beginning the decreasing (for top-down sleeves). For a sweater body, add rows between the ribbing and the armhole bind-off. This will eliminate the need to rework armhole shaping.

Adjusting Length After Knitting

Adjusting length after knitting is more complicated, but it can be done. Most knitters will at some point complete a garment and find that either the body or sleeves are too long or too short for the intended wearer. Instead of ripping it all out, you can add or subtract rows from the bottom edge or from the middle.

To work from the bottom edge, first unpick the cast-on edge, starting from the first cast-on stitch. If the piece was knit flat and seamed, undo an inch or so of the seam on both sides and lengthen each piece separately. If it was knit in the round, continue to work circularly.

After unpicking the cast-on edge, you will be left with a row of open loops. To shorten the garment, rip out rows of knitting. Then put the stitches back on the needle, as shown here, and bind off. To lengthen the garment, after putting the stitches back on the

Adjusting Length

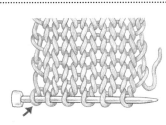

To adjust length from the bottom of a knitted piece, unpick the cast-on edge, insert a needle into the open loops as shown, turn the work and either bind off or begin purling back. Note that the first stitch you pick up should be the half-stitch at the edge.

To work from the center of the garment, divide the fabric. This means that you will remove a row of knitting and place the resulting live stitches on two needles. There are two ways to remove a row. First, you can simply snip one stitch and rip out an entire row, carefully putting the two resulting live rows' worth of stitches on needles. The second method is slightly less scary: Begin by inserting a needle through all the loops on one row, going through the loops from back to front.

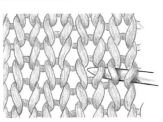

To divide knitted fabric before lengthening or shortening, place one row of stitches on a needle, working from right to left and from back to front of each stitch as shown.

To lengthen the work, turn it and pick up another row of stitches, one row down. Then snip one stitch in the in-between row and pull out that row. You will be left with two needles holding live stitches. Add the required number of rows to the stitches on one of the needles and finally graft the stitches on the two needles together.

To shorten the work, divide the fabric in the same way, removing exactly the number of rows required to achieve the desired length. For example, if the body is 2 inches too long, divide the fabric 2 inches above the top of the ribbing, and begin the ribbing immediately.

needle, turn the work and begin purling back in the other direction. Work to the desired length, then bind off.

When putting the live stitches back on the needle, note that the first stitch to be picked up is the edge stitch, which looks like a half-loop. If you omit this stitch and begin by picking up the first complete loop, the new knitting you add will be a half-stitch off. *See also* BODY FIT; DESIGN; EASE

LET'S KNIT

See MAGAZINES AND JOURNALS (U.K.)

LH

Abbreviation for *left-hand*.

LIFELINE

A temporary strand of yarn inserted through all the stitches in a given row of knitting can later "save your life" if you make a mistake—for this reason they are called lifelines. Lifelines are most commonly used in lace knitting, which is difficult to rip back to a particular point to correct an error. If you insert a lifeline every 10 or 20 rows, or at the beginning of every pattern repeat, you will never have to rip back farther than to the lifeline to correct an error.

To insert a lifeline, thread a yarn needle with a strand of yarn that contrasts in color with the yarn you are knitting with. Use a yarn that is lighter in weight and smooth—scrap cotton yarn is best. After you complete a row of knitting, turn the work as if to start a new row (the needle holding the work pointing to the right). Thread the strand of yarn through every stitch on the needle from back to front. Cut the yarn, leaving a fairly long tail on both ends. Work the stitches as normal, with the lifeline threaded through them. Once you reach the end of the next pattern repeat, remove the previous lifeline and add a new one.

See also CORRECTING COMMON MISTAKES; LACE KNITTING

LIFTED INCREASE

The lifted increase is barely visible and can be used almost anywhere. However, since you are increasing by pulling up a loop from the previous row, the work may pucker if there are fewer than three rows between each increase.

See also INCREASES

LIGON, LINDA (1942-)

Publisher, author and speaker Linda Ligon is the founder and creative force behind Interweave Press. She began the company as sole proprietor in the 1970s, and through her business acumen transformed it from a home-based publication into a diversified company that employs over sixty-five people and has branched into the Internet and social media, television broadcasting and crafts events. Interweave now publishes six craft magazines, including *Interweave Knits,* and has more the 150 craft books in print. In the 1980s, Ligon first made her mark by launching two magazines, the *Herb Companion,* which focused

Lifted Increase

The lifted increase, worked on the knit side.

1. To work the increase on the knit side, turn the work on the left needle toward you so that the purl side of the work is visible. Insert the tip of the right needle from the top down into the stitch on the left needle one row below, as shown.

2. Knit this stitch, then knit the stitch on the left needle.

on the joys of growing and cooking with herbs, and *Herbs for Health*. She also established *Natural Home & Garden* magazine in 1989. In 1990, she was named one of Colorado's Top 10 Business and Professional Women of the Year. Today Ligon, an avid weaver, spinner, crocheter, knitter and tatter, remains creative director at Interweave and lectures on topics such as business leadership, publishing and crafts. She also authored *This Is How I Go When I Go Like This* (Interweave, 2004), a collection of memoiristic essays from *Handwoven* magazine.

See also INTERWEAVE KNITS

Lifeline inserted into a row of knitting

LINEN

Linen is a fiber made from the stem of the flax plant. The plants are pulled from the root, which maximizes the length of the fibers, and then soaked until any non-fibrous material rots away. Only the long fibers of the stems' skins are left, which can be refined and spun into yarn. Linen fabric drapes well and is light, soft and strong. It may seem stiff at first, but the fibers relax a great deal after washing; because of this, it is extremely important to wash and dry swatches before measuring gauge. Linen is especially well suited to lace patterns, since it has very little stretch; its inelasticity means it is not ideal for ribbing or stockinette stitches. The lack of stretch also makes blocking unnecessary. Linen yarn can be difficult to work with: It is slippery (using bamboo or wooden needles is best) and can twist, creating an unintended bias in the fabric.
See also FLAX

LION BRAND YARN CO.

America's oldest continuously running yarn manufacturer, Lion Brand was founded on Manhattan's Lower East Side in 1878 and was later passed down within the Blumenthal family. It is currently run by a fourth generation of Blumenthals. Lion Brand's yarns, including bestsellers "Homespun" and "Wool-Ease," are extremely popular, affordable premium yarns; Lion's needles and notions are also low-price favorites. One virtue of Lion products is their wide availability in crafts chain stores as well as small shops. Another is low price: As a family-run business, Lion has always committed itself to keeping costs down. Additionally, a huge amount of pattern support (much of it free: Lion now offers 3,800 patterns gratis) has helped the company maintain its preeminence. It was also among the first yarn concerns to develop an Internet presence; by 2010, the Lion website had close to a

million subscribers. In 2008, the company opened its first retail store, Lion Brand Studio, near New York City's Union Square; in this chic setting, knitters meet up, take classes and sample yarns wine-bar-style. Lion forged into the twenty-first century developing its crochet-friendly "Vanna's Choice" range, a joint venture with celebrity Vanna White, and its new "LB Collection" of organic and luxury yarns.

LIVELY, BONNIE

See NEEDLE ARTS MENTORING PROGRAM

LIVE STITCH

Stitches that are not yet bound off are considered "live." Live stitches are held on a needle, stitch holder or length of yarn until needed. For example, when completing the back of a sweater, you might leave the stitches at the tops of the shoulders live and attach them later to corresponding stitches on the

front with a three-needle bind-off. Another example is the stitches at the center front or center back of a sweater. Instead of binding them off, leave them live and pick them up when knitting the neckline.
See BIND-OFF

LOCAL YARN SHOP

See LYS

LONG AND SHORT STITCH

Long and short stitch is a form of satin stitch made up of straight stitches of varying lengths. It is used to fill shapes, especially areas that are too large to be covered with satin stitch. It is also used to produce a shaded effect by using two different colors of threads or yarns.
See also EMBROIDERY; SATIN STITCH; STRAIGHT STITCH

LONG-TAIL CAST-ON

In the long-tail, or double, cast-on, yarn is used both from the "tail" and from the ball itself. It is a good

Linen swatch

Long and Short Stitch

Long-tail Cast-On

This cast-on method provides a firm yet elastic edge.

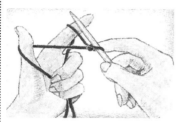

1. Make a slipknot on the right needle, leaving a long tail. Wind the tail end around your left thumb, front to back. Wrap the yarn from the ball over your left index finger and secure the ends in your palm.

2. Insert the needle upward in the loop on your thumb. Then with the needle, draw the yarn from the ball through the loop to form a stitch.

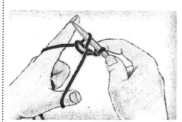

3. Take your thumb out of the loop and tighten the loop on the needle. Continue in this way until all the stitches are cast on.

cast-on for beginners. Be sure to leave a long tail when beginning.
See also CAST-ON

LOOP

See KNITTING FRAME; KNITTING LOOM; KNITTING VS. WEAVING

LOPI

Lopi yarn is produced from the wool of Icelandic sheep. Because of the climatic conditions of Iceland, the wool has certain unique qualities. First, Icelandic sheep, like other fiber-bearing animals in extreme climates, have a double fleece: The protective outer fibers are long and water repellent, and the inner fibers are soft and highly insulating. Strict laws in Iceland prevent the importation of sheep, eliminating the chance of disease and cross-breeding, so the strain has remained pure since the Vikings first brought them to the island in the ninth century.

Lopi yarn is a loosely spun, single-ply yarn; like all animal fibers, it felts well. In addition to its naturally occurring shades of white, black, gray and brown, Lopi takes dye well and is available in a wide range of shades. Traditional Icelandic knits, though, are made using the natural shades, knit into distinctive geometric yoke patterns.

Lopi has a long staple and is often knit as roving. It is also used to produce laceweight yarns.
See also ICELANDIC KNITTING; SHEEP; STAPLE

LORNA'S LACES

First known as Lorna's Laces Yarns, this artisanal hand-dyed fiber business was founded in California in 1986 by Lorna Miser, a skilled seamstress with a love of knitting, spinning and dyeing yarns. In 2003, Beth Casey, a corporate career woman, purchased the business lock, stock and barrel from Miser and moved it to her hometown of Chicago, fulfilling her dream of finding more authentic, hands-on work. Casey was still a driven manager, though, and determined to make a success of Lorna's Laces, she learned every aspect of her craft, hand-dyeing all of the yarns herself in her first year of business. Customers were so satisfied that demand at first outstripped Casey's production, and she has developed a reputation as a leader in the art of hand-dying. The company no longer has a waiting list, but its yarns, especially the superwash "Shepherd" range, continue to be in extremely high demand. Organic materials are used wherever possible. Lorna's Laces yarns are ordered in a slightly unusual way: one first selects the yarn, and this can then be dyed in any of the company's many eclectic solid or variegated colorways.

LOUET

Also known as Louet North America, formerly known as Louet Sales, Louet is a Canadian yarn manufacturer that distributes North American–made yarns. With offices in Prescott, Ontario, as well as Holland, Louet

Swatch knit from Lopi yarn

promotes high-quality natural fibers and unique blends. The company also has a strong emphasis on top-notch customer service. Attention is given to every small detail in the creation of its pattern designs. Louet currently carries various yarn kits, patterns, specialty items and natural yarns. The company was originally founded by Trudy Van Stralen, who learned fibercraft as a child in Holland and operated a retail shop in the 1970s and 1980s. She then launched Louet Sales in 1989 as a spinning and weaving distribution company, which later evolved to supply industry items such as spinning fibers, weaving yarns and dyes. The company began to expand when Trudy's son David Van Stralen joined the operation in 1994. He acquired Euroflax and then developed the GEMS line of worsted yarn. Another interesting yarn line that Louet has distributed in the U.S. is its Nomad camel yarn, originally made by a group of Mongolian women and previously distributed to markets in China by anthropologist Nancy Shand.

LOWE, CATHERINE (1949-)

Knitwear designer, knitting instructor, author and lecturer Catherine Lowe is known for her refined knitting techniques that emphasize the principles and elements of haute couture. Lowe, also a professor of French, lives in upstate New York, where she runs workshops at her design studio. In her career, she extended the hand-knitting vocabulary by distinguishing between "knitting gauge" and "blocking gauge," and became known for her elegant construction and fineness of detail in garments. *The Ravell'd Sleeve/The Journal of The Couture Knitting Workshop* (Catherine Lowe, 2009) is a collection of issues from her well-known journal, uniting her previously published design concepts in a single work. Lowe's Couture Knitting Workshops include knitting retreats, and as a venture are the sole source for her design kits and the complete line of Catherine Lowe Couture Yarns and Notions. Lowe's designs have appeared in *Vogue Knitting* and *Interweave Knits* magazines, and she has also published articles in *Vogue Knitting*. She co-hosted the *Vogue Knitting* Tour of Northern Italy in 2003.

LP(S)

Abbreviation for *loop(s)*.

LYS

This acronym is an abbreviation for "local yarn shop." LYS owners pride themselves on offering a wide range of yarns and tools plus personalized service, assistance and instruction. No matter its size—shops range from one-room storefronts up to the 25,000-square-foot Webs in Northampton, Massachusetts—the twenty-first-century LYS is characterized by a welcoming atmosphere, wall-to-wall fiber, color saturation, plenty of sample garments and yarn swatches, a library of patterns and at least one comfortable spot to sit and knit. Classes, special events and regularly scheduled knitting circles are common. Many LYS owners custom-write patterns for their customers; incorporate locally produced, boutique or house fibers into their inventory; and offer lessons in spinning, felting, dyeing and other crafts that complement knitting and crocheting. Many also sell materials for other crafts, such as quilting and needlepoint. Popping up with increasing frequency is the combination LYS/café, a yarn shop that serves café food, coffee, tea and sometimes beer and wine. LYSes are in constant competition with online vendors, although many have become online stores themselves.
See also INTERNET

M

Abbreviation for *meter(s)*.

M1

Abbreviation for *make one*.
See also INCREASES; MAKE ONE

M1 P-ST

Abbreviation for *make one
purl stitch*.
See also INCREASES

MABLY, BRANDON (1968-)

Perhaps the most painterly fiber
artist never to have formally
studied art and design, Mably is a
designer/author/instructor who
learned on the job as apprentice
to the colorwork master Kaffe
Fassett. Mably, who had no art
training and no knitting or
needlepoint skills, asked Fassett
twice for a job—and was turned
down both times. On his third
request Fassett relented. More
than twenty years later, Mably
still serves as Fassett's studio
manager, although their
relationship has evolved
from mentor/apprentice to that
of equals.

Mably has been interested in
color and design since he was a
child growing up in a small town
on the coast of South Wales. He
has found inspiration in the
objects, architecture and
landscape he's encountered on his
world travels, both with Fassett
and as an acclaimed instructor in
his own right. "I love design that

has movement, which might
mean a wobble—not a strictly
regimented pattern," he explained
to *Rowan* magazine. Hence
intarsia that meanders like
Vietnamese steppes and chevrons
that take wing in a seagull-like
fashion. Mably has authored two
books, *Brilliant Knits* (Taunton,
2004) and *Knitting Color*
(Sixth&Spring Books, 2006), and is
a frequent contributor to *Rowan*
and *Vogue Knitting*. He's taught
extended color inspiration
workshops around the globe and
close to home, at London's
Wormwood Scrubs prison and in
local grade schools. "My job is to
encourage knitters to let go of
their fears," he told *Vogue Knitting*
in 2002. I want them to learn to
play, to be children again, to
make mistakes."
See also DESIGNERS; FASSETT,
KAFFE; ROWAN DESIGN STUDIO

MACHINE KNITTING

A knitting machine is an
apparatus for mechanically
creating knit fabric. It consists of
a row of about 200 needles set
into a needle bed, and a traveling
carriage (sometimes called a cam
box) that is pushed along the row
of needles. The needles, in
contrast to the straight needles
used in handknitting, have a
hook and a locking latch at their
tips. As the carriage passes, the
hook catches the yarn, creating a
stitch, and the latch allows the

new stitch to slip off the needle.
With each pass of the carriage,
an entire row of stitches is
produced.

The modern knitting machine is
the descendent of the knitting
frame, invented in 1589 by
England's William Lee to rapidly
produce silk stockings. For
economic reasons, the frames
were not widely used until the
second half of the eighteenth
century, when variations were
developed to create ribbed
knitting, lace and color changes. In
1867, Isaac Lamb of
Massachussetts introduced the
first modern knitting machine; the
Lamb Knitting Machine
Corporation still manufactures
knitting machines today.

Since this time, knitting
machines have evolved. Lamb's
was a *single-bed* machine that
produced only knit stitches; soon
after, a double-bed machine was
introduced to create purl stitches
and ribbed fabrics. Circular
machines that knit tubes of fabric
instead of flat pieces also became
available not long after the Lamb
machine.

Knitting machines make it easy
to produce multicolored and
textured knits. The earliest
machines required the user to
manipulate the needles by hand;
eventually punch cards were
created to guide the needles.
Today's machines use computer
processors to produce complicated

patterns and are usually designed
to knit a specific weight of yarn:
standard-bed machines knit
laceweight to fingering yarns; mid-
gauge models knit worsted
weight; and chunky models make
fabric from bulky yarns.
See also BRITISH KNITTING;
CARON

**MAGAZINES AND
JOURNALS**

Knitting magazines and journals
deliver dozens of patterns,
technical advice, trend reports,
yarn-industry news, designer
profiles and other feature articles
to knitters on a seasonal basis in
traditional print-periodical format.
Prior to the advent of the Internet,
magazines were handknitters'
main source of current patterns
and crafting news, offering more
updated information than knitting
books could. For much of the
twentieth century, mainstream
magazines such as *McCall's,
Woman's Day* and *Ladies' Home
Journal* included knitting and
crochet patterns and tutorials, but
phased out these features by the
end of the 1980s. Today, knitting
and crochet magazines are niche
publications devoted solely to the
fiber arts.

Knitting magazines arose in the
late nineteenth century in England
and America as part of the new
magazine industry. Early
newsletters dedicated to the
needlearts were put out by

patternmaking companies, who were themselves a fairly new industry. Weldon, a London, England, pattern printer, introduced its short "Practical" series, such as *Weldon's Practical Knitter* and *Weldon's Practical Crochet,* and consolidated them in 1888 into the iconic *Weldon's Practical Needlework.* During the same decade, *McCall's Magazine* was being developed in America to propagate sewing patterns and fashion advice; *McCall's* remained a popular magazine throughout the twentieth century before ceasing publication in 2002, and its special publications of *McCall's Needlework & Crafts* brought knitting and crochet patterns home to American women. In the 1980s, the Simplicity pattern company published *Knitting With Simplicity,* capitalizing on the sweater-knitting boom in that decade. *Family Circle Easy Knitting* was a pattern publication from a mainstream women's magazine.

Vogue Knitting is a quarterly with a history that dates back to the 1930s; it features runway-inspired and classic patterns in a fashion-forward context and has been helmed by knitting luminaries like Nancy J. Thomas and Trisha Malcolm; the magazine offers patterns by Seventh Avenue designers alongside those of famed knitwear designers. *Interweave Knits* was launched in 1997 by the

Loveland, Colorado–based Interweave Press and is now a popular quarterly known for wearable designs. The magazine takes a synergistic approach to the Internet, reinforcing its print efforts with plenty of online support. *Knitter's* magazine offers stylish, casual patterns; excellent diagrams, clear instructions and its School for Knitters section make it a very accessible read. Publisher XRX is the force behind the well-loved and well-attended Stitches events. *Knit 'n Style* and *Creative Knitting* are magazines with easy, generally mainstream patterns, as is *Knit Simple,* a colorful quarterly packed with workshops and tips to help develop skills in knitters with busy lives.

Knit.1 and *Knitscene* are periodicals put out by *Vogue Knitting* and *Interweave,* respectively, that offer patterns with a more edgy, youth-oriented look. A newcomer to the magazine scene is the *Debbie Bliss Knitting Magazine,* a biannual spotlighting the designer Bliss's distinctive patterns and yarns.

Cast On is the official publication of the Knitting Guild of America. The quarterly features patterns, technical articles and guild news and events. *Wild Fibers,* edited by Linda Cortright, is a quarterly that has been dubbed the *National Geographic* of the fiber world. *Yarn Market News* is a trade publication

available to designers, retailers and yarn companies five times a year. *See also* CAST ON (MAGAZINE); DESIGNERS; INTERNET; *INTERWEAVE KNITS;* MAGAZINES AND JOURNALS (U.K.); *MCCALL'S NEEDLEWORK & CRAFTS; KNITTER'S* (MAGAZINE); KNITTING CAMPS AND RETREATS; KNITTING GUILD ASSOCIATION, THE (TKGA); *KNITTY.COM;* STITCHES; *VOGUE KNITTING; WELDON'S PRACTICAL NEEDLEWORK; YARN MARKET NEWS*

MAGAZINES AND JOURNALS (U.K.)

There is a variety of magazines published in the U.K. for the hand knitter, and they differ in general feel from publications for American knitters. British knitting magazines tend to be published monthly, or even weekly, as opposed to quarterly, as their U.S. counterparts often are. British knitting publications tend to present more of a teeming, festive, reader-service atmosphere than do American knitting magazines (which are often heavy on fashion photography, with accompanying text contained in a disciplined way, and with articles delineated from project content). U.K. magazines often arrive in subscribers' mailboxes packaged with bonus gifts (how-to DVDs, needle sets, yarn caddies), and their pages brim with cash prizes,

yarn giveaways, and often with contests.

Simply Knitting, from Future Publishing, is a popular publication with the feel of a homemaker's weekly. Its thirteen yearly issues include ever-in-demand Alan Dart toy patterns, many competitions and giveaways; crosswords and sudoku; and its projects are family-oriented. In contrast, *Let's Knit* is a new magazine from Aceville Publications, billing itself "the U.K.'s Brightest Knitting Magazine"; its patterns are bright and cheery, aimed at younger knitters. *The Art of Knitting* is a weekly publication from Hachette emphasizing learning to knit in step-by-step photo essays; part of the fun of collecting this series is filling up the accompanying binders with issues as you go along.

Knitting magazine, the first to be published, is a more polished monthly from the Guild of Master Craftsmen that bills itself a general-interest read for knitters of all levels, yet presents grist for the serious knitter, with an international perspective and high-end designers. The magazine also sponsors National Knitting Week in October every year. *Knit Today,* from Origin Publishing with thirteen issues a year, contains sophisticated patterns and puts the emphasis on being informative; it offers knitting news,

buying guides, prizes and expert advice.
See also MAGAZINES AND JOURNALS

MAGIC LOOP

The magic loop is a technique for knitting socks and other small circumferences in the round using a very long circular needle, instead of double-pointed needles. The technique was published in a booklet by Fiber Trends, from which the name magic loop probably originates. For this technique, it's best to use a circular needle with a thin, flexible cable that is approximately three to four times the circumference of the knitting. Cast on the necessary number of stitches and push them onto the cable. Find the midway point of the stitches, pull the cable through to form a loop and slide the stitches onto the needles. With the active yarn on the right side, pull the right needle through and

Stitches cast on for magic loop technique

knit the stitches on the left needle. Turn the knitting around, pull the right needle through and knit the other half of the stitches. Continue in this way to knit in the round.

MAKE ONE

The make one increase is made between two stitches and is practically invisible.
See also INCREASES

MAKING UP

See FINISHING TECHNIQUES

MANNING, TARA JON

See CAMPS AND RETREATS; HEALTH BENEFITS OF KNITTING

MANOS DEL URUGUAY

Whenever yarn shops are asked to name their bestselling lines, "Manos" always seems to come up on the list, despite the company's relatively subdued presence in the advertising and marketing forums of the knitting world. But unmistakably, this cooperative of over 800 women in the rural areas of Uruguay supplies silk, Corriedale and merino blends that handknitters find they cannot do without. Founded in 1968 to promote social and economic development through traditional handicrafts, Manos produces and supplies handspun and hand-dyed yarns to customers worldwide, including such major designers as Ralph Lauren, Benetton and DKNY. All yarns produced by Manos are made using all-natural fibers

Make One

This version of the make one increase slants to the right on the knit side. (To knit an increase that slants to the left, insert the left needle from the front to the back and knit it through the back loop instead.)

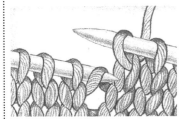

1. Insert the left needle from back to front into the horizontal strand between the last stitch worked and the next stitch on the left needle.

2. Knit this strand through the front loop to twist the stitch.

3. To make the increase on the purl side, insert the left needle from back to front into the horizontal strand and purl it through the front loop.

sourced in South America. Artesano, Ltd., is the distributor for Manos to the United Kingdom, the Republic of Ireland, Germany, Sweden, Denmark, Norway and Finland, while Fairmount Fibers distributes Manos in the U.S. Manos del Uruguay has also been admitted as a full member of the World Fair Trade Organization, recognizing Manos's mission to eradicate poverty through reinvestment in artisans, farmers and producer communities. But ask the average knitter why he or she demands Manos yarn, and the answer is just as likely to be "its stunning colors and texture" as "its social mission."

MAPSTONE, PRUDENCE

See FREEFORM KNITTING/ CROCHET

MARKER

Usually called a stitch marker, a marker is a small ring or coil used to mark the beginning or end of the round, where knitting increases or decreases occur, or to delineate the beginning and ending of a stitch pattern. Markers can be metal, plastic or even a loop of yarn in a contrasting color, a paper clip or a safety pin. Most commercially available markers are plastic and come in a wide variety of colors and shapes. They are slipped from needle to needle along with the stitches—they do not intertwine with the yarn at all—so they should be smooth so as to not snag the work.

Handmade stitch markers often feature beads or other decorative elements attached to the ring. A split-ring type can be attached right to the knitting and is crucial in crochet, where marking a particular stitch is necessary.
See also NOTIONS

MARYLAND SHEEP AND WOOL FESTIVAL

See SHEEP AND WOOL FESTIVALS

MASON-DIXON KNITTING

This popular North/South knitting blog, in which New Yorker Kay Gardiner and Nashvillite Ann Shayne chronicle their knitting and family lives through convivial "letters" to one another, was at the forefront of the online knitting community. Later they would pen two books together. After meeting virtually on the Rowan Yarns message boards in May 2002 and striking up a correspondence, the two women began the joint blog in July 2003 before they'd even spoken on the phone, much less met face to face. "Although it now

seems inevitable, I still wonder how I could find such a kindred spirit at the other end of the DSL connection," Gardiner told *VenusZine* online magazine in 2006.

"It was a peculiar thing to write a book together in such a long-distance, no-contact way, but I never doubted the fact that it would work out well," Shayne says. *Mason-Dixon Knitting: The Curious Knitters' Guide* (Potter Craft, 2006), their first book, did indeed work out well, striking a chord with its light-comic touches, down-home knitting advice and thirty patterns.
See also DESIGNERS; INTERNET

MASSACHUSETTS SHEEP AND WOOL FESTIVAL

See SHEEP AND WOOL FESTIVALS

MASTER KNITTING PROGRAM

The Knitting Guild Association (TKGA) has at its core a "noncompetitive achievement

program" for advanced knitters. Established in 1987, the evaluated correspondence course culminates in the awarding of the TKGA Master Knitter title and pin. While it is not a certification program, completion indicates that a Master Knitter is well versed in the mechanics and techniques of knitting, can write competently about knitting and can properly prepare designs for submission to publications and yarn companies. Well-known designers such as Ann Budd count themselves among the Master Knitter ranks, but most title holders are knitting enthusiasts who do not work in the industry. From October 2001 through November 2006, the first time period in which TKGA collected data about the program, 1,027 candidates submitted materials, with 787 becoming Master Knitters.

Prospective Master Knitters choose to enroll in one of three program categories: handknitting, machine knitting, or Passap machine knitting. The first two are three-level courses of study; Passap machine knitting entails only two levels. Working at their own pace, participants must successfully complete each level, which progress from beginner to intermediate to advanced, before going on to the next. At each level, candidates knit swatches and garments from written instructions, prepare a research notebook and write reports, all of which are evaluated by members

of the Master Knitter committee. The level number corresponds to the number of committee members who review submitted work before it is sent for a final check to a committee co-chair (for example, Level I candidates are evaluated by one member, while Level III knitters are scrutinized by three). The committee often returns submissions to candidates for rework with "constructive suggestions for improvement." The syllabus for the Hand Knitting program includes:
• Level I: Sixteen knitted samples—three swatches each of ribbing, basic stitches and gauge; mirrored increases and decreases, yarn overs, cables and color changes; seventeen questions to research and answer; one hat; two-page report on blocking and care of knits
• Level II: Twenty-one knitted samples—seams, decreases, lace, cables, buttonholes and picked-up stitches; nineteen questions to research and answer; one traditional argyle sock; one Fair Isle mitten; one vest; four book reviews; two-page report on the history of knitting
• Level III: Eighteen knitted samples—invisible cast-on and bind-off, decreases, fancy stitch patterns, work from symbols, duplicate stitch; twelve questions to research and answer; self-designed and self-knit Aran sweater with at least three patterns, or Fair Isle/Scandinavian sweater with at least three colors

Markers come in various materials and can be plain or decorative.

or a nontraditional advanced design; self-designed and self-knit hat or cap that differs in technique from the sweater; two book reviews and two knitting magazine reviews; report on six fibers; report on Aran and Fair Isle traditions

TKGA supports Master Knitter candidates by including an "On Your Way to the Masters" reference article in every issue of the organization's quarterly magazine *Cast On*, as well as via a password-protected, members-only Masters section and forum on the TKGA website. There is a fee for each level of the program, to cover administrative expenses and shipping.

See also CAST ON (MAGAZINE) INTERNET; KNITTING GUILD ASSOCIATION (TKGA), THE

MATTRESS STITCH

This is a sewing technique used for seaming garments together. Also known as invisible vertical seaming or row to row seaming, it is best used for seaming stockinette stitch or reverse stockinette stitch. Mattress stitch is worked from the right side of the garment. It hides the uneven selvage stitches at the edges of the rows and creates an invisible seam. The technique is slightly different for stockinette, reverse stockinette and garter stitch.

See also FINISHING TECHNIQUES; SEAMING

Mattress Stitch on Garter Stitch

The finished vertical seam on garter stitch

Insert the yarn needle into the top loop on one side, then in the bottom loop of the corresponding stitch on the other side. Continue to alternate in this way.

Mattress Stitch on Reverse Stockinette Stitch

The finished vertical seam on reverse stockinette stitch

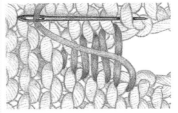

Working into the stitches inside the edge, insert the yarn needle into the top loop on one side, then in the bottom loop of the corresponding stitch on the other side. Continue to alternate in this way.

Mattress Stitch on Stockinette Stitch

The finished vertical seam on stockinette stitch

Insert the yarn needle under the horizontal bar between the first and second stitches. Insert the needle into the corresponding bar on the other piece. Continue alternating from side to side.

MAZZA, CAT

See GUERRILLA KNITTING

MC

Abbreviation for *main color.*

MCCALL'S NEEDLEWORK & CRAFTS

The McCall Pattern Company, founded in 1870, began in the 1880s to market its sewing patterns in a ladies' magazine alongside homemaking and handicraft information. The monthly magazine eventually evolved into the familiar *McCall's*, one of the so-called Seven Sisters, the seven major American ladies' magazines of the twentieth century (which included, for example, *Family Circle* and *Woman's Day*). The Seven Sisters all published supplemental periodicals called "special publications"; *McCall's Needlework & Crafts* was a special that thrived midcentury and offered patterns of high quality and diversity, in knitting, crochet, embroidery, weaving, rugmaking, decorating and other crafts. Many of the projects were visionary, and might include crocheted toys that would later come to be called amigurumi; fine embroidery mimicking historical styles such as Delft china and Colonial Williamsburg; or Native American and Peruvian-style sweaters. Knitters who can locate issues today will find them packed with inspiration.

See also MAGAZINES AND JOURNALS

MEASUREMENTS

Whether you're designing your own garments or following a pattern, good fit starts with an accurate set of body measurements—and a good tape measure. If you are designing for yourself, you'll get a more accurate read if you enlist the help of a friend. Hold the tape snug (but not tight) as you measure and record the following:

Bust (1)

This is the single most important measurement you'll take, as it's the starting point for determining how much ease to allow in the sweater and is often the focal point of the design. Measure around the fullest part of the chest, and don't let the tape slide down your back.

Waist (2)

This measurement will help you determine the overall shape and silhouette of the garment. To find your true natural waistline, tie a piece of string or elastic around your middle and let it fall. Where it settles is where you should take your waist measurement.

Hips (3)

This measurement is essential for skirts, long sweaters and dresses and, like the waist measurement, will help you determine the overall look of the garment. Measure your hips at their widest point below the waist.

Shoulder to Underarm (4)

Measure from the top of the shoulder to the underarm. This gives you the depth of the armhole.

Upper Arm (5)

Most sweaters allow for plenty of room in this area, but if you are creating a very fitted garment it's important to get this measurement right. Measure around your arm at the widest point.

Back Neck to Waist (6)

Measure from the bone at the base of your neck to the waist. This will help you determine the sweater's length. If you are creating a sweater that will fall below the hips, measure from the waist to where you want the lower edge of the sweater to hit and add that amount to the back neck to waist measurement.

Crossback (7)

The crossback encompasses your shoulder and neck width and is a must for sweaters with set-in sleeves. Measure across the back from the tip of one shoulder to the other.

Center Back Neck to Wrist (8)

With the arm extended, measure from the center bone at the back of the neck to the wrist bone, or to the point where you want the sleeve to end. This will be used to determine the length of your finished sleeve.

Wrist to Underarm (9)

With the elbow slightly bent, measure from the wrist bone along the underside of your arm to approximately one inch before the underarm. This measurement will help you determine the length for set-in sleeves.

See also BODY FIT; DESIGN; EASE

MEE, CORNELIA

See BRITISH KNITTING

MEMORIAL FUND FOR KNITTERS

See KNITTING GUILD ASSOCIATION, THE (TKGA)

Measurements

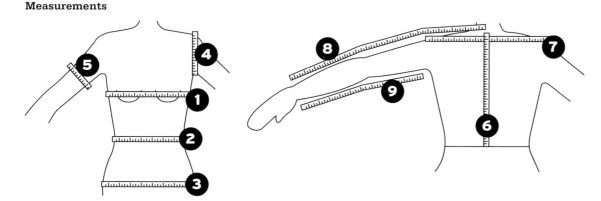

Key measurements to take when knitting a garment

MERINO

The oldest and most prevalent wool-producing breed of sheep, merinos possess a soft, fine, long-staple fiber and are recognizable by the characteristic folds in their skin. Descended from a strain originally bred by the Beni Merines, a nomadic group from North Africa, merinos settled in Spain during Roman times. Merinos thrived in the high altitudes of southern Spain; for many centuries the Spanish Armada guarded the breed, allowing none of the valuable animals to leave the country.

By the 1700s many people actually believed that the merino could thrive only in Spain. When King Phillip V, who shared this belief, began exporting the sheep as gifts to crowned heads throughout Europe, its falsity was soon proved. By early in the next century, breeding stock existed in many European countries. Today most merino sheep live in Australia. The origin of the Australian merino came when Elizabeth I brought some merinos to England, essentially starting the English wool industry there. British colonists began to bring sheep with them to South Africa, New Zealand and Australia, sold by mistake as meat sheep. An early settler in Australia, Captain John Macarther, recognized the worth of these particular sheep, purchased them and began a huge sheep-raising and breeding industry. By the mid-1800s, the sheep were so important to the

Australian merino sheep

Australian economy and society that landed gentry were referred to as "pure merinos." Today Australia is the largest producer of merino wool, with the population of sheep outnumbering that of people. Much of the finest merino is exported to Italy, where it is spun, largely for use in the commercial textile industry.

The fineness or coarseness of wool is determined by the diameter of the fibers, measured in microns (a micron equals one millionth of a meter or one thousandth of a millimeter). The lower the micron count, the finer the fiber. The best merino wool averages 20 microns or less; as a comparison, a sheet of paper is approximately 100 microns thick, and ordinary wools may have fibers as coarse as 30 to 35 microns.

Merino wool is also distin-guished by its tight crimp, or curl. This characteristic makes merino elastic and also contributes to its loft and softness. Merino sheep come in a variety of natural colors, from pure white to darkest brown. *See also* FIBER CHARACTERISTICS; SHEEP; STAPLE; WOOL

MICHIGAN FIBER FESTIVAL

See SHEEP AND WOOL FESTIVALS

MILLS

In reference to hand-knitting yarn, a mill is a facility where fibers are cleaned, carded (or combed into alignment), spun into yarn and/or dyed. A mill may perform just one or any combination of these processes on any given fiber, then deliver the product to another mill for the next step in a chain of events orchestrated by the

manufacturer who will ultimately label and market the yarn as its own. Milling is now a very global operation, and it is typical for yarns to be produced from components from entirely different parts of the world; for example, wool harvested in New Zealand might be spun into a blend in Italy with alpaca sourced from South America. The blend may then be imported by an American manufacturer who packages it as hand-knitting yarn. Among the various operations mills can perform on fiber while turning it into yarn are choosing different lengths of staple, spinning fiber into various numbers of plies, adjusting the tightness and direction of the twist, varying the texture into bouclés, tapes, ribbons, slubbed yarns and others, and adding components such as fringe.

North American mills had their heyday in the nineteenth century in the northeastern United States, where they were built along rivers to harness steam power. Stanley Woolen Mills and Capron Mill, both in Uxbridge, Massachusetts, were examples of river-town mills that throve for many decades under different incarnations, ultimately shutting down in the late twentieth century when production moved overseas. These two businesses still exist as the major hand-knitting yarn manufacturers Berroco and Bernat, respectively. Currently, there are few large spinning mills in North America: Briggs & Little, Canada's oldest woolen mill, still produces yarn in New Brunswick, and Brown Sheep Company of Nebraska is a relatively new large mill founded in 1980 on the "buy American" ethos. Throughout the first decade of the twenty-first century, however, North America saw a resurgence of small-scale mills (or microspinneries) capitalizing on consumers' interest in supporting independent, local producers and eliminating the carbon footprint of global shipping. *See also* BERNAT; BROWN SHEEP; SPINNING; YARN

MINDFUL KNITTING

See CAMPS AND RETREATS

MITERED KNITTING

This knitting technique shapes a corner by means of a series of decreases. Shaped corners, often used on borders or necklines, are knit by decreasing (or, less often, increasing) to form an angle to the original edge. Blankets made up of small mitered squares are common.

The basic unit in mitered knitting is a module formed with a series of decreases. You can knit a simple mitered square using a similar series of decreases. Squares like this can be combined in numerous ways to create easy-to-make but deceptively complicated-looking afghans, pillows and garments, such as shawls and capes.
See also BORDERS; MODULAR KNITTING; SCHULZ, HORST

MITERED SQUARE

See MITERED KNITTING

MITTENS

Coverings for the hand enclosing the four fingers together and the thumb separately, mittens seem to have originated in the cold territories of Northern Europe, and examples dating from the eleventh century have been found in Estonia, Finland and Latvia. They can be knit in the round or worked flat and seamed at the side and are popular for both children and adults. Mittens are often canvases for Fair Isle designs and other colorwork, which is often quite elaborate, especially in folk knitting traditions. Fingerless mittens are a popular variation.
See also BALTIC KNITTING; GLOVES

MM

Abbreviation for *millimeter(s)*.

MODULAR KNITTING

The combination of "modules," shapes such as squares, diamonds, triangles or hexagons, to form garments or other knitted items is known as modular knitting. Each small shape is crafted through a series of decreases. The shapes are then sewn, knitted or crocheted together to form the finished garment. Modular knitting is also known as domino or patchwork knitting.
See also DECREASES; GAUGHAN, NORAH; MITERED KNITTING; SCHULZ, HORST

MÖBIUS STRIP

A Möbius strip is an object with a single, continuous side and a single edge, essentially a loop with a half-twist in it; it is named after August Ferdinand Möbius, the German mathematician who discovered it. A scarf may be knit in this form, as popularized by Elizabeth Zimmermann. To knit a seamless Möbius strip on circular needles, make a half-twist and knit into the bottom of the stitches after casting on and joining the ends. These stitches stay on the needle, so that the needle loops twice through the stitches. When the row is complete there will be twice as many stitches as were cast on; knit these normally in a reversible stitch pattern.

MOHAIR

The fiber from the angora goat is called mohair. Native to Ankara, Turkey, the word means "best fleece" in Arabic. The long-staple fiber is wavy and lustrous, and its softness varies depending on the age of the goat, the first shearing, which is called kid, being the softest. About half of the world's mohair is grown in South Africa;

Mitered square

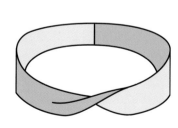

Möbius strip

Swatch knit in mohair yarn

Angora goats are the source of mohair fiber.

Designing With Polygons

by Norah Gaughan

While planning and then writing *Knitting Nature*, I became totally enthralled with building sweaters from hexagons and pentagons.

It started out innocently enough, with pentagons forming a nice yoke, or a string of hexagons adorning the front edges and collar of a sweater coat—polygons as decoration. Then I started thinking about forming whole garments from polygonal pieces. For example, hexagons fit, or tile, together neatly to cover a flat surface beautifully. Most of the sweaters I design are made of flat pieces—a back, a front, sleeves. So I thought about that flat surface made of hexagons and wondered which pieces or sections I could make from polygons. For example, the bodice of the Russian coat shown here is one continuous piece carved from hexagons and triangles.

Then there are pentagons. When pentagons are placed side to side, with no spaces between them, they form a three-dimensional bubble. Turns out that's a pretty good start for a sweater shape too.

Those of you who like jigsaw puzzles, brain twisters or crossword puzzles know how addictive this kind of thing can be. After a while, I found it hard to design something not made from polygons. One of the most amazing things about these shapes is that all of them are actually made up of simple triangles—look closely at the hexagons in the Russian coat and you will see them. And these triangles are both easy to knit and extremely adaptable: simple lace or an ordinary cable repeated five or six times around, once in each triangle, appears richly complex. Only you will know how easy it was to execute.

My Russian coat, which features knitted polygons, appeared in the Holiday 2007 issue of *Vogue Knitting*.

The author of *Knitting Nature* (STC Craft, 2006), Norah Gaughan is currently the design director at Berroco Inc. Her designs appear frequently in *Vogue Knitting* and other major knitting magazines, and she blogs at blog.berroco.com.

Mohair South Africa (mohair.co.za) was formed to support and promote the mohair industry in South Africa. Texas is a large producer in the U.S.

Because it lacks elasticity, much mohair for handknitting is blended with other fibers such as nylon, silk and wool. It is usually brushed, creating a halo effect similar to angora, and when knit loosely produces a light, airy fabric. Mohair yarn comes in all yarn weights from lace to super bulky.
See also FIBER CHARACTERISTICS

MORENO, JILLIAN
See KNITTY.COM

MOSAIC PATTERNS
Mosaic is the term for knitting slip-stitch designs worked in two colors. No bobbins, stranding or changing colors mid-row are required for mosaic knitting; instead, color changes are made at the side edge of every other row. Mosaic patterns can be worked in stockinette, reverse stockinette or garter stitch. Only two colors are used to create the motif, and each color is used alone for two entire rows. The first stitch of the chart is the guide to which color will be worked on that row. The first and last stitch of every row are always worked, never slipped. Right-side rows are usually charted. For the wrong-side row, the stitches are slipped or worked exactly as they were in the preceding row.

The term "mosaic knitting" was coined by Barbara Walker in the 1960s, and a large number of patterns using the technique first appeared in her *Second Treasury of Knitting Patterns* (originally published by Scribner in 1970).
See also MULTICOLORED KNITTING; SLIP-STITCH PATTERNS; WALKER, BARBARA

MOSS STITCH
Often confused with seed stitch, moss stitch is a textured, checked pattern formed by combinations of knit and purl stitches. The names "moss stitch" and "seed stitch" are often used interchangeably to describe knit/purl patterns that form small checked fabrics. In some books and references, patterns that arise from alternate motifs of k1, p2 motifs are considered either moss stitch or seed stitch. In other books and references, moss stitch and double seed stitch describe the same pattern. In yet other references the names moss stitch and double seed stitch describe a pattern of repeated k2, p2 motifs.

Regardless of the exact number of knit and purl stitches in each motif, all these patterns are basically k1, p1 or k2, p2 ribbing that is broken on every row or on alternate rows. The stitches lie flat and do not curl, making them good for borders. They also are reversible. The swatch shown here is knit over a multiple of 4 stitches:
Row 1 (RS) *K2, p2; rep from * to end.
Rows 2 and 3 *P2, k2; rep from * to end.
Row 4 *K2, p2; rep from * to end. Rep rows 1–4.
See also BORDERS; KNIT STITCH; PURL STITCH; SEED STITCH

MULTICOLOR KNITTING
Knitting done with two or more colors of yarn.
See also ARGYLE; CHANGING COLORS; INTARSIA; FAIR ISLE; MOSAIC KNITTING; SLIP-STITCH PATTERNS

MUSEUM OF ARTS AND DESIGN
This museum, located in New York City, focuses on many craft media, including fiber, clay, glass and wood. The museum's permanent collection houses more than 2,000 objects; special exhibits touch on many themes related to fiber and knitting, such as "Beyond the Fringe" (2005), "Radical Lace and Subversive Knitting" (2007) and "Pricked: Extreme Embroidery" (2007–2008).

MUSEUMS
See AMERICAN FOLK ART MUSEUM; BOHUSLAN MUSEUM; MUSEUM OF ARTS AND DESIGN; NATIONAL TEXTILE MUSEUM; TEXTILE MUSEUM OF CANADA; VICTORIA & ALBERT MUSEUM

Swatch knit in a mosaic pattern

Swatch knit in moss stitch

NÅLEBINDING

Also known as *naalbinding, naalebinding* and *nalbinding*, this technique for creating fabric predates both knitting and crochet. Nålebinding (also called "knotless knitting" or "single-needle knitting") is accomplished by forming a loop in a length of thread or yarn and using a needle to pull the thread through the loop. Left loose, the yarn forms a new loop. The needle is passed through the new loop, forming a chain. At the end of a row, the work may be turned, and each stitch passed through both its partner loop and a loop in the previous row. Unlike crochet, where the work is formed only of loops, nålebinding passes the full length of the working thread through each loop. The resulting fabric generally spirals up row by row and can be very elastic or quite stiff depending on the variation and material used.

The earliest known extant examples of nålbinding date from around 6500 B.C. and were found in a cave in the Israeli desert. Some of what were once believed to be early examples of knitted fabric were actually created with nålebinding.
See also HISTORY OF KNITTING

NAMP

See NEEDLE ARTS MENTORING PROGRAM

Nålebinding

1. To form the first row of stitches in nålebinding, loop the thread around your thumb and pull each new stitch through the previous one to form a chain.

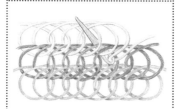

2. To form each new row of stitches, pass the thread through the stitch immediately below in the current row as well as through the previous stitch in the current row.

NATIONAL NEEDLEARTS ASSOCIATION, THE (TNNA)

This nonprofit trade organization was founded in 1974. TNNA represents wholesalers, manufacturers, distributors, designers, publishers and other players in the needlearts industry—not just knitting and crochet but also needlepoint, embroidery, cross-stitch and other such disciplines. Although membership is available to the trade only, TNNA maintains extensive consumer-outreach programs, including the series of Stitch 'N Pitch events held at major-league baseball parks throughout baseball season and its breast-cancer fundraising efforts Stitch to WIN Against Breast Cancer and One Pixel at a Time. The TNNA website points readers to local yarn shops and presents how-to information.

The biannual TNNA trade shows, which encompass a marketplace, a fashion show, an extensive class syllabus and retailer get-togethers—afford distributors and companies a venue to show their new wares at market and retailers the space to see and order potential inventory firsthand. TNNA publishes several industry booklets, including *Starting Out Right*, for those interested in opening a local yarn shop, and commissions annual State of the Needlearts surveys. Pathways into Professional Needlearts is the association's summer college internship program that places budding needlearts professionals in work-study positions at member companies or retailers and sponsors annual Student Design Competitions.
See also MAGAZINES AND JOURNALS; MASTER KNITTING PROGRAM

NATIONAL TEXTILE MUSEUM

This Washington, D.C.–based museum has significant holdings in textiles from around the world. Founded in 1925, the museum began with an impressive collection of Oriental rugs and has since expanded to include textiles from the Far East, the Middle East and South America.
See also MUSEUMS

NATURALLY COLORED YARN

Yarn that has not been dyed is known as naturally colored. The pigments can come in a wide range of shades, depending on the type of fiber. Interest in naturally occurring shades has increased as a result of environmental concerns that the bleaching and dyeing of fibers, yarns and fabrics is harmful to the environment and may pose health threats to wearers of these fabrics.

While sheep produce various shades of wool, historically, sheep were prized for the whiteness of their fleece. Black sheep were traditionally undesirable aberrations, hence the negative connotation of the phrase "black sheep of the family." Shetland sheep are an exception to this rule—Shetland fleeces are prized for their wide range of naturally occurring shades, including grays, browns and blacks. Merino sheep occur in a wide range of natural colors, from nearly pure white to dark brown. Alpaca fleeces also occur in a wide range of tones.

Undyed cotton is off-white; pure white cotton is achieved by bleaching. In recent years growers have been experimenting with naturally pigmented cotton, now available in a small range of greens, tans and light browns and growing in popularity.
See also ALPACA FIBER; COTTON; FIBER CHARACTERISTICS; SHEEP

NEATBY, LUCY
See CAMPS AND RETREATS

NECK EDGING
Stitches or patterns worked along the edge of a neckline form the neck edging. Edgings can be used to cover raw edges or to flatten pieces that have a tendency to curl. They can also serve a purely decorative purpose, especially when worked in a lace pattern. Neckline edgings are usually picked up and knit with a smaller needle than that used for the body of the garment; crocheted edgings are also a popular finish.
See also COLLARS AND NECKBANDS; EDGINGS

NECKLINES/NECKBANDS
See COLLARS AND NECKBANDS; NECK EDGING; V-NECK SHAPING

NEEDLE ARTS MENTORING PROGRAM (NAMP)
This national initiative fosters community and grooms a new generation of needlecrafters by pairing qualified adults with children interested in learning to knit, crochet or needlepoint. Founded in the fall of 2002, NAMP grew out of a handful of after-school fiber-arts programs developed in the late 1990s for at-risk students in Seaside, Oregon, based on research findings that found young people are less likely to succumb to risky behaviors and substance abuse when their growth and achievements are encouraged by trusted adults. Spurred by their regional success, Bonnie Lively, a longtime independent yarn representative, and Marilyn North first began a regional program and then approached industry organizations to fund a broader program. In 2000, with backing from the National NeedleArts Association, the Craft Yarn Council of America and other guilds and fiber companies, the women set up the Helping Hands Foundation, Inc., the charitable, educational corporation that now administers NAMP and other TKGA programs.

As of May 2007, 140 volunteer mentoring programs were in place in twenty-nine states, catering to 3,600 children. Each of the programs run for six weeks; during that time, mentors and students meet in a group setting for one hour at various venues, from elementary schools to youth clubs to summer camps. NAMP advocates teaching small, easy-to-finish projects to young knitters and crocheters, suggesting the introduction of a charity angle by having students make 7-by-9-inch squares that can be sewn into afghans for Warm Up America!.

When a volunteer registers to be a NAMP mentor, Helping Hands either connects him or her with an existing volunteer coordinator in the area or provides tools to start a new chapter. The mentor commits to attending a two-hour training session, and to meeting with his or her student for one hour weekly during the six-week duration.
See also CHARITY KNITTING; CRAFT YARN COUNCIL; KNITTING GUILD ASSOCIATION, THE

Three shades of naturally colored yarn

Metal needle gauge made in England in the late 1800s

(TKGA); NATIONAL NEEDLEARTS
ASSOCIATION, THE (TNNA);
WARM-UP AMERICA!

NEEDLE GAUGE

A tool used to determine the size of a knitting needle, needle gauges often also have a stitch gauge component. Usually a small, flat, cardlike piece of metal or plastic, approximately 3 by 5 inches, a needle gauge has a series of holes labeled to correspond with needle sizes. While most straight needles have the size clearly indicated on the end cap, the number can wear off with frequent use, and circulars and dpns are frequently unmarked.

To determine the size of a needle using the gauge, insert the needle into the round holes one by one until you find the hole into which the widest part of the needle fits smoothly but snugly. Bear in mind that there is some variance in sizing from different manufacturers; some needle gauges don't accommodate half sizes.
See also NOTIONS; STITCH GAUGE

NEEDLES, HOW TO HOLD

See AMERICAN/ENGLISH–STYLE KNITTING; CONTINENTAL/ GERMAN–STYLE KNITTING; KNIT STITCH; LEFT-HANDED KNITTING; PURL STITCH

NEEDLE SIZE

Though needles come in many lengths and configurations, to speak of "needle size" is primarily to discuss the diameter of the needle. Two measurement systems are in common use: American and metric. American sizing uses mostly whole numbers that correspond to a measurement in millimeters; metric sizing describes the needles based on the actual measurement. American sizing commonly ranges from 0 (2mm) to 15 (10mm), and certain novelty needles for very large-gauge yarns can range up to size 35 or more. In addition, lace needles can be found in sizes as fine as 0000. The size of the needle used for a particular project determines the gauge, and most yarns recommend a range of needles to achieve a certain gauge on the ball band. There is a proportionality to the pairing of needle size with yarn thickness; to stray from the natural combinations will yield a different fabric, whether more open or more dense. Swatching will help to determine the best needle size for a given yarn and project.

Needle lengths vary, too, and are sized in inches or centimeters. The most common lengths for straight needles are 10 and 14 inches (25 and 36cm); for double-pointed needles (dpns), common lengths are 5, 7 and 10 inches (12, 18 and 25cm); circular needles commonly come in 16-, 24- and 36-inch (40, 60 and 90cm) lengths, although other lengths as small as 12 inches (30cm) and as large as 60 inches (150cm) are available. The length used is determined by the knitter's preference, or the requirements of a particular project. The cord of a circular needle can accommodate many more stitches than a straight needle, so large-scale projects are best suited to a circular needle.
See also CIRCULAR KNITTING; CIRCULAR NEEDLES; DOUBLE-POINTED NEEDLES; NEEDLE GAUGE; NEEDLE TYPES; YARN WEIGHT

NEEDLE TYPES

There are three main categories of knitting needle styles: straights, double-pointed needles (dpns) and circulars, each of which is best suited to certain types of knitting, or to a knitter's preference.

Straights, or single points, are the most basic type of needle; they have a sharp point on the working end and a knob or flat cap on the other to prevent stitches from falling off. Sold in pairs, they are best used for flat knitting and are often the type of needle people learn to knit with. Straight needles are most often used to knit sweater pieces, such as fronts or backs. They can be awkward to use, as the weight of the knitted fabric becomes cumbersome when it is all on one needle. Also, because they stick out to the side when in use, they are not ideal for use in tight spaces such as commuter trains or airplanes.

Double-pointed needles (dpns), with points on both ends, are sold in sets of four or five needles. Stitches sit on them in a rough approximation of a circle, using one fewer needle than came in the set; this extra needle is the one that is knit onto when knitting. They are typically used to knit small, tubular items such as socks, sleeves or hats.

Circular needles have points on both ends with short lengths of knitting needle, connected by a length of wire or tubing. They can be used to knit in the round or to knit flat pieces by working back and forth. For large flat items uch as afghans, a circular needle is much easier to use than a pair of flat needles, because the weight of the piece can rest

Needle Size Chart

U.S.	METRIC
0	2mm
1	2.25mm
2	2.75mm
3	3.25mm
4	3.5mm
5	3.75mm
6	4mm
7	4.5mm
8	5mm
9	5.5mm
10	6mm
10½	6.5mm
11	8mm
13	9mm
15	10mm
17	12.75mm
19	15mm
35	19mm

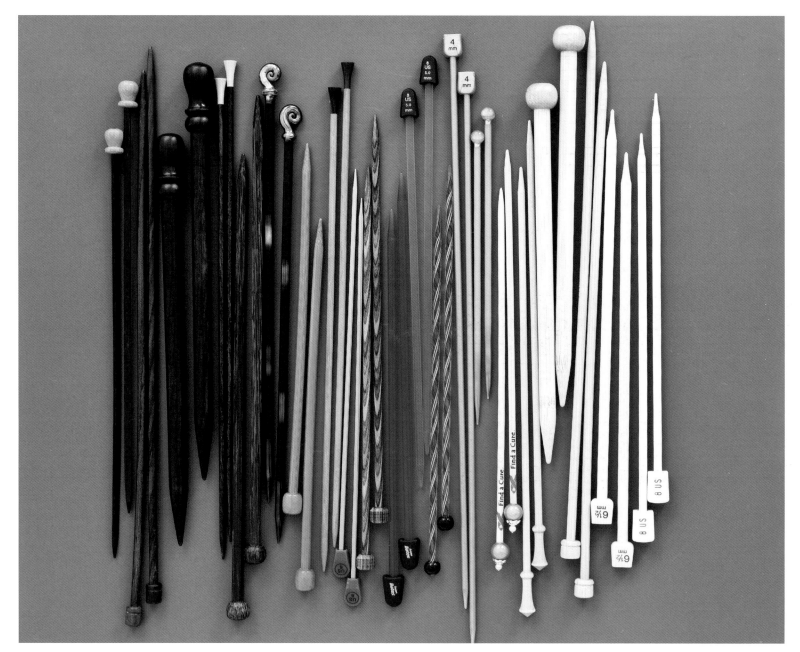

A variety of straight knitting needles demonstrates the wide range of sizes and materials available.

across the knitter's lap rather than falling to one side, and the cord can accommodate many more stitches.

Needles are available in many different materials: metal, plastic, many different types of wood, and even bone. The choice of material is more a question of the knitter's preference and current trends than the demands of a particular project. Each material has certain advantages and disadvantages. The quality of the tip is probably the most important feature—it should be smooth so it doesn't snag the yarn and sharp enough to easily pick up the yarn, but not so sharp that it splits the yarn.

Bamboo needles, first used in Asia, have become popular in the United States and Europe. Smooth, lightweight, quiet and aesthetically pleasing, they are made from a renewable resource and appeal to environmentally conscious knitters. Wood, like bamboo, has become an increasingly popular material for needles. With wooden needles, it is important to check the quality of the finish for smoothness and the strength of the wood itself. Wooden needles are warm to the touch. The wood "grips" the yarn more than a plastic or metal needle does, which is helpful for delicate work such as lace.

Bone needles, no longer manufactured, have become collectors' items. Many were made of whalebone, a formerly abundant byproduct of the whaling industry.

Metal needles, today usually made of aluminum, are widely available, lightweight and very smooth. They tend to make a clicking noise when knitting and can be cool to the touch. Steel, once popular for dpns, has largely been replaced by wood, bamboo, plastic and aluminum.

Plastic was, until recently along with aluminum, the modern material of choice for knitting needles. Inexpensive and widely available in a range of colors,

plastic needles are quieter and warmer to the touch than aluminum. They aren't quite as slick as metal needles.
See also CIRCULAR KNITTING; CIRCULAR NEEDLES; DOUBLE-POINTED NEEDLES; NEEDLE GAUGE; YARN WEIGHT

NETHERLANDS
See DUTCH KNITTING

NEWTON, DEBORAH (1953-)
This designer has repeatedly said that having her first published design, in a 1982 edition of *McCall's Needlework & Crafts*, photographed backward was a less than auspicious beginning. But the error may have augured innovations to come.

Newton grew up in Providence, Rhode Island, and majored in English at Rhode Island College, where after graduation she worked as a costume-design assistant in the theater department, learning design from the ground up, from sketch and fabric through realized garment. "The process itself becomes your teacher," she said in an interview with *Vogue Knitting*.

In 1980 Newton picked up needles again, after having learned to knit as a child. She began knitting fashion garments for herself. Two years later, after *McCall's* bought that first pattern, she embarked on a freelance design career. She knit intently, selling swatches to ready-to-wear

designers and picking up all she could from the masterworks of Barbara Walker and Elizabeth Zimmermann. The 1992 book *Designing Knitwear* (Taunton) sprang from her desire, she said in Melanie Falick's book *Knitting in America* (Artisan, 1996), to share with other knitters what trial and error had taught her about designing knitwear—from tangible issues of fit and silhouette, color and texture to more amorphous concepts such as finding inspiration and making sound choices. Ultimately, "a good sweater design is a marriage of fabric, technique and fashion," Newton told *Family Circle Easy Knitting*, where she also talked about her special affinity for lace and her love of finishing. "I never let anyone else do it. To me that's the end of the process and I want to be there. When a garment is all done, when it's perfect, it will never look that good again." Along with a full career in knitting, Newton remains part of her family business, working as a mapmaker for Maps for the Classroom in Providence, Rhode Island.
See also DESIGN; DESIGNERS; WALKER, BARBARA; ZIMMERMANN, ELIZABETH

NEW YORK STATE SHEEP AND WOOL FESTIVAL
See SHEEP AND WOOL FESTIVALS

NIAMATH, CHERYL
See KNITTY.COM

NICHOLAS, KRISTIN (1958-)
This prolific knitting designer and author lives a crafty life every bit as colorful as her vivid designs. "I try to get the colors to bounce off each other, to become more alive and kind of jump," she said in an interview with *Knit It!* magazine about her vivid colorwork with bright embroidery, bobbles, pompoms and other detailing.

Nicholas was eight when she combined her first two hues—yellow and orange—in a striped pocketbook she felt took too long to complete. So she abandoned the knitting needles until college, though she wielded an embroidery needle throughout her childhood. After earning a bachelor's of science in textiles and clothing design from the University of Delaware, she continued her education at Oregon State University, rediscovering knitting on a cross-country train trip to the East Coast with some hand-spun yarn she'd made and a copy of Elizabeth Zimmermann's *Knitting Without Tears*.

Nicholas served a stint in the New York textile industry and ran her own mail-order yarn and design business, Eden Trail, making sweaters from the wool sheared on the farm of her future husband's family. A desire to live closer to this farm eventually took

Nicholas to a small yarn mill in Massachusetts, whose handknitting division became Classic Elite Yarns. For sixteen years, from 1984 to 2000, Nicholas was Classic Elite's creative director.

During her tenure at Classic Elite, Nicholas was named a Master Knitter of the '90s by *Vogue Knitting*, kitted up her World Knits Collection (small projects with ethnic flair and mix-and-match yarn) and began writing and illustrating books (she is also an accomplished artist and painter). Her titles include *Color by Kristin* (Sixth&Spring Books, 2009), *Knitting the New Classics* (Sterling, 1995), *Knitting Today's Classics* (Lark, 1997), *Kids Embroidery* (Stewart, Tabori & Chang, 2004), *Colorful Stitchery* (Storey, 2005) and *Kristin Knits* (Storey, 2007); she also coauthored *Knitting for Baby* with Melanie Falick (STC, 2002) and illustrated Falick's *Kids Knitting* (Artisan, 1998).
See also CLASSIC ELITE; DESIGNERS; EMBROIDERY;

FALICK, MELANIE; ZIMMERMANN, ELIZABETH

NIDDY-NODDY

The simplest, most traditional type of yarn or skein winder, a niddy-noddy is used to wind yarn from bobbins or hand spindles into skeins (or hanks). Usually made from wood, though sometimes metal or plastic, a niddy-noddy consists of a central bar with crossbars offset from each other at both ends. These tools come in different sizes, and the length of the crossbar determines the length of the skein.
See also HANK; SKEIN

NONTRADITIONAL YARNS

In the 1990s and 2000s, hand knitters began seeking out hypoallergenic, ecologically friendly or simply more novel alternatives to wool, cotton, flax/linen and petroleum-based synthetics such as acrylic. A wide spectrum of nontraditional fibers is now available as a result.

Hardy, highly sustainable crops such as hemp and bamboo provide ideal garment fibers; nettles are also being spun into a comparable fiber. The category of "food fibers" is surprisingly diverse, tending to yield light, breathable yarns; included are fibers spun from soy, such as South West Trading's Soysilk; corn; seaweed, in SeaCell yarn; banana stalks; processed milk solids (casein); and sugarcane, a viscose fiber sloughed during sugarmaking. Animals are a source of nontraditional fibers: the Arctic muskox, yak, American buffalo, Andean vicuña and Mongolian camel all produce warm fibers appropriate for their native climates. Thin strips of beaver, fox, mink and muskrat fur are offered as yarn, usually used as trim; fur plucked from the pelts of New Zealand's populous opossums is being spun and exported around the world. Yarns are not limited to land animals: Chitin, a lofty, light fiber spun from ground shrimp and crab shells, is marketed for its soft hand and antibacterial properties.
See also BUFFALO FIBER; CAMELHAIR; QIVIUT; ORGANIC KNITTING; YAK FIBER

NORO

A Japanese producer of exquisite hand-painted luxury yarns, Eisaku Noro Ltd. is named for its founder

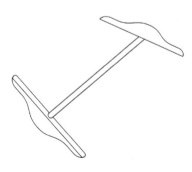

Niddy-noddy

A sampling of Noro's many vivid colorways

and chief designer. Noro's yarns earn almost religious devotion from handknitters the world over for their stained-glass multicolors, organic purity and sensuousness. The collection includes twenty-plus varieties incorporating silks, kid mohair, lamb's wool, ganpi paper, cotton, cashmere, alpaca, camel and angora, as well as felted fabrics. Eisaku Noro, who studied the textile arts, founded his company at age 30, calling his line "The World of Nature" (which is still printed on Noro labels today). He aimed for yarns with emotional impact, as well as all-organic materials; he adapted industrial carding and spinning machines to consume far less energy than the norm. In the 1980s Sion Elalouf's Knitting Fever Inc. became a major distributor of Noro in the U.S. and Europe. Today Noro operates from modest facilities in Ichinomiya in central Japan with a relatively small staff. He and his assistants continually design new dyes and yarns, maintaining an unrushed

creative process. All of the new yarns that go into production are still hand-painted in the traditional way. The company also does brisk business selling yarn and fabric to the fashion industry.

NORTH, MARILYN
See NEEDLE ARTS MENTORING PROGRAM

NORWEGIAN KNITTING
Gansey-style sweaters have been a part of the Norwegian knitting tradition since the mid-eighteenth century, but the precisely patterned color-stranded styles most of us associate with the region didn't begin appearing until about 1830. The sweaters were knit to a very firm gauge, a practice that both created a rich embroidered look and strong wind-resistant fabric ideally suited to the region's long, cold winters. The patterns themselves, stylized stars, flowers and geometrics, are probably German or Dutch in origin. Norwegian knits are likely the inspiration for Fair Isle and Faeroe designs.

The *luskofte*, or "lice," pattern is the most recognizable of the Norwegian styles. Originating around 1840 in the Setesdal Valley, it came to the attention of the rest of the world when it was chosen as the national ski sweater for the Olympic games of the 1930s. The sweaters traditionally begin with a section of white at the bottom followed by a wide band of black,

Norway is located in Northern Europe on the western edge of the Scandinavian Peninsula.

Sweater knit in the traditional Norwegian "lice" pattern

color-stranded stars, or flowers. The ground then changes to black crossed by several narrow bands of white geometric designs. This central ground is decorated with white flecks (the "lice" for which the sweater is named) and the shoulders are worked with elaborate bands of geometric designs. The upper and lower sleeves are decorated with similar bands with a ground of "lice" between. The cuffs and neckline are finished with embroidered felted fabric and the neckline usually closes with pewter clasps.

The Fana region developed a distinct style, a woman's cardigan knit in the round and cut open down the front of the sweater. The lower edge sports a checkerboard band followed by stripes of alternating colors with contrasting specks in each stripe. Nordic stars decorate the shoulders, upper arms and cuffs, while the sleeves repeat the body pattern of the sweater. The edges are usually bound and the cardigan closes with pewter clasps.

Another popular Norwegian style is the coastal jersey, which evolved around 1900. It uses a star design on the lower edge, shoulders and upper arms; the body is worked in an overall design, usually checkered. A two-color, twisted-purl cast-on is often used, and the neckline is cut and edged with woven fabric.
See also FAIR ISLE KNITTING; FOLK KNITTING; SETESDAL SOCKS; STEEKS

NOSTEPINNE

Also called a *nostepinde* or *nystepinne*, this tool is used to wind yarn into a center-pull ball. A *nostepinne* is basically a shaped stick of wood. To use it, begin by wrapping the yarn around it a few times, between the handle and the tapered part at the top. Holding the handle in your left hand (if you are right-handed), wrap the yarn around the nostepinne until you have about 1–2 inches (2.5–5cm) of parallel wraps. Now begin winding in an X pattern around

the nostepinne. Keep the tension even and not too tight, and turn the nostepinne to make it easier to wrap. When all the yarn is wrapped, slip the ball off the nostepinne. With a little practice, you will be able to wind very fast and to shape the center-pull ball to your preference: football shape, flat or round.
See also BALL; BALL WINDER

NOTIONS

Notions is the general term used in sewing and the needlearts to describe the peripheral items used for the craft including buttons, hooks, scissors, stitch holders, stitch markers, pins, tape measures and point protectors to keep knitting from sliding off the needles when not in use.
See also MARKER; NEEDLE GAUGE; PINS; STITCH GAUGE; STITCH HOLDER

NOVELTY YARN

Specially produced yarn that is not in a tight pile or standard strand is referred to as "novelty yarn."

Nonstandard shapes such as small ladders or even a strand with protruding, perpendicular strands (eyelash) are all novelty yarns. Even certain bouclé yarns can be considered novelty yarn. Working with novelty yarn is generally not as easy as with standard yarn; stitch definition is hard to discern and the yarns have a tendency to twist on themselves. Often they are held with a standard worsted-spun yarn to increase stability and yet still use the fun qualities of the novelty yarn. Novelty yarns are nearly always made out of a synthetic fiber that can hold up to the different processing they take.
See also BOUCLE; EYELASH YARN; FIBER CHARACTERISTICS; FUN FUR YARN; RIBBON YARN; YARN; YARN WEIGHT

Nostepinne

An assortment of knitting notions, including tape measures, yarn needles, scissors and point protectors

O

P

OFFINGER MANAGEMENT COMPANY

See KNITTING GUILD ASSOCIATION, THE (TKGA)

OKEY, SHANNON (1975-)

This designer is the consummate fiber-entrepreneur hyphenate: knitter-spinner-dyer-author-designer-publisher-knit blogger-retailer-instructor. "If you want to put out your own CD, put out your own CD; if you want to put out your own zine, put out your own zine," Okey told *Vogue Knitting* in 2007 about her take-charge business ethos. She paid homage to this in the title of her blog and in her first book, *Knitgrrl* (Watson-Guptill, 2005), a primer for tweens/teens that spawned a sequel, *Knitgrrl II* (Watson-Guptill, 2006), and, she said, taught young women to "make your own thing that reflects you as a person."

The daughter of artists, Okey began knitting "one scarf literally for years." In 2002, living in Boston, she visited the Cambridge LYS Mind's Eye Knitting and told owner Lucy Lee that she wanted to knit a cardigan. Instead of herding her into a typical beginner's project, Lee got her started knitting and, not long after, spinning.

Since that breakthrough book, Okey has coauthored *Spin to Knit* (Interweave, 2006), *Felt Frenzy* (with Heather Brack; Interweave, 2007), *Crochet Style* (Creative Homeowner, 2006), *Just Socks* and *Just Gifts* (both Potter Craft, 2007), *AlterNation* (with Alexandra Underhill; North Light, 2007), *The Pillow Book* (Chronicle, 2008), *How to Knit in the Woods* (Skipstone, 2008) and *Alt-Fiber* (Ten Speed Press, 2008). She founded and co-owns Stitch Cleveland, a studio/workshop space with educational and retail components, and she produces a call-in radio show/podcast, *The Knitgrrl Show*.
See also DESIGNERS; INTERNET

ONLINE RESOURCES
See INTERNET

OPENWORK PATTERNS
See EYELET PATTERNS, FAGGOTING, LACE STITCHES, YARN OVER

ORENBURG LACE

Exquisitely patterned Russian lace shawls made with ultrafine yarn traditionally spun from goat hair, the famed Orenburg lace shawls are often called "spiderweb" or "cobweb" shawls and date back to at least the seventeenth century. During the severe Russian winters, women wore these shawls every day, especially in the country. Each woman owned a minimum of two shawls: one for everyday wear and one for holidays. The shawls used for everyday wear are commonly plied with silk for strength to withstand daily use.

The shawls' designs (and the yarns used to create them) are of

Orenburg lace shawl, knit circa 1900

Modern-Day Wonders

By Amy R. Singer

You've probably seen strange food-related fibers on your local yarn shop's shelves. What the heck are soy, bamboo, corn and milk doing in yarn?

Actually, they're not just a marketing gimmick; these fibers are improving the knittability and wearability of handknitting yarns, especially nonwool yarns.

Most of the new knitting fibers owe their existence to the development of Lyocell (invented in 1992), an improved version of rayon. Lyocell is made by grinding cellulose fibers (wood, cotton) into a pulp that is processed with solvents into a gelatinous solution. This solution is extruded through a spinneret (a nozzle with tiny holes), and what comes out the other end is firmed up and spun into yarn. Modal (invented 1930) is another improved version of rayon using, specifically, beechwood. Some fibers are protein based (like soy or milk) or sugar based (like corn). All of these base fibers can be processed into yarn that's strong, soft, absorbent, breathable, drapey and wrinkle resistant.

One of the best things about these new fibers, beyond their coolness against the skin, is that many of them are kind to the environment. Soy fiber is made from the waste products of the tofu process. Chitin comes from shrimp and crab shells. Some fibers, such as bamboo, are made from plants that grow quickly without any fertilizers or pesticides. Some, such as corn, can be used in place of petroleum products. SeaCell fiber contains seaweed, and, says the company that created it, "the structure of SeaCell facilitates the active exchange of substances between the fiber and the skin—nutrients such as calcium, magnesium and vitamin E are released by the natural body moisture when the fiber is worn, thereby creating a complete sense of well-being." Wow. Meanwhile, from the jewelry aisle, pearl fiber was recently developed in China, and surprisingly soft jadeite fiber is available in a yarn blended with wool and silk. Wonders, they do not cease.

Amy R. Singer is the founder, editor and publisher of *Knitty.com*, which has had more than 45 million site visits since its launch in 2002. She has written four books: *Knit Wit* (HarperCollins, 2004), *Big Girl Knits*, cowritten with Jillian Moreno (Potter Craft, 2006), *No Sheep for You* (Interweave, 2007) and *More Big Girl Knits*, cowritten with Jillian Moreno (Potter Craft, 2008).

such a delicate quality that the entire shawl can be passed through a wedding ring. The yarn used in traditional designs comes from Ural Mountain goats, whose exceptionally soft and light down is combed out each winter to be hand-spun into yarn. The softer and finer the fiber, the more valuable the shawl. The shawls were historically made in the natural colors of the goats—white, gray or brown—and each knitter developed her unique pattern of lace and ornaments.

See also FOLK KNITTING; LACE KNITTING; SHETLAND LACE

ORGANIC KNITTING

The push to live a more "green" life is not exclusive to knitting. Organic knitting is a growing movement in line with society's burgeoning eco-consciousness in which you knit with yarn made from renewable fiber sources and/or produced by means of environmentally sound methods. Organic cotton is grown and harvested without being treated with toxic agrochemicals; organic wool comes from sheep fed only with organic feed and not sprayed with insecticides. Choosing local yarn leaves a smaller carbon footprint. Among the industry leaders in organic and all-natural wool and cotton are Blue Sky Alpacas, Green Mountain Spinnery and the Vermont Organic Fiber Company, which produces the O-Wool line of yarn.

Renewable and sustainable sources increasingly being tapped for fiber use include soy (introduced to knitters in 2001 in the South West Trading Company mainstay Soysilk), hemp, corn, bamboo, linen, nettle, recycled silk, chitin (shrimp and crab shells), banana fiber, pineapple ramie, kenaf and milk protein. *Knitty.com* editor Amy R. Singer delves into the attributes of many of these sources in *No Sheep for You* (Interweave, 2007), her book about knitting without wool. Recycled knitting—stitching with yarn from unraveled vintage sweaters, cut-up T-shirts or even plastic grocery bags cut into strips—also has its proponents.

See also FIBER CHARACTERISTICS; NONTRADITIONAL YARNS; SINGER, AMY R.; YARN SUBSTITUTION

OZ

Abbreviation for *ounce(s).*

P

Abbreviation for *purl.*
See also PURL STITCH

P1FB, P1F&B, PFB

Abbreviations for *purl into the front and back of a stitch.*
See also INCREASES

P2SSO

Abbreviation for *pass two slipped stitches over.*
See also DECREASES

P2TOG

Abbreviation for *purl two together.*
See also DECREASES

PADEN, SHIRLEY (1952-)

Shirley Paden is a teacher, hand knitwear designer and owner of Shirley Paden Custom Knits. She has been featured on HGTV and *Knitting Daily TV*, and her designs have appeared in *Interweave Knits, Interweave Crochet, Vogue Knitting, Family Circle* and *Knit It!* She is the author of *Knitwear Design Workshop* (Interweave Press, 2010), a print version of her popular "Knitwear Design" class, in which she teaches students to alter commercial patterns and design their own garments.

Besides being an expert in knitwear couture, colorwork, cables and finishing techniques, Paden is an internationally acclaimed master of lace knitting, and her articles on the topic have informed the readers of *Vogue Knitting* magazine, among others. Her designs are built with small-scale details and exquisite patterning, shaping up into refined silhouettes that reflect a classic, timeless urban sophistication.

PAIRED INCREASES AND DECREASES

See DECREASES; INCREASES; REVERSE SHAPING

PARKES, CLARA (1969-)

This author and website editor has made a career out of encouraging each and every knitter to become a "yarn whisperer," someone who can study a skein and intuit what it wants to become. She's well positioned to do this as the publisher of *Knitter's Review*, a weekly e-magazine that features exhaustive reviews of yarn, needles, books, yarn stores and trade shows, and as the author of *The Knitter's Book of Yarn: The Ultimate Guide to Choosing, Using and Enjoying Yarn* (Potter Craft, 2007) and *The Knitter's Book of Wool: The Ultimate Guide to Understanding, Using, and Loving This Most Fabulous Fiber* (Potter Craft, 2009). These books unspin fiber ply by ply and include patterns designed to maximize the attributes.

Taught to knit by her grandmother and taken to her first yarn shop at the age of eight, Parkes felt her passion for knitting exert greater pressure during the decade she worked in Silicon Valley as an editor at a high-tech magazine. In May 2000 she left California to move to her great-aunt's farmhouse in Blue Hill, Maine, which she renovated and from which she launched *Knitter's Review* that September, sending the first issue to seventy-four people. Readership exploded to nearly 35,000 within seven years.

Knitter's Review offers much more than just the newsletter; it encompasses a thriving message board and online boutique, and it

sponsors an annual fall retreat.
See also INTERNET; *KNITTER'S
REVIEW;* MAGAZINES AND
JOURNALS; WEBSITES

PASSAP MACHINE KNITTING

See MACHINE KNITTING;
MASTER KNITTING PROGRAM

PAT(S), PATT(S)

Abbreviations for *pattern(s)*.

PATCHWORK KNITTING

See MITERED KNITTING;
MODULAR KNITTING

PATONS

Patons Australia has a long history
and roots that extend back to 1920,
when two mill-owning
entrepreneurs, John Patons and J.
Baldwin, merged forces to form
Patons & Baldwin. With that
merger "Beehive Wool" was born, a
brand that grew into a handknitting empire of sorts in
Australia, New Zealand and
Canada. A new mill was built in
Tasmania in 1923, and another in
Toronto in 1931. For many
decades, Beehive Wool was the
knitting or crocheting housewife's
staple. But toward the end of the
twentieth century, hard times fell
on many textile mills as
manufacturing shifted to Asia, and
in 1996, out of necessity, Patons
merged with Alliance Textiles of
New Zealand. In the year 2000, the
company was rejuvenated when
the Australian Country Spinners
acquired Patons, creating Patons
Australia. The company is located

in Melbourne, and its operations
include a mill site in Wangaratta,
Victoria. In 1999 Patons gave
Spinrite the rights to the company
name and distribution in North
America, but in other parts of the
world, including Asia, Patons
Australia has exclusive marketing
rights. Some of Patons' more
unusual yarns are blends made
with bamboo, corn and soybean.

PATRICK, MARI LYNN (1951-)

Mari Lynn is a designer who is
living her childhood dream—
becoming a high-fashion knitwear
designer. She learned to knit at the
age of seven from her grandmother
and, after delving through copy
after copy of old *Vogue Knitting*
magazines at a friend's house,
began designing couture knitwear
for her younger sister's Barbie
dolls. (That sister is Carla Scott,
who herself has made a career as
an editor of knitting magazines.)

Patrick's first job was at the
American Thread Company, which
produced knitting books and
leaflets for a major chain store and
where she leaned the importance
of assiduous measuring, charting,
pattern-testing, pattern-checking
and writing, skills she later took to
the needlework company
Columbia Minerva. Patrick was
instrumental in the relaunch of
Vogue Knitting in 1982, designing
several sweaters and acting as the
issue's technical editor, even
though she was then living in
Turkey. She has continued
designing and writing for *VK* as

well as other knitting, crochet and
craft magazines, and she authored
Total Knitting Fashions (Leisure
Arts/MQ, 2005). "I never run out of
ideas; it's something in me," she
told *VK* in 2007. "It's like true love."
See also DESIGNERS; SCOTT,
CARLA

PATTERN

The written instructions for
knitting a garment or other item
are known as a pattern. Patterns
cover all aspects of knitting a
project, from the yarn and needles
required to the final seaming of the
knitted pieces. Style and format
vary from book to book, magazine
to magazine and manufacturer to
manufacturer, but most use the
same basic construction sequence
and standard terminology and
abbreviations. Patterns can be
made up of text only, diagrams
with labels only (a system that is
particularly popular in Japanese
patterns), or a combination. All the
elements will be defined (special
stitches; all symbols) somewhere
either within the pattern or, in the
case of a pattern book, in the book.
Often a specific combination of
stitches used within a pattern is
called the "stitch pattern," but the
catchall term "pattern" also applies
to the whole.

Read through the entire pattern
before you begin. This will help
you decide whether the pattern is
suited to your technical ability,
eliminate any surprises, and avoid
having to drop everything to look
up an unfamiliar term or
technique—or worse, start over. A

lot of information is contained in a
pattern, and the shorthand and
other tricks for condensing the
data may initially appear confusing
or like a different language.
Reading it over carefully is the
surest way to avoid mistakes. Look
for any special notes or materials
that you'll need to complete the
project, and circle or highlight the
information that pertains to your
size to aid you.
See also ABBREVIATIONS;
CHARTS; SCHEMATIC

PATTERN DESIGN

See DESIGN

PEARL-MCPHEE, STEPHANIE (1968-)

Best known as the Yarn Harlot,
the name she shares with the
enormously popular knit blog she
writes from her home in Toronto,
Canada, knitting humorist
Stephanie Pearl-McPhee was
taught to knit at the age of four by
her grandmother. Pearl-McPhee
began blogging and landed a
book deal in 2004. "I never met a
yarn I didn't like," she told *Yarn
Market News* in 2005, about the
genesis of the moniker Yarn
Harlot, a reference to her inability
to knit projects "monogamously."
She became a leader of the online
knitting community. As she told
the *Christian Science Monitor* in
2006, "Up until blogging, if you
knit a [bad] buttonhole you might
be stuck until you could get to a
knitting store. Now I can take a
picture of a buttonhole, put it up
online, and in 10 minutes I can

have someone from Atlanta writing to say, 'I did that last week. You need to do a yarn over.' I'm definitely a better knitter because of it."

Pearl-McPhee's vast readership, who log on to Yarn Harlot at the rate of 30,000 times a day, have bought her books with equal verve: Her bestsellers include *At Knit's End: Meditations for Women Who Knit Too Much* (Storey, 2005), *Yarn Harlot: The Secret Life of a Knitter* (Andrews McMeel, 2005), *Knitting Rules!* (Storey, 2006), *Stephanie Pearl-McPhee Casts Off: The Yarn Harlot's Guide to the Land of Knitting* (Storey, 2007) and *Things I Learned from Knitting (Whether I Wanted To or Not)* (Storey, 2008). On her extensive book tours, hundreds of knitters turn out to hear her read and speak about knitting activism. Pearl-McPhee spearheaded two of the major Internet community-knitting endeavors of the mid-2000s: the Knitting Olympics and Tricoteuses Sans Frontières. The Winter Olympics in 2006 saw more than 4,000 "knit-letes" cast on a personally challenging project during the opening ceremonies of the Torino Winter Games and attempt to finish it by the closing ceremonies. The tradition has continued through the subsequent Olympic games. Tricoteuses Sans Frontières (Knitters Without Borders) is a charity effort that, as of 2007, had netted more than $430,000 on behalf of Médècins Sans Frontières/Doctors Without Borders.
See also INTERNET

PENCE JUG

Small knitted pitchers used as change purses or to hold small items, pence jugs date back to at the latest the late 1700s, and patterns, or "recipes," for them were very popular during the Victorian age.
See also VICTORIAN KNITTING

PERUVIAN CAP

See ANDES REGION KNITTING; HATS

PHILLIPS, MARY WALKER (1923-2007)

A textile artist who bridged the gap between craft and art by elevating knitting to an art form, Phillips created large, abstract hangings using nontraditional materials such as tape, wire, bells and even seeds. Her work was exhibited worldwide and is part of the permanent collections of the Museum of Modern Art, the

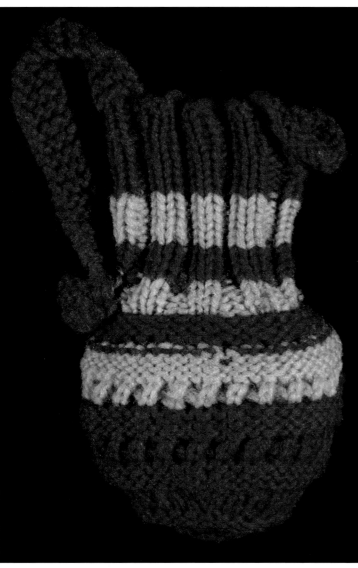

English pence jug from the mid-1800s

Phoney Seam

To create a phoney seam, drop a stitch all the way down the length of the garment (or as far as you want the phoney seam to extend) to create a ladder. Insert a crochet hook through the bottom stitch, catch the next 2 dropped stitches, and pull them through the first stitch, then pull one stitch through these 2. Repeat, alternating hooking one and 2 stitches, up the length of the garment.

Cooper-Hewitt National Design Museum and the Art Institute of Chicago. She was a fellow of the American Craft Council.

Phillips began as a weaver. She studied at the Cranbrook Academy of Art in Michigan and worked in San Francisco and Switzerland. She wove fabric for clothing and household items, including the draperies for Taliesin West, Frank Lloyd Wright's home in Arizona. When she turned to knitting in the 1960s, she created huge pieces that resembled tapestries or lacework and then enriched them with delicate lattices and textured patterns.

See also MUSEUMS

PHONEY SEAM

A phoney seam is a false seam added to a garment that has been knit in the round to create fold lines or to give the garment a more tailored look. Phoney seams are useful when knitting in stockinette or garter stitch, but are more difficult to incorporate successfully into garments with color or texture patterns.

See also LADDER

PICKING UP AND KNITTING

This instruction, sometimes given as simply "pick up," means to create a new stitch along the edge of a knitted piece and knit it.

See also PICKING UP STITCHES

Picking Up Stitches Along a Horizontal Edge

1. Insert the knitting needle into the center of the first stitch in the row below the bound-off edge. Wrap the yarn knitwise around the needle.

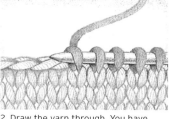

2. Draw the yarn through. You have picked up one stitch. Continue to pick up one stitch in each stitch along the bound-off edge.

Picking Up Stitches Along a Vertical Edge

1. Insert the knitting needle into the corner stitch of the first row, one stitch in from the side edge. Wrap the yarn around the needle knitwise.

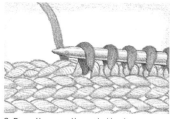

2. Draw the yarn through. You have picked up one stitch. Continue to pick up stitches along the edge. Occasionally skip one row to keep the edge from flaring.

Picking Up Stitches With a Crochet Hook

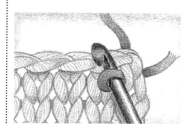

1. Insert the crochet hook from front to back into the center of the first stitch one row below the bound-off edge. Catch the yarn and pull a loop through.

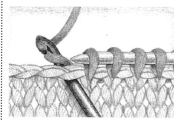

2. Slip the loop onto the knitting needle, being sure it is not twisted. Continue to pick up one stitch in each stitch along the bound-off edge.

PICKING UP STITCHES

To bring yarn through the fabric along the edge of a knitted piece in order to create new stitches is called picking up stitches. It is important to pick up stitches evenly to make a smooth join between the two sections and to prevent any puckering or gaps. The neatest and easiest method is to work from the right side of the garment and to knit each new stitch, using a new strand of yarn (often written as "pick up and knit"), rather than simply placing loops on the needle and working

them on the next row or round. Start at the right-hand edge of the piece. You can use a crochet hook or a knitting needle, but in either case, use a tool that is one or two sizes smaller than the size used for the body of the piece to prevent unsightly holes. Change to the correct needle size for the next round or row.

To pick up stitches evenly, place a marker (a strand of yarn, a stitch marker or a safety pin) every 2 inches (5cm) around the entire edge. Count the number of sections and divide that number

by the total number of stitches to be picked up. For example, if a neckline is 20 inches (50cm) around, and the instructions say to pick up 120 stitches, measure off ten 2-inch sections and pick up 12 stitches within each section.

If the instructions don't indicate the number of stitches to pick up, here is an easy rule of thumb: Pick up one stitch in every bound-off stitch, plus 2 stitches in every 3 rows (for medium- to bulky-weight yarns), or plus 3 stitches in every 4 rows (for lightweight yarns).

PICKING UP WRAPS

This is the method used in short-row shaping to hide the wraps formed in the construction of partially knit rows. It can be tricky to "pick up" a wrap in order to work it with the stitch it wraps, but through careful manipulation of the stitches—sometimes moving a stitch back and forth from the left to the right needle—it can be done. The wraps serve to "fill in" any potential gaps that could be created at the edge of a short row.

See also SHORT ROWS; SHORT-ROW SHAPING; WRAP AND TURN

PIERROT (1957-)

Pierrot is the knitting alias of French designer Pierre Carrilero, whose cheeky knits grace the frames of Hollywood stars, including Sarah Jessica Parker and Mimi Rogers. Born in Lyon, France, Carrilero started knitting at the age of nine, when a soccer accident kept him bedridden for a month. He continued knitting all through his years in the Paris punk movement, selling clothes to New York boutiques under the label Pierrot.

After moving to New York in the early 1990s, where he worked as a nanny and model, he again picked up the needles professionally, creating knitwear for designer Miguel Adrover before branching out on his own in a Fashion Week group show in 2000. His first solo show in 2001 was such a success that the Japanese group Onward Kashiyama licensed his designs and sold them to major department stores. His partner, stylist Eric Daman, introduced Carrilero to *Sex and the City* costume designer Patricia Field, who consistently used his clothes on that groundbreaking TV show. He also designed knitwear for movies and extended his clientele through his line for QVC, Voila by Pierrot, and his collection of wintry knits for Lion Brand Yarn. Carillero is unusual among designers in that he knits every stitch in his collection himself:

He's an extremely fast knitter who can finish a sweater in just over a day. "I'm not very technical or innovative," he told *Vogue Knitting*. "I just use a lot of imagination."

See also DESIGNERS

PINS

Small pieces of metal wire, pins are usually hardened brass or high-carbon steel coated with nickel or gilt. With their sharp edges, pins are perfectly suited to fasten fabrics together, and they are available in a variety of shapes and sizes. Steel wires are plated to strengthen them against rust and corrosion; brass wire will not rust. Straight pins are made of hardened metal wire, usually stainless steel, with a cylindrical, straight shaft, a flat or round head on one end, and a very sharp point at the other. They come in a variety of sizes and can be used to pin finer-gauge knits together in preparation for seaming. Many knitters prefer straight pins with colored plastic heads that are easier to see against the knitted fabric.

T-pins are larger and made of heavier-gauge metal than straight pins, which makes them more effective for pinning together bulky knitted garment pieces. They are also the best pins to use for blocking, because they hold garment pieces firmly in place. T-pins come in several sizes, the most common being 2 inches long.

Other types of pins include plastic basting pins, which can be used similarly to T-pins, and two-pronged pins that are ideal for working with pieces knit in bulky yarns.

See also BLOCKING; NOTIONS

PITA LACE

See AZORES LACE

PITTI FILATI

Pitti Filati is the yarn industry's premier international trade show, held biannually in the summer and winter in Florence, Italy. The exhibition emphasizes a couture viewpoint and serves as a showcase for all the major fashion-brand yarns, fibers and knitted fabrics, in every imaginable color, surface texture and blend. The event is sponsored and organized by Pitti Immagine, an Italian consortium promoting a range of fashion events from its headquarters in Florence's Palazzo Pitti. Pitti Filati is eagerly attended by fiber manufacturers, buyers and designers from the world over, not least because Italy is the historical center of textile spinning, and presents a lovely venue for attendees. During Pitti Filati there are countless product debuts, awards for competitions, presentations, couture shows, parties and other social events throughout the city and its environs.

PLACE MARKER

See MARKER

From left to right: Plastic basting pins, straight pins and two-pronged pins

PLACKET

A slit at a neckline is known as a placket. Usually a placket is knitted in either vertical or horizontal ribbing to make it lie flat. A placket may be worked with or without buttons and buttonholes.

See also COLLARS AND NECKBANDS

Horizontal Ribbed Placket

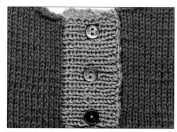

To work a horizontal placket, pick up stitches along the side edges and work to the depth of the placket width. Bind off evenly for a neat edge.

Vertical Ribbed Placket

To work a vertical placket, leave the stitches on a holder until the piece is complete. Pick up stitches behind the stitches on the holder.

Sew the side edges once the band is complete.

PLAIT

A cable that includes more than two strands that cross close together is called a plait. The words "plait" and "braid" are used interchangeably in knitting. Knitted plaits are common in Aran-style knitting and may contain three, four, five or more interlocking strands. Although they may look complex, they are all relatively simple to knit once you master the basics of cable knitting.

The plait shown below is knit over nine stitches and worked as follows:

6-st RC Sl 3 sts to cn and hold to back, k3, k3 from cn.
6-st LC Sl 3 sts to cn and hold to front, k3, k3 from cn.
Rows 1 and 5 (RS) Knit.
Row 2 and all WS rows Purl.
Row 3 6-st RC, k3.
Row 7 K3, 6-st LC.
Row 8 Purl.
Rep rows 1–8.

See also CABLE PATTERNS; CABLES

Swatch showing plait-style cable

PLEAT

Pleats are folds of even width made by folding fabric back on itself. Knitted pleats are best executed in stockinette or another plain stitch using a fine-weight yarn that will retain its shape. Pleats consist of three layers, each of which has the same number of stitches—the face, the fold-under and the underside. Each underside joins with the face of the next pleat, and slip stitches and purl stitches are used to define the folds. Where you place the purl stitch will determine whether the pleat folds to the left or to the right.

To determine the number of stitches to cast on for a pleated garment, multiply the stitches needed for one pleat (face, fold-under, underside, plus a slip stitch and a purl stitch) by the number of inches in the piece. To create the pleat, determine the desired width of the finished pleat and multiply by the stitch gauge.

See also EMBELLISHMENTS

Pleat

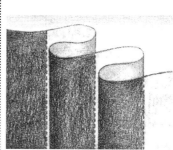

This illustration shows how the three layers of a pleat fit together. The face is shown in blue, the fold-under in dark gray, and the underside in light gray. All three sections have the same number of stitches. The underside of each pleat is continuous with the face of the next pleat.

The face (right) of a left-folding pleat is edged with a slip stitch that is purled on wrong-side rows. The fold-under portion (center) joins the underside (left) with a purl stitch. For a right-folding pleat, reverse the slip stitches and purl stitches.

PLY

Ply is another word for "strand." A yarn is described by how many plies are twisted together to form it. For example, two-ply yarn is made up of two single strands twisted together.
See also SPINNING

PLYMOUTH YARN CO.

In 1964 Richard W. Power, Sr., and two partners created Fidelity Fibres to process fibers for woolen and worsted spinning mills in the U.S. Soon afterward, the Plymouth Yarn Company was officially organized and set up in Bristol, Pennsylvania, to sell American-spun yarn on commission to mill-outlet and retail stores. Today, Plymouth has grown to employ over 60 people in its 50,000-square foot-facility in Bristol, and it prides itself on having provided yarns to independent shops for over 45 years. Today the company imports more than 90 percent of its product mix, and is the sole U.S. distributor for a variety of Italian brands, including Adriafil, Lane Cervinia and Le Fibre Nobili, as well as the Peruvian Indiecita alpaca yarns and the Australian lines Cleckheaton and Panda. Some of the Plymouth yarns that American knitters rely upon are Encore, Alpaca Grande, Galway, Dreambaby and Fantasy Naturale. Plymouth Yarn's design director Joanne Turcotte manages the production of 200 or so leafleted patterns per season. Turcotte and Christine Welsh Forester maintain blog sites on behalf of the company where they discuss all aspects of the yarn industry. The company also carries an interesting line of shawl sticks, pins and buttons in wood, shell and horn.

PM

Abbreviation for *place marker.*
See also MARKER

POCKET

When a shaped piece of knitted fabric applied inside or outside a garment forms a pouch, it is a pocket. The two most common types of pockets are patch pockets, which are applied to the outside of a garment, and inset pockets.

Pockets on women's garments are roughly 5½ to 6½ inches (14 to 16cm) square. Add an inch (2.5cm) for men's garments; subtract an inch for children's pockets. On a woman's sweater, place the pocket so that the lower edge is no farther than 21 to 22 inches (53 to 56cm) from the shoulder and 2½ to 4 inches (6.5 to 10cm) from the center front edges.

Patch pockets are the easiest to make: Simply knit a square or rectangle in the size, color and stitch pattern (noncurling stitches such as garter or seed stitch work best) of your choice, then sew it to the finished garment piece. Patch pockets work best with stable yarns that support their weight. Patch pockets can be left plain or accented with flaps applied slightly above the pocket opening.

Before attaching the patch pocket, block it, making sure the final stitch and row gauges match those of the piece you will attach it to. Pin the pocket in place, then use a slip-stitch seam to attach it.
See also EMBELLISHMENTS

POCKET EDGING

A decorative band or border applied to a pocket, pocket edgings can be made of ribbing, garter stitch, seed stitch or reverse stockinette. Most pocket edgings are worked in the same stitch and with the same size needles as the garment's edgings, but many decorative treatments are possible as well. A pocket edging may be either picked up or sewn on.
See also BORDERS; EDGINGS; EMBELLISHMENTS; DESIGN; POCKET

PODCAST

Independently produced audio shows distributed via the Internet, podcasts are an aural form of online interaction that complements written blogs. Software to record podcasts became widely available in late 2004, giving individuals the ability to record their own radiolike broadcasts on their home computers, and to syndicate them over websites and through aggregators like iTunes. From these sites, listeners can subscribe to a podcast, automatically receiving new episodes, or download individual shows to be loaded onto an MP3 player or listened to directly through a computer.

KnitCast, the first knitting podcast, debuted in February 2005; on it, host Marie Irshad, a BBC Radio journalist and knit blogger, interviewed high-profile knitwear designers and Internet personalities. The second major podcast, Cast On, hosted by Brenda Dayne, premiered in November 2005, bringing more of a magazine feel, with essays, regular segments and music. Cast On was the first knitting podcast to be sponsored by advertisers. Since then, many knitting podcasts have been produced. Most take the form of an *ear blog,* with the podcaster extemporizing about his or her knitting projects, technical tips, yarn, yarn shops, the knitting community, magazine and book reviews, cyber-knitting information and, frequently, personal information. Popular podcasts have included Lime & Violet, a duo of friends who riffed humorously about yarn obsession; Sticks and String, "by a Australian bloke who knits"; Knit Picks, hosted by Kelley Petkun, VP of the Knit Picks mail-order company;

Knitting in Media

by Vickie Howell

If I had my way, knitting (and all handicrafts, for that matter) would be portrayed and perceived as every bit as relevant as reciting lines on screen, performing music on stage, or painting on canvas.

Knitting deserves to be seen for what it is: a delicious, ageless, genderless vehicle of self-expression that stands proudly amongst all other "legitimate" art forms. Our challenge, however, is that the modern mentality, which is largely driven by mass media, is slow in accepting the idea that knitting can convey deeply personal meaning.

I was hired to host DIY's *Knitty Gritty* to demonstrate that being a knitter doesn't mean that one is unhip. Although my indie-eccentric brand of crafting may not be everyone's cup of tea, my job is done if my presence in the community opens eyes to the fact that putting one face on all knitters is like putting one face on all members of a gender. It's impossible to confine the art form this way.

However, media is changing. We no longer have to depend solely on broadcast radio and television, so more voices are able to be heard, collectively speaking louder about the scope of the craft. Instead of broadly stroking a market in hopes of reaching a general audience, we can now—via webcasts, blogs and online forums—speak directly to the niches we individually connect with. I started producing my own podcast, *Craft.Rock.Listen,* to do just that—to have a dialogue with others who see knitting, music, pop culture and fashion as interconnected rather than mutually exclusive. And our ways of connecting are evolving as new social media sites offer us fresh ways to communicate.

It's a great gift to be able to do that and one that others can benefit from. Whether your interests lie with intricate lace shawls, free-form gallery pieces, new and luxurious yarns or recycled and reinvented fibers, there is something in new media for you to read, look at or tune in to. As this diversity continues to blossom, I hope and expect that it will feed back into older broadcast media and reinvigorate them so that they ultimately reflect the creative side of us all.

Vickie Howell is the host of the TV show *Knitty Gritty* and has penned columns in *knit.1* and *KIWI* Magazines. She produces the podcast *CRL* and is author of a number of books including *Knit Aid: A Learn It, Fix It, Finish It Guide for Knitters on the Go* (Sterling, 2008).

Ready, Set, Knit!, the podcast of the Northampton, Massachusetts yarn emporium Webs; Stash and Burn, musings on the needlearts by two San Francisco women who purport to be working through their stashes; CraftLit, an episodic broadcast of great literary works read aloud; and The Knitmore Girls, a show by a mother-daughter knitting duo with a sizable following on Ravelry.

Podcasting is a marketing tool for yarn stores and yarn companies as well as a means of self-expression. Because podcasts are typically produced by individuals on their own time and dime (though many hosts put a "donate" button on their sites, allowing listeners to contribute toward production costs), it's not unusual for a show to "podfade," or peter out. Even if that happens, back episodes tend to stay available through iTunes.
See also INTERNET

POLO
See COLLARS AND NECKBANDS

POLYESTER
A manufactured fiber made from polymers of polypropylene and polyethylene, which are petroleum byproducts, polyester was developed in the 1950s. Polyester resembles nylon (polyamide) and has many of the same qualities of other man-made fibers in that it is strong and inexpensive to produce. Polyester, also known by its British trademark Terylene, has good stability when washed and is wrinkle resistant. It virtually revolutionized the textile industry in the 1960s when "drip-dry" polyester-blend fabrics were introduced. Unlike nylon and acrylic, polyester is usually blended with other fibers for handknitting yarns to add strength and keep cost down.
See also FIBER CHARACTERISTICS

POMPOM
Small puffy balls made out of cut pieces of yarn, pompoms (also spelled *pompons*) are typically used for decorative trim at the top of a hat, the end of a cord or on a child's garment. You can make a pompom using a commercially produced pompom maker or create your own template. To make a pompom, cut two pieces of cardboard in identical circles the diameter you want your pompom to be. Cut a hole in the middle of each circle and a notch that goes from the edge to the center. Holding the two circles together, wrap yarn tightly around the radius of the circle until the center is filled. Cut the yarn between the two templates, then slip a piece of yarn between the two halves and tie it tightly. Remove the cardboard and fluff and trim the pompom. Try mixing up the distribution of yarn colors for more colorful effects.

PONCHO
A poncho is a blanketlike cover-up with an opening in the center for the head. Originating as a workers' garment in Central and South America, the poncho moved out of folkwear and into the fashion scene in the 1960s and '70s, when knit and crochet versions were favored by hippies and disco divas alike. The poncho then slipped to the sidelines until the 1990s, when lush knitted versions began parading down the fashion runways and into stores. Knitters were quick to take to the trend, creating endless patterns that ranged from simple garter-stitched rectangles to elaborately patterned pieces worked in cables and textural stitches. Since they require little or no shaping and generally have a one-size-fits-all approach, they tend to be easy to create, even for beginning knitters. They often feature fringed trim and pockets.
See also SERAPE; SHAWL

POPCORN
See BOBBLE

PORTER, J. P.
See FLORENTINE JACKET

PORTUGUESE PATTERNS
See AZORES LACE; FOLK KNITTING; SPANISH KNITTING

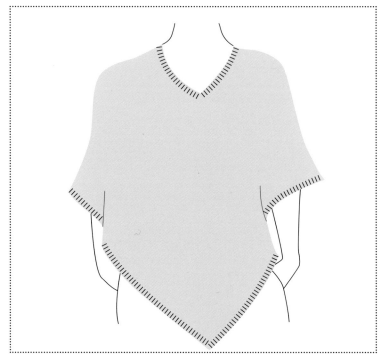

Poncho

PRECIOUS PALS

See KNITTING GUILD
ASSOCIATION, THE (TKGA)

PREPARATION ROW

See FOUNDATION ROW

PREV

Abbreviation for *previous*.

PRISM

Prism Arts is the venture of
fiberarts maven Laura Militzer
Bryant, who has had an eclectic
career spanning from rock concert
promoter to sailboat racer to
bookkeeper. Bryant, a graduate of
the Michigan School of Art, found
that after the art boom of the
1980s, she needed other income in
addition to painting. So she picked
up several yarn lines and
established herself as a yarn rep in
upstate New York. Bryant
formulated ideas for hand-dyeing
yarns and at a TNNA proposed to
Tahki director Diane Friedman a
line of yarns hand-painted "by
Prism for Tahki." The line was so
successful that Bryant decided to
purchase a quarter-ton of undyed
mohair and put her painting
talents to work on her own line.
She began selling her Prism yarns
very successfully, dyeing each
skein herself and utilizing her
bookkeeping skills to grow the
company. She then moved her
operations from a garage to a large
studio space in Florida. Prism
differentiates itself from other
premium hand-paints by focusing
on mohair and novelties such as its
Stuff yarns, including Wild Stuff.
These unique skeins meld
stretches of different fibers within
one skein, as well as the different
hues characteristic of hand-paints.

PROBLEM AREAS AND SOLUTIONS

See CORRECTING COMMON
MISTAKES; DARNING; FROGGING;
GAUGE

PROVISIONAL CAST-ON

When a design calls for adding
further knitting onto a cast-on edge
(typically in a lace shawl or scarf),
starting with a provisional cast-on
makes the job easy and invisible.
There are many different methods
for provisionally casting on; the
most common are the crochet
chain cast-on, the open cast-on,
and knitting with waste yarn.

The latter is the easiest method.
Simply begin knitting with waste
yarn, casting on in any method
you choose, and knitting one or
two rows. At the beginning of a
row, switch to the main-color yarn.
Complete the section of the
garment according to instructions.
When you are ready to pick up the
open stitches from the cast-on,
unravel the stitches knit in waste
yarn. You will be left with a row of
live stitches. Carefully place them
on a needle and begin working in
the other direction.

See also CAST-ON

Chain (Provisional) Cast-On

With waste yarn, make a crochet chain
a few stitches longer than the number
of stitches to be cast on. With main-
color yarn, pick up one stitch in the
back loop of each chain. To knit from
the cast-on edge, carefully unpick the
chain, placing the live stitches one by
one on a needle.

Open (Provisional) Cast-On

1. With two needles held together,
make a slip knot. Hold waste yarn
beside the working yarn. Loop, working
yarn under waste yarn, then over the
needles as shown.

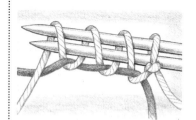

2. Continue looping under waste yarn
until all stitches are cast on. Withdraw
one needle, knit into the front loops on
first row. Leave waste yarn in place
until stitches are needed.

PSSO

Abbreviation for *pass slipped
stitch over*.

See also DECREASES

PULLOVER

A sweater that pulls over the head
with no front or back opening is
called a pullover.

See also DESIGN; SWEATER

PURL STITCH

A basic building block of knitting,
the purl stitch is one of the two
basic stitches used to form a fabric
in knitting. It is the reverse of the
other basic stitch, the knit stitch.
Each loop is called a stitch.

There are two ways to form a
purl stitch: the American/English
method and the Continental
method. In American/English
knitting, you hold the yarn in your
right hand; in the Continental
method, you hold it in your left. In
a normal purl stitch, you work into
the front loop of the stitch from
right to left while holding the yarn
to the front.

See also AMERICAN/ENGLISH–
STYLE KNITTING; CONTINENTAL/
GERMAN–STYLE KNITTING;
KNIT/PURL PATTERNS; KNIT
STITCH

English-Style Purl Stitch

1. As with the knit stitch, hold the working needle in your right hand and the needle with the stitches in your left. The yarn is held and manipulated with your right hand and is kept to the front of the work.

2. Insert the right needle from back to front into the first stitch on the left needle. The right needle is now in front of the left needle and the yarn is at the front of the work.

3. With your right index finger, wrap the yarn counterclockwise around the right needle.

4. Draw the right needle and the yarn backward through the stitch on the left needle, forming a loop on the right needle.

5. Slip the stitch off the left needle. You have made one purl stitch. Repeat these steps in each subsequent stitch until all stitches have been worked from the left needle. One purl row has been completed.

Continental-Style Purl Stitch

1. As with the knit stitch, hold the working needle in your right hand and the needle with the stitches in your left. The yarn is held and manipulated with your left hand and is kept to the front of the work.

2. Insert the right needle from back to front into the first stitch on the left needle, keeping the yarn in front of the work.

3. Lay the yarn over the right needle as shown. Pull down on the yarn with your left index finger to keep the yarn taut.

4. Bring the right needle and the yarn backward through the stitch on the left needle, forming a loop on the right needle.

5. Slide the stitch off the left needle. Use your left index finger to tighten the new purl stitch on the right needle. Continue to repeat these steps until you have worked all of the stitches from the left needle to the right needle. You have made one row of purl stitches.

PURLWISE

When a stitch is handled as if it were to be purled, it has been worked *purlwise*. Most often this term is used to explain how to slip a stitch from the left needle to the right. Some knitting instructions will state "slip as if to purl." However, slipping purlwise often goes without saying: If it doesn't specify throughout, purlwise is always assumed, as slipping purlwise does not twist or alter the stitch.

See also DECREASES; KNITWISE; SLIP-STITCH PATTERNS

To slip one stitch purlwise, insert the right needle through the next stitch on the left needle as if you were purling it. Pull this stitch off the left needle to transfer it to the right needle. The stitch on the right needle will be untwisted.

PURSE

A purse is a bag used to carry personal items, often made in leather or woven fabric but sometimes made in knit or crochet fabric. Handcrafted knit purses are usually based on a square or rectangle; some have gussets, while others are pouchlike with oval or circular bottoms and drawstring closures. Bags with round or circular bottoms may be knit flat in separate pieces or in the round in one piece. Handles and straps may be knitted, crocheted, constructed from I-cord or purchased; among the choices of purchased handles are plastic, wood and bamboo. Clutch, envelope, shoulder and sack designs are just some of the purse options. Various yarns can be used for bag knitting, but the knitted fabric should be firm. Felting is a popular technique for bag and purse knitting because of the sturdy fabric it produces.

See also BEAD KNITTING; FELTING; TOTE

PUT-UP

"Put-up" refers to the way in which yarn is wound into units for sale. The three most common put-ups are balls, hanks and skeins.

See also BALL; HANK; SKEIN

PWISE

Abbreviation for *purlwise*.

See also PURLWISE

Various put-ups, clockwise from top: hank, large skein, small skein, ball

Simple purse made by folding a rectangle in half and sewing the sides

Felted bag with rounded bottom

Flat-bottomed drawstring purse

Q
R

QIVIUT

The soft, gray-brown fiber from the undercoat of the Arctic muskox is called qiviut. Pronounced "ki-vee-ut," the word means "down" or "underwool" in the Eskimo language, and it is sometimes spelled qiviuq, qiviuk, or qiveut.

A large animal that lives only in the Arctic tundra of Alaska, northern Canada and Greenland, the qiviut has a dual coat that sheds naturally each spring. An adult yields between four and six pounds of fiber per year. The fiber is lanolin-free, so it is easy to clean, but the undercoat must be separated from the coarse outer hairs before spinning. Warmer than wool and extraordinarily lightweight, qiviut is often compared to cashmere. Because of the limited supply, the fiber is even costlier than cashmere. Most qiviut sold for handknitting is laceweight and is often undyed, although it does take dye well. *See also* FIBER CHARACTERISTICS

Qiviut is the soft underwool of the muskox

Arctic Gold

By Linda Cortright

They snort. They belch. They shake their heads and stamp their feet, and for six months of the year they never see the sun, because it never rises above the horizon of their far northern homelands.

They are called muskoxen, and their woolly undercoat is called *qiviut*—the ultimate fiber for handknitters and connoisseurs of luxury wear. Yet most people have never seen a muskox, much less had the exquisite pleasure of knitting with its fiber. With a price tag that rivals the finest-quality cashmere, there is a reason why knitters call it their stash of Arctic gold.

Unlike cashmere, which is produced by millions of goats that live everywhere from the high Himalayas to the backlands of Texas, qiviut is rare. There are only approximately 130,000 muskoxen on the planet, and 80 percent of them live in the Canadian Arctic. Because of their scarcity, they have been protected by the Canadian government since 1917.

Every year, about the same time the sun finally sneaks above the horizon to signal the beginning of spring, the muskox sheds its downy undercoat, taking on the appearance of a woolly mastodon draped in dryer sheets. In parts of northern Alaska, Canada and Greenland, these delicate clouds of fiber are gathered by hand and then carefully dehaired before being processed into yarn. The insulating value of qiviut is six to eight times greater than that of wool, and as a result, a laceweight qiviut sweater has the same warming capacity as a bulky wool pullover, yet with the added appeal of no-itch fiber.

But the benefits of qiviut extend beyond its delicate touch: Muskoxen represent environmental stewardship and the preservation of traditional ways of life. In Alaska, the Oomingmak Knitting Cooperative supports its two hundred members through the sale of handknit qiviut garments through its storefront in Anchorage, and in the far reaches of the Canadian Arctic, the muskox herds are protected by the Inuvialuit Group of the Northwest Territories and are managed in a way that combines tradition and sustainability, to ensure their unthreatened existence.

Linda Cortright is the editor and publisher of *Wild Fibers* magazine, a quarterly publication dedicated to promoting the natural fiber industry throughout the world. Her work has also appeared in *Interweave Knits* and *Yarn Market News*. In addition to being a knitter and handspinner, she maintains a small herd of cashmere goats on her farm in Maine.

R

RAFFIA

Sometimes called raffia straw, the fiber from the raffia palm native to Madagascar, Africa, is traditionally used to make rope, string and baskets. The fiber, which is soft, pliable, strong and does not shrink when wet, is torn in thin strips from the palm leaves. After being dried in the sun, raffia takes on a yellowish-tan hue, but it is often dyed other colors.

Raffia can be knit or crocheted and is best suited for bags, mats and items where an organic, rustic look is desired.

See also FIBER CHARACTERISTICS

RAGLAN SHAPING

A raglan armhole slants from the neck to the underarm, so the shaping must be calculated to traverse that slope. There is no shoulder seam—the sleeve cap becomes the shoulder of the sweater. The sleeve must match the front and back body shaping, and the sleeve cap must have exactly the same number of rows as the back and front pieces of the armhole. For more definition at the shoulder, a dart can be worked up the center of the sleeve cap.

In the simplest raglan shaping, the front and back pieces are exactly the same depth. In this case, the top of the sleeve cap will be straight. In other methods, the front piece is shorter than the back piece to accommodate a curve at the neck. The two sides of the sleeve cap are then shaped differently to match the corresponding front and back pieces. Shaping on the cap of the right and left sleeves must be reversed for proper fit around the neck.

See also ARMHOLE SHAPING; SLEEVE CAP; SLEEVES

RAGLAN SLEEVE

Often, but not always, worked from the top down, a raglan sleeve has a long slanting seam that runs from the neck to the armhole.

See also RAGLAN SHAPING; SLEEVE CAP; SLEEVES

RAVELRY

Ravelry, launched in 2007, took the tradition of online knitting forums and usergroups and transformed it into a comprehensive networking website for knitters, crocheters, spinners and weavers. Ravelry was founded by knitter and blogger Jessica Forbes and her husband, Casey Forbes, a web designer. Originally invitation-only but now open to any and all, Ravelry had more than 800,000 members as of September 2010. The site functions as a social network on a user-centric Web 2.0 platform, so that essentially it is the crafters themselves, rather than the Ravelry company, who shape the content of the site. Ravelry offers organizational tools, reference sources, links to yarn businesses and, most importantly, extensive means of connecting with like-minded crafters. Users can message one another, view each other's projects, "friend" others on the site, participate in forum discussions, research favorite designers, seek out and purchase new yarns, search through patterns, stay updated on events, and much more. Groups are an important component of Ravelry, offering places for knitters to congregate and discuss topics, from cities to patterns to publications to podcasts. The site also enables users to keep an inventory of needle and yarn collections and a photo album of projects. Users can post comments, advice and ratings of patterns and yarns, and patterns are available both for sale and as free downloads.

See also INTERNET; *KNITTY.COM*; PODCAST

RC

Abbreviation for *right cross*.
See also CABLES

RECYCLING YARN

Recycling yarn is the practice of

Recycling Yarn

Mitten before recycling

Unraveling the mitten

Tying the yarn to prepare for soaking

Recycled yarn ready for knitting

unraveling knitted objects in order to reuse their fiber. A knitter might choose to recycle yarn to save money (for example, to try out a luxury fiber she cannot afford in its new state); to honor the objects of the past by reusing them; to help the environment by keeping old knits out of the landfills and reducing demand for the production and shipment of new yarn; or simply to reap the serendipity that can occur when a project adapts itself to a given fiber rather than the other way around. Secondhand stores, yard sales and almost anybody's attic or storeroom are all likely places to find knit and crocheted garments and blankets to unravel.

When choosing objects for recycling, try to select pieces whose yarn is in good condition, without stains, matting, holes or pills. Remove the seams from the garment or object carefully; the goal is to maximize the length of the strand(s) you will unravel. (You might have to cut into neckbands and shoulders, but only do so as a last resort, advised Leigh Witchel in his article "Frugality Is the New Black" in *Vogue Knitting,* Spring/Summer 2009.) After seam removal, frog the yarn, then soak it to smooth out the kinks. To soak the yarn, wind it loosely over your arm into several skeins; tie each one loosely in three places with yarn in a contrasting color. Soak skeins in warm, soapy water for about an hour, avoiding any agitation that may cause felting.

Rinse the yarn, remove excess moisture by rolling it in a towel, and air dry. Recycled yarn may be recolored, usually by *overdyeing.* Several Ravelry groups dedicated to recycling yarn can provide helpful information.
See also FROGGING; ORGANIC KNITTING; RAVELRY; UNRAVELING

RED CROSS
See AMERICAN RED CROSS KNITTING CAMPAIGNS

REM
Abbreviation for *remain(s).*

REP
Abbreviation for *repeat(s), repeating.*

REPEAT
To repeat is to perform the same action again. In knitting patterns, a repeat is a specific series of stitches worked more than once. The stitch pattern may repeat horizontally or vertically. This is an easy way to condense a knitting pattern's written directions—describe the action just once, and have the crafter repeat it the proper number of times. A repeat may be indicated in several different ways. The most common is the abbreviation "rep," such as "rep row 4." This means to follow the directions given for row 4 one more time.

Asterisks (*) are often used to indicate repeated actions in knitting patterns. For example, the direction "*K1, p1; rep from * to

end" means to repeat the k1, p1 across the entire row. Parentheses and brackets are also used in pattern writing to separate out the elements that will be repeated: K1, (k1, p1) 3 times, k1. Brackets are used similarly to parentheses.

When a pattern is represented in chart form, the whole chart may be repeated—in which case that will be explained—or just a part of it may be meant to be reworked, and that area will be outlined in some way (usually red) so that the reader can easily find the portion to repeat. Occasionally directions for repeating will be noted at the bottom of the chart rather than with an outline.

When a pattern repeat is many stitches wide, it may be useful to place stitch markers between the repeats, to alert the knitter to the change in pattern and to make it easy to spot mistakes.
See also ABBREVIATIONS; PATTERN

RETREATS
See CAMPS AND RETREATS

REV
Abbreviation for *reverse.*

REVERSE SHAPING
To work a knitted piece while mentally swapping the previous instructions is to use reverse shaping. It's a common directive in patterns for cardigans, sweater backs and fronts and some sleeve caps, though there is a shift in pattern writing away from this

method. To do it, you'll be mirroring the previous work, so work the shaping at the opposite end from where it was worked for the previous side. For example, if you began to shape a cardigan armhole by binding off stitches at the beginning of a right-side row for the left front, you would bind off stitches at the beginning of a wrong-side row for the right front. If you are increasing or decreasing at the beginning of a row for one front, you would increase or decrease at the end of the row for the other front. For very professional looks, the direction of the decrease should also be reversed. For that reason, many patterns now specify exactly how to work the shaping on both sides, to ensure the best and most clear results.
See also PATTERN

REVERSE STOCKINETTE STITCH
If stockinette stitch is made by working alternating rows of knit and purl and shown with the "knit" side on the right side, reverse stockinette is the opposite of that—the same sequence of rows is worked, but the purl side is considered the right side. The fabric has the same qualities as stockinette as far as curling and density, but the look is that of small bumps rather than the smooth Vs of stockinette. Often cable stitches are worked on a background of reverse stockinette to make the stockinette cables "pop" more. To

work reverse stockinette stitch, cast on any number of stitches:

Row 1 (RS) Purl.

Row 2 (WS) Knit.

Repeat rows 1 and 2.

See also KNIT STITCH; PURL STITCH; STOCKINETTE STITCH

REVOLUTIONARY KNITTING CIRCLE

See GUERRILLA KNITTING

REV ST ST

Abbreviation for *reverse stockinette stitch*.

See also REVERSE STOCKINETTE STITCH

RH

Abbreviation for *right-hand*.

RHINEBECK

See SHEEP AND WOOL FESTIVALS

RIB

Abbreviation for *ribbing*.

See also RIBBING

RIBBING

A ribbed fabric is made up of both knits and purls but has all its knit stitches lined up vertically and all its purl stitches lined up vertically. Most ribbing patterns consist of even numbers of stitches, such as ribbing formed by one knit stitch and one purl stitch (sometimes called "1x1" or "k1, p1" ribbing) or two knit and two purl stitches ("2x2" or "k2, p2" ribbing).

Ribbing can also be constructed from uneven numbers of knit and purl stitches, such as two knit stitches and three purl stitches. More than one color of yarn can be combined in ribbing.

Having approximately (or exactly) equal numbers of knit and purl stitches in the fabric means ribbing is reversible and will not curl—however, the fabric will tend to pull in, which gives it elasticity and stretch suitable for cuffs and bottom borders on sweaters or other garments. The fewer stitches in the repeat, the tighter the ribbing; 1x1 will be more taut than 4x4, for example.

See also BORDERS; EDGINGS; KNIT STITCH; PURL STITCH

RIBBON YARN

Ribbon yarn is a novelty yarn that is actually a narrow strip of woven fabric and is available in a range of fibers including wool, cotton, rayon and silk. It comes in many weights, from fine to bulky, and in colors ranging from solid to variegated. Ribbon yarns are most often used for accessories, accents or fringe and the occasional summer top. It can be somewhat tricky to knit with as it easy to pierce the ribbon with a needle and the yarn tends to twist while being knit due to its flat construction. In addition, the finished item tends to be stretchy and have little resilience.

See also NOVELTY YARN; YARN

RIGHT-HAND CARRY

See AMERICAN/ENGLISH–STYLE KNITTING

RIGHT-HAND VS. LEFT-HAND KNITTING

See AMERICAN/ENGLISH–STYLE KNITTING; CONTINENTAL/ GERMAN–STYLE KNITTING; KNIT STITCH; PURL STITCH

RIGHT-SLANTING DECREASE

See DECREASES

RND(S)

Abbreviation for *round* or *rounds*.

ROBERTS, PATRICIA

See BRITISH KNITTING

ROBINS, FREDDIE

See GUERRILLA KNITTING

ROSENBERG, NINA

See GUERRILLA KNITTING

ROUND

In circular knitting, one complete circle of stitches knit on either circular needles or double-pointed needles is called a "round." It is distinguished from the "row" that is worked when knitting back and forth.

See also CIRCULAR KNITTING; CIRCULAR NEEDLES; DOUBLE-POINTED NEEDLES

Reverse stockinette stitch swatch

K1, p1 (1x1) ribbing

K2, p2 (2x2) ribbing

Swatch knit in ribbon yarn

ROUND HEEL
See HEELS

ROVING
See CARDING; SPINNING

ROWAN DESIGN STUDIO
Rowan is one of the world's foremost handknitting-yarn manufacturers and pattern houses, headquartered in an ancient mill in Holmfirth, West Yorkshire, England. From its inception in the early 1980s, when the small firm of Rowan Weavers capitalized on the explosive popularity of one of its Kaffe Fassett sweater kits to become Rowan Yarns, the studio has carefully cultivated the brand's exclusivity through selected distribution of its yarns, as well as through its kits, the high caliber of its designers, and its beautiful *Rowan Knitting & Crochet Magazine* (pattern books shot in moody Dales landscapes). Fassett's designs helped create the Rowan mystique to a large degree, but the company has since been the incubator of many a storied knitwear career, including those of Debbie Bliss, Kim Hargreaves, Martin Storey, Erika Knight, Zoë Mellor and many others. The company's fibers exemplify products native to the United Kingdom, such as Shetland wool, heathers and tweeds. Rowan runs many workshops at its picturesque mill headquarters, and has an extremely loyal following among its retailers and hand knitters.
See also BLISS, DEBBIE; FASSETT, KAFFE; STOREY, MARTIN

ROWAN KNITTING AND CROCHET
See MAGAZINES AND JOURNALS (U.K.); ROWAN DESIGN STUDIO

RS
Abbreviation for *right side*.

RUCHING
The method used to add bands of gathering to a garment is called ruching. Ruching creates a fabric with a rippled appearance, and can be created in knitting as easily as in sewing. Bands that gather are created by changing the number of stitches (increasing, then decreasing a few rows later) and the needle size. The pattern, a 14-row repeat, is worked over any number of stitches.
See also EMBELLISHMENTS; PLEAT

RUNNING STITCH
Small, straight embroidery stitches worked over one knitted stitch and under the next, running stitches can be used as an embellishment (they're especially useful for outlining) or as a basting stitch. The stitches can be worked vertically, horizontally, or diagonally in equal or varying lengths.
See also EMBROIDERY, SEAMING

RUSSIAN PATTERNS
See FOLK KNITTING

RYKIEL, SONIA (1930-)
Sonia Rykiel is a French fashion designer known as the "Queen of Knits." With no formal training, Rykiel began designing clothing when she became pregnant in 1962 and could not find maternity clothes to her liking. Her first sweater, now iconic, was a shrunken pullover that later came to be known as the "poor boy" sweater. Her knitwear is very distinctive looking, and is characterized by a vibrant color palette, stripes, long and skinny or cropped shapes, raw hems and inside-out seams.

Swatch knit in a ruching pattern

Running Stitch

S

S2KP

Abbreviation for "slip two stitches together knitwise, knit one stitch, pass the two slipped stitches over the knitted stitch."
See also DECREASES

SATIN STITCH

Satin stitch is an embroidery stitch that completely covers an area of fabric.

SC

Abbreviation for *single crochet.*
See also SINGLE CROCHET

SCANDINAVIAN PATTERNS

See BERGEN MUSEUM; BOHUS KNITTING; FOLK KNITTING; ICELANDIC KNITTING; FAROE KNITTING; NORWEGIAN KNITTING; SETESDAL SOCKS; SWEDISH KNITTING

SCARF

A strip of fabric that wraps around the neck is called a scarf. Traditionally a rectangular strip of wool stitched in stockinette, ribbing or cables, and originally intended as a winter layering piece, the scarf has evolved into an accessory that is more about fashion than function. Style options are limitless—from the classic muffler designed to chase the winter chill to fur, metallic and openwork designs that are necklace-like in both appearance and function. Since little or no shaping is involved in most scarf designs and sizing is not needed, they are excellent beginner projects. Basic garter stitch patterns knit with novelty yarns were wildly popular in the early twenty-first century, and "the scarf craze" fueled much of the knitting boom at the turn of the century. Scarves continue to be popular items for knitters of all skill levels.
See also SHAWL

SCHEMATIC

The line drawings in a pattern representing a finished knitted piece, including all the measurements as well as any special notes, are called schematics. They serve as a mini visual representation of the pieces that need to be knitted to complete a project. Drawn to scale, schematics are labeled with the name of the piece (back, sleeve, left front, etc.) and its exact measurements. The sample schematics on the next page show the standard measurements that are given on most schematics. Here is a description of these measurements:

Diagram 1

A—the width across the back, or the width across the front at the bust. This measurement is usually the same for back and front in a pullover. When doubled, it gives you the finished bust measurement. You'll notice that the line extends past the ribbing at the lower edge, as the ribbing usually pulls in and doesn't match this width measurement.

B—the depth of the ribbing. The depth of the ribbing or other lower edge detail corresponds to the instructions. It's the first vertical measurement given on the right side of the schematic. It will also tell you the depth of a hem that is later turned up to the inside. The turning line will be indicated by a horizontal broken line.

C—the length to the underarm. This is measured above the lower edge ribbing and up to the underarm. Notice that each of the measurements on the schematic's right side is an increment and is marked between two dots. These marked increments are particularly helpful if you are planning to shorten or lengthen your sweater.

D—the depth of the armhole to the shoulder. This measurement is given in the instructions for the back under "armhole shaping" to "shoulder shaping." Whether the armhole is straight or curved, take this measurement flat, and vertically from the first armhole bind-off. Do not curve your tape measure along the shaped armhole edge.

E—the length from lower edge to first neck shaping.

F—the depth from front neck to

Satin Stitch

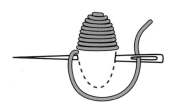

Draw the needle up through the fabric and across the area to be covered, taking care to keep the fabric taut and the stitches close together.

Scarf knit in an openwork pattern with fringed ends

Kid mohair scarf knit in a twisted-cable pattern

Striped scarf knit in a chevron pattern

back neck. This increment, when added to "G," gives you the number of inches/centimeters that the front neck is dropped from the shoulder edge.

G—the depth from back neck to shoulder. This shows how much the back neck is dropped compared to the shoulder at the armhole edge. This doesn't reflect the slope of the shoulder, which is a slant of about ½–1 inch (1.5–2.5cm)—shoulder slope is determined by stepped bind-offs, not this depth measurement.

H—shoulder width. Shoulder width is determined by the number of stitches bound off for each shoulder divided by the stitch gauge.

I—width of the neck. Neck width is measured straight across, not along the depth or curve of the neck, front or back. It is determined by the total number of stitches bound off for the neck divided by the stitch gauge. Add "I" and both "H's" together and you'll get the cross back measurement (the width across the back between the shoulders).

Diagram 2

J—width of the lower sleeve. This measurement is taken above the cuff ribbing and includes any increased stitches on the first row above the ribbing.

K—depth of the cuff ribbing. This measures the ribbing before the stitch pattern begins.

L—sleeve length to underarm. This is the length that is knit, in

Sample Schematics

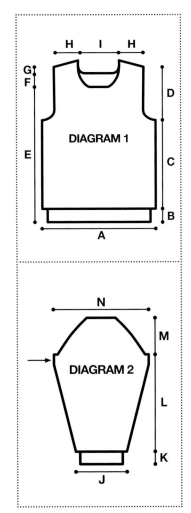

Sample body (Diagram 1) and sleeve (Diagram 2) schematics

pattern, above the cuff and up to the underarm. If you plan to change the sleeve length, the schematic shows you where to add or subtract at the top of the sleeve—this is done in the straight portion just beneath the shaping at the underarm (indicated by our arrow).

M—sleeve cap depth. This length measurement is determined by the number of rows needed to arrive at the top of the sleeve cap shaping, and is proportionate to the depth of the armhole.

N—sleeve width at upper arm. This measures the sleeve at the upper arm, and is figured according to the final number of stitches in the sleeve after all increases are made. You'll also see this measurement given under "Knitted Measurements" in the instructions. If you have fitting problems at the upper arm, compare this measurement to your figure as a check before you knit. *See also* ASSEMBLING; MEASUREMENTS; PATTERN

SCHIAPARELLI, ELSA
(1890-1973)

Elsa Schiaparelli was an Italian fashion designer, heavily influenced by and involved with the Surrealist art movement, who was a contemporary and competitor of Coco Chanel. She caused a sensation in the fashion world and shaped knitwear trends with her 1927 *trompe l'oeil* Bow-Knot sweater, whose pattern was designed to make it look as though the wearer had a scarf tied around her neck. The sweater was knit using a double-layered stitch, now know as the Armenian technique, in which a contrasting color of yarn is stranded across the knitted fabric and picked up in every third stitch, giving the fabric a tweedy appearance. The double-layered

stitch, in addition to being aesthetically interesting, created a sturdy fabric that retained its shape better than other knitwear being produced at the time. *See also* FRENCH KNITTING

SCHULZ, HORST

One of the pioneers of modular patchwork knitting, Schulz's colorful circles, triangles, rectangles and shells are worked directly onto the previous shape, avoiding the need for an abundance of seaming. "Everything that surrounds us consists of individual parts. Why then must a piece of knitting consist of only one part?" he ponders in his knitting workshops. "As a house is built brick by brick until it's as big as you want, you place planks next to planks to create a floor of a room until it is finished. This is exactly how I have arranged my knitting work—patchwork unit attached to patchwork unit and strip attached to strip."

Schulz and his family fled his native Germany during World War II and spent four years at a detention camp in Denmark, where an elderly woman taught him to knit a lace tablecloth using stone-sharpened wire as a circular needle and unraveled potato sacks as yarn. Settling in postwar Germany, he spent time as an upholsterer, interior designer and, finally, ad-man for a clothing store that sold wool yarn.

His two books on patchwork knitting—*Patchwork Knitting*

(Saprotex International, 1997) and *New Patchwork Knitting: Fashion for Children* (Saprotex International, 2000), originally published in German, have been translated into four languages. Schulz began giving workshops in the United States in 1999 and taught at Stitches events in the early 2000s, spreading his knitting ethos: "I would wish that people would share and stimulate each other as it used to be in the days of spinning, quilting and knitting get-togethers. We often smile about those days. In our world of hectic days, knitting creativity is a balm." *See also* DESIGNERS

SCOTT, CARLA (1956-)

Carla Scott is the executive editor and longest-serving staff member of *Vogue Knitting* magazine and editor in chief of *Knit Simple* magazine. She has been knitting since the age of seven, learning from her grandmother and sister, designer Mari Lynn Patrick. While she and her sister were growing up, the family frequently moved around on the East Coast of the United States. Scott appears regularly on *Knit & Crochet Today* on PBS, hosted by Brett Bara. She is a member of the Craft Yarn Council's Standards Committee and has worked with the council to organize annual Knit-Outs. Scott is featured in the instructional section of the *Art of Knitting Vol. 2* DVD. She also travels extensively, giving seminars and workshops on specialized knitting techniques and hosting annual *Vogue Knitting* tours all over the world. *See also* PATRICK, MARI LYNN; *VOGUE KNITTING*

Scrumble knit and crocheted by Prudence Mapstone

SCRUMBLE

The basic unit of freeform knitting and crochet, a scrumble can be knit, crocheted or both. *See also* FREEFORM KNITTING/ CROCHET

SEAMING

The process of sewing knitted pieces together to complete the garment or item is collectively known as "seaming," sometimes also "finishing." There are several methods of seaming. Generally the same yarn used to knit the project is the yarn used to seam the pieces together. If, however, the yarn is particularly bulky yarn or a novelty, the seams are best sewn with a flat, firm yarn comparable in color to that used in the project. This ensures the best results and least chance of unraveling or unsightly seams.

Block the pieces to size and line them up how they should be joined together. Use pins to hold them together, or loosely baste with scrap thread. Next, count up about ten rows on each side and

Swatch knit in seed stitch

pin the corresponding stitches together. On projects worked all in one piece (a hat, for instance), the rows should line up exactly. When you are pinning two separate pieces (a sweater back and front, for example), you may have to ease in extra rows if one piece is slightly longer than the other. Using a tapestry needle and a piece of yarn no more than 18 inches in length, firmly and evenly stitch the pieces together. Mattress stitch is an invisible and common stitch for joining pieces side to side; if stitches are live, grafting, also called Kitchener stitch, provides an invisible join. *See also* BACKSTITCH (SEAMING); FINISHING TECHNIQUES; GRAFTING; MATTRESS STITCH; RUNNING STITCH

SEED STITCH

A textured stitch, seed stitch is created by working a series of knit and purl stitches, alternated on every row. The simplest form of seed stitch consists of alternate rows of k1, p1. It is the first textured stitch most knitters learn, after mastering garter stitch, stockinette stitch and perhaps attempting a ribbing.

Many items can be knit solely with seed stitch, but often it is used to separate other motifs, such as cables. Because it does not curl, it is a good choice for sweater borders. Some knitting books and references use the term "moss stitch" as a synonym for seed stitch. The swatch shown on page 185 is knit over an even number of stitches.

Row 1 (RS) *Knit one, purl one; repeat from * to end.

Row 2 Purl one, knit one; repeat from * to end.

Repeat rows 1 and 2.

See also ARAN KNITTING; BORDERS; CABLE PATTERNS; CABLES; KNIT STITCH; MOSS STITCH; PURL STITCH

SELVAGE

The edge of a knit fabric that will be absorbed into the final seaming is known as the selvage (U.K.: selvedge). In knitting it is generally considered the first and last stitch of the front or back of a piece, and that one stitch is usually set apart from the body of the work by changing the stitch pattern at the beginning and end of every row. Selvages stabilize the fabric and prepare it for seaming. Selvages also give knitted pieces that are not seamed a finished edge.

Usually a selvage consists of one stitch, which you can add to an existing pattern or when designing

One-Stitch Selvages

Garter Stitch Selvage (Left Side)
This selvage is best worked on stockinette stitch fabrics and is the easiest selvage for beginners.

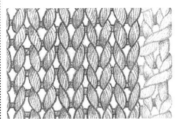

Garter Stitch Selvage (Right Side)
The selvage looks slightly different on the right edge, as shown here. Work left and right edges as follows: **Row 1** Knit one, work to the last stitch, knit one. Repeat this row.

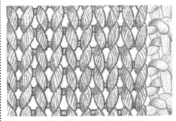

Reverse Stockinette Stitch Selvage
Suitable for stockinette stitch, this is easy for beginners. Work both sides as follows: **Row 1 (right side)** Purl one, work to the last stitch, purl one. **Row 2** Knit one, work to the last stitch, knit one. Repeat these 2 rows.

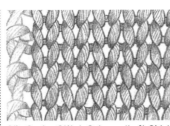

Slip Garter Stitch Selvage (Left Side)
This selvage is similar to the garter stitch selvage, only firmer. It is ideal for patterns that tend to spread laterally. The left side shown above is slightly different than the right side.

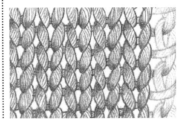

Slip Garter Stitch Selvage (Right Side)
Work both sides of the slip garter stitch selvage as follows: **Row 1** Slip the first stitch knitwise, work to the last stitch, knit one. Repeat this row.

Chain Stitch Selvage
This selvage is for garter stitch and is worked as follows:
Row 1 With the yarn in front, slip the first stitch purlwise, with the yarn in back, knit to the end. Repeat this row.

Slip-Stitch Selvages

This method has three variations. All of them make a chain stitch edge, with each chain loop representing two rows. It is perfect to use when you must later pick up stitches.

English Method
Row 1 (RS) Slip the first stitch knitwise, work to the last stitch, slip the last stitch knitwise.
Row 2 Purl one, work to the last stitch, purl one. Repeat these 2 rows.

French Method
Row 1 (RS) Slip the first stitch knitwise, work to the last stitch, knit one.
Row 2 Slip the first stitch purlwise, work to the last stitch, purl one. Repeat these 2 rows.

German Method
Row 1 (RS) Knit the first stitch, work to the last stitch. With the yarn in back, slip the last stitch purlwise.
Row 2: Purl the first stitch, work to the last stitch. With the yarn in front, slip the last stitch purlwise. Repeat these 2 rows.

your own garments. Examples of one-stitch selvages are shown on the previous page. Another common type of selvage is the slip-stitch selvage. The knots and chains created on every other row of this selvage can help you keep track of your rows. Multiple-stitch selvages are used most often to prevent curling on non-seamed pieces, such as scarves.
See also GARTER STITCH; KNIT STITCH; PURL STITCH; SCARF; SLIP STITCH

SERAPE

This poncho-like garment (sometimes called a *zarape*) is typically woven, but knitted

Serape

versions are also made. It can be rectangular and worn around the shoulders like a shawl or have a hole for the head like a poncho. Originating in Mexico and other areas of Latin America, serapes are usually striped in bright colors.
See also PONCHO

SETESDAL SOCKS

Socks knit in the traditional Norwegian *lusekofta* or "lice" pattern from Norway take the name Setesdal socks.
See also FOLK KNITTING; NORWEGIAN KNITTING

SET-IN SLEEVE

Sleeves fitted and sewn into the

armhole of a garment, rather than simply attached to the edges of a straight body shape, are considered "set in" as opposed to "drop." For the sleeve to sit properly in the armhole (the *armscye* or *armseye*) with no bumps or bulges, the measurements along the curved edge of a set-in sleeve must be equal to that of the measurement along the armhole edge. Also, the first bind-off should be the same as the armhole bind-off at the underarm of the body. Shaping begins with an even slant, then continues with a sharper decreasing angle toward the top, ending with bound-off stitches in the last few rows to curve the top of the sleeve cap.

The design of a set-in sleeve requires a bit more math, but the fit is more professional and polished. A drop sleeve tends to give a more boxy shape overall, rather than the custom-fit appearance of a set-in sleeve. There are online set-in sleeve calculators to aid in determining the best rate of decrease to get the best shape.
See also ARMHOLE SHAPING; ASSEMBLING; FINISHING TECHNIQUES; SLEEVE CAP; SLEEVES

SEWING

See SEAMING

SHAKER PATTERNS

See BRIOCHE; FOLK KNITTING

SHAPING

Techniques used to modify rectangular pieces knit on straight needles or tubular pieces knit on circular needles to make the knitted pieces conform to body shape or to the requirements of the finished item encompass the term "shaping." Shaping is used in garments to create a more professional final piece—one that appears to be custom-knit rather than a one-size-fits-all pattern. Shaping is typically accomplished using increases or decreases, or short rows, but knit pieces also can also be shaped by combining different pattern types. For example, ribbing and cable patterns tend to pull in, whereas lace patterns and knit-purl patterns tend to expand. Another way to shape a garment is to change the needle size as you knit the piece.
See also DECREASES; INCREASES; KNIT/PURL PATTERNS; RIBBING; SHORT ROWS

SHARP, JO (1959-)

Prominent Australian knitting designer and author Jo Sharp began her career selling finished knitwear, but soon, in the early '90s, developed her own line of wool yarn and hand-knitting patterns. The Jo Sharp line, including kits and pattern booklets simply titled *Knit,* quickly became a mainstay in Australian yarn shops. Her garments have a relaxed look that suits the creative modern woman, and an innate practicality that enables them to fit into casual yet hectic lifestyles. Sharp's many yarns are characterized by natural fibers, graceful colors, earth tones and touchable texture. Her latest book, *Rugyard Story: Hand Knitting Collection,* melds the landscape and beauty of Western Australia with the natural colors in her collection. Earlier pattern books that Sharp authored include *Knitting Bazaar, Knitting Emporium* and *Knitted Sweater Style,* all featuring her own yarn. Her company runs a flagship store in Cottesloe, outside of Perth.

SHAWL

Similar to a scarf, a shawl is a wrap that provides extra warmth. Shawls are larger than scarves, however—often large rectangles, triangles or circles. They can be draped loosely over one's arms, or even wrapped around the neck more closely. Shawls are often worked in lacework patterns, but can be knit in any pattern.

See also ORENBURG LACE; SCARF; SHETLAND LACE

SHAYNE, ANN

See MASON-DIXON KNITTING

SHEEP

Ruminant quadrupeds with a woolly fleece, sheep *(Ovis aries)* are bred for both food and their fleece, which is spun into wool yarn. There are many breeds of sheep, but they are generally sub-classable as wool, meat or dairy breeds. Dual-purpose breeds are bred for both wool and meat. Major wool breeds include merino, Rambouillet, Romney, Shetland, Leicester and Lincoln. Wool sheep are further classifiable as fine, medium, long or carpet wool breeds. Most fine wool sheep are merinos or breeds derived from merinos, such as Rambouillet. Long wool breeds, such as Lincoln and Leicester, are larger and have a relatively slow rate of wool growth. Their wool is the easiest to spin, and thus well suited to hand-spinning. Most medium wool sheep raised for fiber rather than meat are crossbreeds between fine and long wool breeds, developed with quality and high production rates in mind. Examples are the American Columbia, a cross between the Rambouillet and the Lincoln, and the Corriedale, an Australian-developed crossbreed of merino and Lincoln. Carpet wool breeds, which include the Icelandic sheep, are usually double-coated; their long, coarse outer coats yield durable fibers suitable for carpets or tapestries. Hair-class sheep shed their coats, which are not usable as fiber.

After China, the largest producers of sheep products are in the southern hemisphere: Australia, New Zealand and the Patagonian regions of Argentina, Uruguay and Chile. In the United Kingdom, the importance of the wool trade was at one time so significant to the economy that in the upper chamber of Parliament (the House of Lords), the Lord

Columbia

Icelandic

Leicester

Lincoln

Merino

Rambouillet

Romney

Shetland

A Life With Sheep

by Kristin Nicholas

Thirty years ago, my husband-to-be, Mark, and I purchased four white Romney ewes from a farmer in northern Vermont.

We chose Romneys because they're a dual-breed sheep—they grow nice, long, beautiful wool and produce lambs that are good to eat. They are also particularly beautiful, classic-looking sheep with lovely dispositions, and the ewes are excellent mothers. We borrowed a truck and drove our four sheep back to the farm Mark grew up on in western Massachusetts. We named them Putney, Betsy, Addie and Frieda (after my grandmother).

No one Mark knew had ever had sheep. He was an animal science major and had lived on a dairy farm for most of his life, so he knew animals. But he didn't know sheep. I grew up in the suburbs and didn't know the first thing about sheep, except that their wool would make lovely yarn to handknit with. We learned together.

When you start raising sheep, the idea is that you will eventually have more sheep to increase your flock. For that you need a ram. We heard of a Romney ram for sale a couple of hours from the farm. We picked up Edward and waited to see what would happen. The next spring, three little lambs were born. I remember how excited we were. They were healthy, sturdy animals, and the ewes took good care of them. Now there were eight sheep.

Whenever I visited the farm, I would spend hours with the sheep—watching them graze, watching the babies nurse and grow bigger, smelling the green grass they were eating, helping to care for them. I learned that sheep have distinct personalities—one was the leader of the group, one was noisy, one was always last.

Now it is almost thirty years later. We have over 150 ewes, all descended from those first five sheep. Our sheep have birthed literally thousands of lambs over the years. We aren't nearly as attached to individual animals as we were in the beginning—in fact, it's hard for me to tell them apart, although Mark can. We sell the lambs at a livestock auction, primarily for the Easter lamb market. We sell the fleeces to hand-spinners when we can.

To this day, the most rewarding part of raising sheep is looking out at a beautiful green field in the evening and watching the sheep browse around nibbling at a particularly fine patch of grass with their lambs at their sides. Their lovely wool coats are slowly growing as the year progresses, keeping them warm in the winter and cool in the summer. It's a good and rewarding life feeling close to nature and seeing how it all goes 'round.

Kristin Nicholas designs, knits, blogs (getting-stitched-on-the-farm.blogspot.com) and writes books on a farm in western Massachusetts. She is the author of several books, and her patterns appear frequently in major knitting magazines.

Chancellor sits on a bench known as the Woolsack.

The color of sheep fleece varies, with white being the most prevalent and prized. Of all the wool-producing breeds, Shetland sheep probably have the most naturally occurring colors, although Icelandic sheep are also valued for their tonally varied fleeces. Other variables from breed to breed include staple length and strength, fineness, crimp and amount of lanolin.

Once a year, sheep are sheared of their fleece of wool, which is then processed (cleaned) to be ready for spinning into wool, whether by hand-spinners or for commercial use.
See also FIBER CHARACTERISTICS; LANOLIN; LOPI; MERINO; WOOL

SHEEP AND WOOL FESTIVALS

Agricultural sheep and wool festivals are events at which livestock—typically sheep, goats, alpacas—and sheepdogs—are shown and judged, classes are given, food is served and demonstrations in sheep-shearing and the like entertain. There has always been a fiber-arts element to these festivals. As knitting has exploded in popularity, the yarn aspect has grown exponentially, with many vendors—mostly small, independent fiber companies—attending and setting up sales booths. Sheep-to-shawl competitions, in which contestants complete a sweater with yarn they spun from fleece they sheared that day, are often held at sheep and wool festivals, which can range from one-day to weekend affairs.

Sheep and wool festivals are held from May through November throughout the country, but the Northeast hosts its share of exceptionally well-attended ones that have become destination trips for knitters. First up for the season is the biggest, the Maryland Sheep and Wool Festival (sheepandwool.org), held the first weekend of May at the Howard County Fairgrounds in Maryland. Ending the month is the Massachusetts Sheep & Woolcraft Fair (masheepwool.org). Ending the season on the Atlantic side of the country is the New York State Sheep and Wool Festival (sheepandwool.com) in Rhinebeck, New York, a favorite of vendors and bloggers alike.

Other notable fiber festivals include the Black Sheep Gathering (blacksheepgathering.org) in Eugene, Oregon, in June; the Michigan Fiber Festival (michiganfiberfestival.info) in Allegan, Michigan, in August; and the Wool Festival at Taos

The Shetland Islands are an archipelago off the northeastern coast of Scotland.

Shetland lace shawl

(taoswoolfestival.org), in Taos, New Mexico, in October.

International festivals include the Australian Sheep and Wool Festival held each July in Victoria; the Textilhandwerksmarkt in Berlin, Germany; the New Zealand Fibre and Fleece Festival; and the U.K.'s Woolfest, held each summer in Cockermouth, Cumbria.

Knitter's Review posts a sheep and wool festival primer on its website (knittersreview.com). *See also* CAMPS AND RETREATS; *KNITTER'S REVIEW*; TRAVELING WITH KNITTING; TOURS

SHETLAND LACE

This fine form of lace knitting was established in the Shetland Islands, particularly the isle of Unst. Situated at the northernmost point of Britain, the Shetland Islands are just about equidistant from Scotland and Scandinavia and follow in the knitting traditions of both. Sailors more than likely brought the craft to the islands, and the inhabitants took it up with incredible skill. By the early eighteenth century, the islanders had established a booming knitwear business, supplying the merchants who frequented their ports with quality knitted stockings, blankets and shawls.

The fine lace knitting for which the Shetlands are famed didn't emerge until the 1840s, when improved transportation began bringing both travelers and aspiring entrepreneurs to the Isles. The latter brought along fashionable lace items from home

and asked the island's skilled knitters to reproduce them. On Unst, the most northerly of the Isles, the knitters began producing a finely spun yarn that they worked into intricate openwork shawls and scarves. Called "wedding ring shawls" because they were so finely knit that the entire piece could be passed through a wedding ring, they played into the romantic visions so many had of life on the islands and were soon both in fashion and in demand.

Shetland lace shawls begin with a single stitch and work the edging on the bias. There is no discernable cast-on or cast-off edge. The stitch patterns, which have evocative names like "Fern," "Cat's Paw," "Fir Cone " and "Print o' the Wave," are worked both on garter and stocking stitch grounds, and different families often have their own names for the patterns. *See also* BRITISH KNITTING; FAIR ISLE KNITTING; FOLK KNITTING; KNITTED LACE; LACE KNITTING; LACE STITCHES; ORENBURG LACE

SHORTENING A GARMENT

Because patterns are written for use by many people, and no one garment could fit everyone equally well, to ensure the most flattering fit, sometimes customization is needed. People smaller than a typical model may find that shortening the garment makes the final object fit better.

To make a sweater body shorter, you can simply subtract rows

between the lower edge and the armholes. Sleeve shortening takes a little more work, as the increases that shape the sleeve must be recalculated: Figure out how long the sleeve will be, then use your row gauge to determine how many rows will be in the new sleeve length. Divide that number by the number of increase rows given in the original pattern. This will give you the approximate new spacing of increases. To create a short or three-quarter length sleeve, take the measurement of your arm at the point at which you want the sleeve to end (taking ease into account), then multiply it by your stitch gauge. This will give you the number of stitches to begin with.

Take care when shortening a garment that, should there be a stitch pattern, the shortening does not negatively affect the final look. *See also* DESIGN; LENGTH, ADJUSTING; PATTERN

SHORT ROWS

Partial rows of knitting are called *short rows*. They are used to shape or curve sections or to compensate for patterns with different row gauges. The result is that one side or section of a knitted piece has more rows than the other, but no stitches are decreased.

Short rows can be used to shape shoulders, eliminating the jagged edges that result when binding off a series of stitches. Short rows can also be used for darts at the bust and to shape collars, back necks on circular yokes, hats and medallions with circular pieces.

They are perhaps most famously used in socks, where their natural qualities create the turn of the heel. They can also be used in a specific technique known as the *short-row heel* or *short-row toe* in place of a heel flap or another toe construction.

Because the work is suddenly halted and turned, there is a likelihood that a hole will appear where the turn occurred. For this reason, knitters employ various methods to *fill* the holes. The most common is known as a *wrap and turn*, but the *yarn over* method is also popular. In either case, an additional wrap of yarn is placed at the point of the turn and then is worked into the stitch as if it weren't there, providing bulk to the stitch and thus a filling of the hole. Each creates its own unique look and knitters are known to prefer one over another for aesthetic reasons. *See also* HEELS; PICKING UP WRAPS; TOE; WRAP AND TURN

SHORT-ROW SHAPING

The process used to construct short rows, also called wrapping and turning. *See also* SHORT ROWS; WRAP AND TURN

SHOULDER SHAPING

The increases and/or decreases that shape the shoulder area of a garment are logically called the shoulder shaping. The outside of the shoulder should be lower than the inside neck edge to conform to the natural slope of the shoulder. Shoulders can be shaped by binding off a series of stitches over a number of rows. The more rows in the shoulder shaping, the greater the slope of the shoulder. Short-row shaping can also be used.

See also ARMHOLE SHAPING; SHORT-ROW SHAPING; SLEEVES; SWEATER

SHRUG

Smaller than a cardigan but more structured than a scarf, a shrug fits over the arms and covers the shoulders without adding a lot of bulk. It is the ideal garment to go over a light dress or formal gown once the temperature starts to drop. Knitters like shrugs because they can often be made out of one skein of yarn.

See also CARDIGAN; SCARF

SIDE-SPLIT COLLAR

See COLLARS AND NECKBANDS

SILK

A natural protein filament obtained from cocoons made by the larvae of the silkworm *(Bombix mori)*, silk is a continuous filament, as opposed to a fiber which has a set length or staple. Sericulture, or the cultivation of silk, is an enterprise that can be traced back to ancient China, and China is still the world's foremost producer of silk.

Cultivated silkworms feed solely on mulberry leaves, which have no tannins. The filaments are soft, strong, lustrous and brilliantly white—and absorb dye really well. Tussah, or wild silk, is produced from silkworms that feed on leaves containing tannins, resulting in filaments that are duller, and as a result the dyed colors aren't as clear.

Silk for Handknitting

The lightness, sheen and drape of silk make it a popular fiber for spring and summer yarns. It is not itchy, so it can be worn close to the skin, and it has good stitch definition. The downside of silk is its lack of resilience and tendency to pill. The quality of silk varies dramatically; it is best to use the higher-quality yarns as they tend to hold up better.

The longer the fibers the yarn is spun from, the more sheen it will have and the less likely it will be to pill. The best-quality silk yarn, called reeled silk, is made by unwinding the silk from the cocoon to yield long, unbroken strands. Lower-quality silk yarn is made by crushing and then combing the cocoons, which yields shorter fibers. Silk can also be combined with other fibers, such as wool or cotton, to yield less expensive yarns.

See also FIBER CHARAC-TERISTICS; YARN WEIGHT

SIMPLICITY KNITTING MAGAZINE

See MAGAZINES AND JOURNALS

SIMPLY KNITTING

See MAGAZINES AND JOURNALS (U.K.)

SINGER, AMY R. (1962–)

Amy Singer is the founder of *Knitty.com*, the preeminent knitting-pattern magazine on the Internet. Taught to knit at age six by her grandmother Lillian, whose needles grace every *Knitty* page, Singer continued knitting and crafting as she grew older. In 2002, while Singer was working as an editor and proofreader in the advertising industry, penning a knit blog and surfing the Web, she experienced her lightbulb moment: She noticed there were many budding knitwear designers who would create something interesting and pop the pattern on the Internet with no fanfare. She put out a call for submissions on her blog—which, at the time, got "one hundred hits a day, so it's amazing it took off at all," she reminisced on the *Ready, Set, Knit* podcast—and received enough response to launch *Knitty*.

Singer has also written books geared to traditionally unserved segments of knitters: *Big Girl Knits* (Potter Craft, 2006) and its sequel, *More Big Girl Knits* (Potter Craft, 2008), coauthored with friend and *Knittyspin* editor Jillian Moreno,

Shrug

Swatch knit from silk yarn

Bombyx mori silkworms

Cocoons ready for reeling

caters to women size 14 and up;
No Sheep for You (Interweave,
2007) focuses on wool alternatives
for knitters who, like Singer, are
allergic or sensitive to wool or
other animal fibers. She also pens
the "Web Watch" column for
Interweave Knits.
See also DESIGNERS;
KNITTY.COM; INTERNET;
INTERWEAVE KNITS

SINGLE CAST-ON

The single cast-on is the simplest
method and therefore a good one
to use when teaching children.
However, it does not provide the
neatest edge.
See also CAST-ON

SINGLE CROCHET

One row of single crochet, shown
at far right, makes a neat, narrow
edge; several rows form a firm
edge. You can also use it as a base
for other crochet edges.
See also CHAIN; CRAB STITCH

SK

Abbreviation for *skip.*

SK2P

Abbreviation for "slip one stitch,
knit two stitches together, pass the
slipped stitch over the two stitches
knitted together."
See also DECREASES

SKACEL KNITTING

Skacel is a yarn and needle
distributor and manufacturer
based in Seattle that makes many

Single Cast-On

Single cast-on edge

1. Place a slipknot on the right needle,
leaving a short tail. Wrap the yarn from
the ball around your left thumb from
front to back and secure it in your palm
with your other fingers.

2. Insert the needle upward through the
strand on your thumb.

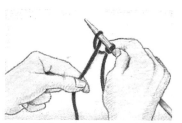

3. Slip this loop from your thumb onto
the needle, pulling the yarn from the
ball to tighten it. Continue in this way
until all the stitches are cast on.

Single Crochet

Single crochet edge

Single crochet can be worked on a
slip-stitch base, as shown here.

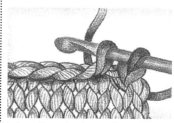

1. Draw through a loop as for a slip
stitch, bring the yarn over the hook,
and pull it through the first loop.
*Insert the hook into the next stitch
and draw through a second loop.

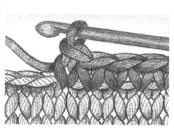

2. Yarn over and pull through both
loops on the hook. Repeat from the * to
the end.

fine German knitting materials
available to the American
consumer market. In 1987, Hans
and Ingrid Skacel sold the
Volkswagen dealership they had
been running and returned to the
yarn-importing business they had
first worked in when they
immigrated to the U.S. in 1957.
When the opportunity presented
itself, the couple purchased the
Schaffhauser line of yarn from the
importer Qualitaet. As the
handknitting industry boomed,
Skacel Collection added more
brands, including Schoeller &
Stahl, Zitron, Schulana and
eventually their own Skacel label
and collection. They also
introduced the speedy, top-of-the-
line Addi Turbo needles to the U.S.
market, as well as the full Addi
line. In 2007, the Skacels retired,
and their daughter Karin, who had
been operating a retail pottery
shop, took over as CEO of the
family business. Since then she
has taken the company in new
directions, importing yarns from
mills in Peru, Germany and Italy
and emphasizing customer service
to independent yarn shops. Skacel
is also well known for sponsoring
events that encourage people to
knit. They are active participants
in shows such as TKGA
conventions and the consumer
show Stitches.

SKEIN

Sometimes used interchangeably
with hank, a skein is a single unit

of yarn. Different manufacturers produce skeins of different sizes, though generally 50-gram or 100-gram sizes are the most common. When not wound into a ball, yarn comes in what is called a skein. Before it can be knit, it must be wound into a ball to prevent it from becoming tangled. A swift and ball winder make easy work of this, although an extra pair of hands or the back of a chair are also good options.
See also BALL; BALL WINDER; HANK, SWIFT

SKIRT

Garments worn to cover the legs that have a single opening are known as skirts, and they are worn almost exclusively by women. Knit or crocheted skirts are not unheard of, though care must be taken to make the right choices as to fit, yarn and pattern to avoid unsightly tugging or sagging. Given the knit stitch's propensity to lengthen in height, skirt patterns that do not place the stitches in a vertical alignment are the most flattering—

try for side-to-side construction or even bias work.

SKP

Abbreviation for "slip one stitch, knit one stitch, pass the slipped stitch over the knitted stitch."
See also DECREASES

SL

Abbreviation for *slip*.

SL 1K, SL1K

Abbreviations for "slip one stitch knitwise."

SLEEVE CAP

The uppermost point of a sleeve is known as the *sleeve cap*. The cap fits into the armhole of the sweater body. Sleeves for straight, square or angled armholes have no true cap; the top of the sleeve is simply worked straight. Cap shaping is worked for set-in and raglan sleeves only. A shaped armhole and set-in sleeve cap is one of the most complex types of shaping, as the measurement of the curved edge of the cap must

be equal to that of the armhole edge. For a raglan sleeve cap, the sides of the cap must have exactly the same number of rows as the back and front pieces of the raglan armhole.
See also RAGLAN SHAPING, SET-IN SLEEVE, SHAPING, SLEEVES

SLEEVES

The parts of a garment that cover the arm are the sleeves. Sleeve style for sweaters varies greatly, from feminine ruffled caps and flowing bell sleeves to sophisticated set-in styles and rugged raglans. When planning sleeves and their accompanying armholes, think about them in relation to other aspects of the design. A tailored, fitted silhouette, for example, demands a set-in sleeve. If you are using a chunky yarn, you may want to reduce bulk at the underarm by choosing a square or angled armhole. A deep armhole requires a wider, fuller sleeve.

Raglan Sleeve

A raglan sleeve extends in one

piece fully to the collar, leaving a diagonal seam from underarm to collarbone. It is named after the first Baron Raglan (a British soldier, 1788–1855), because it was designed to fit his coat for the arm he lost in the Battle of Waterloo.

Set-in Sleeve

A set-in sleeve is joined to the body of a garment by a seam that starts at the edge of the shoulder and continues around the armhole.

Drop Sleeve

A drop sleeve has a shoulder line that hangs down from the natural shoulder line. It is often used in relaxed, loose-fitting garments.

Saddle Shoulder

A saddle shoulder is a variation of a raglan sleeve, in which the shoulder portion forms a straight band that is continuous with the sleeve.
See also ARMHOLE SHAPING; RAGLAN SHAPING, SET-IN SLEEVES, SLEEVE CAPS

Large and small skeins

Sleeve Styles

Raglan Sleeve

Set-in Sleeve

Drop Sleeve

Saddle Shoulder

SLICER-SMITH, JANE

(1959–)

Born in Bradford, England, Jane Slicer-Smith learned to knit around the age of five at school but put it down again until, at seventeen, she designed her very first garment, a three-quarter-length Aran coat, on the needles without a pattern. She has since traveled the world picking up inspiration for her colorful knitwear. "I love the process of knitting," Slicer-Smith told *Knitter's* magazine. "It puts your mind in a different space. Knitting helps you sort things out—and not just in your swatch, but in your mental filing and sorting."

While working on her knitwear-design degree from Trent University in Nottingham in 1980, Slicer-Smith won the British Knitting Export Council Award for color, with the expectation that she would go to Paris or New York. Instead, she convinced the committee to allow her to backpack through Africa for sixteen weeks, seeing some of the earliest examples of knitwear in Egypt and soaking in the colors, patterns and culture of the continent. "Everyone in the group thought it crazy to be knitting a sweater through red-hot Egypt and Sudan, but I got to wear it when

we reached the equator: Kenya and Kilimanjaro were quite high and quite cold," she recounted in *Knitter's*. On her journey, she became friends with several Australians, whom she decided to visit in 1982—and ended up staying. In 1983 she began designing for the largest Japanese importer of British wool; two years later, she launched her own line of designs, kits and, eventually, merino wool, Signatur Knits, introduced to the U.S. market in 2000 and distributed by Trendsetter Yarns. Slicer-Smith has taught at the Stitches East show and the 2004 *Vogue Knitting* cruise to Alaska. She's best known for her impeccably tailored swing coat with bright intarsia graphics and her mitered designs.
See also DESIGNERS; STITCHES; TOURS

SLIPKNOT

A simple knot made on the needle used to begin most cast-on methods, a slipknot is counted as the first cast-on stitch. For the long-tail cast-on, leave a length of yarn about three times the width of the cast-on edge before making the slip knot. For other cast-on methods, leave an 8–10 inch (20–25cm) length to weave in later.
See also CAST-ON

SLIPPERS

Coverings for the feet that are more sturdy than socks but less structured than shoes are called

Slipknot

1. Hold the short end of the yarn in your palm with your thumb. Wrap the yarn twice around the index and middle fingers.

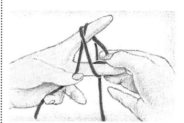

2. Pull the strand attached to the ball through the loop between your two fingers, forming a new loop.

3. Place the new loop on the needle. Tighten the loop on the needle by pulling on both ends of the yarn to form the slipknot.

slippers. Knit slippers are often felted for durability; sometimes, if the slippers are designed to be worn outdoors, leather soles are added, or other measures taken to protect the knitted fabric.
See also FELTING; SOCKS

SLIP STITCH

A stitch passed from one needle to the next without being worked is called a slip stitch. Slip stitches are often used when decreasing, as well as working color or slip-stitch patterns. Stitches may be slipped knitwise or purlwise. A stitch slipped knitwise has been twisted, but a stitch slipped purlwise retains its original orientation. Patterns will generally specify which method to use, but if it does not specify, purlwise is intended.
See also DECREASES; KNITWISE; PURLWISE; SLIP-STITCH PATTERNS

SLIP-STITCH PATTERNS

Patterns that use slip stitches to form vertical or horizontal textured designs are called slip-stitch patterns. When used with one or more colors, slip-stitch patterns produce a fabric with a woven appearance. Colorwork is made easy with slip-stitch patterns because only one color is used in any given row or round.
See also INTARSIA; MOSAIC KNITTING; MULTICOLOR KNITTING; SLIP STITCH

SL P, SL1P

Abbreviations for *slip one stitch purlwise.*

SL ST

Abbreviation for *slip stitch(es).*

SMOCKING

Smocking, also called the butterfly stitch, is a geometric design that is commonly used in sewing but also can be created in knitwear. To create smocking, a needle is used to weave through vertical ribs and to join adjacent ribs together to form a pattern that is reminiscent of a honeycomb. The pattern

Smocking

1. Beginning with the second knit rib at the lower right edge, bring the needle up the right side of that rib to the fourth stitch.

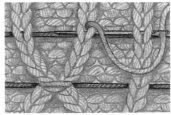

2. *Insert the needle from right to left into the fourth stitch (shown here after a few stitches have been smocked) of the first and second ribs. Bring the needle through and pull to join the ribs; repeat from the * once to complete a smocking stitch.

3. Bring the needle up the next 4 stitches on the left side of the second knit rib and work the smocking stitch, joining the second and third ribs by inserting the needle from left to right. Repeat steps 2 and 3 to the top of the piece.

decreases the width of the piece by about one third, and thus can be used to gather and shape a garment.
See also EMBELLISHMENTS

SOCKS

The earliest known socks knit on two needles (as opposed to having been created with a technique called *nålebinding,* which uses a single needle and short lengths of yarn) were discovered in the Middle East and date from sometime between the thirteenth and sixteenth centuries. By the start of the sixteenth century, people all over Europe were knitting socks. Royalty and aristocracy wore fine silk stockings crafted on slender metal needles, while commoners wore coarse hose made from wool they spun themselves and knit on larger needles.

Much of the history of American sock knitting is tangled up in war. Starting with the Revolutionary War, women knit socks for soldiers. After World War II, hand-knitting largely gave way to machines in the production of socks. In the past twenty years, however, there has been a resurgence of sock knitting as crafting and DIY have become popular in North America and throughout the world.

To avoid the need for seams, most socks are worked in the round, either on a set of four or five double-pointed needles, or on one or two circular needles. There are two ways to knit socks: from the top down, or from the toe up.

In this vertical slip-stitch pattern, the working yarn is held to the back as a stitch is slipped from the left needle to the right to form the vertical column of slip stitches.

In this horizontal slip-stitch pattern, the yarn is held in front as the stitches are slipped to create the horizontal stranded appearance of the fabric.

For socks knit from the top down, it is important to choose a method for casting on that will give a firm but stretchy edge, such as the standard long-tail or cable cast-ons. For toe-up socks, use a provisional cast-on such as crochet cast-on. Casting on with waste yarn and removing the cast-on row after the toe is completed will allow you to begin working in the round with the correct number of live stitches.

To shape the socks, paired decreases and short rows are used. Short rows are used to shape curved sections, such as toes and heels. Toe-up socks use wrapping and turning and working (or picking up) the wraps; top-down socks use a streamlined technique that does not require wrapping and working the wraps.

To finish a top-down sock, the Kitchener stitch (or grafting) is used to close up the toe. This method forms an invisible join and leaves no rough edges inside the sock. If the sock is worked toe-up, it will be necessary to bind off the last row of stitches. Be sure to bind off loosely so that the top of the sock stretches to fit comfortably. Go up one or two needle sizes if necessary. When the sock is completed, turn it inside out and weave in the loose yarn ends using a yarn needle.

Parts of a Sock

Cuff or Top Treatment

This is the part that holds the top to the leg so that the top does not slip down. It is often made in stretchy ribbing, plain or fancy, and the length can be varied. Elastic thread or round elastic can be worked with the yarn to ensure the stretch.

Leg

This is the part that covers the leg down to the start of the heel and is the area most visible when the sock is worn. This area is the main showcase for colorful or textured design elements.

Heel Flap

To create the heel flap, you work back and forth on approximately half the leg stitches. The other half of the stitches rest while you work the heel flap and heel. The heel flap gets a lot of wear from shoes, so it is usually worked in a stitch pattern that adds some durability, such as a slip-stitch pattern. Often additional fibers (such as Wooly Nylon) are added to make the flap more durable. Some sock yarns come with a tiny skein of reinforced thread that you use to knit the heel flap.

Turned Heel

Turning a heel simply means knitting a sort of "cup" in which the heel will fit. The process is called "turning" because most methods call for short rows that are turned frequently. Contrary to what you may have heard, turning a heel is actually an easy and fun process.

Gusset

Once you turn the heel, you must rejoin the heel stitches to those resting stitches so that the foot can be completed. Pick up stitches along both edges of the heel flap, then join the heel stitches and the resting stitches and begin knitting in rounds once more. Because of the picked-up stitches, you will now have more stitches on your needles that you had earlier. The gusset consists of a series of decrease rows in which you remove those extra stitches.

Foot

This is the part that covers the foot—the instep and the sole. Because this part is usually worn

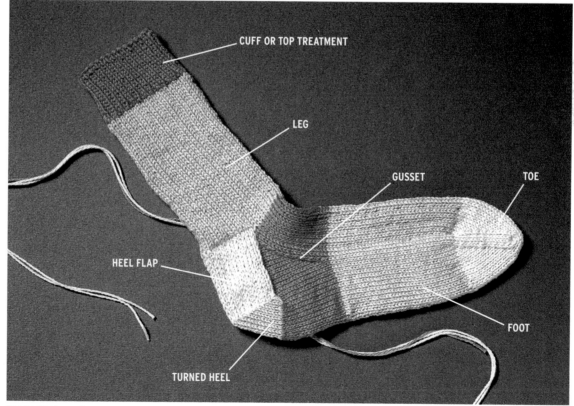

The parts of a sock

within a shoe, bumps and lumps in a pattern should be avoided. The sock's foot should be worked to the exact length of the wearer's foot. Therefore, begin shaping the toe when the sock foot is about 2 inches (5cm) shorter than the person's foot, measured from the back of the heel to the tip of the longest toe. The sock's length is very important. If it is too long, the sock will bunch up in the shoe and create blisters. If it is too short, the toes will be cramped and painful.

Toe

There are many ways to shape a toe. The most common method is to work a series of paired decreases, with each decrease row usually separated by an even row. The gradual narrowing of the piece creates a shaped toe. Most toe shapings are worked so that left and right socks are interchangeable.

See also AMERICAN RED CROSS KNITTING CAMPAIGNS; CIRCULAR KNITTING; CIRCULAR NEEDLES; DECREASES; DOUBLE-POINTED NEEDLES; GRAFTING; HEELS; HISTORY OF KNITTING; MAGIC LOOP; NÅLEBINDING; SHORT ROWS; TOE

SOCK SUMMIT

The Sock Summit was a convention for sock crafters held in 2009 that drew a large attendance of about four thousand knitters, spinners and crocheters, as well as more than one hundred and fifty vendors and dozens of "sock celebrity" instructors, to the Oregon Convention Center in Portland. Interest in the summit was so great that when registration opened online, thirty thousand would-be applicants crashed the organizers' server. This intense interest reflected sock knitting's rise throughout the '00 decade into a fiscally important category of the knitting arts. Portland's mayor was clued in to this popularity, taking time to attend the summit and officially declaring "Sock Knitting Week" in Portland. Classes, lectures and panel discussions were held at the summit, and, to add to the excitement, a Guinness World Record was set for the most people (935) knitting simultaneously. A second Sock Summit took place in 2010, indicating a possible longstanding future for the festival.

SPANISH KNITTING

Although it is unclear when knitting arrived in Spain (having made its way via North Africa), it was well established there by the ninth century. Most of the early knitting done in Spain was in service of the Catholic church. A prime example, a pair of altar gloves dating from the sixteenth century, is now in the collection of the Victoria & Albert Museum.

By the sixteenth century, Spanish knit stockings were the ultimate luxury item, prized by Queen Elizabeth I. It's likely that lace knitting originated in Spain, as the names of many of the original lace patterns are Spanish.

Shipwrecked sailors of the Spanish Armada are often given credit for the colorful patterns of Fair Isle knitting, but the story is based more on the romantic notions of nineteenth-century knitting historians rather than actual fact. However, sailors probably did have something to do with the spread of three-dimensional embossed designs

Spain, along with Portugal, is part of the Iberian Peninsula, located between the Atlantic Ocean and the Mediterranean.

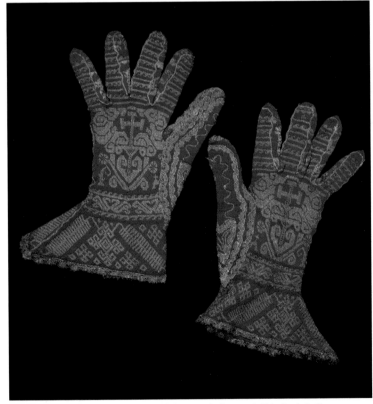

These red-and-gold silk gloves with religious symbols were knit in Spain in the sixteenth century.

such as cables, bobbles, trellises and honeycombs to Bavaria and the British Isles, though the technique and patterns themselves probably originated in the Islamic world.

See also FAIR ISLE KNITTING; FOLK KNITTING; GLOVES; LACE KNITTING

SPIDERWEB STITCH

A woven embroidery stitch used to create a flower motif.

See also EMBROIDERY

SPINNING

The twisting together of fibers to create yarn, spinning can be done by hand or machine. The earliest method probably involved simply twisting the fibers in the hand. A thread was pulled out of a bundle of fleece or fibers and twisted between the palm and thigh, and the twisted fibers were wound onto a short, straight stick. Eventually the stick was notched to hold the thread, and a "whorl," a weight made of clay or wood, was added to increase

Andean woman spinning fiber on a drop spindle

momentum. This mechanism is known as a drop spindle. The spinning wheel, which was probably invented in India between 500 and 1000 A.D. and arrived in Europe sometime in the Middle Ages, improved on the drop spindle.

The spinning jenny was invented in 1764 by James Hargreaves. A machine that could spin eight threads of cotton yarn, it threatened the livelihoods of handspinners and led to an uprising.

The Industrial Revolution saw the rise of mechanized spinning powered by water or steam, and eventually electricity. These days, new techniques including open-end and rotor spinning can produce yarns at rates in excess of 40 meters per second per spinning head.

In recent years handspinning has experienced a resurgence among both hobbyists and artisan spinners who create small quantities of one-of-kind yarn for their own use or for sale to others.

Spiderweb Stitch

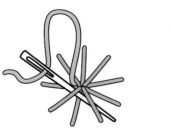

Create an odd number of "spokes" using straight stitches.

Weave the yarn or thread over and under the spokes, starting in the center and working out.

Spinning Is More Than Twisting Fibers by Shannon Okey

Spinning is so much more than the act of twisting fibers together to make yarn.

It is a celebration of color, skill and texture all wrapped up together, an opportunity to direct a project's development from the beginning without relying on the personal tastes or bottom line of a yarn company. Spinning, in short, frees you to decide not only what you want to knit but also exactly how it should look and feel. Whether you use a drop spindle or a wheel matters not: It's the fibers you choose and how you spin them that make the yarn sing.

And the fibers! We are so lucky to have access to the finest merino, camel, angora and alpaca just a mouse click away. In addition, there's soy fiber, bamboo, Lyocell and many organic spinning fibers that were unheard of just a few years ago. Experiment with these new choices if you're already spinning; if you're not already spinning, why not? What are you waiting for? Spinning is neither as difficult nor as time consuming as you may think, and the joy of creating your own yarn far outweighs any negatives.

I once overheard Lynne Vogel tell a student who was just learning to spin that her (lumpy, uneven) yarn was "designer yarn," and that she'd never be able to spin that way again, so she should treasure it. Wise advice! Save that first skein to remind yourself how far you've come—and to get inspiration. Plenty of projects look best knit in thick-and-thin yarns with a rustic, homespun quality.

For me, dyeing is often a part of spinning, because directing how a piece of multicolor fiber is divided during the spinning process determines what the final yarn will look like as much as your actual technique. Also, there are dozens of ways to split the same piece, so individual spinners can even put their own stamp on identically dyed bits of fiber. It's all these small decisions that add up to create the artistry of a single handspun yarn. Hand-spinning is compelling, creative and the end product is yarn—what's not to love?

Shannon Okey is the author of *Spin to Knit* (Interweave, 2006) plus almost a dozen other fiber and fabric-related books. Her website, knitgrrl.com, is popular with knitters, spinners and other fiber fanatics.

See also DROP SPINDLE; FIBER CHARACTERISTICS; SPINNING JENNY; SPINNING WHEEL

SPINNING JENNY

In Lancashire, England, in 1764, James Hargreaves invented a new machine that was capable of spinning eight threads of cotton yarn. Called the *spinning jenny,* it could do the work of eight people, something that caused some anger among local hand-spinners, who feared a loss of work. In 1768, a group of spinners broke into Hargreaves's house and destroyed his machines. Hargreaves decided to move, and he settled in Nottingham, where he found a partner, Thomas James, and set up a small spinning mill. The spinning jenny and spinning wheel continued to be used in homes until well into the nineteenth century.

See also DROP SPINDLE; FIBER CHARACTERISTICS; SPINNING; SPINNING WHEEL

SPINNING WHEEL

The spinning wheel, which was probably invented in India between 500 and 1000 A.D. and arrived in Europe sometime in the Middle Ages, improved on the drop spindle. The spindle was horizontally mounted in bearings and rotated by a cord encircling a large, hand-driven wheel. The larger the wheel, the faster the spindle would turn. The size of the wheel grew to 6 feet or larger in diameter, and it became known as the "Great Wheel" or "Walking Wheel." As time progressed, a foot pedal was added to the wheel. This allows the spinner to sit and spin, rather than move back and forth to wind fiber onto the spindle.

See also DROP SPINDLE; FIBER CHARACTERISTICS; SPINNING; SPINNING JENNY

SPINRITE

The Spinrite company of Stratford, Ontario, has a long history, starting before World War I under the name Perfect Knit Mills. It capitalized on the demand for wool for soldiers' uniforms and thrived only as long as the war lasted. The company then changed ownership, renamed as Maitland Mills, and did well again in World War II, and again languished afterward. In 1952, David Hay bought Maitland Mills, located in Stratford, Ontario, and renamed it Spinrite Yarn and Dyers, Ltd. At that point the company was already a major producer of yarn for the clothing industry, but retail played only a small part of their business. Today, Spinrite's market has grown very large in the wholesale and retail arenas, producing some of North America's most iconic brands, especially for crocheters. For example, Lily Sugar 'n Cream has a huge market share in cotton fibers sold for handicrafts; Bernat is a very influential brand, and Spinrite also owns the North American license for the distribution of the brand Patons.

SPLIT AND SPLICE

See JOINING YARN

SPOOL KNITTING

See ARABIC KNITTING; KNITTING NANCY

SPORTWEIGHT

See YARN TYPES

SPP

Abbreviation for "slip one stitch, purl one stitch, pass the slipped stitch over the purled stitch."
See also DECREASES

Engraving of a spinning jenny from the early 1800s

Spinning wheel

SQUARE-NECK COLLAR

See COLLARS AND NECKBANDS

SQUARE-NECK SHAWL COLLAR

See COLLARS AND NECKBANDS

SSK

Abbreviation for "slip two stitches knitwise one after another, then knit these two stitches together."
See also DECREASES

SSP

Abbreviation for "slip two stitches knitwise one after another, then purl these two stitches together."
See also DECREASES

SSSK

Abbreviation for "slip three stitches knitwise one after another, then knit these three stitches together."
See also DECREASES

STAPLE

The length of a natural fiber, such as wool or cotton, is called the staple. In general, longer staples are easier to spin and thus more desirable; longer staple length also indicates a higher-quality strand. Merino wool has the longest staple, typically 3–5 inches (7.5–13cm) in length, and is considered to be the highest-quality wool. Pima cotton is the longest staple cotton, typically 1½ inches (3.5cm) in length. The table at right gives the staple length of various fibers used in handknitting, in order from shortest to longest.
See also COTTON; FIBER CHARACTERISTICS; MERINO; SPINNING; WOOL

STARMORE, ALICE (1952-)

A knitwear designer revered for her expertise in Fair Isle and Aran knitting, Alice Starmore was born and still lives on Stornoway, on the Isle of Lewis in the Outer Hebrides. Starmore grew up steeped in the Scottish fishing port's culture and traditions and is still inspired by the landscape. Her mother taught her to knit at the age of three or four, and she continued throughout her life, turning professional in 1975, when she sold her first collection in London boutiques. Three years later she traveled to Norway, Sweden and Finland on a Winston Churchill Fellowship to study Scandinavian textile traditions and, upon her return, began a writing career that has produced some of knitting's gold-standard references and includes her own system of charting.

Starmore's books featuring her subtle colorwork and twist on traditional patterning, many of which are out of print and fetch high prices on the Internet, include *Scandinavian Knitwear* (Bell & Hyman, 1981), *Knitting From the British Islands* (Bell & Hyman, 1982), *Children's Knitting From Many Lands* (St. Martin's Press, 1983), *Alice Starmore's Book of Fair Isle Knitting* (reissued by Dover, 2009), *Sweaters for Men* (Ballantine, 1988), *The Celtic Collection* (Trafalgar Square, 1992); *Charts for Colour Knitting* (Windfall Press, 1992), *Fishermen's Sweaters* (Trafalgar Square, 1993), *Celtic Needlepoint* (Trafalgar Square 1994), *In the Hebrides* (Windfall Press, 1996), *Aran Knitting* (Interweave, 1997), *Pacific Coast Highway* (Windfall Press, 1997) and *Tudor Roses* (Windfall Press, 1998). *The Children's Collection* (Interweave Press, 2000) was co-authored with her daughter, Jade, her partner in Virtual Yarns, their Internet-based design/yarn business (virtualyarns.com).
See also ARAN KNITTING; FAIR ISLE KNITTING; DESIGNERS; INTERNET

STEAM BLOCKING

See BLOCKING

STEEKS

A vertical column of extra knitted stitches designed to be cut open when a garment is being finished is called a steek; to knit using steeks is referred to as *steeking*. Often used in Fair Isle knitting, steeks are used to create armholes and the fronts of cardigans when knitting in the round. An extra 8 to 10 stitches are cast on at the beginning of the armhole or

Staple Lengths

FIBER	STAPLE LENGTH
Buffalo	1"/2.5cm
Yak	1¼"/3cm
Qiviut (Muskox)	1½-2¾"/3.5-7cm
Cashmere (Kashmir Goat)	2-2¾"/5-7cm
Angora (Angora Rabbit)	2¾-5"/7-13cm
Mohair (Angora Goat)	3-6"/7.5-15cm
Wool (Sheep)	2¾-7¾"/7-20cm
Pima Cotton	1½"/3.5cm

Steeks

1. To work a steek, place eight stitches on a holder, then cast on eight stitches. When the body is complete, use the holder stitches plus picked-up stitches to work the band or the sleeve.

2. Pick up stitches through the inside loop of the first stitch before the steek by inserting the needle into the stitch and wrapping the yarn around the needle.

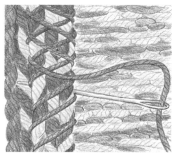

3. Once the steek is trimmed to a two-inch width, fold it back and sew in place with a finer yarn. Overcast the steek in one direction and then in the other direction as shown.

cardigan opening, the first and last of which serve as edge stitches to be picked up later. When the knitting is complete, the armhole or sweater front is cut up the center of the steek. The steek will then create a small facing that can be slip-stitched down. While seemingly fragile, when worked in 100 percent wool that slightly fulls amongst the interlaced stitches, a steek provides a sturdy, unravelable edge even after being cut. For more slippery yarn, which does not grab the adjacent stitches, sewing along the edge can "lock" the fabric, creating reliable steeks.
See also CIRCULAR KNITTING; FAIR ISLE KNITTING; FIBER CHARACTERISTICS

STITCH COUNT

The number of stitches per inch/centimeter is the stitch count. In some knitting directions, stitch count also is used refer to the total number of stitches in a row or a round.
See also GAUGE, GAUGE SWATCH

STITCHES

Stitches shows are knitting conventions open to the public, run by XRX, Inc., publisher of *Knitter's Magazine.* Stitches shows are held annually in four regions nationwide: Midwest, East, West and South. These are indoor events running for four days, usually held on the same general dates in the same cities: Stitches Midwest, for example, takes place in August in Schaumburg, Illinois. Stitches shows attract hobbyists of all skill levels to attend classes taught by prestigious teachers on a diverse variety of subjects, from Japanese stitches to buttonholes to steeking to mosaic knitting or Fibonacci knitting. Student events and fashion shows are on tap, as are professional-development programs for yarn shop owners, designers and others. The colorful Market is a particularly fun aspect of Stitches, offering a huge variety of knitting merchandise from hundreds of attending vendors, as well as product demos, book signings and cash giveaways. Some Stitches shows are followed by two-day intensive workshops called Stitches Etc.

STITCH FORMATION

The construction of a new knit stitch or purl stitch by pulling a loop of yarn through an existing stitch on another needle is its stitch formation.
See also AMERICAN/ENGLISH–STYLE KNITTING; COMBINED KNITTING; CONTINENTAL/GERMAN–STYLE KNITTING; EASTERN KNITTING; KNIT STITCH; PURL STITCH

STITCH GAUGE

A tool for measuring the gauge of a piece of knitting, a stitch gauge is primarily used when making a gauge swatch prior to beginning a knitting project. Sometimes it is a simple ruler-like object about 5 inches (13cm) long with a window in the center, other times it can be part of a needle gauge, a flat, card-like piece of metal or plastic, approximately 3 by 5 inches (7.5 by 13cm), with ruler marks on one edge and/or a window cutout. The

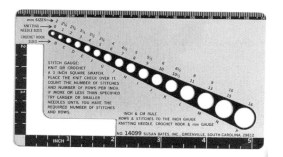

Stitch gauge

The Knitting Technician

by Meg Swansen

Knitting dazzles and inspires me with bright, exuberant colors and design motifs—with large, dramatic garments and extreme fashion/art knitting.

For my actual, real-life knitting, however, I am drawn to traditional styles such as lace, twisted stitches, two-end knitting, Latvian color patterns and Armenian knitting because of the different, and often unique, techniques involved. Some of my greatest knitting satisfaction comes from small, unnoticeable things backstage: specific techniques that, to me, are essential to the final success of the design.

I well remember the excitement created at Knitting Camp the first time a crocheted steek was demonstrated. To the casual viewer, it matters not whether a garment was knitted flat and sewn together, or knitted in the round and steeked; there is especially no interest in whether the steek was wrapped, machine-stitched, hand-stitched or crocheted. To the Knitting Technician, however, a well-executed steek is a thing of beauty and self-satsfaction.

Many techniques are even more subtle: Will anyone ever notice that your paired sleeve increases (or decreases) are mirror-images? Most likely not. Those small pleasures are for you, the knitter, alone. Even something as simple as switching your method of producing a left-leaning decrease from slip-one-knit-one-psso to ssk can give you a smile. If you are fortunate, you have an equally obsessive knitting buddy who will understand and appreciate these bits of knitting minutiae.

It is not surprising that many so-called new techniques result from misunderstanding the original instructions. In the There Are No Mistakes In Knitting mode, consistency can convert a "mistake" into a new design/technique/concept. The above-mentioned crocheted steek is a prime example: Amy Detjen's chain-stitch crochet (instead of the originally instructed single crochet) resulted in an easier-to-execute and less bulky finished product. Likewise, in an interpretation of Barbara G. Walker's ssk (slip, slip, knit), Dee Barrington "mistakenly" slipped the second stitch as if to purl, which led to a smoother left-leaning decrease for many knitters.

A technician's life is not a flashy one, since executing a knitting sleight-of-hand is usually not noticed, you must be content with an inner sense of achievement often known only to you.

Meg Swansen is the owner of Schoolhouse Press, author of five books, including *A Gathering of Lace* (XRX, 2000), and runs Knitting Camp, now in its thirty-sixth year. She writes frequently for *Vogue Knitting*, and her patterns have appeared in all major knitting publications.

gauge is placed on top of the knitting, and the stitches can be seen in the window and easily counted. Because the stitches are isolated from the rest of the knitting, they are easier to count than with a measuring tape. Most stitch gauges are marked with both inches and centimeters.
See also GAUGE; NEEDLE GAUGE; NOTIONS

STITCH HOLDER

Any tool that holds stitches when not in use is called a stitch holder. Usually a length of bent metal resembling a safety pin, a stitch holder may come in many styles, but need not be high-tech: A length of yarn can also be used.
See NOTIONS

STITCH MARKER

See MARKER

STITCH MOUNT

The stitch mount refers to the way in which stitches are placed on a needle. In Western knitting, which includes American/English knitting and Continental/German knitting, the leading leg is at the front, while the trailing leg is at the back. In Eastern knitting, the style of knitting common in eastern Europe, the Islamic world and South America, the leading leg of the stitch is at the back of the needle and the trailing leg is in front.
See also AMERICAN/ENGLISH-STYLE KNITTING; COMBINED KNITTING; CONTINENTAL/GERMAN-STYLE KNITTING; EASTERN KNITTING; WESTERN KNITTING

STITCH 'N BITCH

This term—both formal and generic—is given to groups of knitters that meet on a regular basis. According to Anne Macdonald's book *No Idle Hands: The Social History of American Knitting* (Ballantine, 1988), the term stretches back at least as far as World War II, when soldiers' wives would get together, knit and wait for news about their husbands. In 2000, the Chicago Stitch 'N Bitch group started a website to track the national network. In September 2003, Debbie Stoller's seminal *Stitch 'N Bitch: The Knitter's Handbook* (Workman) was published, giving the new wave of knitting its first blockbuster book, inspiring hundreds of SNB chapters to form across North America and landing on the *New York Times* bestseller list. Stoller's *Stitch 'N Bitch* sequels—2004's *Stitch 'N Bitch Nation*, 2006's *Stitch 'N Bitch Crochet: The Happy Hooker*, 2007's *Son of Stitch 'N Bitch: 45 Projects to Knit and Crochet for Men* and 2010's *Stitch 'N Bitch Advanced* (all from Workman) have extended the brand and continue to promote knitting to a wide audience.
See also DESIGNERS; HISTORY OF KNITTING; INTERNET; STOLLER, DEBBIE

STOCKINETTE STITCH

The basic knit and purl pattern formed by alternating knit rows with purl rows is called stockinette stitch. In stockinette stitch, the knit stitches are on the right side of the work and the purl stitches are on the wrong side, producing a fabric with a smooth surface. It has a propensity to curl in on itself due to the added surface on the purl side of the fabric—this can be combated in many ways in pattern design. For stockinette stitch, cast on any number of stitches. To knit with straight needles:
Row 1 (RS) Knit.
Row 2 Purl.
Repeat rows 1 and 2.
To knit stockinette in the round, knit every round.
See also KNIT STITCH; PURL STITCH; REVERSE STOCKINETTE STITCH

STOCKING CAP

See HATS

STOCKINGS

See SOCKS

STOLLER, DEBBIE (1963-)

Debbie Stoller is at the forefront of those bringing knitting to the next

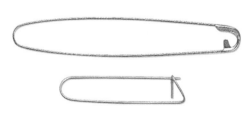

Two sizes and styles of stitch holders

Swatch knit in stockinette stitch

generation. With her enormously influential and popular *Stitch 'N Bitch* series of books, the co-creator of the feminist pop-culture magazine *Bust* exploded the myth of knitting as a stodgy pastime. "The only reason knitting had such a bad rap was because it had traditionally been done by women," Stoller told *Newsweek* in 2004.

Stoller, the descendant of many generations of Dutch needleworkers, holds a Ph.D. in the psychology of women from Yale. Though she learned to stitch as a child, she didn't become fully hooked until 1999, around the time she began publishing crafts in *Bust*. "There were already a number of threads going in the culture that were pointing toward a new generation becoming interested in 'women's work' type of things that had been rejected for a while," she told *Vogue Knitting* in 2007. "And that's when I found myself feeling more and more interested in these subjects," an interest she indulged in *Stitch 'N Bitch: The Knitter's Handbook*, published by Workman in 2003.

With its downtown design sensibility, instinctive how-to sections and cool photography, *Stitch 'N Bitch* spoke to a new generation of knitters in their own language, inspiring the rapid expansion of the loose-knit network of Stitch 'N Bitch knitting groups throughout North America. It spent time on the *New York Times* bestseller list and launched three sequels—2004's *Stitch 'N Bitch Nation*, 2006's *Stitch 'N Bitch Crochet: The Happy Hooker*, 2007's *Son of Stitch 'N Bitch: 45 Projects to Knit and Crochet for Men* and 2010's *Stitch 'N Bitch Advanced*, all published by Workman. *See also* DESIGNERS; INTERNET; STITCH 'N BITCH

STOREY, MARTIN (1958-)

A native of Yorkshire, Storey attended Middlesex University in the early 1980s, earning a degree in fashion and textiles. He got his start at the innovative knitwear design house Artwork, where he continued to work for fifteen years. He then left to become chief designer for Jaeger Handknits, his designs winning wide acclaim and contributing to the company's success. Today, Storey has become one of Britain's most foremost handknitting designers, being especially skilled at interpreting trends into styles for men. Storey is now a designer at Rowan, with his patterns featured in the Classic series of brochures for men, women, children and babies. He also contributes designs to *Rowan Knitting & Crochet Magazine*. Additional Rowan books that Storey has authored include *Classic Knits for Real Women*, *Classic Knits for Men* and *Knitting Goes Large*.

STORING YARN

Proper storage of yarn is essential, especially for wool. The most important things about storing yarn are: keeping it away from direct sunlight to prevent fading; keeping it away from dust and dirt; and protecting it away from pests, like moths and mice. In addition, it is essential that yarn be kept dry, as dampness can cause mildew and rot. Natural fibers need to breathe and so should not be stored in airtight containers.

Traditionally, woolen clothing was stored in cedar chests, as cedar repels moths. However, most knitters like to be able to see the yarn they have, and store it on open shelves, in baskets or in clear plastic containers, all of which are suitable if the previous points are considered. Spot clean before storing finished garments. Fold, don't hang, sweaters and knitted garments.
See also CARE; FIBER CHARACTERISTICS

STOVE, MARGARET (1940-)

This esteemed lace knitter/designer from New Zealand has done a great deal to catalog the history of lace knitting, and she developed a way to spin merino wool into a lofty laceweight yarn. Taught the knit stitch by her grandmother at an early age, by five years old she was adept enough that her teacher deemed her worthy of learning to purl. As an adult, she was drawn to lace and researched the topic assiduously, documenting her findings.

Stove earned acclaim when she designed and knit the lace christening shawl that was the national gift of New Zealand to Prince William of Wales in 1982. She is the author of three books: *Handspinning, Dyeing and Working with Merino and Superfine Wools* (Interweave, 1991), *Creating Original Hand-Knitted Lace* (Lacis, 1995) and *Wrapped in Lace* (Interweave, 2010). She produces her own line of laceweight yarn, Artisan, with her daughter, Kristine Sullivan. Stove's work is displayed at galleries and private collections around the world.
See also DESIGNERS

STRAIGHT STITCH

A basic embroidery stitch used for outlining and creating straight lines.

STRANDED KNITTING

See BOHUS KNITTING; FAIR ISLE KNITTING

ST(S)

Abbreviation for *stitch(es)*.

ST ST

Abbreviation for *stockinette stitch*.
See also STOCKINETTE STITCH

SUI, ANNA

See VOGUE KNITTING

SUPERWASH

"Superwash" is used in reference to wool, and it is a designation trademarked by the Wool Bureau. It is a treatment or process that allows wool fibers to be washed by machine without the risk of felting or shrinking. Wool felts and shrinks when the microscopic scales on its fibers interlock; superwashing works by eliminating the possibility of this scale activity. Wool can be superwashed either by being coated with a polymer resin that smooths out its natural scales, or by undergoing an enzyme bath to tame the scales' interlocking propensity.

Superwash yarn is made to be washed and dried by machine, but should still be handled with care, and objects made from it should be washed on the gentle cycle and air dried when possible.
See also FELTING; WOOL

Straight Stitch

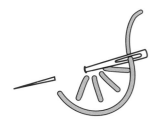

Draw needle up. In one motion, insert needle a short distance away and draw up again.

SUSAN BATES

The Bates Company, a major force in American needlemaking, was founded by Carlton Bates in Chester, Connecticut, in 1907 to manufacture crochet hooks, knitting needles and manicure sets. The company later became C. J. Bates & Son, but sold its products under a persona named Barbara Bates (a marketable fictional female much like Betty Crocker) until the 1940s, when the moniker was changed to Susan Bates. In the 1990s Bates stopped production of its own needles but continued to import and sell tools. Coats & Clark later acquired the brand, and the Susan Bates line forged forward to remain one of the most inexpensive, easily found lines of stitching tools, including the popular Silvalume and Quicksilver series and countless notions and accessories.

SWANSEN, MEG (1942–)

A master knitter in her own right,

Sweden is located in Northern Europe between Norway and Finland in the Scandinavian Peninsula.

Meg Swansen is the daughter of knitting trailblazer Elizabeth Zimmermann. Swansen studied drawing at a German art school in the early '60s, finding on her travels around Europe Icelandic wool that her mother later imported for the Wisconsin-based mail-order business Zimmermann founded, Schoolhouse Press. After returning to the States and marrying composer Chris Swansen, she received sweater commissions from such jazz luminaries as Stan Getz. Swansen joined Zimmermann at Schoolhouse Press in the late '70s and, on her mother's retirement in 1989, took the helm of the business, growing its activities and product development based on a knitter's instinct. Among the titles Swansen is proud to have published are all seven of Barbara Walker's previously out-of-print books. Her other endeavors include publishing the semiannual newsletter *Wool Gatherings,* increasing the number of Knitting Camp summer sessions to four, converting the instructional videos she and Zimmermann made to DVD, and penning a regular technique column for *Vogue Knitting.* Swansen's son Cully Swansen has carried on the family tradition by becoming a knitter; in 2010 *Vogue Knitting* published one of his hat patterns that explored intertwining colors and cables.

Other books that Swansen has either authored or coauthored include *Handknitting with Meg Swansen* (Schoolhouse Press, 1995), *Meg Swansen's Knitting* (Interweave, 1999), *A Gathering of Lace* (XRX, 2000), *Sweaters From Camp* (with Amy Detjen and Joyce Williams; Schoolhouse Press, 2002) and *Armenian Knitting* (with Joyce Williams and Lizbeth Upitis, Schoolhouse Press, 2007). Like her mother, Swansen is an acolyte of circular knitting and prefers to instruct in ways that beg interpretation from the individual knitter.
See also CAMPS AND RETREATS; DESIGNERS; *VOGUE KNITTING;* ZIMMERMANN, ELIZABETH

SWEATER

The sweater is a garment that is worn over the torso and is likely the most common knitted item. Sweaters can take many forms and styles, including cardigans and pullovers.
See also ARMHOLE SHAPING; COLLARS AND NECKBANDS; CARDIGAN; DESIGN; GANSEY; SHRUG; SLEEVES; YOKE

SWEDISH KNITTING

Knitting styles and patterns characteristic of Sweden are similar to those of Norway. Sweden introduced the technique of *tvåändsstickning,* or two-end knitting. This circular technique, in which both ends of the same ball of yarn are used and the strands twisted between each stitch, produces a firm, warm, wind-resistant fabric. Sweden is also home to two notable knitting cooperatives, the Halland Knitting Cooperative, which began producing Binge knitting (stranded garments worked in red, white and blue), and Bohus Stickning, which became world-famous for its sweater designs. *See also* BOHUS KNITTING

SWIFT

Sometimes called an umbrella swift, a swift is a collapsible wooden or metal device used to hold a hank (skein) of yarn while it is being wound into a ball. Most swifts are clamped to a table when in use, although there are some freestanding models available. A swift comprises a center post and six or eight collapsible arms that

when extended form a V-shaped groove that holds the yarn. Used with a ball winder, or wound by hand, the swift freely rotates while the yarn is being wound, eliminating the need for a person or chair to hold the yarn. *See also* BALL; BALL WINDER; HANK; SKEIN; WINDING YARN

SWISS DARNING

See DUPLICATE STITCH

SYMBOLS

When representing knitting in chart form, each stitch is formed using a single symbol. These symbols are unique to knitting, and are becoming standardized across the discipline. The table at right shows the standard symbols adopted by members of the Craft Yarn Council. *See also* ABBREVIATIONS; CHARTS

Winding a ball of yarn with a swift

Standard Knitting Symbols

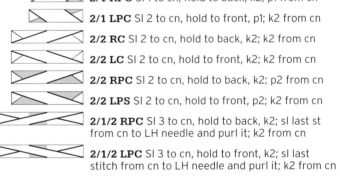

□	K on RS, p on WS	Ω̲	P1 tbl on RS, k1 tbl on WS
▨	P on RS, k on WS	●	Bobble
▬	P on RS, k on WS on a color chart	▪	Sts do no exist in these areas of chart (70% shade)
O	Yarn over (yo)	M	Make 1 (M1) knitwise on RS, M1 purlwise on WS
╱	K2tog on RS, p2tog on WS		
╱	P2tog on RS, K2tog on WS	**M**	Make 1 (M1) purlwise on RS, M1 knitwise on WS
╲	SSK on RS, SSP on WS	Ⅴ	Inc 1-to-3
╲	SSP on RS, SSK on WS	Ⅳ	Inc 1-to-4
⅄	Right-slanting inc	Ⅴ	Inc 1-to-5
⅄	Left-slanting inc	⍓	Dec 4-to-1 (right-slanting)
Ⅴ	Sl 1 purlwise with yarn at WS of work	⍓	Dec 4-to-1 (left-slanting)
Ⅴ	Sl 1 purlwise with yarn at RS of work	⍓	Dec 4-to-1 (vertical)
⁄₃	K3tog on RS, p3tog on WS	⍓	Dec 5-to-1
⅄	SK2P, SSSK on RS, SSSP on WS	℞	K1, wrapping yarn twice around needle
⅄	S2KP2 on RS, S2PP2 on WS		
Ω	K1 tbl on RS, p1 tbl on WS	⌒	Bind off

2/1 RPC Sl 1 to cn, hold to back, k2; p1 from cn

2/1 LPC Sl 2 to cn, hold to front, p1; k2 from cn

2/2 RC Sl 2 to cn, hold to back, k2; k2 from cn

2/2 LC Sl 2 to cn, hold to front, k2; k2 from cn

2/2 RPC Sl 2 to cn, hold to back, k2; p2 from cn

2/2 LPS Sl 2 to cn, hold to front, p2; k2 from cn

2/1/2 RPC Sl 3 to cn, hold to back, k2; sl last st from cn to LH needle and purl it; k2 from cn

2/1/2 LPC Sl 3 to cn, hold to front, k2; sl last stitch from cn to LH needle and purl it; k2 from cn

TAHKI•STACY CHARLES, INC.

Known for its very broad coverage of the American hand-knitting market with yarns both elegant and casual, TSC was formed in the year 2000 by the merger of two established American yarn companies, Stacy Charles and Tahki Imports. The melding of these two companies was an extraordinary success. Stacy Charles, Inc., was founded in 1984 when Stacy Charles began importing two high-quality Italian novelty fiber lines, Filatura Di Crosa and Filpucci. Many well-known fashion designers have sourced these lines for their knitwear collections. Tahki Imports, Ltd., launched as a mail-order business in 1968, operating out of the home of its cofounder Diane Friedman. Tahki Imports has had great winners in its natural-fiber brand Tahki, which includes the beloved "Donegal Tweed" and "Cotton Classic" yarns. In addition to these classic lines, the merged company carries the couture-quality S. Charles Collezione, an outgrowth of Charles's original Missoni line, with luxury fibers, colors and textures designed to be mixed and matched. With its new Loop-d-Loop yarn collection by Teva Durham, TSC has added an urbane, ecologically conscious dimension to its offerings with yarn for this progressive designer's cutting-edge designs. TSC prints patterns for its yarns in spring and fall.

TAILS
See WEAVING IN

TARTAN KNITTING

A type of intarsia knitting that uses squares, rectangles or diamonds to create a plaid fabric, Tartan knitting is an old technique. In some cases, the vertical lines are added using duplicate stitch. Argyle patterns are examples of Tartan knitting, as are plaid designs, such as the one shown below.
See also ARGYLE; DUPLICATE STITCH; FOLK KNITTING; INTARSIA

TATTING

A lacemaking technique that uses a shuttle and thread to create durable knotted lace, tatting is now largely considered an "old-fashioned" craft. It was traditionally used to make edgings, doilies and collars and is a cousin of macramé. Like many so-called lost arts, tatting is enjoying something of a resurgence. Probably evolved from the decorative rope work of sailors, it was popular in England during the reign of Queen Mary and can be seen in paintings of Madame Adelaide, the daughter of Louis XV of France.

Unlike knitted or crocheted lace, both of which are stretchy, tatted lace is stable and therefore not as delicate. It is usually made with fine-gauge cotton or linen thread and is suitable for collars and decorative motifs that can be applied to knitted garments.
See also LACE KNITTING

TBL
Abbreviation for "through the back loop(s)."
See also KNIT THROUGH THE BACK LOOP

TEA COZY
A hat-like cover used to keep the tea in a china teapot warm during and after steeping, a tea cozy (spelled *cosy* in Britain) is de rigueur at a classic British tea. The Irish, English and Danes have all been given credit for the tea cozy's origin, but the most popular legend of its invention dates back to seventeenth or nineteenth century in Ireland. It seems a tired farmer leaned across the table one evening, causing his hat to drop from his head and land atop the family teapot. The hat was left where it fell, and when the farmer removed it some time later to pour himself another cup, the tea was still warm—voilà! The cozy was born. In later years, cozies were a necessary part of any quality set of table linens, coordinated to the tablecloth, napkins and even china

This tartan box-jacket appeared in the Fall/Winter 1951 issue of the *Vogue Knitting Book*.

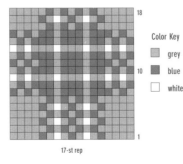
Color Key
▨ grey
▨ blue
☐ white
17-st rep

Swatch knit in a plaid Tartan pattern

patterns. Today's cozies take on many shapes, styles and fabrics, but knit versions remain popular, often updated with wild colors, stripe patterns, pompoms, embroidery and other accents. Cozies can be knit in the round or back and forth on straight needles, left plain or felted. Wool (prized for its insulating abilities) is usually the yarn of choice, but acrylics, cottons and even some novelty yarns find their way into the mix.

TENSION

See GAUGE; GAUGE SWATCH

TERIOKHIN, VLADIMIR (1960-)

After a successful career as a ballet dancer, Vladimir Teriokhin leapt

into knitting. The Russian-born Teriokhin spent ten years with the Bolshoi Ballet after being accepted to its Academy School in Moscow at the age of nine. He and his wife, ballerina Elena Stepaneko, emigrated to New York in 1989 and, after dancing for a while with the Los Angeles Classical Ballet Company, Teriokhin decided to try his hand at knitwear. "Ballet gave me the discipline and training to be a designer," having designed ballet costumes while with the Bolshoi, he told *Vogue Knitting* in 2002.

His feminine yet strong garments combine the romanticism of ballet with the fortitude of a highly structured dancer's life. "Knitwear has a long tradition, and I like the challenge of

Knit tea cozy designed by Kristin Nicholas (from *Color by Kristin*, Sixth&Spring Books, 2009)

trying to create something totally new." Along with designing regularly for *Vogue Knitting*, Teriokhin has created knitwear collections for such major Seventh Avenue designers as Vera Wang, Oscar de la Renta, Donna Karan and Isaac Mizrahi, making the cover of *Women's Wear Daily* (the first of many times) with one of the sweaters he designed for Ralph Lauren in 1998.
See also DESIGNERS

TEST SWATCH

See GAUGE SWATCH

TEXTILE MUSEUM OF CANADA

This museum located in Toronto, Canada, whose motto is "Connecting cloth, culture, and art," has a permanent collection that includes more than twelve thousand objects that span two thousand years of history and two hundred world regions.

TEXTILE MUSEUMS

See MUSEUMS

TEXTURED KNITTING

A pattern in which one type of stitch is used as background and another type stands away from the background is known as a textured knitting pattern.
See also BOBBLE, CABLE PATTERNS; CABLES; HONEYCOMB STITCH, KNIT/PURL PATTERNS, MOSS STITCH, RIBBING, SEED STITCH, SLIP-STITCH PATTERNS, TRAVELING STITCHES, TWISTED-STITCH PATTERNS

THOMAS, NANCY J. (1946-)

Writer, author and knitwear designer Nancy J. Thomas has been editor at several top knitting magazines, including *Vogue Knitting, Knitter's* magazine and *Family Circle Easy Knitting*. Formerly the creative director at at Tahki•Stacy Charles, Thomas is now creative director at Coats & Clark. Thomas's book *Tweed: More Than 20 Contemporary Designs to Knit* (Potter Craft, 2007) is the first of its kind, offering, in addition to its patterns, a guide to working with tweed fibers and tracing the history of tweed from its humble beginnings to the variety of present-day applications both classic and contemporary. Thomas has also cowritten with Adina Klein a series of *Just* knitting books and pattern-card sets for the Lion Brand Yarn Company, including *Just Scarves: Favorite Patterns to Knit and Crochet* (2005) and *Just Hats: Favorite Patterns to Knit and Crochet* (2005), both published by Potter Craft.

THREE-NEEDLE BIND-OFF

This bind-off is used to join two edges that have the same number of stitches, such as shoulder edges, which have been placed on holders.
See also BIND-OFF

THROW

See AFGHAN

TINK

The opposite of "knit," the slang term "tink" means to undo your knitting stitch by stitch. It is not the same as "frogging" or "ripping" your knitting, which is to remove rows at a time.
See also FROGGING; UNRAVELING

TKGA

See KNITTING GUILD OF AMERICA, THE

TNNA

See NATIONAL NEEDLEARTS ASSOCIATION, THE

Three-Needle Bind-off

Three-needle bind-off

1. With the right side of the two pieces facing each other, and the needles parallel, insert a third needle knitwise into the first stitch of each needle. Wrap the yarn around the needle as if to knit.

2. Knit these 2 stitches together and slip them off the needles. *Knit the next 2 stitches together in the same way as shown.

Slip the first stitch on the third needle over the second stitch and off the needle. Repeat from the * in step 2 across the row until all the stitches are bound off.

TOE

The toe of a knitted sock can be worked in a number of ways. The first consideration when deciding which type of toe to use is whether the sock is worked from the top down or the toe up. Three of the toe types described below can be worked with top-down socks: the flat toe, the wide toe and the pointed toe. Toes for top-down socks are usually shaped by working a series of paired decreases, each decrease row usually separated by an even row. The short-row toe is used for socks worked from the toe up.

Socks, and therefore toes, are almost always worked in the round, usually using double-pointed needles or the magic loop method. Most toe shapings are worked so that left and right socks are interchangeable.

In her book *Knitting Vintage Socks* (Interweave, 2005), Nancy Bush takes classic sock patterns from *Weldon's Practical Needlework* and updates them for the modern knitter. Patterns for

the flat toe, the wide toe and the pointed toe, as well as several others, are included.

Flat Toe

The flat toe is a popular toe shape that is worked over an even number of stitches divisible by four. In each decrease round, four stitches are eliminated. The toe can be finished with either three-needle bind-off or grafting.

Wide Toe

The wide toe is similar to the flat toe, but more stitches are worked between the decreases on each side of the toe. It is finished in the same way as the flat toe.

Pointed Toe

The pointed toe is also worked over an even number of stitches that is divisible by four. Four stitches are eliminated in each round in a pattern that creates a spiral at the tip of the toe. The toe is finished by gathering the remaining stitches together with a yarn needle.

Types of Knitted Toes

Flat toe

Wide toe

Short-row Toe

The short-row toe is worked by casting on half the total number of stitches using a provisional cast-ton, decreasing by working wrapped short rows and then picking up the wrapped stitches to increase to the full toe width. *See also* BUSH, NANCY; HEELS; DECREASES; DOUBLE-POINTED NEEDLES; GRAFTING; MAGIC LOOP; PAIRED DECREASES; PROVISIONAL CAST-ON; SHORT ROWS; SHORT-ROW SHAPING; THREE-NEEDLE BIND-OFF; WRAP AND TURN; SOCKS; *WELDON'S PRACTICAL NEEDLEWORK*

TOG

Abbreviation for *together*.

TOTE

A tote is a large handbag or carryall. Knitted totes are generally worked in a sturdy yarn and stitch pattern, though large open meshes can work well as grocery bags. Many bags are felted to increase sturdiness.
See also PURSE

TOURS

Knitting as a holiday unto itself gained a great deal of traction in the mid-2000s, with big-name designers teaching on cruises, in European capitals and exotic South American locales, and at luxury-resort retreats. Knitting tours soon turned into a true business. Itineraries change from year to year, but several travel companies specialize in planning knitting-niche trips—domestic, international and oceanic— including Craft Cruises (craftcruises.com), Craft World Tours (craftworldtours.com), Stitchaway Tours (stitchawaytours.com) and Tactile Travel (tactiletravel.com). Traveling Together (travelingtogether.net/Traveling/ knitting.cfm) books the annual *Vogue Knitting* adventure.
See also CAMPS AND RETREATS; SHEEP AND WOOL FESTIVALS

TOYS

By nature, knitted toys are plush and soft, making them perfect for newborns up to adults. Knitted stuffed animals have been popular for ages, but the Japanese "cute" craft of *amigurumi* (literally, knitted stuffed toy) transformed the practice, spawning ever more cute dolls, animals and inanimate objects with large features and small bodies. Though often crocheted, knitted amigurumi is popular as well. A crocheted amigurumi is generally worked all in single crochet in continuous spirals; the shapes are dramatically rounded to enhance their cuteness.

Toys are generally stuffed with polyester or cotton fiberfil, and the knitting is done at a dense gauge to ensure that the stuffing does not escape.
See also AMIGURUMI

TRAVELING STITCHES

Stitches that are moved from one position to another in a knitted piece are said to be traveling. In traveling stitch patterns, the stitches are crossed without a cable needle. Many traveling stitch patterns consist only of traveling stitches; others combine traveling stitches with other types of stitch patterns. In the example below, traveling stitches are formed by twisted-stitch pairs.
See also ALPINE REGION KNITTING; CABLES; STOCKINETTE STITCH

TRAVELING WITH KNITTING

Packing knitting projects and supplies for travel presents specific challenges to knitters.

Packing

The consensus among knitters for packing needles, yarn and notions is to either use a separate dedicated yarn travel bag or to stow everything in plastic baggies so the contents are protected from leaking bottles and so clothing doesn't get snagged by needle points.

Flying With Knitting

Ever since the terrorist attacks on September 11, 2001, knitters have

Pointed Toe

Short-row toe

In this swatch, traveling stitches are formed by twisted-stitch pairs.

struggled with packing knitting projects for air travel. For a time after the attacks, knitting needles and crochet hooks were prohibited as carry-on items on flights originating in the United States. The rules have since changed, with the U.S. Transportation Security Administration now allowing needles and hooks in both checked and carry-on baggage; however, the policy is subject to change at any time in response to the given security climate, and individual security officers always have, according to the detailed TSA bulletin on "Transporting Knitting Needles and Needlepoint," "the authority to determine if an item could be used as a weapon and may not allow said item to pass through security." To reduce the risk of confiscation, consult the TSA website (tsa.gov) for current guidelines. It's a good idea to bring along a self-addressed stamped envelope to mail implements home in order to retain your belongings in case of confiscation.

Knitting on Public Transportation

Many knitters knit on public transportation and as passengers in cars to while away a commute. Simple travel etiquette keeps your project—and elbows—close at hand and away from being a nuisance to fellow travelers. Small, portable projects and circular needles allow for less physical encroachment upon a seatmate's personal space. Scissors should, if possible, remain stowed; sudden stops could make for a dangerous situation otherwise.
See also CAMPS AND RETREATS; TOURS

TRENDSETTER YARNS

In 1989, Barry Klein and his mother, Myrna Klein, launched the importing company Trendsetter Yarns, an industry leader specializing in bringing upscale fashion yarns from around the world to the American market. The Kleins were no strangers to the business when they founded Trendsetter: In the 1970s, Myrna operated a needlepoint store and traveled to Italy, where she was inspired to launch the importing company Fantacia, one of the first firms to distribute Italian hand-knitting fashion yarns in the United States Barry became increasingly involved in Fantacia as a pattern designer, sales agent and TNNA representative. Three years after Myrna disbanded Fantacia in 1985, she and Brian reconnoitered fresh sources in Italy, then formally debuted Trendsetter. Trendsetter's yarns are exemplified by classic wool lines such as Naturally from New Zealand and luxury lines such as the Italian Mondial. Trendsetter offers substantial pattern support for its yarns, publishing frequent pattern booklets and seasonal collections and securing designs from such established names as Fayla Reiss and Jane Slicer-Smith. The Kleins have also worked tirelessly in industry organizations to promote of the craft of knitting. Recently the company expanded its operations to the United Kingdom and Canada.

TRUNK SHOW

An assemblage of rotating merchandise that travels from store to store, allowing consumers to sample wares firsthand before they buy, may or may not be delivered in a trunk but is still called a trunk show. The concept of this common marketing tool, adopted by the yarn industry from high-end fashion and jewelry designers, is centuries old, taken from the days when peddlers hawked their wares in trunks they hauled from town to town. Today fiber-related trunk shows are shipped overnight from one LYS to the next on the list, usually in boxes, not trunks.

Yarn-shop owners sign up to receive trunk shows presented by yarn companies to support seasonal lines, designers to support fresh pattern collections, or knitting and craft publishers to support book launches and specific magazine issues. A trunk show typically encompasses a dozen or so sample garments and their corresponding patterns; the retailer is encouraged to carry the yarn specified for each project, giving consumers immediate soup-to-nuts availability. Designers sometimes travel with their trunk shows and sign books or speak, using the garments as visual aids. Retailers benefit by exposing their customers to the latest designs and fibers; knitters and crocheters benefit by being able to try on garments and experience the way a particular skein of yarn works up pre-purchase. Retailers interested in receiving trunk shows should contact their distributors to see which companies currently offer such a program.
See also DESIGNERS; LYS; MAGAZINES AND JOURNALS

TUNIC

Long blouses or sweaters are called tunics.
See also SWEATER

TURKISH PATTERNS

Some speculate that the Turkish tradition of sock knitting dates to the seventeenth century, but its origin is largely unknown. As in the Balkans, the designs on the socks identified the wearer's community and social rank, and they were often given as gifts.

The striking geometric designs used in the socks resemble those of the Turkish kilim (rugs or carpets). Worked upward in stockinette, often employing a twisted stitch, they have a triangular toe and heel and can employ anywhere from four to eight colors in a single round. The entire sock, sole included, is decorated with patterns of stars, diamonds, hooked triangles, diamonds and other geometric

shapes. The pattern names, such as "apple slice," "watch chain," "beetle," "nightingale," and "moth," vary from region to region, and a single motif may have many names.
See also BALTIC KNITTING; FOLK KNITTING

TURN

When knitting instructions say "turn," they are directing you to reverse the position of your work so that the side that was away from you is now facing you. In flat knitting, you always turn the work upon completion of a row.
See also SHORT ROWS; SHORT-ROW SHAPING; WRAP AND TURN

TURTLENECK

See COLLARS AND NECKBANDS

TVÅÄNDSSTICKNING

See SWEDISH KNITTING

TWINKLE (1967-)

Twinkle is the company name of ready-to-wear/knitwear designer Wenlan Chia. Twinkle's signature

Turkey is located between the Mediterranean and the Black Sea.

look juxtaposes chunky yarn with slender silhouettes and feminine accents. "It's youthful and slightly bohemian," Chia told the *Washington Post* about her design ethos. "The chunkiness makes it feel less precious but still very sumptuous and rich." Intarsia is also a Twinkle trademark, both in her knits and her ready-to-wear.

Born in Taipei, Taiwan, Chia earned a B.A. in sociology from Taiwan University before coming to the United States in 1991, completing her education with an M.A. in art history from New York University. Her entrée into fashion began when she took a course in needlepoint at New York's Fashion Institute of Technology. Building on this needlework base, Chia started designing chunky knits for herself; the response she received when she wore the sweaters convinced her to start selling her wares, and a small Twinkle knitwear collection was launched in fall 2000. Since then she has branched out with full ready-to-wear lines shown each Fashion Week at the Bryant Park Tents, plus collections of home-décor items, accessories and jewelry. Among Chia's accolades: winning the Onward Kashiyama

Turkish socks in a market. Some traditional designs are even more intricate.

New Design Prize (Tokyo) and the Competition of Young Fashion Designers (Paris), and being nominated for the Fashion Group International Rising Star Awards. *Vogue* named her one of five "Spring's Leading Ladies" in 2005.

In 2007 Classic Elite Yarns began distributing Twinkle by Wenlan, a line of yarns developed by Chia to correspond to her design sensibility and support her instantly recognizable designs, which are often knit in the round. "This technique eliminates bulky seams, which is common when knitting chunky sweaters," she told Craft Blog in 2007. Chia frequently contributes patterns to *Vogue Knitting* and *Interweave Knits* and has written two books of her own: *Twinkle's Big City Knits* (Potter Craft, 2007) and *Twinkle's Weekend Knits* (Potter Craft, 2008). "For me, it all starts with the sweater," she explained to *Fashion Wire Daily* in 2003. "That's the thing about a great sweater…all you have to do is put it on."
See also DESIGNERS; *INTERWEAVE KNITS; VOGUE KNITTING*

TWISTED CORD

See CORDS

TWISTED RIBBING

These are ribbing patterns that are formed from combinations of twisted knit and purl stitches. To make a twisted knit or purl stitch, you must knit or purl through the back loop. In some twisted ribbing patterns, you work into the back loop of just the knit stitches; in others, you work into the back loops of both the knit and purl stitches.
See also KNIT STITCH; KNITTING THROUGH THE BACK LOOP; PURL STITCH; RIBBING; TWISTED-STITCH PATTERNS

TWISTED-STITCH PATTERNS

Textured patterns formed by twisting two or more stitches around each other without using a cable needle are considered twisted-stitch patterns. They give the look of cables or other intricate work but are usually quite simple to execute.
See also ALPINE REGION KNITTING; TWISTED RIBBING

In this twisted rib pattern, only knit stitches are twisted.

TWO-ENDED KNITTING

See SWEDISH KNITTING

TWO-HANDED KNITTING

Two-handed knitting is a technique for stranding, or knitting with two colors of yarn simultaneously. In this technique, each hand holds one strand of yarn, and yarns are picked up alternately over and under one another across each row. When knitting with the yarn that is held in the right hand, the American/English style of knitting is used; when the yarn held with the left hand is being used, the Continental/German style is employed.
See also FAIR ISLE KNITTING

TWO-STRAND KNITTING

To knit with two strands of yarn held together is to perform two-strand knitting. Sometimes misleadingly called doubled knitting (in true double knitting, a piece with two "right" sides is created and the fabric is made of two interlocked layers), this technique can be used to create a heavier gauge from an existing yarn or to create texture and interest by working two different yarns together, such as a plain worsted and a fur, ribbon, or other novelty. The two strands of yarn are treated as one as you work the piece. You can work in this manner from two separate balls of yarn or rewind both yarns into a single ball. Great care must be taken if unraveling a work done with two strands held together, lest the yarn become impossibly tangled.
See also DOUBLE KNITTING; FOLK KNITTING; NOVELTY YARN; WINDING YARN

TYROLEAN KNITTING

See ALPINE REGION KNITTING

UFO

The acronym used amongst knitters for an "unfinished object." Often used by knitting bloggers to describe uncompleted projects that have been put aside.
See also FO

UNRAVELING

When the work must be taken out entirely, or to a certain point well back from the live stitches, the work must be unraveled. For the easiest and least stressful unraveling, use a contrasting yarn or stitch marker to mark the row with the error. Remove the knitting needle and pull out the stitches to that row.
See also CORRECTING COMMON MISTAKES; FROGGING; TINK

V

W

V&A

See VICTORIA & ALBERT
MUSEUM

VAN DER HURK, L.J.A.M.

See ESCH FRAGMENTS

VARIEGATED YARN

Multicolored yarn that has been
space-dyed in sections. When
knit the yarn may create random
streaks of color or a set pattern,
such as stripes.
See also DYEING

VICTORIA & ALBERT MUSEUM

This decorative arts museum in
London was conceived by
England's Prince Albert as a way
to improve the standards of
British design by making the
finest models available for study.
It was opened by Queen Victoria
in 1857, and the V&A is now
considered the world's greatest
museum for the decorative arts.
The museum houses an extensive
collection of textiles, including
knitted garments, swatches,
needles and tools from antiquity
to the present day.
See also MUSEUMS

This panel, which was knit by a blind person, was displayed at the Great Exhibition of 1851 in Victorian England. The "Prayer for the High Court of Parliament" from the Book of Common Prayer is knit in twenty-seven lines of purl stitch.

VICTORIAN KNITTING

Knitting abounded in the Victorian
era. Around 1835, knitting
changed from a craft of utility to a
fashionable pursuit. There were
several contributing factors to
knitting's change in status. The
primary factor was the increasing

Skein of variegated yarn and swatch knit from yarn

mechanization of fabric production, including knitted goods. Freed from the tedium of knitting interminable stockings, socks and outerwear, women were able to indulge their interest in the decorative arts. Coverlets and doilies became popular projects, and lace knitting, termed the "height of the knitter's art" by Mary Thomas in her *Book of Knitting Patterns*, flourished. The defeat of Napoleon opened up trade with Saxony (Germany) and introduced English and Scottish knitters to "fancy" wool, a high-quality silky merino that took dyes well. It did knitting no harm, either, that Prince Albert came from the center of German wool country, and Queen Victoria enjoyed knitting for him. (Victoria learned fine knitting from her German governess. Interestingly, there are almost no published mentions of Queen Victoria knitting until toward the end of her life.)

The first English knitting books began appearing in 1840; by 1846 they were being printed at an alarming rate. Small and often filled with mistakes, these so-called drawing-room books rarely mentioned gauge or needle size and expected the knitters purchasing them to be skilled enough to work out the often sketchy instructions. Many of these volumes offered moral and religious guidance along with patterns for bonnets, doilies and shawls.

The upper classes weren't the only ones seeing a change in the craft. Knitting also became more enjoyable for the working class as needles and yarn improved. The knitting sheath passed out of favor, as speed was no longer as important and the focus turned more toward design. Monthly magazines, such as *Weldon's Practical Needlework*, introduced the lower classes to decorative knitting. Typically, each magazine had sixteen pages and was a tutorial on a particular type of needlework, such as crochet, tatting, smocking or various types of lace and embroidery.

The Great Exhibition of 1851 is often cited in discussions of Victorian knitting. Although it displayed knitting curiosities, such as a little lace dress made with six thousand yards of fine sewing cotton and a panel knit by a blind person (shown on previous page), its main attraction was machine knitting—not handknitting.
See also BRITISH KNITTING; *WELDON'S PRACTICAL NEEDLEWORK*

V-NECK SHAPING

When shaping creates the slanted "V" shape at the neckline it is commonly known as V-neck shaping. As with raglan shaping, a V-neck is worked gradually over a number of rows from the point of the V up. When splitting for the two sides, if you have an odd number of stitches, the V-neck can be shaped by binding off a center stitch; if the stitch count is even, the neck can be separated without a center stitch. Place a marker at the center of the piece and work to 2 stitches before the marker, decrease one stitch, and join a second ball of yarn. Decrease one stitch and work to the end. Work one row even, then decrease one stitch on each side of the neck every right-side row or as specified in your pattern.
See also COLLARS AND NECKBANDS; NECK EDGING

VOGUE KNITTING

Vogue Knitting is a knitting magazine with a storied history. It features more than thirty runway-inspired and classic patterns per issue, presented in a fashion-forward context. Designs are by leading designers of hand-knitting wear, including Nicky Epstein, Shirley Paden, Meg Swansen, Mari Lynn Patrick and Norah Gaughan, as well as Seventh Avenue designers such as Michael Kors and Anna Sui. *VK*'s patterns range from the technically advanced to the "Very Easy Very Vogue" designation for beginners. Each issue also features articles on topics such as fiber production, techniques,

Vogue Knitting through the decades (from left to right): 1930s, 1940s, 1950s, 1960s and the first issue of the relaunched magazine from 1982.

retail shops and art knitting. Epstein and Swansen pen regular technique columns. In addition, *VK* reviews new knitting books, yarns, needles and notions.

First published in the 1930s through the late '60s as the *Vogue Knitting Book* by Conde Nast, publisher of *Vogue, VK* was relaunched in 1982 as a division of the Butterick sewing-pattern company that in 2001 morphed into SoHo Publishing Company, the current publisher. At first published twice per year, *VK* now produces five issues each year. The editors in chief of *Vogue Knitting* have included many hand-knitting luminaries: Polly Roberts (tenure 1982–1985), Marilyn F. Cooperman (1985–1986), Lola Erlich (1986–1988), Margaret C. Korn (1989), Meredith Gray (1990–1991), Sonja Dagress (1991–1992), Nancy J. Thomas (1992–1995), Margery Winter (1995–1996), Carla Scott (1995–1996), Gay Bryant (1996–1997), Trisha Malcolm (1997–2007 and 2008–present) and Adina Klein (2007–2008). Carla Scott, now executive editor, has had a long tenure at the company. She selects garments for each issue in cooperation with editor in chief Trisha Malcolm, who guides the magazine's direction and vision. Creative Director Joe Vior oversaw magazine design during the 1980s and returned to the artistic helm in 2005. *Vogue Knitting's* editors have also produced authoritative bestselling books, including *Vogue*

Knitting: The Ultimate Knitting Book (Sixth&Spring Books, 1989/2002).
See also EPSTEIN, NICKY; GAUGHAN, NORAH; KORS, MICHAEL; MAGAZINES AND JOURNALS; PADEN, SHIRLEY; PATRICK, MARI LYNN; SCOTT, CARLA; SWANSEN, MEG; THOMAS, NANCY J.

W

WALKER, BARBARA (1930-)
Barbara Walker revolutionized the modern knitting-reference library. A self-taught knitter who first picked up needles and learned out of a Bernat instructional book at the age of thirty-five, Walker became fascinated with stitch patterns and spent the next thirteen years recording them, utilizing the skills she amassed as a journalism student at the University of Pennsylvania. Conducting research from knitting magazines and books, yarn-company patterns and out-of-print titles dating back to 1830 she found in the Library of Congress—augmented by patterns she collected from knitters around the world and devised herself—Walker swatched and meticulously

transcribed more than 1,000 stitch patterns in her four stitch-pattern compendia, all originally published by Scribner and reprinted by Schoolhouse Press: *A Treasury of Knitting Patterns, A Second Treasury of Knitting Patterns, Charted Knitting Designs: A Third Treasury of Knitting Patterns* and *A Fourth Treasury of Knitting Patterns*. She also created the reversible slip-stitch colorwork technique known as mosaic knitting, was one of the first knitters to promote the top-down method of knitting garments, devised her own method of charting patterns, coined the now-common abbreviation "ssk," knits socks with her own two-needle

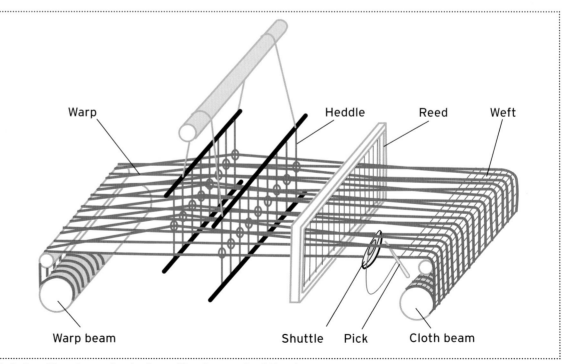
Illustration of loom for weaving showing position of warp and weft threads

technique, and has stitched six hundred or so doll outfits.

Once she completed her study of knitting and extrapolating upon the symbols she found within the craft, Walker moved on to exhaustively document other topics, many involving their own sets of symbols, including tarot, feminism, minerals, goddess lore and I Ching. Along with her *Treasury* quartet, her still influential knitting books include *The Craft of Lace Knitting* (1971), *The Craft of Cable-Stitch Knitting* (1971), *Knitting From the Top* (1972), *The Craft of Multicolor Knitting* (1973), *Learn-to-Knit Afghan Book* (1974) and *Mosaic Knitting* (1976) (all originally from Scribner).
See also DESIGNERS

WALTERS, JAMES
See FREEFORM KNITTING/
CROCHET

WARM UP AMERICA!
Warm Up America! (WUA!) is a charity founded in Wisconsin in 1991 by Evie Rosen. Individual volunteers or groups are recruited to knit or crochet small rectangles, which are joined together to make afghans. Volunteers are encouraged to distribute afghans or handknitted garments within their own communities, though the foundation also maintains a list of agencies that provide services to battered women, veterans, the homeless and other people in need, through which afghans can be distributed. WUA! also runs the website teachknitandcrochet.org, which gives guidelines and tips on how to teach knitting and crochet and lead a group in the creation of an afghan for charity. This kind of project has become popular in school and youth groups, community organizations, churches and businesses.
See also CHARITY KNITTING;
NEEDLE ARTS MENTORING
PROGRAM

WARP
In textiles, the vertical threads are called the warp. In weaving, there are two sets of yarn: the warp and the weft. The warp yarns run lengthwise on the loom and the weft threads run horizontally.
See also KNITTING VS. WEAVING

WARP KNITTING
This term is used when referring to machine knits in which the yarns interface vertically. Knitting machines employ a system of individual needles for each loop or stitch, which produces a very stable fabric that can't easily unravel.

WATCH CAP
See HATS

WATTS, MISS
See BRITISH KNITTING

WEAVING IN
Tucking or sewing loose ends of yarn into the reverse side of a knitted fabric is called weaving in. There are many ways to weave in loose ends, and the method you choose should secure the end so it will not unravel and not be visible on the right side of the work. As you attach a new ball of yarn to your work, leave a 6-inch tail to use for weaving in. A convenient method in flat knitting is to thread that tail onto a yarn needle and sew it into a seam. Another method is to thread the yarn onto a yarn needle and sew it into the bumps on the wrong side of the work. You can tuck the ends in horizontally or vertically. Trim ends with approximately ½ inch of length so that the end does not pop out to the right side.
See also FINISHING TECHNIQUES;
SEAMING

WEBSITES
See INTERNET

WEDDING RING SHAWL
See ORENBURG LACE; SHETLAND LACE

WEFT
In textiles, the filling threads that run perpendicular to the warp are the weft. In weaving, a shuttle is used to move the filling yarn across warp threads in a preset

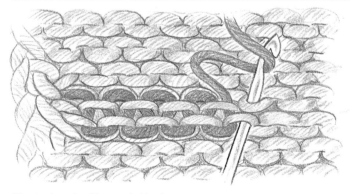
Weaving in ends with a crochet hook

pattern that can be either simple, as in a plain weave, or complex. Most handknitting is weft knitting—that is, the linking of a series of loops horizontally. In handknitting the basic weft knitting stitch is called stockinette. In machine knitting it is called jersey.
See KNITTED FABRIC; KNITTING VS. WEAVING

WELDON'S PRACTICAL NEEDLEWORK

The Weldon paper company began printing, in 1885, a monthly newsletter called the Practical Knitter Series. Each one featured patterns and techniques for the subscribers. Later, in 1888, larger books were printed called *Weldon's Practical Needlework*. These books and booklets feature hundreds of Victorian patterns current to the time.
See also VICTORIAN KNITTING

WELSH KNITTING

The cottage knitting industry of Wales probably began sometime in the sixteenth century. Welsh cattle drivers brought knit stockings to sell at English fairs, and the trade of stockings from Wales was well established by the late seventeenth century. In the eighteenth century, the sight of countryfolk knitting along the roadsides and at markets was a common one. In the winter months women gathered in groups known as *cymmorth gweu* (knitting assembly) to knit for the markets, often accompanied by the playing of a harp or the telling of ancient tales. The Welsh cottage knitting industry flourished until well into the 1850s, surviving the Edwardian years, but because of the advent of the railroad and better machine knitting technology, it had all but vanished by the 1920s.
See also BRITISH KNITTING; FOLK KNITTING

WELT

The welt is the lower edge of a garment, constructed from horizontal ridges that run across the fabric. Welts are the equivalent of horizontal ribbing. Welts are formed by alternating rows of knit and purl stitches, and they are mostly used as borders on knitted garments.
See also BORDERS; KNIT STITCH; PURL STITCH; RIBBING; WELT PATTERNS

WELT PATTERNS

Patterns formed from alternate rows of knit and purl stitches are called welt patterns. Simple welt patterns, like the one shown below, consist of alternating rows of knit and purl. More complex, broken welt patterns can have combinations of knit and purl stitches in the same horizontal row.
See also BORDERS; KNIT STITCH; PURL STITCH; RIBBING; WELT

WESTERN KNITTING

Western and Eastern knitting refer to different ways in which stitches are mounted on needles and the stitches are worked. In Western knitting, the stitches are mounted on the needle so that the leading leg of the loop over the needle is at the front, as opposed to Eastern knitting, in which the leading leg is at the back of the needle and trailing leg is in front. In Western knitting, the knitter forms a knit stitch by inserting the needle from front to back, passing the yarn under the right needle and drawing the new loop through to make a knit stitch. To make a purl stitch, the knitter inserts the yarn into the front loop of the stitch from back to front, passes the yarn over and under the needle and pulls the loop through. The American/English and Continental/German knitting styles are the two main types of Western knitting.
See also AMERICAN/ENGLISH–STYLE KNITTING; COMBINED KNITTING; CONTINENTAL/GERMAN–STYLE KNITTING; EASTERN KNITTING

WIGGINTON, CAROL

See KNITTING GUILD ASSOCIATION, THE

WILD FIBERS

See MAGAZINES AND JOURNALS

Swatch knit in a welt pattern

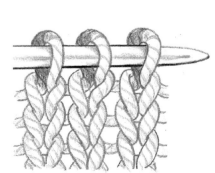

Western stitch mount

Swatches knit in plied (top) and unplied (bottom) wool

WINDING YARN

The process of transferring yarn from hanks into balls or skeins, either by hand or using a swift and ball winder, is the act of winding yarn.

The hand-winding method can utilize two people or one person and a stationary object such as a chair back. Robert Service refers to the two-person method in his poem *Winding Wool*: There are "two active and two passive hands." The passive hands simply hold the untwined, untied hank loosely, allowing the active hands to wind the yarn into a ball. With the one-person method, the hank is draped over a chair back and wound into a ball.

With the swift and ball winder method, a hank of yarn is untwined and untied and placed loosely into the V-shaped groove formed by the expandable arms of the swift. The outer end of yarn is inserted into the groove of the ball winder, which is cranked carefully until the hank is completely unwound. A center-pull skein is formed.

Diameter/Fineness and Staple Lengths of Wool by Sheep Breed

BREED	DIAMETER/FINENESS	STAPLE LENGTH
Merino	18-24 microns	2¾-4"/7-10cm
Rambouillet	18-24 microns	2-4"/5-10cm
Shetland	20-25 microns	2-4¾"/5-12cm
Columbia	23-29 microns	4-6"/10-15cm
Corriedale	25-31 microns	3¼-6"/8.5-15cm
Romney	32-39 microns	6-8"/15-20cm
Leicester	32-38 microns	6-8"/15-20cm
Lincoln	34-41 microns	8-14¾"/20-37.5cm

See also BALL; BALL WINDER; HANK; SKEIN; SWIFT

WIP

WIP is the acronym for a "work in progress." The term is used by knitting bloggers to describe projects currently underway.

WOMAN'S DAY

See MAGAZINES AND JOURNALS

WOOL

The fiber from the domestic sheep is called *wool*. This term is sometimes incorrectly used to describe other protein fibers, such as mohair and angora. Wool has two qualities that distinguish it from hair or fur: It has scales that overlap each other, and it is crimped. It is these two properties that make it easy to spin and felt—they help the individual fibers attach to each other so that they stay together. Because of the crimp, wool fabrics have a greater bulk than other textiles and retain air, which causes the product to retain heat. The amount of crimp corresponds to the thickness of the wool fibers. A fine wool like merino may have up to one hundred crimps per inch, while coarser wools like karakul may have as few as one to two crimps per inch.

Wool is generally a creamy white color, although some breeds of sheep produce natural colors such as black, brown, silver and random mixes. Wool straight off a sheep contains a high level of grease that contains lanolin as well as dirt, dead skin, sweat residue and vegetable matter. This state is known as "grease wool" or "wool in the grease." Before the wool can be used for commercial purposes, it must be scoured, or cleaned. Semi-grease wool can be worked into yarn and knitted into particularly water-resistant mittens or sweaters, such as those of the Aran Island fishermen. Lanolin removed from wool is widely used in the cosmetics industry, such as in hand creams.

After shearing, the wool is separated into five main categories: fleece (which makes up

Microscopic Views of Wool Fibers

Detail of a wool fiber as it would appear under a microscope. Each fiber can have up to thirty crimps per inch.

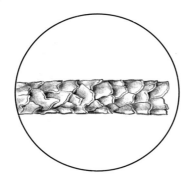

The microscopic overlapping scales of a wool fiber help the fibers attach to each other.

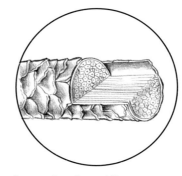

Cross-section of a wool fiber

the vast bulk), pieces, bellies, crutchings and locks. These are then sold to different consumers—hand-spinners prize fleeces. The quality of wool is determined by a technique known as wool classing, whereby a qualified woolclasser groups wools of similar gradings together.

There are three systems for determining wool grade, or the quality (fineness or coarseness) of the fiber. The oldest method of grading wool is the blood system, which is based on the bloodline of the sheep from which the wool came. Wool from merino and Rambouillet sheep was fine, and coarser wool from animals that were crossbred with other breeds was rated as ½ blood, ⅜, ¼, low ¼, or common. Another way to grade wool is by wool count, which is the number of hanks (560 yards) that can be spun from one pound of wool. While this system is still used among hand-spinners, the most common system for wool grading now is the micron system, which measures the diameter of wool in micrometers. While a high wool count indicates a finer wool, a high micron measurement indicates a coarser fiber. For

comparison, a human hair has a diameter of about sixty microns. Fine wool has a diameter of less than twenty microns, whereas the coarsest wool, called carpet wool, is nearly twice as thick. In general, coarser wool also has a longer staple length. The chart on page 223 gives the diameter/fineness and staple lengths of the wool of various sheep breeds in order of diameter/fineness.

Wool for Handknitting

Wool has been so widely used for handknitting that for many years the words "yarn" and "wool" were used interchangeably. Wool can be soft and fine enough for baby clothes and tough enough to be worn by sailors and firefighters. Wool does tend to shrink and felt, and for many years textile chemists worked to develop "superwash" wools that can be machine-washed. However, the felting properties of natural wool are regarded by many as an advantage, and in recent years the popularity of felting has been a boon to the wool industry.

It is crucial to carefully read the care instructions on the label prior to washing any wool yarn.

See also FIBER CHARACTERISTICS; LANOLIN; SHEEP; SUPERWASH

WOOLEN-SPUN YARNS

See WORSTED-SPUN YARNS

WOOL FESTIVAL AT TAOS

See SHEEP AND WOOL FESTIVALS

WORKING FLAT

See FLAT KNITTING

WORKSHOPS

Workshops are intensive classes on knitting and/or crochet, most often held at local yarn shops or organized guild events or trade shows. Workshops differ from typical LYS classes in that they are longer and tend to be more focused on a particular technique or garment. Many designers and knitting authors support their latest projects and books by traveling to various yarn shops and giving classes across the country. Major knitting events like Stitches, TKGA's Knit & Crochet Show and the TNNA trade show markets offer comprehensive course listings with top designers.
See also CAMPS AND RETREATS;

CRAFT YARN COUNCIL; DESIGNERS; KNITTING GUILD ASSOCIATION, THE; LYS; NATIONAL NEEDLEARTS ASSOCIATION, THE

WORLD WARS

See AMERICAN RED CROSS KNITTING CAMPAIGNS; BRITISH KNITTING

WORLD WIDE KNIT IN PUBLIC DAY

This movement was started in 2005 by knitter Danielle Landes to transform knitting from a solitary act into a public one and get knitters "out into fresh air." WWKIP Day, as it is usually abbreviated, is a concept rather than a specific program run by any centralized organization. Anybody may run a Knit in Public Day event, anywhere they choose, during the designated WWKIP week in June. As such, it has become the largest knitter-run "happening" in the world: The number of events held worldwide grew from 25 in the year 2005 to 751 in 2009. Events range from guild-sponsored gatherings at flea markets to marches (or "crawls") through the streets of London, needles and

Measuring WPI (wraps per inch; from left to right): a fingering-weight yarn with a WPI of 23; a sport-weight yarn with a WPI of 14; a bulky yarn with a WPI of 7

projects in hand. The common denominator is that participants be knitting, outside, where people will see them.

WORSTED-SPUN

Yarn spun in a specific way using long-staple fibers of uniform length that have been carded so that they lie parallel to each other is called "worsted spun." Worsted spun yarns tend to be of higher quality than their counterparts, woolen-spun yarns, which utilize shorter staple fibers carded in a random fashion. Do not confuse this with worsted-weight yarn, which describes a specific weight of yarn, whether or not the fiber was processed via the worsted method. *See also* YARN WEIGHT

WORSTED WEIGHT

See YARN WEIGHT

WPI

This abbreviation for "wraps per inch" is a measure of the thickness of a strand of yarn. The higher the WPI, the finer the yarn. For example, a laceweight yarn might have a WPI of 30 or higher, while a bulky yarn might have one of less than 8.

To determine WPI for any yarn, wind it loosely around a ruler and count how many strands there are from one inch mark to the next. When substituting yarns, it is best to choose a yarn with a very similar WPI to the original. *See also* YARN SUBSTITUTION; YARN WEIGHT

Wrapping Stitches (Knit Side)

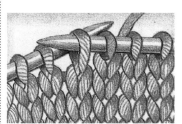

1. To prevent holes in the piece and create a smooth transition, wrap a knit stitch as follows: With the yarn in back, slip the next stitch purlwise.

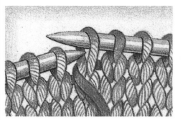

2. Move the yarn between the needles to the front of the work.

3. Slip the same stitch back to the left needle. Turn the work, bringing the yarn to the purl side between the needles. One stitch is wrapped.

4. When you have completed all the short rows, you must hide the wraps. Work to just before the wrapped stitch. Insert the right needle under the wrap and knitwise into the wrapped stitch. Knit them together.

Wrapping Stitches (Purl Side)

1. To prevent holes in the piece and create a smooth transition, wrap a purl stitch as follows: With the yarn at the front, slip the next stitch purlwise.

2. Move the yarn between the needles to the back of the work.

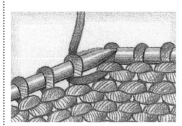

3. Slip the same stitch back to the left needle. Turn the work, bringing the yarn back to the purl side between the needles. One stitch is wrapped.

4. After working the short rows, you must hide the wraps. Work to just before the wrapped stitch. Insert the right needle from behind into the back loop of the wrap. Place it on the left needle, as shown. Purl it together with the stitch on the left needle.

WRAP AND TURN

One of a few common methods used to create short rows is the wrap and turn. When you add an extra row into a knitted piece, you must make a smooth transition between the edge where one row is worked and the edge that has an extra row. You can do this by wrapping a slipped stitch, using one method for knit stitches and another for purl, as shown at right. *See also* SHORT ROWS; SHORT-ROW SHAPING

WRAPPED COLLAR

See COLLARS AND NECKBANDS

WRAPS PER INCH

See WPI

WRONG SIDE

The side of a garment that faces inward when the garment is worn is called the wrong side. In general, the wrong side of a garment will not show the pattern stitch, and all ends will be woven in on the wrong side. *See also* RIGHT SIDE

WS

Abbreviation for *wrong side*. *See also* WRONG SIDE

WYB, WYIB

Abbreviations for *with yarn in back*.

WYF, WYIF

Abbreviations for *with yarn in front*.

X
Y
Z

XRX

See KNITTER'S (MAGAZINE);
STITCHES

YAK FIBER

The yak is a member of the bovine family native to high-altitude regions of Tibet, Mongolia and south central Asia. Like other high-altitude fiber-bearing animals, the yak has an outer coat of coarse guard hairs and a softer undercoat. The animals shed in the spring and the fibers are collected and separated. The coarsest are used to produce rope. The softer short-staple fibers are spun for export, or exported as fiber to be blended and spun with other fibers. Yak doesn't bleach or dye very well and is usually used in its natural hues of brown and

Yak

black. The spun yarn is prized for being delicately soft, and it commands a high price.
See also FIBER CHARACTERISTICS; STAPLE

YARN

Yarn is a continuous length of twisted fibers or filaments used for the creation of fabric. Yarn has been spun for approximately 20,000 years, at first with spindles; in the Middle Ages, the spinning wheel made production faster; and finally the invention of the spinning jenny in 1764 led to modern mechanical yarn spinning. In the context of knitting, yarn can be spun from animal fibers (wool, cashmere, angora, silk, mohair), plant fibers (cotton, linen, bamboo), synthetic fibers (acrylic), or a blend of fibers that incorporates the best properties of each. Yarns are composed of plies, or single spun threads, twisted together to add strength. They are usually dyed and wound into hanks, skeins or balls, and are sold by weight and categorized by thickness, ranging from 0 (laceweight) to 6 (superbulky).
See also ACRYLIC; AFGHAN WEIGHT; ALPACA FIBER; ANGORA FIBER; ARAN WEIGHT; BALL; BUFFALO FIBER; BULKY YARN; CAMELHAIR; CASHMERE; CHENILLE; CHOOSING YARNS; COLORWAY; COTTON; DYEING; DYE LOT; FELTED YARN; FELTING; FIBER CHARACTERISTICS; FUN FUR YARN; HAND-PAINTED; HEMP; JUTE; LACEWEIGHT YARN; LOPI; MERINO; MOHAIR;

Various Types of Yarns

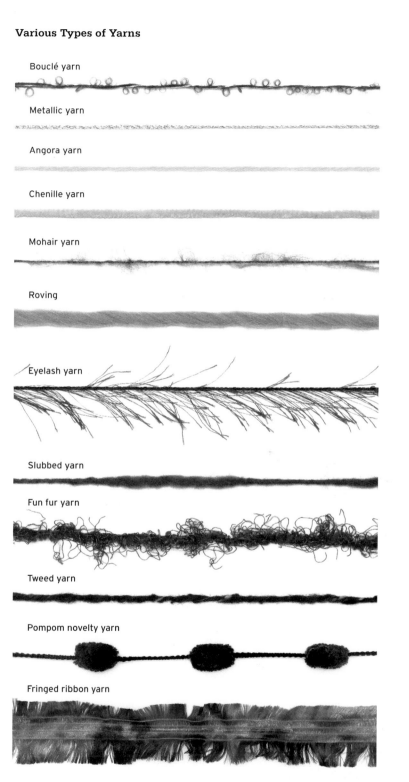

Bouclé yarn

Metallic yarn

Angora yarn

Chenille yarn

Mohair yarn

Roving

Eyelash yarn

Slubbed yarn

Fun fur yarn

Tweed yarn

Pompom novelty yarn

Fringed ribbon yarn

NATURALLY COLORED YARN; NONTRADITIONAL YARNS; NOVELTY YARN; ORGANIC KNITTING; POLYESTER; QIVIUT; RAFFIA; RECYCLING; RIBBON YARN; SILK; SPORTWEIGHT; STORING YARN; VARIEGATED YARN; WINDING YARN; WORSTED-SPUN; WORSTED WEIGHT; YAK FIBER; YARN REQUIREMENT; YARN SUBSTITUTION; YARN WEIGHT

YARNDEX

This online yarn directory (yarndex.com) is provided by online yarn retailer Yarnmarket, LLC. Yarndex launched in 2003 as a website that allows visitors to search for yarns based on name, brand, color, fiber content (cotton, mohair, alpaca, silk blend, etc.), weight (fingering, bulky, etc.) and texture (ribbon, chenille, plied, metallic, etc.). Each entry offers full information on the fiber, including color-card photos, yardage and other descriptors, and sometimes links to retailers. The site is used by the public and by yarn-industry professionals as a reference; it indexes more than five thousand yarns, including most brands available in America.

YARN GROUP OF TNNA, THE

This subgroup of TNNA (The National Needlearts Association) formulates industry directives for production, marketing and retailing of yarn. Members of the TNNA trade association, who may be wholesalers, shop owners, pattern designers, publishers, manufacturers' representatives, teachers and more, have the option to join "product segment" subgroups that liaise throughout the year and convene at TNNA's semiannual conventions and markets. The Yarn Group, one of these product segment cagetories, focuses on issues concerning yarn and its arts, and strategetizes plans, programs and goals to benefit the future of yarn crafting.
See also NATIONAL NEEDLEARTS ASSOCIATION, THE (TNNA)

YARN HARLOT

See PEARL-MCPHEE, STEPHANIE

YARN LABELS

Sometimes called a ball band label, the paper label attached to a ball, hank or skein of yarn is known as the yarn label and contains various amounts of information about that particular yarn. The name of the yarn and manufacturer, fiber content and country of origin, dye lot, yardage, gauge, recommended needle and crochet hook size—in both American and metric—are standard on commercially produced yarn labels. In addition, care recommendations and international care symbols are usually included as well.

Some yarns produced by small manufacturers, such as farm-produced yarns and cottage industry spinners and dyers, have less comprehensive labeling and often only include fiber content and yardage along with dye lot.
See also DYE LOT; FIBER CHARACTERISTICS; GAUGE; YARN WEIGHT

YARN MARKET NEWS

This trade magazine brings domestic and international fiber-industry news to professionals in the yarn market—retailers, manufacturers, representatives, designers and teachers. Originally debuted as a newsletter by Albuquerque yarn purveyors Kate Mathews and Rob Pullyn in 1978, *YMN* moved to Asheville, North Carolina, shortly thereafter and was helmed by Jeane Hutchins through the 1980s, a boom decade for knitting. However, when that boom waned, the magazine folded in 1988. It was reinaugurated in May 2005 by SoHo Publishing Company under the editorship of Karin Strom. The magazine advocates communication in the industry, and to that end is an important player at trade shows and organizations, as well as holding its own Smart Business conferences.
See also MAGAZINES AND JOURNALS

YARN OVER

The yarn over is a decorative increase made by wrapping the yarn over the needle. There are various ways to make a yarn over, depending upon where it is placed and the number of times the yarn is wrapped around the needle. It is abbreviated "yo," "yon" and sometimes "yrn," which means *yarn 'round needle.*
See also DECREASES; DROP-STITCH PATTERNS; EYELET PATTERNS; FAGGOTING;

Sample Yarn Label

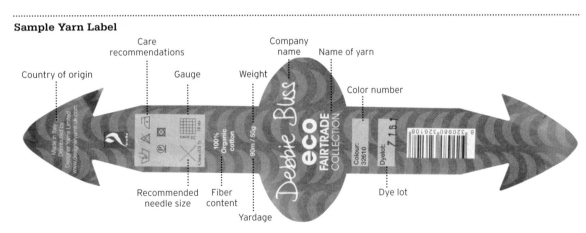

Country of origin · Care recommendations · Gauge · Weight · Company name · Name of yarn · Color number · Recommended needle size · Fiber content · Yardage · Dye lot

Yarn Overs

A yarn over is a decorative increase made by wrapping the yarn around the needle. There are various ways to make a yarn over depending on where it is placed.

Between Two Knit Stitches

Bring the yarn from the back of the work to the front between the two needles. Knit the next stitch, bringing the yarn to the back over the right needle as shown.

Between a Knit and a Purl Stitch

Bring the yarn from the back to the front between the two needles, then to the back over the right needle and to the front again as shown. Purl the next stitch.

Between a Purl and a Knit Stitch

Leave the yarn at the front of the work. Knit the next stitch, bringing the yarn to the back over the right needle as shown.

Between Two Purl Stitches

Leave the yarn at the front of the work. Bring the yarn to the back over the right needle and to the front again as shown. Purl the next stitch.

At the Beginning of a Knit Row

Keep the yarn at the front of the work. Insert the right needle knitwise into the first stitch on the left needle. Bring the yarn over the right needle to the back and knit the next stitch, holding the yarn over with your thumb if necessary.

At the Beginning of a Purl Row

To work a yarn over at the beginning of a purl row, keep the yarn at the back of the work. Insert the right needle purlwise into the first stitch on the left needle. Purl the stitch.

Multiple Yarn Overs

1. For multiple yarn overs (two or more), wrap the yarn around the needle as for a single yarn over, then wrap the yarn around the needle once more (or as many times as indicated). Work the next stitch on the left needle.

2. Alternate knitting and purling into the multiple yarn over on the subsequent row, always knitting the last stitch on a purl row and purling the last stitch on a knit row.

INCREASES; KNIT STITCH; LACE STITCHES, PURL STITCH

YARN REQUIREMENT

The amount of yarn needed to make a particular garment is the yarn requirement. The charts on the next page give estimates for a variety of garments, sizes and yarn weights. Remember that many factors affect the amount of yarn you ultimately need: your gauge (if you knit very tightly, you will use more yarn than the estimate indicates), the stitch pattern (heavily cabled garments can require up to 50 percent more yarn than garments knitted in stockinette stitch), and any adjustments you decide to make to your pattern (for example, shorter sleeves or longer body length). In general, textured stitch patterns such as ribbing, seed stitch or cables require more yarn than stockinette; lace stitches require less. So remember that the tables below are estimates only, and always round up when deciding how many skeins to buy. Purchase enough skeins of the same dye lot to ensure you'll have enough yarn to finish your project.

Yarn weight also greatly affects yardage requirements. The finer the yarn, the greater the yardage required for a given garment. For example, you might require 1,800 yards (1,600m) of worsted-weight yarn to knit a medium-size man's sweater. Using bulky yarn, you might complete the same sweater using only around 1,300 yards (1,150m).

Yarn Requirements for Various Garments

Hat

	Infant	Child	Woman	Man
3 Light weight	125 yd (112m)	175 yd (160m)	225 yd (200m)	275 yd (250m)
4 Medium weight	100 yd (90m)	150 yd (135m)	200 yd (180m)	250 yd (225m)

Mittens

	Infant	Child	Woman	Man
3 Light weight	75 yd (66m)	100 yd (90m)	150 yd (135m)	175 yd (160m)
4 Medium weight	50 yd (45m)	75 yd (66m)	125 yd (113m)	200 yd (180m)

Gloves

	Child	Woman	Man
3 Light weight	300 yd (270m)	350 yd (315m)	400 yd (360m)
4 Medium weight	200 yd (180m)	250 yd (225m)	300 yd (270m)

Socks

	Infant	Child	Woman	Man
1 Super-fine weight	125 yd (112m)	225 yd (200m)	350 yd (315m)	450 yd (405m)
2 Fine weight	100 yd (90m)	200 yd (180m)	300 yd (270m)	400 yd (360m)

Scarf

	6 x 40 in (15 x 100cm)	8 x 54 in (20 x 135cm)
2 Fine weight	450 yd (400m)	675 yd (600m)
3 Light weight	350 yd (315m)	525 yd (475m)
4 Medium weight	200 yd (180m)	300 yd (270m)
5 Bulky weight	150 yd (135m)	225 yd (200m)

Sweater

	Infant 16" (40cm) chest	Child 24" (60cm) chest	Woman 40" (100cm) chest	Man 48" (120cm) chest
2 Fine weight	500 yd (450m)	750 yd (675m)	2,100 yd (1900m)	2,700 yd (2,400m)
3 Light weight	400 yd (360m)	550 yd (500m)	1,600 yd (1,450m)	2,100 yd (1,900m)
4 Medium weight	325 yd (300m)	500 yd (450m)	1,400 yd (1,250m)	1,800 yd (1,600m)
5 Bulky weight	250 yd (225m)	350 yd (315m)	1,000 yd (900m)	1,300 yd (1,150m)

YARN STORAGE

See STORING YARN

YARN SUBSTITUTION

To use a yarn other than what is specified in a pattern is to perform a yarn substitution. To make a yarn substitution it is crucial to match the gauge that is called for in the pattern. In addition, patterns are designed with a certain type of yarn in mind, so factors such as drape and sheen should also be considered. If a silk yarn is called for in the pattern and it is knit in angora, even if the gauge is identical, the finished garment will differ radically from the one photographed in the recommended yarn.

Most yarn labels carry gauge symbols that conform to the Craft Yarn Council's Standard Yarn Weight System ranging from 0 (Laceweight) to 6 (Super Bulky). Patterns in most current magazines and many books utilize this system and indicate on the pattern the recommended category.

To substitute another yarn of the same weight as the one called for in the pattern, first determine the number of yards (meters) per skein for each yarn. For example, suppose your pattern calls for 10 skeins of a yarn with 200 yards (180m) per skein. You want to substitute a yarn that is put up in 150-yard (135m) skeins. First, determine how many yards (meters) you need: 200 yd (180m) x 10 = 2,000 yd (1,800m).

Next, divide the total amount

needed by the amount per skein in the new yarn: 2,000 yd (1,800m) ÷ 150 yd (135m) = 13.3 skeins.

Round this up to the nearest whole number, which gives you 14 skeins of the substitute yarn.

See also FIBER CHARACTERISTICS; GAUGE; WPI; YARN LABEL; YARN WEIGHT

YARN WEIGHT

Yarn comes in many different thicknesses; the thickness is referred to as the yarn weight. The weight classifications are designated by the Craft Yarn Council Standard Weight System.

Laceweight, the newest designation in the Craft Yarn Council's Standard Yarn Weight System, represented by the symbol 0, includes yarns with a gauge of 33–40 stitches to 4 inches on size 000 to 1 needles. This category also includes 10-count crochet thread traditionally used for doilies.

Fingering weight is super fine-weight yarn, called two- or three-ply in Britain, and is number 1 on the CYC Standard Weight System. This classification includes sock, baby and some lace yarns. It typically knits up at 27–32 stitches to 4 inches in stockinette on size 1 to 3 needles. This weight category also includes some of the traditional crochet cottons used for lace and doilies.

Sport, or fine-weight, yarn includes many sock yarns. Number 2 on the CYC Standard Weight System, this classification includes yarns that knit up to 23–26 stitches to 4 inches using size 3 to 5 needles. In addition to socks and gloves, this weight is suitable for babies' and children's clothes, tailored garments and lightweight sweaters.

Light worsted, number 3 on the CYC Standard Weight System chart, includes the British DK yarns. Light worsted knits up to 21–24 stitches to 4 inches on 5 to 7 needles. This is a popular sweater weight and is often used for Fair Isle type knitting.

Worsted, probably the most widely used weight of yarn, is a medium-weight yarn, number 4

STANDARDS & GUIDELINES FOR CROCHET AND KNITTING

Standard Yarn Weight System

Categories of yarn, gauge ranges, and recommended needle and hook sizes

Yarn Weight Symbol & Category Names	0 Lace	1 Super Fine	2 Fine	3 Light	4 Medium	5 Bulky	6 Super Bulky
Type of Yarns in Category	Fingering 10 count crochet thread	Sock, Fingering, Baby	Sport, Baby	DK, Light Worsted	Worsted, Afghan, Aran	Chunky, Craft, Rug	Bulky, Roving
Knit Gauge Range* in Stockinette Stitch to 4 inches	33–40** sts	27–32 sts	23–26 sts	21–24 sts	16–20 sts	12–15 sts	6–11 sts
Recommended Needle in Metric Size Range	1.5–2.25 mm	2.25–3.25 mm	3.25–3.75 mm	3.75–4.5 mm	4.5–5.5 mm	5.5–8 mm	8 mm and larger
Recommended Needle U.S. Size Range	000 to 1	1 to 3	3 to 5	5 to 7	7 to 9	9 to 11	11 and larger
Crochet Gauge* Ranges in Single Crochet to 4 inch	32–42 double crochets**	21–32 sts	16–20 sts	12–17 sts	11–14 sts	8–11 sts	5–9 sts
Recommended Hook in Metric Size Range	Steel*** 1.6–1.4mm Regular hook 2.25 mm	2.25–3.5 mm	3.5–4.5 mm	4.5–5.5 mm	5.5–6.5 mm	6.5–9 mm	9 mm and larger
Recommended Hook U.S. Size Range	Steel*** 6, 7, 8 Regular hook B–1	B–1 to E–4	E–4 to 7	7 to I–9	I–9 to K–10½	K–10½ to M–13	M–13 and larger

* GUIDELINES ONLY: The above reflect the most commonly used gauges and needle or hook sizes for specific yarn categories.

** Lace weight yarns are usually knitted or crocheted on larger needles and hooks to create lacy, openwork patterns. Accordingly, a gauge range is difficult to determine. Always follow the gauge stated in your pattern.

*** Steel crochet hooks are sized differently from regular hooks--the higher the number, the smaller the hook, which is the reverse of regular hook sizing.

This Standards & Guidelines booklet and downloadable symbol artwork are available at: **YarnStandards.com**

Various Weights of Yarns

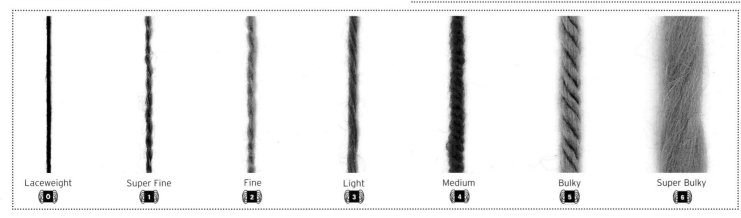

| Laceweight 0 | Super Fine 1 | Fine 2 | Light 3 | Medium 4 | Bulky 5 | Super Bulky 6 |

on the CYC Standard Weight System. The word "worsted" actually refers to the way the wool is spun but has become synonymous with this weight of yarn. Used for garments, afghans and accessories, worsted-weight yarn is widely available in a range of fibers, qualities and colors. It knits up to 16–20 stitches to 4 inches on 7 to 9 needles. Heavy worsted, sometimes called "medium-heavy weight," also a very popular weight of yarn, falls under the worsted category on the CYC chart, knitting up at about 18–20 stitches to 4 inches.

Bulky, category 5 on the CYC's Standard Weight System, includes craft, chunky and rug yarn. It typically knits up at 12–15 stitches to 4 inches on 9 to 11 needles. Bulky yarns work up quickly and are suitable for beginners' and quick projects such as hats, scarves, blankets and chunky sweaters.

Super-bulky, or extra-bulky, weight is category 6 on the CYC Standard Weight System and refers to the heaviest yarns, 6–11 stitches to 4 inches in stockinette using size 11 needles and larger. This weight isn't typically used for clothing other than extremely chunky sweaters and coats. Super bulky yarn or roving is sometimes used for rugs and home furnishing items. *See also* AFGHAN WEIGHT; ARAN WEIGHT; BULKY; LACEWEIGHT; SPORT WEIGHT; WORSTED-SPUN

YD

Abbreviation for *yard(s)*.

YFWD

Abbreviation for *yarn forward*. *See also* YARN OVER

YO, YON

Abbreviations for *yarn over*. *See also* YARN OVER

YO2, YO (2)

Abbreviations for *yarn over twice*. *See also* YARN OVER

YOKE

A section of a garment that joins the front, back and sleeves at the underarm, and then continues to the neckband, is called the yoke. Yokes are usually knit in the round and become the garment's sleeve cap, shoulders, front and back. A circular yoke must include the

Each swatch is knit in a different weight yarn. From top to bottom: fingering, sport, light worsted, worsted, bulky.

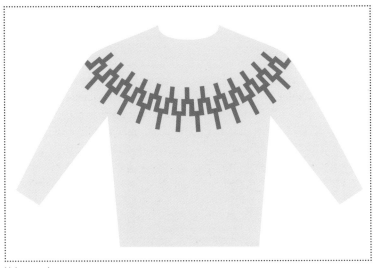

Yoke sweater

Placing Stitches on a Holder for Underarm

1. If you need 8 stitches for the total underarm at each side seam, place 4 stitches to the left of the seam marker and 4 to the right onto a holder. Be sure to end at the left underarm on the back piece.

2. Place 4 stitches on either side of the sleeve seam marker on a holder. Place each sleeve so the stitches on the holder face the underarm stitches on the body piece. You are ready to join the yoke.

Joining the Yoke

Joining all the pieces is the first crucial step in making a circular yoke. The underarm stitches should be left on holders until the yoke is complete.

armhole as well as the shoulder, so it should be slightly deeper than the length of the armhole. Traditionally yokes are worked in colorwork pattern bands with plain decrease rows in the main color between them.

The most important step in making a circular sweater with a yoke is joining the body and the sleeves. It is shown here in several steps.

Placing Stitches on a Holder for Underarm

Work the body piece and both sleeves to the underarm. At this point, leave a number of stitches unworked for the underarm on both the body and the sleeves. The unworked stitches usually equal 2–3 inches (5–7.5cm), depending on the weight of the yarn and the size of the sweater, and are centered on the marker. These stitches are left on a holder and are grafted together when the yoke is complete to join the side and sleeves at the underarms.

Joining the Yoke

Before you join the yoke, mark the front or back of the pieces at the lower edge. Beginning at the left front underarm, work across the front, ending at the right underarm. Join one sleeve by working across all stitches except those on the holder. Beginning at the right back underarm, join the back by working across to the left underarm. Join the other sleeve by working across all stitches, omitting those on the holder. Place

a new marker to indicate the beginning of the round.

Joining all the pieces is the first crucial step in making a circular yoke. The underarm stitches should be left on holders until the yoke is complete.
See also BOHUS KNITTING; FAIR ISLE KNITTING; ICELANDIC KNITTING; NECKLINES

YRN

Abbreviation for *yarn around needle*.
See also YARN OVER

ZIMMERMANN, ELIZABETH (1910-1999)

The single most influential knitter of the twentieth century, Elizabeth Zimmermann demystified and deconstructed the craft of knitting, becoming an icon for generations of devoted fans. "I rarely knit the same thing twice," wrote the multifaceted author/designer/TV personality/knitting entrepreneur in *The Knitter's Almanac* (Dover, 1981), and her work bore out that statement.

Zimmermann eschewed slavish pattern replication in favor of an individual design-it-yourself philosophy based on her patented Elizabeth Percentage System (EPS)—a no-frills mathematical

formula to determine the number of cast-on stitches necessary for optimum garment proportion— and often incorporating garter stitch, no-seam circular-knitting techniques, and traditional stitch patterning and yoke colorwork. She was a staunch advocate of natural materials, especially wool, and she put knitters at ease by writing instructions for her self-described "unventions" in a relaxed, conversational voice. "She gave us license, I think, to be chatty, and to be informal—and funny," says designer Kaffe Fassett, whose knitting life was inalterably changed after Zimmermann introduced him to circular needles.

Born Elizabeth Lloyd-Jones near Devon, England, in 1910, Zimmermann claimed that one of her first memories was being taught to knit, English style, by her mother as a reward for good behavior; she later learned her favored Continental method from a Swiss governess. Zimmermann humorously wrote in *The Knitter's Almanac* that her unconventional education, provided by governesses and at several private schools, "means that my head contains some very odd pieces of information, indeed, and little formal knowledge." Always creative, always knitting to her own drumbeat, at seventeen she attended art school in Lausanne, Switzerland, and not long after was accepted into a pre-Akadamie Art School program in Munich, Germany, where she met Bavarian master brewer Arnold Zimmermann through a mutual friend. Elizabeth and Arnold began dating, and when Arnold felt it necessary to flee to England after an SS officer overheard him denigrating Hitler, Elizabeth went, too. They were married in England in 1937 and later that year moved across the pond to New York, bouncing around the United States for a while before settling permanently in Wisconsin with their three children, Meg, Lloie and Thomas. In Wisconsin—where she was known to knit on the back of Arnold's BMW 900 CC motorcycle—Zimmermann found herself wondering why she alone among the friends with whom she knit felt confident enough in her skills to stitch off-pattern.

In 1955 Zimmermann sent her first knitting designs—colorfully yoked Norwegian-style dropped-shoulder sweaters—to *Woman's Day* and other magazines. A few years later the *Vogue Pattern Book, Vogue Knitting*'s sister publication, ran an Aran sweater of Zimmermann's design, later credited as the first Aran-sweater design to be commercially published in the United States. As payment for the pattern, Zimmermann was listed as the source of the natural unbleached wool she used for the garment. That brief mention led to the 1959 founding of Schoolhouse Press, the mail-order business named for the dilapidated schoolhouse in Babcock, Wisconsin, that the Zimmermann family had

Elizabeth Zimmermann

renovated as their home and through which Zimmermann sold yarn, knitting books and knitting supplies. Under the Schoolhouse Press umbrella, Zimmermann began publishing her own knitting newsletter, eventually titled *Wool Gathering,* at long last retaining control over both her designs and her inimitable writing style.

In the thirty years she ran Schoolhouse Press, Zimmermann also hosted *The Busy Knitter*, a nationally syndicated PBS series in the mid-'60s; wrote a regular column for *Vogue Knitting* in the '80s; and authored four books, popular to this day, that document her unorthodox yet highly intuitive knitting ethos: *Knitting Without Tears* (Scribner, 1971), *The Knitter's Almanac* (Dover, 1975), *Elizabeth Zimmermann's Knitting Workshop* (Schoolhouse Press, 1981) and *Knitting Around* (Schoolhouse Press, 1989). Her daughter, Meg Swansen, joined Schoolhouse Press in 1965, and in

1974 Zimmermann instituted a now legendary summer knitting camp in Green Lake under the auspices of the University of Wisconsin, where she taught knitters to understand the EPS so they could concentrate more on design elements and be less intimidated by construction issues.

Among Zimmermann's most notable knitting innovations and revelations: the aforementioned EPS, a formula that lets a knitter multiply the gauge of a chosen yarn by the wearer's widest circumference to calculate how many stitches to cast on for each section of a circularly knit sweater to achieve a proportionate custom-fit; the widespread use of tubular garment construction, allowing a knitter to avoid seaming; unset yoke sleeves; constructive use of I-cord, which was so named after Zimmermann dubbed it "idiot cord"; the championing of Continental knitting as a particularly efficient stitching method; the Pi shawl, shaped by regularly spaced increases based on the mathematical constant pi; and the Baby Surprise jacket, knit flat in one piece and strategically folded to form fronts and back.

"Please bear with me, and put up with my opinionated, nay, sometimes cantankerous attitude. I feel strongly about knitting," Zimmermann requested in *The Knitter's Almanac*, and her readers have obliged. Though Zimmermann retired at seventy-nine in 1989 and died at age

eighty-nine ten years later, her legacy remains strong. Swansen has embraced and enhanced the knitting heritage left to her by her mother, continuing to run Schoolhouse Press and the knitting camp (now in Marshfield, Wisconsin); compiling a decade's worth of Zimmermann's earliest newsletters (1958–1968) in *The Opinionated Knitter* (Schoolhouse Press, 2005); converting segments from *The Busy Knitter* and other videos Zimmermann had made into DVDs; and taking over the writing of both Wool Gathering and the *Vogue Knitting* column. A 2006 exhibition at the University of Wisconsin-Madison, "New School Knitting: The Influence of Elizabeth Zimmermann and Schoolhouse Press," paid tribute to Zimmermann's ongoing impact on the knitting world. A knit-along blog called Zimmermania, where hundreds of cyber-savvy knitters document their progress as they tackle classic Zimmermann projects (zimmermaniacs. blogspot.com), acknowledges her as the "innovator, engineer, wisewoman, teacher, godmother of the craft in North America." Perhaps most telling, Zimmermann was the first career knitter to warrant a full obituary in the *New York Times*, which credited her not only with her many tangible accomplishments but also because "She gently urged knitters to challenge the limits of their imaginations."
See also AMERICAN/ENGLISH-STYLE KNITTING; ARAN KNITTING; ARMHOLE SHAPING; CAMPS AND RETREATS; CIRCULAR KNITTING; CIRCULAR NEEDLES; CONTINENTAL/GERMAN-STYLE KNITTING; CORDS; DESIGNERS; EPS; FASSETT, KAFFE; GAUGE; INTERNET; MAGAZINES AND JOURNALS; NEEDLE TYPES; NORWEGIAN KNITTING; STITCH GAUGE; SWANSEN, MEG

ZIPPER

A slide fastener used for joining two pieces of fabric is called a zipper. Zipper styles and types have multiplied exponentially over the years, and many are suitable for sweater designs. Regular non-separating zippers are appropriate for skirts or the back of close-fitting necks; for front-opening, half-zip styles you may want to use one of the more decorative zippers on the market. Separating zippers are used for jackets and cardigans.

Zippers should be sewn to handknits by hand, not machine. The opening for the zipper in the finished garment needs to be the same length as the zipper so that the seam does not stretch or pucker. To prepare the edges, work a selvage. You may need to add a crocheted slip-stitch edging to smooth out the edges. Place the zipper a stitch or row from the edge to prevent the teeth from showing and sew it down with a backstitch.
See also CLOSURES; EDGINGS; SELVAGE

Zipper

Whipstitch the zipper in place on the wrong side, then backstitch it on the right side close to the edge of the knit fabric.

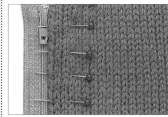

1. To apply the zipper, work from the right side of the piece or pieces with the zipper closed. Pin the zipper in place so that the edges of the knit fabric will cover the teeth of the zipper and meet in the center.

2. After pinning, baste the zipper and remove the pins. Turn the zipper to the wrong side and whipstitch in place. Turn the zipper to the right side and backstitch in place.

Types of Zippers

Five types of zippers (from left to right): One-way separating zipper adorned with rhinestones; invisible non-separating zipper that hides in a seam; all-purpose one-way separating zipper; all-purpose non-separating zipper; one-way separating brass jeans zipper for heavier knits.

PHOTOGRAPHY & ILLUSTRATION CREDITS

Illustrations by Phoebe Gaughan; Anders Wenngren; Uli Monch; and Kate Simunek, Chapman Bounford and Associates, UK (from *Vogue® Knitting: The Ulimate Knitting Book,* Sixth&Spring Books) unless otherwise noted below.

All maps by Sally Mara Sturman

p. 2: David Lazarus
p. 6: David Lazarus
p. 8: Marcus Tullis
p. 10 (acrylic): Marcus Tullis
p. 10 (afghan): From *Cover Up with Nicky Epstein* by Nicky Epstein (Sixth&Spring Books); photograph by Marcus Tullis
p. 11 (alpaca fiber–Suri): ©Alexander Fortelny/iStockPhoto
p. 11 (alpaca fiber–Huacaya): ©*Wild Fibers Magazine*
p. 11 (alpaca fiber–swatch): Marcus Tullis
p. 12 (Alpine Region Knitting): From *Twisted-Stitch Knitting* by Maria Erlbacher (School-house Press); photograph by Meg Swansen; courtesy of Schoolhouse Press
p. 12 (American Red Cross): ©Corbis
p. 13 (amigurumi): Paul Amato for LVARepresents.com
p. 13 (Andes region knitting): Steve Axford
p. 14 (angora fiber–stole): ©Condé Nast Publications, Inc.; photograph by Fred Baker
p. 14 (angora fiber–rabbit): ©Maria Dryfhout/Shutterstock
p. 14 (angora fiber–swatch): Marcus Tullis
p. 15 (Aran knitting): ©Condé Nast Publications, Inc.
p. 17 (argyle–sweater): ©Condé Nast Publications, Inc.; photograph by Fred Baker
p. 17 (argyle–swatch): Jack Deutsch
p. 18 (armhole shaping): Original illustrations by Diana Huff; redrawn by Loretta Dachman
p. 20 (Azores lace): ©V&A Images/Victoria & Albert Museum, London
p. 21: Jack Deutsch
p. 22 (ball): Marcus Tullis
p. 23 (Baltic knitting): From

Latvian Mittens by Lizbeth Upitis (Schoolhouse Press); photograph by Alvis Upitis
p. 24 (basket-weave stitch): Jack Deutsch
p. 25 (bathing suits, knitted): ©Condé Nast Publications, Inc.; photograph by Fred Baker
p. 26 (bead knitting): ©V&A Images/Victoria & Albert Museum, London
p. 27 (beads): Jack Deutsch
p. 29 (blocking): Marcus Tullis
p. 32 (bouclé yarn): Marcus Tullis
p. 33 (brioche): Jack Deutsch
p. 33 (British knitting): ©V&A Images/Victoria & Albert Museum, London
p. 35 (buffalo fiber–buffalo): ©*Wild Fibers Magazine*
p. 35 (buffalo fiber–yarn): Jack Deutsch
p. 38 (buttons): Marcus Tullis
p. 39: David Lazarus
p. 40 (cable needle): Jack Deutsch
p. 40 (cable patterns) Jack Deutsch
p. 41 (camelhair): Marcus Tullis
p. 43 (care): Textileaffairs.com
p. 44 (cashmere–goat): ©*Wild Fibers Magazine*
p. 44 (cashmere–swatch): Marcus Tullis
p. 47 (charts): Jack Deutsch
p. 48 (chenille): Marcus Tullis
p. 50 (circular needles): Marcus Tullis
p. 51 (clasps): Marcus Tullis; clasps available at nickyepstein.com
p. 55 (swatch): Courtesy of Brandon Mably
p. 55 (painting): ©Kaffe Fassett
p. 59 (cotton–field): ©Gonul Kokal/Shutterstock
p. 59 (cotton-boll): ©Jerry Horbert/Shutterstock
p. 59 (cotton–swatch): Marcus Tullis
p. 60 (Cowichan knitting): Cowichan Valley Museum & Archives 1997.10.3.1
p. 62 (crochet hook): Marcus Tullis
p. 63: Marcus Tullis
p. 70 (double-pointed needles): Marcus Tullis
p. 71 (drop spindle–photo): Marcus Tullis
p. 71 (drop-stitch patterns): Jack Deutsch
p. 72 (Dutch knitting): ©V&A Images/Victoria & Albert

Museum, London
p. 73: David Lazarus
p. 75 (embroidery): From *Color by Kristin* by Kristin Nicholas (Sixth&Spring Books); photograph by Jack Deutsch
p. 77 (entrelac): Marcus Tullis
p. 79 (eyelash yarn): Marcus Tullis
p. 79 (eyelet patterns): Jack Deutsch
p. 80: Marcus Tullis
p. 81 (faggoting): Marcus Tullis
p. 82 (Fair Isle knitting): *Portrait of HRH The Prince of Wales,* 1925 (oil on canvas) by John St. Helier Lander (1869-1944) © Leeds Museums and Galleries (Lotherton Hall) U.K./The Bridgeman Art Library
p. 83 (Faroe knitting): Courtesy of Edward Fuglø (artist) and the Faroese Postal and Stamps Company
p. 85 (felting): Marcus Tullis
p. 88 (Florentine jacket): ©V&A Images/Victoria & Albert Museum, London
p. 89 (freeform knitting/crochet): Courtesy of Prudence Mapstone (knotjustknitting.com)
p. 90 (French knitting): ©V&A Images/Victoria & Albert Museum, London
p. 91 (frog closure): From *Knitting Never Felt Better* by Nicky Epstein (Sixth&Spring Books); photograph by Jack Deutsch
p. 92: Marcus Tullis
p. 93 (garter stitch): Marcus Tullis
p. 96 (German knitting): Bildarchiv Preussicher Kulturbesitz/Art Resource, NY
p. 101: Marcus Tullis
p. 102 (halter): ©Condé Nast Publications, Inc.; photograph by Fred Baker
p. 102 (hand-painted): Marcus Tullis
p. 102 (hank): Marcus Tullis
p. 103: Courtesy of Elaine Eskesen
p. 106-107 (heel): Marcus Tullis
p. 109 (history of knitting): ©V&A Images/Victoria & Albert Museum, London
p. 111 (honeycomb stitch): Marcus Tullis
p. 112: Jack Deutsch
p. 113 (Icelandic knitting): ©CSLD/Shutterstock
p. 114 (intarsia): Jack Deutsch

p. 115 (interchangeable needles): Jack Deutsch
p. 119: Marcus Tullis
p. 121 (knit/purl patterns): Jack Deutsch
p. 123 (knitted lace): Jack Deutsch
p. 125 (flower): stock.xchng
p. 125 (drawings): From *Creating Original Hand-knitted Lace* by Margaret Stove (Lacis); courtesy of Margaret Stove
p. 125 (gown): ©Margaret Stove/Museum of New Zealand Te Papa Tongarewa
p. 128 (knitting journal): ©V&A Images/Victoria & Albert Museum, London
p. 128 (knitting loom): Jack Deutsch
p. 128 (knitting nancy): David Lazarus
p. 132: Marcus Tullis
p. 133 (lace knitting): ©V&A Images/Victoria & Albert Museum, London
p. 133 (lace stitches): Jack Deutsch
p. 138 (linen): Marcus Tullis
p. 139 (lopi): Marcus Tullis
p. 141: David Lazarus
p. 144 (magic loop): Marcus Tullis
p. 145 (marker): Marcus Tullis
p. 147 (measurements): Craft Yarn Council's YarnStandards.com
p. 148 (merino fiber): ©John Carnemolla/Shutterstock
p. 149 (mitered knitting): Marcus Tullis
p. 149 (mohair fiber–goats): ©*Wild Fibers Magazine*
p. 149 (mohair fiber–swatch): Marcus Tullis
p. 15: Rose Callahan
p. 151 (mosaic patterns): Marcus Tullis
p. 151 (moss stitch): Jack Deutsch
p. 152: Marcus Tullis
p. 154 (naturally colored yarn): Marcus Tullis
p. 154 (needle gauge): ©V&A Images/Victoria & Albert Museum, London
p. 156 (needle types): Marcus Tullis
p. 158 (Noro): Rose Callahan
p. 159 (Norwegian knitting): ©Stanislav Sokolov/Shutterstock
p. 160 (notions): Marcus Tullis and Jack Deutsch
p. 161: Marcus Tullis
p. 162 (Orenburg lace):

Textile Museum of Canada
p. 166 (pence jug): ©V&A Images/Victoria & Albert Museum, London
p. 169 (plait): Jack Deutsch
p. 175 (purses): From *Vogue Knitting On the Go! Bags and Backpacks* (Sixth&Spring Books); photographs by Brian Kraus and Juan Ríos; designs by (from left to right): Chris Lipert, Elaine Mehl, Jane Livingston
p. 175 (put-up): Marcus Tullis
p. 176 (qiviut): ©*Wild Fibers Magazine*
p. 176: Marcus Tullis
p. 180 (reverse stockinette stitch): Marcus Tullis
p. 180 (ribbing): Marcus Tullis
p. 180 (ribbon yarn): Marcus Tullis
p. 181 (ruching): Marcus Tullis
p. 182: Marcus Tullis
p. 183 (scarf): From *Vogue Knitting On the Go! Scarves Two* (Sixth&Spring Books); photographs by Jack Deutsch; designs by (from left to right): Karen Connor, Irina Poludnenko, Carol Gillis
p. 185 (scrumble): Courtesy of Prudence Mapstone (knotjustknitting.com)
p. 185 (seed stitch): Jack Deutsch
p. 188 (sheep–Icelandic): ©Gunnar Már Halldórsson/Shutterstock
p. 188 (sheep–Leicester): ©Shane White/Shutterstock
p. 188 (sheep–Lincoln): ©Sharon Kingston/Shutterstock
p. 188 (sheep–merino): ©*Wild Fibers Magazine*
p. 188 (sheep–Shetland): ©willmetts/Shutterstock
p. 188 (sheep–Columbia): Courtesy of Imperial Stock Ranch/Imperial Yarn; photograph by Jeanne Carver
p. 188 (sheep–Romney): Courtesy of Kristin Nicholas
p. 188 (sheep–Rambouillet): Courtesy of Mountain Meadow Wool Mill; photo-graph by Cheyenne Greub
p. 190 (Shetland lace): ©V&A Images/Victoria & Albert Museum, London
p. 192 (silk–swatch): Marcus Tullis
p. 192 (silk–silkworms): ©Brian K. Tan/Shutterstock
p. 192 (silk–cocoons): ©Suzan

STITCHES AND PATTERNWORK

TECHNIQUES

ACKNOWLEDGMENTS

Developing a comprehensive resource like *Knitopedia* is truly a group effort. The following writers lent their expertise and skills to this project: Marjorie S. Anderson, Daryl Brower, Cheryl Krementz, Elaine Silverstein, Erin Slonaker, Kristina Sigler and Karin Strom. Some of the text on knitting technique first appeared in *Vogue® Knitting: The Ultimate Knitting Book* and was written by Nancy J. Thomas, Carla Scott, Joni Coniglio and others.

Many knitting-world luminaries shared areas of their personal interest and expertise by contributing essays on myriad topics. They are: Debbie Bliss, Linda Cortright, Nicky Epstein, Elaine Eskesen, Norah Gaughan, Vickie Howell, Brandon Mably, Tara Jon Manning, Kristin Nicholas, Shannon Okey, Clara Parkes, Mari Lynn Patrick, Amy R. Singer, Alice Starmore, Margaret Stove and Meg Swansen.

Of course the words that make up *Knitopedia* are only part of the story. The hundreds of beautiful and instructive photographs and illustrations that grace the pages come from dozens of sources. Photographers Marcus Tullis and Jack Deutsch took the majority of still-life photographs. Phoebe Gaughan, Uli Monch, Sally Mara Sturman and Anders Wenngren created artwork expressly for *Knitopedia*. Many of the technical illustrations first appeared in *The Ultimate Knitting Book* and were drawn by Kate Simunek, Chapman Bounford and Associates (UK). Many museums, publishers and individuals were instrumental in providing images that illustrate history, knitting traditions, fiber sources, knitting tools and other topics. Linda Cortright of *Wild Fibers Magazine*, Margaret Stove, Meg Swansen of Schoolhouse Press and the Victoria & Albert Museum in London were particularly generous with their time and assistance.

Organizing and editing all of the text and hundreds of images that make up *Knitopedia* was a monumental task. Over the several years that this book this book has been in the making, several editors have taken on the challenge: Elaine Silverstein, Erin Slonaker and Michelle Bredeson, with the able assistance of Kristina Sigler, Marina Kastan, Mirlande Jeanlouis and Lily Rothman. Managing editor Wendy Williams facilitated the production of the book. Art director Diane Lamphron worked with designer Chi Ling Moy to assemble the massive amount of text and images into a coherent whole that is both beautiful to view and eminently useful.

In addition to all of the writers, editors, photographers and designers throughout the years from *Vogue Knitting* whose contributions are reflected in this book, several current staff members had a direct hand in the creation of *Knitopedia*. Editorial director Trisha Malcolm and executive editor Carla Scott developed the original concept for the book and carefully reviewed the text and illustrations. Associate editor Faith Hale knit many of the swatches and, along with yarn editors Tanis Gray and Renée Lorion, was instrumental in procuring the gorgeous yarns and knitting tools for photography that were generously provided by a number of companies.

NORTHVILLE DISTRICT LIBRARY

3 9082 11761 3177